BLOOD AND SAND

Love, Death and Survival in an Age of Global Terror

FRANK GARDNER

BANTAM PRESS

LONDON · TORONTO · SYDNEY · AUCKLAND · JOHANNESBURG

TRANSWORLD PUBLISHERS
61–63 Uxbridge Road, London W5 5SA
a division of The Random House Group Ltd

RANDOM HOUSE AUSTRALIA (PTY) LTD
20 Alfred Street, Milsons Point, Sydney,
New South Wales 2061, Australia

RANDOM HOUSE NEW ZEALAND LTD
18 Poland Road, Glenfield, Auckland 10, New Zealand

RANDOM HOUSE SOUTH AFRICA (PTY) LTD
Isle of Houghton, Corner of Boundary and Carse O'Gowrie Roads,
Houghton 2198, South Africa

Published 2006 by Bantam Press
a division of Transworld Publishers

A catalogue record for this book is available from the British Library.
ISBNs (hb) 0593055780
9780593055786 (from Jan 07)
(tpb) 059305699X
9780593056998 (from Jan 07)

Typeset in 11½/14½pt Sabon by
Falcon Oast Graphic Art Ltd

Printed in Great Britain by
Clays Ltd, St Ives plc

1 3 5 7 9 10 8 6 4 2

Papers used by Transworld Publishers are natural, recyclable products made from
wood grown in sustainable forests. The manufacturing processes conform to the
environmental regulations of the country of origin.

For Amanda

CONTENTS

FOREWORD

This is an important book about one of the dominating issues of our time: the rise of violent Islamic fundamentalism, and its collision with Western society. It is also a desperately sad and personal book. Frank Gardner was partially paralysed as a result of a murderous and entirely unprovoked attack by a group of Al-Qaeda gunmen while he was filming in Saudi Arabia in 2004; his cameraman, Simon Cumbers, an Irishman who was a great favourite with everyone in British television who knew him, was murdered in cold blood. Frank himself survived only through the most remarkable good fortune. Now he has woven together the two strands of his story, the personal and the geopolitical, into a compelling and sometimes disturbing narrative.

But this is not all about bombs and bullets. Frank's twenty-five years in the Middle East encompass many happy experiences: living with the Bedu in the deserts of Jordan, learning Arabic with a family in the backstreets of Cairo, or riding for two days down to Khartoum on the roof of a train. In this book he reveals a little-known side of the Arab world that he feels privileged to have seen.

There are plenty of good books about militant Islamism, but Frank is able to provide us with a unique understanding of the phenomenon: as an Arabic-speaker, as a correspondent who has lived in the Arab world, and as a professional observer of international terrorism. And finally, we could add, as someone who has come close enough to be marked by it for life.

The world has been plagued by political or religious terrorism – the two have often been deeply intertwined – since the 1960s. Yet in the past the most violent organizations had specific aims, and specific enemies; even if many, perhaps most, of those who were killed as a result of their actions had nothing to do with the basic cause. And somewhere in the minds of the activists and their apologists there was usually a faint sense that murdering innocent passers-by was something to be ashamed of, or at the very least explained away.

For more than a decade now, the religious terrorism which Osama Bin Laden has espoused from his refuges in Afghanistan and Pakistan has troubled itself very little about who, precisely, it has killed. There have been disputes within the Al-Qaeda movement about the value of indiscriminate killing, but it still goes on. Hundreds of those who died in the Twin Towers attack on 11 September 2001 were not Americans; some of those who died or were injured in the London bombings of 7 July 2005 were Muslims. None of it mattered. The aim was to kill as many people as spectacularly as possible. Politicians and newspapers have used the word 'terrorist' to describe just about every act of political violence since the early 1970s, and it has therefore come to be an undifferentiated term of abuse. Yet attacks like those on the World Trade Center and the public-transport systems of Madrid and London were, in the precise sense of the word, planned with the intention of causing terror.

Frank Gardner and Simon Cumbers were attacked because they happened to be Europeans and their attackers happened to spot them. The gang that shot them was later involved in the savage murders of two Americans. All of them, Frank, Simon and the Americans, were targets, not because of what they did, but because of their ethnicity. That has always been a defining characteristic of Al-Qaeda. Any Westerner who worked along-side or reported on the *mujahideen* uprising against the Soviet occupation of Afghanistan quickly learned how dangerous some jihadists could be: even though the common enemy was supposedly the Russians. The extremists hated all non-Muslims, regardless of their origin or motivation.

For his part, Frank Gardner has had a lifelong respect for and love of the Islamic world, like so many of us who have worked in Muslim countries. Nothing that he has experienced has changed that. His perspective on Al-Qaeda and the threat it poses is a unique one: not only does he have an authoritative insight into the Al-Qaeda phenomenon, he has looked an Al-Qaeda team in the face and survived. In understanding what happened to Frank and to Simon Cumbers, and honouring them both accordingly, we can begin to appreciate more about the causes and nature of the threat which people like their attackers present to us.

John Simpson,
BBC World Affairs Editor.
January 2006

1

Hit for Six:
Getting Shot

'DO YOU HAVE TIME FOR SOME supper?' called Amanda from the kitchen.

I looked at my watch. It was Tuesday 1 June 2004 and the car taking me to Heathrow airport would be here in twenty minutes, but I was packed and ready to go. 'I'll be right down,' I replied, and walked out of our bedroom, unaware that that was the last time I would ever see it.

Three days earlier there had been a bloodthirsty raid by Al-Qaeda fanatics in the eastern Saudi town of Al-Khobar. A small but well-armed team of terrorists had gone on the rampage, looking for Westerners and non-Muslims to kidnap and kill. First they found a prominent British expatriate, Michael Hamilton, as he arrived at his office. They shot him dead in his car, then tied his body to their car bumper and dragged it around town for over a mile in some kind of grisly parade of their power. Then, masquerading as government security forces, they marched into the Oasis compound, a large residential complex housing many Westerners, Indians and Filipinos who worked in jobs administrating the country's vast oil industry, meeting no resistance at the poorly defended gatehouse. They worked their way methodically through the buildings, rounding up all those they suspected of being non-Muslims. Having questioned them on their religion, according to the testimony of survivors, the militants coolly slit the throats of the 'non-believers', Al-Qaeda's usual term for non-Muslims. The siege appeared to end in front of local TV cameras with the arrival of Saudi commandos who landed by helicopter on the roof of one of the buildings. But in fact the Saudi authorities had done a deal with the terrorists, believing it was the only way to spare massive bloodshed. Fearing that Al-Qaeda had several hundred hostages at their mercy, the Saudi authorities allowed three of the four terrorists to escape from the premises. But by the time order was restored in Al-Khobar, twenty-two people had been killed.

The raid came as a shock to most Saudis. Yes, there had been suicide bombings and attacks on Westerners before, but almost none here, in the normally tranquil Eastern Province of the country. Al-Khobar was a quiet, dull place that existed to serve the oil industry. Its grid-patterned streets were laid out like a small US city, its neon signs advertised Kentucky Fried Chicken and other fast-food outlets. There was no entertainment and very little for expatriate Westerners to do other than drive across the nearby causeway to free-wheeling Bahrain or fantasize about the next annual leave in Bangkok.

Saudi Arabia's charismatic ambassador to London at the time, Prince Turki Al-Faisal, had wasted no time in touring the TV news studios to defend his government's record in tackling terrorism. I interviewed him on Monday night for the ten o'clock news. A former Saudi spymaster, Prince Turki was unusually open and frank. He took the view that his country had nothing to hide and encouraged British journalists to visit, helping with urgent visa requests. I was to go there to report for BBC News together with Simon Cumbers, a freelance Irish cameraman and trusted veteran of countless BBC assignments.

That night Amanda and I sat up talking late into the night. My wife was understandably anxious about my forthcoming trip; clearly there were people on the loose in Saudi Arabia who hated Westerners with a passion. 'Do you *have* to go to Saudi?' she asked. I did not. Unlike some other TV networks, the BBC is quite reasonable about asking people to go to difficult places and I have never personally been told the equivalent of 'Go to Baghdad or pick up your P45.' It had been nearly a year now since I had last been to Riyadh, a great deal had happened there since then and people in News felt this was the right moment to update viewers on what was going on in this under-reported country. Besides, Saudi Arabia was not considered a high-risk-category country like Iraq or Afghanistan; I knew of no visiting journalists who had ever been threatened there.

'Then are you taking a flak jacket?' asked Amanda. This was a touchy subject between us: she has always maintained I agreed at our wedding never to be a flak-jacket journalist, a pledge I have no recollection of making. In truth, though, I have never seen myself as a 'war correspondent', believing that no story is worth getting shot for, although there are occasions when it is wise to wear a flak jacket as a precaution. But I did not feel this was one of them: no civilians wore flak jackets in Saudi Arabia and if anything it would only attract unwelcome attention. But Amanda's concerns troubled me, not just because I did not want her to worry while I was away but because she has an uncanny knack of being right about places she has never even been to. 'So what are you going to say when terrorists have got a gun to your head?' she asked me. I tried to reassure her – and myself, for that matter – that I would not get into such a situation, that we were going to tread extremely carefully on this trip, going nowhere without a government escort. We would have absolutely no contact with anyone hostile to the government and we would put ourselves entirely in the care of our Saudi minders, and knowing how over-cautious they tend to be, our only problem should be not getting enough access to interesting subjects. One of the last things I packed was a miniature copy of the Koran, one of several I keep to give as presents to hospitable Muslim hosts, a gesture that always brings great appreciation.

I kissed my wife and children goodbye and watched them recede through the car's back window on that warm summer night. I tried to dismiss the feeling of unease I had in the pit of my stomach, reminding myself that Saudi Arabia was a country I knew well and had been to countless times since 1989, and that I'd always felt safe there. Soon I was at Terminal Three, helping Simon heft heavy cases of camera equipment on to the scales at check-in. He and his wife Louise had their own freelance TV production company, Locum Productions, and with his innate sense of fair play Simon had recently felt bad about asking one of his cameramen to go to Baghdad. He had resolved that when the next filming trip to the Middle East came up he would take it on himself.

We flew overnight to Manama, where a man from the Saudi Interior Ministry met us to escort us over the causeway that connects the island of Bahrain to the Saudi mainland and the oil town of Al-Khobar. When we drew up at the local five-star hotel, the Al-Khobar Meridien, I could hardly believe it: Saudi security had set up a sandbag gun emplacement outside, backed by an armoured car. This was a businessmen's hotel which I had often stayed in in my former incarnation as a Gulf banker, but even during the dark days of the Gulf War in 1991 there had never been anything like this atmosphere of brooding tension. I had only been away eleven months and already this was not the Saudi Arabia I knew.

The next few days were a blur of hastily filmed and edited reports for our television news bulletins. Having got a team into Saudi Arabia, the BBC was keen to use us to the max. Not surprisingly, the attack in Al-Khobar had sent the global oil markets into jitters, sparking fears that any more brazen attacks like this would damage the output of the world's biggest oil producer and exporter. But the Saudi authorities believed they had nothing to hide from our news camera. They allowed us, under close escort, to get right into the heart of their oil-producing and exporting industry and it gave them the opportunity to show off their tight security. We had even been allowed to film one of their most highly guarded sites, the loading terminal on the Gulf coast at Ras Tanura, one of the Kingdom's economic lifelines.

So in my TV reports I had made the point that while Al-Qaeda-linked groups had successfully attacked a relatively small number of Westerners and other non-Muslims living here, they had so far failed to make any impact on Saudi Arabia's oil production itself. I wanted to dispel the myth that the Saudi oil industry would collapse the day after Western expertise departed. In fact Saudi Aramco, the state oil company, employs a majority of Saudis. Westerners, mainly Americans, tend to be involved more in long-term planning and finance than in day-to-day production. In the Eastern Province our days passed in a whirlwind of filming, driving and frantic editing in our hotel room, followed by a dash up the motorway to the nearest satellite uplink station in time to make the one, six or ten o'clock TV news in Britain; in other words, pretty much typical of a foreign newsgathering trip following a major event.

Simon seemed to have endless patience and good humour. With the clock ticking against us he would juggle two conversations at once, talking down the phone to the satellite intake desk in London while simultaneously cajoling the local Saudi technicians into trying a failed connection one more time. Once, when we had been out filming all day and had just sat down to a plate of sandwiches, Simon looked at me and said mildly, 'Do you realize we've only got forty minutes left to cut this film for the six o'clock news? That's not very long, is it?'

In the middle of this schedule I was invited to attend the memorial service for Michael Hamilton, the first Westerner found by Al-Qaeda on their murderous spree a few days earlier. The service was held in a schoolhouse in Al-Khobar and I sat at the back, as discreetly as I could, taking notes for the report I needed to file for the Radio 4 six o'clock news. I had never known Michael Hamilton, but was overwhelmed by the sadness and futility of his death. One had only to look round the room at his mourners to judge his popularity: Saudis, Britons, Bahrainis and Indians had all come to pay their respects. The British ambassador, Sherard Cowper-Coles, read a deeply moving tribute and that night we interviewed him in his hotel room, sharing my packet of Walkers short-bread fingers for which the ambassador admitted a weakness. Cowper-Coles's previous posting had been as ambassador in Tel Aviv and he had a refreshing tendency to tell it how it is. 'Saudi Arabia does have a serious problem with terrorism,' he said, 'and I predict there will be more attacks on Westerners.' Prescient as he was, he could not have foreseen that Simon and I were to be Al-Qaeda's next victims.

On the Friday we took the short flight to Riyadh and spent the afternoon at a barbecue with British expatriates in their walled compound. Friday is the day off in Saudi so this was half work, half pleasure. Our intention was to film a slice of Western expatriate life and interview Britons about their new fears of Islamist terrorism. Life here had recently taken a turn for the worse, they said. They had accepted for some time the risk of being caught up in a suicide bombing but now there was a new horror: being taken hostage and then executed in cold blood, on the basis of one's religion or the colour of one's skin. The expats had been hearing reports of Al-Qaeda scouts marking Westerners' number plates with chalk to indicate them as potential targets. (Within ten days there were to be two separate kidnappings and executions of Americans in Saudi, but I would not be conscious to report on them.)

When we checked into our Riyadh hotel we saw similar security precautions to those in Al-Khobar. A chicane of concrete roadblocks zigzagged across the road up to reception, presumably to deter truck-bombers, but I noticed there was no visible armed guard on duty and this worried me. If Al-Qaeda decided to raid this hotel and go through it room by room, I did not believe there would be much to stop them. As soon as I was allocated my room I went over to the window and decided that if there was to be an armed raid I could probably jump down on to the tree below, which would break my fall. I felt that a raid was unlikely, though; not because Al-Qaeda might be put off by the security – they had been growing increasingly brazen in their attacks – but the summer heat meant there were so few Western guests in the hotel it would hardly have been worth their time.

Simon and I had come to Riyadh with the aim of reporting on the deeper story of how the Saudi authorities were combating the country's Al-Qaeda-inspired terror cells. The previous summer I had been granted unprecedented access to Saudi's counter-terrorist teams in training, filming them on my own in 45-degree heat at a secret base on the outskirts of Riyadh. We were hoping to build on this by interviewing senior security officials who could brief us on their strategy now that Al-Qaeda had raised the stakes by attacking the hinterland of the oil industry. We spent a morning traipsing round various offices in the Ministry of Information, applying for permission to film. Saudi Arabia does not allow unescorted film crews, partly for their own safety. Many Saudis still have a xenophobic view of outsiders, making them deeply suspicious of foreigners with cameras, convinced they are trying to film their women or pass the footage to some Western government.

We asked to film three things: checkpoints and other physical security measures; an interview with a senior official; and a general view towards Al-Suwaidi, a restive area of south Riyadh where there had been a shoot-out six months earlier between police and an Islamist cell leader, Ibrahim Al-Rayyes, who had been killed. The area was now calm, we were assured, but still we had no wish to go into it, only to film from a distance to give the viewer an impression of what the place looked like.

Arab government ministries tend to close down at two p.m., so having lodged our filming applications we went back to our hotel for lunch and a swim. The Ministry of Information had not been very encouraging about the chance of meeting our requests, and since we had already had a good run in Al-Khobar, getting our reports on to every major news bulletin, we had decided to call it a day in Riyadh and fly home the next day. I took a call from BBC2's *Newsnight*, asking me if we could stay on to film extra footage and do a story for them, but I replied that we were reluctant to hang around in Riyadh in this tense atmosphere when we had nothing firmed up to film.

So it was somewhat to our surprise that permission came through mid-afternoon to film around Riyadh, including the district of Al-Suwaidi. Reluctantly – because we had mentally finished our Saudi trip – we roused ourselves from the pool and went up to our rooms to change. I watched a few minutes of the D-Day sixtieth-anniversary celebrations on TV, admiring the veterans in their berets and medals and pleased that my father had made the trip back there with my mother and a friend. We then went down to the car park to pile our camera gear into a government minivan. Mubarak, a black Saudi, one of thousands of Arabs with African ancestry, was at the wheel. Beside him was Yahya, our assigned 'minder' from the Ministry of Information. I had never worked with him before but he assured me immediately that he was an old hand at chaperoning foreign film crews. He seemed very easy-going and far more eager to help than most of the government minders I have encountered in the Arab world. We were free to go wherever we chose in Riyadh, he said, but we could not film checkpoints. Simon and I did not need ordinary land-marks and street scenes – the BBC had plenty of those on tape back in London – so we asked to go straight to the edge of Al-Suwaidi. With Mubarak at the wheel and Simon filming out of the window, we drove south through the suburbs of Riyadh. They were unremarkable to look at: low, white-washed, flat-roofed buildings, usually above a row of shops selling cold drinks, fabric and spare car parts. People were just starting to emerge on to the streets after the mid-afternoon siesta; a few of the men, I noticed, wore the short robes and long beards of devout fundamentalists. Here and there was a neon-lit fast-food joint, a sandy backstreet, an overflowing litter bin. One could sense this was a poorer part of town, but the poverty was not extreme.

When we drew up on the edge of Al-Suwaidi district it looked exactly like every other residential housing area I have known in the Gulf states: two- or three-storey cream-coloured villas surrounded by high walls topped by purple bougainvillea. Patches of flat stony wasteground separated the buildings, and while there was some graffiti on the walls there were also several expensive four-wheel-drive cars parked in the shade. There was not a soul around, although after a while some laughing children appeared and wanted us to film them. Simon got me to do what is known as a 'walking piece-to-camera', one of those earnest, strolling soliloquies from the reporter that is supposed to set the scene in context, or at least prove to the viewer that the reporter has been there.

Simon and I had agreed in advance that we would spend no

more than ten minutes here, but Yahya was very relaxed and certainly there was nothing to suggest any kind of threat – no furtive figures darting into doorways, no twitching curtains – so we did several takes from different angles to get the filming just right. Again and again I strolled across the wasteground towards the camera, pausing to deliver my words and point out the villas in the background where the police had traded fire with the militants six months earlier.

After about half an hour of this we were on the verge of packing up and driving back to the hotel when a car pulled up close to our minivan. I was vaguely aware of some people in the distance, but when a young Saudi got out of the vehicle there was nothing suspicious about him at first. Like every adult male Saudi, he wore the traditional white *thaub* dress, essentially a smart shirt that extends all the way down to the ankles. He looked very young, perhaps even still in his teens, and had a kindly face with a hint of a smile, almost as if he knew us or our two Saudi escorts. Was he coming to ask directions? Perhaps he knew the driver and had come to chat. Looking straight at me, he called out, '*Assalaamu aleikum*' ('Peace be upon you'). All over the Arab and Islamic world this is the traditional Muslim greeting, a reassurance to a stranger that you wish him no harm. I replied with the standard response: '*Wa aleikum assalaam wa rahmatullah wa barakaatuh*' ('And upon you the peace and the mercy of God and His blessings'). The man paused, a curious look on his face, then with no sign of haste he reached his right hand into what must have been a specially extended pocket sewn into the breast of his *thaub*. I did not need to see the weapon to know what was coming next. It was like a film with a predictable ending. 'No! Don't do this!' I shouted instinctively in Arabic. Simon must have heard my shout but I did not see him. My eyes were fixed on my attacker, who was now pulling out a long-barrelled pistol. Oh my God, I thought, this cannot be happening, these people have come here to murder us in broad daylight.

There was no time to make a plan; instinct took over. I ran for my life, sprinting away from our van and into the deeply conservative quarter of Al-Suwaidi. There was a loud crack from somewhere behind me and I felt something sting my shoulder. I didn't know it then but that first bullet passed clean through, hitting the shoulder bone on the way. My adrenaline must have been pumping because I remember it being no more painful than a bee sting, and I ran on, trying to put as much distance as possible between me and the gunman. For a few brief, happy seconds I thought I was actually going to make it, trusting in the power of my legs to outrun my attackers. I felt almost euphoric at the prospect of escaping them, and I began to look ahead for cover. There was not much. Everywhere I looked there were high, windowless walls, locked doors and wide open spaces. But it was academic – I never made it that far.

There was another loud bang and the next thing I knew I was down on my front on the tarmac, felled by a bullet in the leg. I had run slap into the terrorists' second team; they had overtaken me in a minivan to cut off my escape. Now they were crowded inside the open sliding door of their van while I lay prone and helpless on the ground, looking up in horror at this group of Islamist gunmen. These men appeared very different from my first attacker; they had made no attempt to disguise their *jihadi* appearance. Their thin, pale faces were framed by wispy, unkempt beards in the style of most extremists and they had the look of people who spent all their time indoors. Instead of the neatly arranged headdresses with a sharp crease in the middle worn by ordinary urban Saudis, these men wore theirs wound tightly round their foreheads like a bandage. It was the *isaaba*, the dress worn by *jihadi* fighters who consider they are about to go into battle, the same style worn by the 9/11 suicidal hijackers in their video testimonies and by Mohammed Siddique Khan, the leader of the 7 July London bombers, in his posthumous video warning to the West. I realized then that I was doomed. These men were no casual, have-a-go amateurs, they were the real thing: a hardcore Al-Qaeda terror cell bent on attacking their government, killing Westerners and 'cleansing the Arabian peninsular of infidels'.

In that instant I glimpsed faces driven by pure hatred and fanaticism. I pleaded with them in Arabic, as so many hostages have done in Iraq, while they held a brief discussion as to what to do with me. It did not take long. They responded to my pleas by opening fire once more. Even then it crossed my mind how unfair this was. I had spent four years studying Islam for my degree, learning Arabic, reading and translating the Koran and other Islamic texts. I had lived happily amongst Arab families, fasted with Bedu tribespeople in Jordan, taught English to the impoverished family of an Egyptian taxi driver in a verminous Cairo slum. For the past few years I had tried hard to explain the complexities of the Middle East and the thinking behind the Al-Qaeda phenomenon to Western and international audiences. And this was my reward? A bunch of bullets in the guts from men who had convinced themselves they were killing in the cause of Islam. It just did not seem right.

From somewhere close behind me, a gunman stood over me and pumped bullets into the small of my back, hitting my pelvis and sacral bones and causing immeasurable damage to my internal organs. I don't remember it hurting at the point of impact, just a deafening noise each time he squeezed the trigger and a sickening jolt as the bullets thudded into my guts. Each time he fired it was as if a giant hand had picked me up and slammed me down on the tarmac. It rocked my whole inner body frame, like the chassis of a car in a head-on collision. Bloody hell, I thought, I'm really being shot. I'm taking a lot of rounds here. So is this where I float gracefully up into the sky and look down at my body sprawled out below? What an idiot you are. You're supposed to report on Al-Qaeda, not get so close to them you end up getting killed!

But there was one thought in my head that overrode all the others. I *have* to survive this, I told myself, for the sake of Amanda and my girls. I cannot leave them on this earth without a husband and a father. I closed my eyes and kept as still as I could, face-down on my front. The shooting had stopped and there was a discussion going on in Arabic. One of the terrorists was getting out of the van and walking towards me. I held my breath, playing dead while I listened to his footsteps drawing closer. I felt a hand reach into the back pocket of my trousers and remove Simon's radio microphone (which they left at the scene). Then he fished into the other back pocket and took out that miniature copy of the Koran that I had remembered to pack in London.

There followed a terrifying few seconds when any number of horrors could have been inflicted on me. In the previous week this same cell had dragged Michael Hamilton's lifeless body from the back of their vehicle. Would they now be tempted to do the same to me? The week after the attack on us an American helicopter technician, Paul Johnson, would be kidnapped in Riyadh and beheaded, his captors filming his execution then keeping his severed head in the family freezer for days until it was discovered in a police raid. I have no idea if the discovery of that Koran in my pocket saved my life or if the terrorists were by now convinced they had finished me off.

For me, lying punctured and bleeding on the ground, there suddenly came the sweetest sound in the world: the noise of my attackers revving up their engine and driving off. They were leaving me for dead. There followed total silence. No wail of sirens, no crying of children, no clatter of approaching feet. Ominously, there was no sign of Simon, the minder or the driver either. It seemed I was completely alone. Why wasn't anybody coming to my rescue? I felt many things at once: I was relieved and amazed to be still alive, I was furious at the injustice of this attack, yet I was surprisingly calm. I waited until I thought the coast was clear then I flipped over on to my back, supporting myself half upright with extended arms so I could call out more effectively for help. As I turned I felt my legs roll over like two dead logs, my feet flopping flat and lifeless against the ground. My right leg was bent in and out at crazy angles and I could feel nothing below the waist. 'Damn,' I remember thinking, 'that's not good. If I survive this I'm going to need some serious physiotherapy.' Unseen by me, someone was discreetly photographing me with a mobile phone and this was the grainy image that appeared in newspapers and on TV within hours.

By now the adrenaline had worn off and I was in the most excruciating, indescribable pain. The clean white shirt I had pulled on an hour ago for the piece-to-camera was saturated in blood. I had lost count of the number of times I had been shot. In a cracked and desperate voice I cried out in Arabic for help. My cries were of base, animal pain. I was emitting sounds I did not even recognize. At first no one came; the place was deserted. Then a handful of local Saudi men drifted on to the scene and my heart leaped. With their straggly beards and loosely wrapped headdresses they looked disturbingly like the people who had just shot me. Had they come to finish me off? Before I had time to think about it they were joined by a dozen more locals. Despite the pain, I felt reassured by the crowd, which was now getting sufficiently large that if anyone was carrying a concealed weapon he was unlikely to pull it out in front of so many witnesses.

And then, the strangest thing happened. Nobody helped me. In Muslim society, charity and hospitality are legendary. I have known Egyptians cross four lanes of rush-hour traffic to help with a flat tyre; an Omani minister once gave me his prized walking cane inscribed with his title in silver;

Indonesians have slaughtered their sole goat to share with me. And yet here I was, lying in the road, obviously very badly injured, and yet nobody came to help. That is one of the things I remember most about this ordeal: the terrible feeling of loneliness, the sense that I was completely on my own, that I could not rely on anyone to help me. I was obviously an object of interest: there was plenty of discussion and pointing at the empty cartridge cases that lay all around me. But something to staunch the blood? A pillow? A glass of water? Even a few words of comfort? Forget it. The only charitable explanation I can think of is that perhaps nobody dared come near me lest they get dragged off to the police station as a witness.

Staying alive became an endurance test. I feared that if I blacked out and lost consciousness I would be dead by the time I reached hospital, so I willed myself to stay alert. I had never considered myself to be particularly tough (I have always been a complete wuss about cold showers), but I had had some experience of endurance challenges, having run two marathons at university and completed Hong Kong's 100-km Macclehose Trail in under twenty-four hours. But this was different, it was like nothing I had ever known in my life. Bizarrely, though, I do remember thinking, 'Ah, but Frank, you have never given birth and that must be quite an ordeal.'

When the police finally showed up after about half an hour, alerted by somebody in the neighbourhood, they joined a growing throng of people all gawking at me from a distance. It was strange that in years of broadcasting I had never felt self-conscious, despite knowing that millions of people were watching. Yet here I was, being closely observed by thirty or so people, and it did not feel good, perhaps because they had shown no sign of wanting to help. By now I had lost a lot of blood. I was still conscious, but there was no sign of an ambulance or any medics; the policemen seemed unsure of what to do with me. Somebody asked me if I had noted down the number plate of the attackers' van. I think I replied that I had been too busy getting shot to notice, but I did tell them I was British. I knew that Britain was almost as unpopular in some quarters here as America, because of the Iraq invasion, but I hoped that someone would get word to the British Embassy. I was then manhandled by several khaki-clothed policemen into the back of their patrol car. Aware that I was a bloody mess of broken bones and gunshot wounds, they laid me lengthways on some kind of plank contraption. They did the best they could, but the length of my body was greater than the width of their car. And so I remember my head and shoulders protruded ludicrously from one of the back windows.

The police car drove off at speed, sirens blaring, lurching initially over rough bumpy wasteland. I had no idea where they were taking me, but I was in too much pain to care. On top of the agony the bullet wounds were causing me, I now had to grip on to the roof of the car to stop my head getting knocked about.

We pulled up at last at the Al-Iman hospital – not, I learned later, one of Riyadh's finest. There was a huge commotion at the doorway as everyone argued how best to extract me from my rear compartment and on to a hospital trolley, while I lay groaning and writhing but still conscious. At one stage I was being pulled in opposite directions. Then I was rushed through the hospital doors and into the operating theatre. My last memory was of looking up at the faces of the surgeons. They wore an expression close to panic. Then my pleas for painkillers were answered. A needle slid into my arm and I sank at last into oblivion.

2

Early Encounters

ﺷﺒﺎﻙ ﻓَﻨّﻲ
ﺇﺳﻼﻣﻲ

MY FASCINATION WITH THE ARAB world began when I was sixteen. One wintry day in 1977 my mother and I sat on a London bus, clutching our shopping bags and glad to be out of the rain. As the double-decker sloshed its way down Oxford Street we noticed a tall, impeccably dressed man in his sixties giving up his seat to a woman half his age. When he turned his head my mother recognized him immediately. It was Sir Wilfred Thesiger, the veteran Arabian explorer and author of *Arabian Sands* and *The Marsh Arabs*. They had known each other briefly in the 1950s; in fact my mother even suspected his mother of trying to pair them off at one stage, but Thesiger was not the marrying kind. His craggy weatherbeaten face cracked into a smile of recognition. This was a man, explained my mother, who had made journeys previously thought impossible, travelling on foot with his Bedu companions across the vast and inhospitable Arabian desert known as the Empty Quarter. Thesiger's face looked as if it could tell a thousand stories. His piercing eyes glinted beneath bushy eyebrows and his broken nose, a souvenir from his boxing days at Oxford, resembled that of a hungry bird of prey. 'You must come to tea,' he said, so we did.

Sitting in Thesiger's Chelsea flat, trying not to spill his scalding tea, I was mesmerized by the curved Arab daggers that hung from the walls. There were battered old camel saddles and a shrivelled water gourd that seemed to speak of desperate times in far-off places. On his desk were piles of manuscripts for a forthcoming book. On the wall hung large black-and-white photographs taken by him, showing lonely camel trains traversing giant dunes. The lined face of a Bedu nomad stared out at me, framed by a scruffy headscarf, his hand clutching an antiquated rifle. As a teenager just starting to take an interest in travelling, I was fascinated.

'It's all gone now,' said Thesiger wearily, interrupting my reverie. 'That world has vanished, completely ruined by oil. The people I travelled and explored with in the forties and fifties now live in villas and towns. They have lost all connection with their desert past. People there today know nothing of the hardship and nobility of those times.'

I was not fully convinced. 'But surely there must still be some places worth visiting?' I ventured.

It was as if I had pressed a button; Thesiger went into full flow. He had apparently just come back from a disastrous trip to the Gulf, where the quaint, mud-walled villages and forts he had known in the fifties had morphed into prosperous modern cities, where his bête noire, the 'motor car', was everywhere. He did his best to persuade me to forget about the Arab world; East Africa with the Samburu tribe, he said, was the place to be.

I was completely unperturbed. Although I had never been to the Middle East and had yet to read any books by the celebrated explorers Burton, Doughty and Freya Stark, I had a curiosity about the Arab world that was part romantic, part hard-nosed pragmatism. I had seen posters in a travel agent's of Jordan's camel-mounted border guards patrolling the red sands of Wadi Rumm, and I'd listened in awe to my school-friend Alex recounting what it had been like to live in Amman, where his father worked for the UN, during the recent 1973 Yom Kippur War. On the practical side, the Arabs had oil, and it was likely to last well beyond my lifetime, so it seemed to me that there was always going to be a job for someone who spoke their language and knew about their culture. Arabic was the lingua franca in twenty countries from North Africa to the Indian Ocean. It was yet to be taught at secondary-school level in Britain, but when term time came round again in the sixth form at Marlborough College I enrolled in an extracurricular course on Islam and the Middle East. It was run by an English literature teacher, John Osborne, who had fallen in love with Iran and its exquisite Islamic architecture. His enthusiasm soon rubbed off on our small class and we sat rapt at his slide shows of the mosques, caravanserais and bazaars of Isfahan and Shiraz. I found myself doodling Arabic and Persian calligraphy during history lectures when I should have been paying attention to how Pitt the Younger formed his cabinet. By the time I took my A-levels I was determined to read Arabic at university.

My parents had mixed feelings about this. They were not overjoyed at the prospect of their only child making a career in a part of the world that had just fought two major wars in the space of six years. Neither of them had any first-hand knowledge of the Middle East beyond brief port stops at Aden and Port Said on a voyage back from Singapore; the Middle East was an intractable mystery to them and neither had any affinity with the region or its culture. But as career diplomats they harboured hopes that I would one day follow in their footsteps and apply to join the Foreign Office, where Arabic would obviously be an advantage. Already I had inherited their love of languages. My father Neil had learned German while living with a family in the Sudetenland on the eve of the Second World War and he would recount watching the Nazi parades in the cobbled streets just months before he was mobilized on the other side of the Channel. Soon after D-Day he was putting his German to use in Normandy, where his unit was tasked with questioning recently captured German POWs. My mother Grace had read modern languages at Cambridge and had a voracious appetite for French novels. As only the third woman to get into the Diplomatic Service she was asked what her preferences were for an overseas posting. 'Anywhere but behind the Iron Curtain,' she replied, so they sent her to Budapest. Hungary was going through a brutal period of Stalinist repression in the fifties but my mother quickly picked up Hungarian and made several lifelong friends, although some were dragged off in the middle of the night by the secret police, accused of 'anti-communist' activities and incarcerated for years. Back in 1958, when my parents married, the Foreign Office expected its few female diplomats to resign when they married. This absurd rule was not rescinded until the 1960s, but my mother got round it by working for them part-time.

My memories of being a small child in London in the 1960s are of the family crowding round the transistor radio to listen to the prime minister, Harold Wilson, and hearing the announcement of Sir Winston Churchill's death. I always seemed to be having my hair severely combed for children's parties and being told 'Don't forget to say thank-you when you leave.' There were piano lessons at school with a woman called Mrs Lloyd Webber (the mother of Andrew; sadly their family talents never rubbed off on me), and I can remember getting the gamut of children's illnesses – mumps, measles and chicken pox – and my devoted gran peeling grapes at my bed-side. To toughen me up I was taken weekly to Mr Sturgess's gym in South Kensington, where the no-nonsense Mr Sturgess would make us jump up and swing from the monkey bars at the age of five. Once I got into a fight with a boy behind me, who I thought was trying to queue-barge in front of me, which ended with my biting his hair and us having to be separated. My mother was appalled. 'Do you know who that boy is?' she hissed. 'It's Prince Andrew.' When I learned this I was genuinely frightened; apparently I replied, 'Does that mean I'm going to go to prison?'

When I was six my father was posted to the British Embassy in The Hague, where we lived for the next three years. My earliest memory of foreign travel is of our little family boarding the overnight ferry from Harwich to the Hook of Holland and waking up beside a porthole, through which I could see a gas flare burning beside the shores of the North Sea. This seemed the height of exoticism at the time. One of the first towns we drove through on the Continent was called Monster, which made it even more of an adventure. Holland may be almost next door to Britain on the map, but to me it was a strange and exciting place: there were wild boar roaming in the dark woods, seals on the beaches, and in winter it was cold enough to skate along the canals beside the windmills then warm up afterwards with hot pancakes in a seventeenth-century farmhouse. The Dutch had their own version of Christmas called St Nicholas, when friends and neighbours would deliver anonymous presents of glazed patisserie to our door, ringing the bell then vanishing before we opened it. At the international school my best friend was Dutch and I made a stab at learning his guttural language – some consonants are not dissimilar to Arabic – although this was quite pointless as the Dutch all seemed to speak perfect English. Two years later I was sent to boarding school in Kent, travelling unaccompanied on the flight from Rotterdam to Gatwick. Flying home to Holland for Christmas at the end of my first term I was horribly airsick, then the plane was diverted by snow to Amsterdam and for much of the night my parents drove frantically around the Lowlands trying to locate me, while I was happily ensconced in a waiting room with a stewardess, playing with model aeroplanes. As an only child I had learned to amuse myself and I don't remember ever being bored or lonely. I did, though, resent the large number of diplomatic parties my parents were expected to go to in the evenings in The Hague, and they did their best to get out of them without giving offence.

At prep school I was something of a goodie-two-shoes: head prefect, scholar, captain of shooting, victor ludorum in athletics, winner of obscure prizes like Chess and Reading. I left with an Exhibition (a minor scholarship) to Marlborough, but then my academic prowess took a nose-dive. Suddenly there seemed to be so many distractions, especially drama which I threw myself into. Since I seemed to be good at shooting and running, the school contacted the British biathlon Olympic ski team and over two winters I trained hard with the Army in the Austrian Alps before deciding I did not fancy dedicating the next eight years of my life to a sport which was always dominated by Nordic and East European countries. Anyway, I was an average rather than exceptional biathlon skier and the Olympic team needed supermen.

Almost my sole achievement was to become captain of shooting (again) and win a place on the British cadet rifle team to Canada, which included a summer canoe trip in the woods and lakes of upstate Quebec with the Canadian army. The night before we were due to return to civilization I had a nightmare that my long-awaited A-level results had been dreadful: a C and two Ds. The next day I duly rang home and there was a long pause. 'It's not good news,' said my mother. 'You got a C and two Ds.'

Amazingly, this was no barrier to my pursuing my ambition to learn Arabic. I found out that of the few British universities to offer a degree course in Arabic and Islamic Studies, Exeter actually sent its students off to Cairo for a whole year instead of expecting you to fix up something yourself in the summer holidays. I took a train down to Devon to see the head of department, the Egyptian Professor Shaban. Either Shaban was a shrewd judge of a student's potential or he was simply desperate to boost numbers on the course, which at the time were only just nudging double figures. It must be said that he was very odd to look at: almost bald, but retaining a few silky wisps that cascaded down the back of his head, all neatly combed into a ducktail, giving him the appearance of a well-groomed Pekinese. His white moustache was out of control, with several rogue hairs escaping up into his nostrils, causing him to snuffle uncontrollably at the end of each sentence. Most confusing of all, he would often make a statement that ended with a sort of chortle. Out of politeness, I would laugh too, noticing too late that his eyes were not smiling, but were in fact angry at my impertinence. But right then I could have kissed him because he gave me a place on the course. I had walked into his office with a dim view of my chances and walked out an undergraduate with a future.

I now had several months left of the fabled gap year between school and university and resolved to get myself out to the Middle East. I applied for menial jobs in several hotels around the Arab world and to work on a kibbutz in the Negev desert in Israel. While I waited for replies I got work wherever I could find it, including stacking bricks at a factory in Hampshire (£54 a week, less tax, less board and lodging at my parents). The Arab hotels and Israeli kibbutz people all sent letters politely declining my services, so when I had scraped together enough to go travelling I went up to London to buy a cheap InterRail pass that would take me by train to both Morocco and Istanbul.

It was a warm day in May and walking through Hyde Park I stopped to investigate what was going on in Prince's Gate. The whole street appeared to have been closed off to traffic and there were police and cordons everywhere. Hundreds of Iranian Muslims had taken over the road outside the Albert Hall and were squatting on the tarmac, holding collective prayers. Out of sight, a few yards away, a group of Arabic-speaking terrorists from the oil-rich Iranian province of Khuzestan had seized control of the Iranian embassy in Prince's Gate, taking everyone inside hostage at gunpoint. While the police opened negotiations, the Army's Special Air Service (SAS) Counter-Terrorist Unit was preparing for the possibility that its soldiers might have to retake the embassy by storm. The SAS team leader on the spot was Major Peter de la Billiere. Descendant of a French Huguenot family and known as 'DLB', he was already a veteran of counter-insurgency operations in Malaya, Oman and Aden. I was eighteen at the time and had no idea that twelve years later we would both be investment bankers, attending meetings together with Gulf rulers.

The Iranian embassy siege ended abruptly and violently a few days after it began. As soon as shots were heard from inside the building it was obvious the gunmen had started to execute their hostages. The time for talking was over. Black-clad SAS troopers abseiled down from the roof, lobbed stun grenades through the windows, shot the terrorists and freed the hostages. It was a seminal moment in more ways than one. This was the first most people had heard of the secretive crack unit called the SAS, and the regiment soon found itself subject to a lot of unwanted attention. But the incident also brought Middle Eastern terrorism home to Britain. Londoners had grown used to the threat of IRA bombings, but few expected the complex feuds of the Islamic world to spill over to these shores. Suddenly counter-terrorism was the new buzzword and the Thatcher government determined to make Britain too hard a target for foreign terrorists to tackle. Looking back now, twenty-five years later, those were easy days in counter-terrorism compared with the challenges now facing the security forces. Who could have predicted then that Britain would be targeted by an elusive transnational force called Al-Qaeda, or that some of its followers would turn out to be British citizens hiding unnoticed amidst the rest of the population?

But thoughts of terrorism were far from my mind as I set off by rail with a rucksack for Morocco in the summer of 1980. Most of my friends had either started their first jobs or had already taken off on their own gap years, so I was initially alone on this trip. My parents bore this well. I suppose they could hardly complain since they had done so much travelling themselves, but it is only now I am a parent myself that I can begin to appreciate the anxieties they must have suffered over the years each time I was out of contact for a while, anxieties which of course were realized in the summer of 2004.

On a backpacker's budget I wound my way slowly down through the stunted spring vineyards of Andalucia to the port of Algeciras and the ferry for Tangier. As the wind whipped round the Straits of Gibraltar I stood on the deck, clustered together with other wary-looking Europeans, watching the coastline of Europe recede and the shores of North Africa draw closer. As the boat nosed into Tangier harbour we glimpsed white-walled houses climbing up the gentle hillside. Here and there stood the square, crenellated minarets of mosques, and for the first time I heard the haunting sound of the call to prayer. It drifted out from the town and across the water to reach us where we stood on the deck. We were certainly in another world from the one we had left behind in Spain, and the difference jumped out at us as soon as we passed through Customs.

'*Psst! Chef! Hashish? Tu veux acheter le keefi?*' The first drug-peddler latched on to our little group of European back-packers before we were even off the jetty. Dressed in crotch-hugging flares, stack-heeled shoes and an open shirt complete with medallion, he was the archetypal seventies-revival man. Except that we were only just out of the seventies and people really did dress like that. This one looked like trouble, though. His eyes darted shiftily above pockmarked cheeks and his face bore a scar that looked like a slash from a knife. I had read about the drugs industry here: 'keefi' was the local Moroccan word for hashish. Grown extensively up in the Rif mountains, it was illegal, but it was widely smoked. Unfortunately for Western backpackers, a lucrative income was to be had by informing on tourists, then claiming a reward. And an even more lucrative income could be made by persuading terrified tourists, once caught, to bribe their way out of trouble.

Together with a young Dutch couple and a roll-up-smoking German, I ignored him but he followed us past the French-built pavement cafés that lined the harbour, *psst*-ing and *chef*-ing all the way, like something out of *Thomas the Tank Engine*. When we turned left up into the *kasbah*, the old quarter, he turned left as well. Of course it was his city and he knew every backstreet, so there was no shaking him off, but he was starting to ruin the place for us. The Dutch couple decided to buy him off; this was a mistake. They did not get arrested, but as soon as they had parted with their money and bought themselves an unwanted packet of weed other peddlers swarmed around them, attracted by the sight of hard Western currency. We had to take refuge for almost the entire afternoon in an upmarket café overlooking the bay, and suddenly our fortunes changed. The café staff were friendly and welcoming and we ordered glass after glass of delicious mint tea, poured sweet and steaming at some height from a brass teapot with a long curved spout into thin cracked glasses. We lay back on plump cushions and listened to the strange halftones and quavers of Arab music coming from a radio somewhere. We had all of Morocco to explore if we wanted, and life at that moment seemed pretty good.

In fact I saw only a small fraction of the country, preferring to visit first the capital Rabat, with its spectacular Mosque of Mohammed V and its guard of costumed Arab lancers, then Meknès, a former royal capital rich in historic architecture. I liked nothing better than to sit there at a street café, listening to the strange, abrasive North African accents all around me, savouring the scent of the jasmine-sellers and gazing abstractedly at those mysterious keyhole-shaped doorways through which beggars, donkeys and a dozen veiled women seemed to pass in the blinking of an eye. I liked the leisurely Moroccan lifestyle, their habit of going home at lunchtime for a big meal and a decent siesta, then staying up late to mingle and gossip in the covered souk. Not all the Moroccans I encountered were after my meagre backpacker's savings. Many were genuinely hospitable, eager to show me their city for free, or inviting me to meet their families and share a dish of steaming tagine. One man's sister still wrote to me months later – though we exchanged little more than a glance as she brought in the meal – ending her letters with the poetic French words: *'Je te quitte avec mon stylo mais pas avec mon coeur!'*, 'I leave you with my biro but not with my heart.' I knew that what little I had seen of Morocco was far from typical of the rest of the Arab world, that it was only one of over twenty Arab countries. But that taste was enough to reassure me that I had made the right decision. I wanted more than ever to get to know the Arab world, its language, its culture, its religion and its history.

By the time term started at Exeter University in September 1980 I had a smattering of Arabic vocabulary, I could recognize the shapes of some of the letters and I felt I had reaffirmed my commitment to study what was then still considered to be an obscure language. By now the Iran–Iraq War had broken out and there was a buzz of excitement in the Faculty of Arabic and Islamic Studies. A lot of the postgraduate students in our building were Iraqi, some of whom were later reported to be agents of Saddam's regime, tasked to spy on the Iraqi community in Britain for any signs of anti-Saddam behaviour. By invading Iran in the summer, Saddam Hussein had reckoned he could redress in his favour the border treaty he had made five years earlier with Iran's now-deposed Shah Reza Pahlavi. The Iranian military, once the best-run and best-equipped in the Gulf, was in turmoil following the purges of the Islamic Revolution. Many of the most competent officers had been executed, while others had found themselves promoted on the basis of their revolutionary zeal rather than any martial skills. Iran also had an equipment crisis; under the Shah the 'imperial' forces had looked to America and Britain to supply their hardware, but Ayatollah Khomeini had declared America 'the Great Satan' and relations with Britain were hardly any better, so even in peacetime spare parts were going to be a problem, let alone when fighting a full-scale war against a large, well-equipped army like Iraq's. It was hardly surprising Saddam thought he could bring Iran to its knees by the end of the year.

On the campus at Exeter there was a book fair at which Iraqi students proudly leafed through glossy brochures supplied by their embassy and their compatriots in the Iraqi Cultural Centre in London's Tottenham Court Road. The brochures showed Iraqi tanks charging through sand berms into Iranian territory down in the marshes just north of Kuwait. Crowds of cheering, gun-clenching Iraqi soldiers rode on the tanks, flashing victory signs, acting like it would all be over within weeks. 'You will see,' said one moustachioed student to me, 'it will be a great victory.' But Saddam had underestimated the Iranians and their capacity to throw wave after wave of poorly equipped but fanatical soldiers at the front. The ayatollahs cultivated the idea of the *baseej*, the volunteer martyr. The volunteers – who were often just boys – would tie scarves bearing holy verses round their foreheads then march knowingly into minefields, clearing the way for the more experienced – and less expendable – troops then to engage the Iraqis. The suicidal *baseej* were given little plastic keys to hang around their necks, symbolizing the keys to the gates of Paradise. It is ironic that twenty-five years later Iraq has again become the battleground for suicidal volunteers to throw themselves at an enemy, in this case the US-led Coalition and its Iraqi allies.

For eight years, from 1980 to 1988, Saddam's generals fought the Iranians with clouds of poison gas, power cables immersed into the marshes to electrocute the wading Persian infantry, air raids on oil terminals far down the Gulf, and eventually Scud missiles aimed at the capital Tehran. The Iraqis even had the advantage of US intelligence on their side, with Washington feeding them a steady stream of satellite images of Iranian positions. Yet despite all this Iraq's early gains soon petered out and the war descended into one of attrition, with each side gaining a few hundred metres of use-less, shell-blasted marshland, then losing it the next month. It was the First World War all over again, it was to cost the lives of nearly a million men, and it was to end in a stalemate.

At Exeter University, I was itching to start the year abroad in Cairo and somehow, illogically, I was hoping the Iran–Iraq War might prompt our tutors to send us to Egypt sooner than planned. But they had no intention of letting us off the two initial years of hard slog in the classroom, getting to grips with glottal stops, throat-rasping consonants and the various other joys of Arabic grammar. Some people claim that Arabic is one of the hardest languages to learn, but I think this is an exaggeration. We learned the alphabet in a week – even the word itself comes from Arabic, with *alif*, *ba*, *ta* being the first three letters of the Arabic alphabet. True, it is written from right to left and each letter changes its shape according to whether it's at the beginning, middle or end of a word. True, there are a handful of sounds quite alien to the Western palate, like the *kh* as in Khartoum, and yes, it's most un-helpful that Arabic is usually written and printed without the inclusion of vowels, leaving you to guess where they go. But hey, there are only twenty-eight letters to cope with, not thousands as in Japanese. Arabic is not tonal, like Thai or other Oriental languages; it is pronounced as it is written. Plus it does follow a certain logic. Most Arabic words are based on a 'root' of three consonants. For example, anything with the letters k, t, b in it is going to be connected with writing. So *kitaab* is a book, *maktaba* is a library, *kaatib* is a writer, and so on.

Still, this was always going to be a rather unusual four-year degree course, compared with, say, English Literature or Chemical Engineering. For a start, there were only fifteen of us. I looked round the tiny lecture room, wondering what had made my fellow undergraduates take on this language. One was obvious: Neil Hawkins lived in Damascus, where his father was the UN Refugee and Works Agency (UNRWA) rep, so he already had a head start on the rest of us. Neil cared passionately about the Palestinians and years later went on to work on the Oslo Peace Accords, for the UN, then eventually as an adviser to the Australian government. There was Andrew Cunningham, a tall, lanky student with a penchant for Levantine dancing and embroidered waistcoats picked up on his gap year travelling through Iran. Andrew later did the exact opposite of what I did: he started out as a journalist then moved across to the financial world, assessing Middle Eastern banks for credit agencies, which I can't help feeling was a waste of his talents. Then there was Peppy, an attractive girl from Oxford who confessed on day one that she had no career ambitions beyond graduating, yet lived in perpetual terror of the exams. She and I would silently pass each other notes of gossip scribbled in our recently learned Arabic; I think it was some months before either of us understood the other's messages. There was Natalie, who decided the course was not for her and left almost immediately. Sharon too dropped out, but not until the third year when she ran off with an Irish oilman in Cairo and was last heard of living happily in Beirut. There was Rosemary, a good-time party girl who eventually followed up her good degree in Arabic and Islamic Studies by joining Club 18–30, a sequitur I could never quite fathom out. Then there were Janet, Jane and Louise, three girls who rarely spoke but sat demurely on a couch at the back of the room taking copious notes; one of our tutors nicknamed them '*Ahl Al-Kanaba*', 'The Couch People', and during class discussions he would address questions to all three collectively: 'Do the Couch People have a view on this one, perhaps?' But my favourite, despite my initial misgivings, was a student called Peregrine Muncaster. He looked unpromising: nerdy anorak, glasses, pale freckly face devoid of all expression. Yet he turned out to have a brilliant sense of humour and a totally irreverent attitude to homework, which he got away with by fooling the lecturers with his outwardly serious demeanour. We were to become lifelong friends and explore several countries together. There was one other undergraduate I noticed that first term. Tony Fleming was a mature student in the year above us; he had served in the SAS in the Dhofar campaign in Oman, where he had been shot in the back by Marxist insurgents and paralysed. He was a familiar sight in the Arabic department, furiously pushing himself along corridors in his wheelchair and resolutely refusing to have doors held open for him. What must it be like, I remember thinking, to get shot and have to spend the rest of your life in a wheelchair?

Now that I was enrolled I found it hard to understand why neither the coursework nor the lecturers seemed to have much connection with the realities of the modern Middle East. Like many true academics, theirs was a world of intricate grammar, of historical texts, of early pre-Islamic poetry. I yearned to learn how to speak the language of the street or to analyse the latest speech by an Arab leader, but I was told rather haughtily that if that was what I wanted then I should attend a polytechnic, not a university. To be fair, they did give us a superb grounding in the rich treasure trove that is Arabic literature. We painstakingly translated *qasida*, sad and moving verses by the pre-Islamic Arabian poet Imru'l Qais. He would describe his odyssey of unrequited love across the sands of the Nejd desert in what is now Saudi Arabia, searching always for his beloved whom he kept missing by just a few hours. The poet would come across an abandoned camp fire in the dunes where she and her tribe had spent the previous night and he would pick over the ashes, thinking of her, gazing at the dimples in the sand where she may have lain her perfect head.

We were taught how Arabic novel-writing had evolved over the last century from the historical to the romantic to the realistic. We translated and read *Midaq Alley* by the Nobel prize-winning author Naguib Mahfouz, a beguiling story of how a girl from the backstreets of Cairo in the 1940s got sucked into a life of sleaze in wartime bars with off-duty British soldiers. We read literature from the golden age of the Islamic caliphates, when art, science, architecture and writing flourished under the patronage of caliphs in Baghdad and Cairo.

Above all, we studied the Muslim holy book, the Koran, which was 'revealed' to the Prophet Muhammad, who was illiterate. We were taught about the life of the Prophet and his *Ansar* – his companions – the birth of Islam, its early struggle to convert people in a largely godless society dominated by idol-worshippers and greedy merchants, and then the incredible, explosive speed with which Islam's armies conquered all before them. Within little more than a century of the Prophet's death in AD 632 the Muslim armies had plunged deep into Europe, reaching Poitiers in France, while to the East they spread right across Arabia, into Persia and down into India. It is easy to overlook it now but Spain was under Muslim rule for more than seven centuries, a period from which the Moorish palace of the Alhambra in Granada is just one example. Islam, we learned, was not just a religion, but a way of life, a system of order and stability that, although sometimes introduced at sword-point, often replaced anarchy and barbarism.

But although we were unknowingly being given the keys to the world of Arab and Islamic culture, it was still a relatively dry, academic course and I needed something a little more down-to-earth to keep me motivated towards getting my degree. In the first spring holiday I bought a bucket-shop ticket to Tunis, figuring this was the nearest and cheapest place for me to try out my new-found Arabic. Once again, I opted to travel alone, deciding that this would make me more receptive to people around me. Landing at Tunis-Carthage airport I quickly discovered that everyone spoke French and they expected me to as well. I decided that the further I travelled away from the Mediterranean boulevards and whitewashed villas of the capital the more I would have to use Arabic. So I hopped on a bus and headed south to the troglodyte village of Matmata, a place so other-worldly in appearance that it was chosen as one of the sets for the Hollywood blockbuster *Star Wars*.

At first glance, the landscape was unremarkable, just a series of low arid hills and the odd clump of date palms. Then I spotted the sunken, underground houses for which Matmata is famous. With no warning at all the ground would stop abruptly at your feet, giving way to a great carved-out hollow, several storeys deep. Arranged around this open-air 'well' were a number of caves set into the earth and connected by steps, ladders or sometimes even just a long rope with knots in it. In the caves that were still inhabited, Berber women strung out washing and sang to each other while their husbands sat and smoked in the spring sunshine. At least two of these cave-houses had been made into subterranean hotels and I checked into one of them. My room was on the first floor, if you were to work upwards from the bottom of the central pit, or minus three if you were to measure it downwards from ground level. The dry-mud floor was swept clean and on my bed was a woven Berber rug to keep out the cold of the desert night. That evening there was a folklore show to entertain a coachload of German tourists bussed in from the nearby port of Gabes. The Tunisians banged drums, blew on strange pipes and played bagpipes, to the delight of the Germans. When it was all over and I could hear the coach driver revving his engines up above, I felt immensely smug retiring to my cave bedroom just a few yards away.

I spent the next day getting to know the local Tunisians, who struck me as kind, decent people. Dressed in cool, loose-fitting robes, they invariably wore the *chech*, a red felt skullcap with a tiny tassel on the top. They quickly corrected me on a major faux pas I had been making. The standard Tunisian greeting is '*laa bas*', meaning 'no harm' or 'no evil'. Unfortunately I had been saying '*libas*', which I was told meant 'garments' or 'underwear'. Touring a country saying 'pants' to everyone you meet is probably not the best way to ingratiate yourself; it is a wonder nobody knocked me into the gutter.

When I had set off from Gatwick for Tunis I did not have a firm itinerary in mind, just two weeks in which to explore and pick up as much Arabic as I could. But the further south I travelled the more I felt lured by the mystique of the Sahara. Just over the border in Algeria lay the massive sand dunes of the Grand Erg Oriental and according to my Michelin map there was a road that could take me there. In the far south-west corner of Tunisia I hitched a lift with a French family across the vast salt lake known as the *Chott El Djerid*. The blinding white crusts of salt stretched out to the horizon, sculpted by the wind to form frozen waves. It seemed there was no life there at all: nothing stirred, there were no tufts of grass, no lonely sparrow. It was an awesome place and not one you would ever want to break down in.

Our crossing into Algeria did not go well. The French family had brought their own car over from Marseilles and it had French number plates. Not a problem in Tunisia, but apparently an invitation to trouble on the other side of the border. At the very first Algerian village we drove through the children started throwing stones at the car, not just idly but with real determination. After gentle, peaceful Tunisia this came as a shock, but I reminded myself that Algeria had gone through a bitter war of independence from France that even decades later had obviously left bad blood between them in some quarters.

The French family dropped me off at the market town of Ouargla, a name which sounded to me like someone being strangled. Despite the trading that was going on in the market square it looked significantly poorer than Tunisia. Men swathed in khaki turbans rode dilapidated donkey carts, and the inevitable mangy camel sat beneath a tattered banner that read in Arabic: '*Min Ash-sha'ab ila Ash-sha'ab*', 'From the People to the People'. One look at Ouargla told me there was not very much going to the people here.

I managed to hitch a lift to the next town, Touggourt, with another Frenchman, an aid worker, this time in a van with Algerian number plates, and we headed deeper into the sea of white Saharan dunes. This was the formidable desert known as the Grand Erg, which must have one of the lowest population densities on earth. Yet we stopped by the road to visit Ali, a shepherd he knew, right in the middle of nowhere. In the blazing noon heat the shepherd served us tea in his tiny hut, then brought out a sprig of the best dates I have ever tasted. They were called *deglat nour*, 'fingers of light', and they were so tender and sweet they literally melted in the mouth. The shepherd then entertained us by showing us how to find a scorpion from its imprints on the sand. It took him a minute or two to find the tracks, then his weatherbeaten hands began to move quickly over the ground. Suddenly he shouted *'Shouf! Shouf!'*, 'Look! Look!', and there sure enough was a vicious-looking yellow scorpion sprinting over the sand. Ali's hand moved like a snake and he grabbed it, opening his fist just enough for us to see it squirming inside, its ugly, beady eyes looking at us from the top of its flat head. Scorpions were clearly a part of the scenery around here: just over the border in Tunisia a shop had been selling postcards of the Zookeeper of Tozeur, a man who had become immune to the venom of scorpions and who proudly displayed about eight of them clinging to his open palm.

The Frenchman dropped me at a huge permanent tent that served as a travellers' resthouse on the outskirts of Touggourt. Here I was in luck. I found a group of French lycée students about the same age as me who were touring Algeria, and they immediately adopted me. At dusk we sat up on the crest of a huge dune, gazing out at the expanse of the Sahara, a soft warm breeze rippling across the sand and the aroma of grilled lamb drifting up from the guesthouse. That night I tasted my first couscous, the cracked wheat that is the staple diet in North Africa, but I passed a sleepless night. The French students had all been allocated their own sleeping quarters but I was given a patch of sand just beside the tent flap. I spread out my sleeping bag, wriggled into it and thought how great it was to be out here in the Sahara. Just then I became aware of a group of Algerians I had not seen before gathering round my sleeping bag. One of them whispered, 'Is he asleep yet?' Convinced they were out to rob me, or worse, I decided the only thing for it was to pretend I was having a violent nightmare. I put on quite a performance, groaning loudly, thrashing my arms and twisting my head this way and that. It did the trick as they recoiled in alarm, but after that I kept my guard up until the sun's first rays peeped over the dunes and I fell asleep until breakfast.

Travelling with the French students ensured I attracted a lot less attention than if I had been on my own. Osman, the teacher in charge of the group, was himself Algerian, an imposing man built like a bear but with the easy smile of a football star. He did all the bargaining on behalf of the students and kept any leering local youths at bay. The French girls did not seem to have made any compromises to their dress code on account of being in a Muslim country, and their bare arms and legs drew a combination of disapproving and wistful looks. It was as if the local Algerians could not make up their minds whether they wanted to scold them or sleep with them.

But mostly our experiences of eastern Algeria were peaceful, not confrontational. We spent a day picnicking at an oasis which we reached in a convoy of *charrettes* – donkey carts. In the dappled shade of a dozen date palms we lazed on rocks, splashed in the cool clear water and ate fresh oranges. In dusty marketplaces we shopped for desert roses, curious petalled crystalline formations that occur in the Sahara, and I spent hours sketching the local mosques. The architecture here had a distinctly African element, with sticks poking out from mud-walled minarets where doves would alight in flocks. At one point I squatted down to get comfortable only to hear a loud ripping sound. My trousers had torn at the seam all up the back. Escorted by two of the French girls who had to 'cover me', I made a hasty dash for a tailor's shop where I was kitted out with a pair of fantastically baggy khaki pantaloons. I have to say they were not my first choice, but they were all he had so I put them on, quickly discovering that the crotch was somewhere down between my knees and my ankles. As soon as I set foot outside there were roars of laughter; apparently nobody had been wearing these sort of trousers since the sixties. Still, it was an excellent way of diffusing tensions: I looked so ridiculous that people forgot to leer at the French girls.

Our Algerian foray ended in Ghardaya, an enchanting white and blue-walled Saharan oasis town where we slept on the mud roof of a restaurant. Ghardaya was so well hidden in the cleft of a dried-up river valley that you could almost miss it from above, but down at street level it was a labyrinth of twisting passageways and sandy backstreets. Like most of Algeria away from the Mediterranean cities, it was also very conservative. I came across a priceless notice at the entrance to the kasbah: 'Gentlemen, please respect our customs,' it began reasonably enough, 'and do not go without shirt as it will drive the women into great excitement.' Really? I was curious to witness the frenzied women of Ghardaya, but thought better of it. For female tourists there were stricter warnings still, and even our casually dressed lycée girls grudgingly draped a shawl over their tanned and bare shoulders.

I missed my chance to see more of Algeria under peaceful conditions after that. In the early 1990s the military-backed government held elections across the country, which it fully expected to win. But instead the popular vote went to the Islamist party, FIS (Front Islamique de Salvation). The government, however, decided it quite liked being in power and was not going to step down and let the Islamists take over, so it cancelled the elections. There was barely a murmur of protest from the West about this brazen overturning of a democratic election result, because nobody fancied the idea of a strict Islamic government in Algiers. The country then sank into the abyss of a decade-long civil war that claimed an estimated 150,000 lives, possibly more. Most of Algeria became off-limits for Western travellers throughout the 1990s, and as recently as 2003 a group of European tourists was held hostage in the Sahara by an Algerian terrorist group vaguely linked to Al-Qaeda. Reportedly, they only escaped with their lives because a hefty ransom was paid through Libyan intermediaries. Algeria is now slowly creeping back on to the tourist map – *Country Life* has even run a feature on the well-tended gardens of Algiers – but the civil war has left such a legacy of bitterness that it will take at least a generation for society there to heal. I was lucky: my formative year in the Arab world was to be in a place far removed from such troubles, amongst a people so good-natured it often seemed as if the whole country was sharing one huge collective joke.

3

Living in Cairo

عربـة الخضار جنب الأزهر، مصر   ٨٢/٤/٦٦

B ACK ON THE ARABIC COURSE AT EXETER, WE WERE BUSY immersing ourselves in the finer points of Arabic grammar and Islamic history, when over in Cairo the class above us were given a nasty shock. Every year in October the Egyptian military celebrates what it calls its 'victory' over Israel in the 1973 Yom Kippur War. Although it was indeed a psychological victory for the Arabs when they attacked Israel by surprise, the war resulted in their military defeat. Israel ended up in control of the entire (Egyptian) Sinai Peninsula, the (Palestinian) West Bank and the (Syrian) Golan Heights, so it has always rather baffled me as to how that can be called a victory. But by the late 1970s Egypt's President Anwar Sadat had decided there was no point being enemies with Israel, a country that after all possessed nuclear weapons, and that they might as well sign a peace deal and live side-by-side as good neighbours. In the eyes of the Arab world Sadat then

40

committed treason by flying to Israel and addressing the Knesset, the Israeli parliament. On the White House lawn the Camp David treaty was sealed between Sadat and Israel's Prime Minister Menachim Begin before a beaming US President Jimmy Carter and the world's press. But back in Egypt there were some who had already made up their minds that their president must now pay the ultimate price for befriending the Zionist enemy, Israel.

On 6 October 1981, President Sadat sat in a raised reviewing stand on the outskirts of Cairo, surrounded by his top generals, various ambassadors and assembled defence attachés. He watched with pride as his fighter jets roared overhead in formation and tanks clattered past with commanders saluting him from the turrets. When a column of infantry went past in open trucks, Sadat saw one of the soldiers jump down and he assumed he was going to make an over-enthusiastic salute. Sadat even stood up to receive it, but the soldier had other ideas. His name was Khaled El-Islambouly and he was part of an Islamist cell bent on assassinating Sadat and turning Egypt into an Islamic republic. (Iran's ayatollahs so applauded this idea they named a street after Islambouly in Tehran, close to the British Embassy.)

Islambouly jumped to the ground with his loaded Kalashnikov already at the aim and let rip a burst of machine-gun fire into the centre of the reviewing stand. His accomplices also opened fire and hurled grenades, one of which landed next to the vice-president, Air Force General Hosni Mubarak, but failed to go off. There was pandemonium in the reviewing stands as people tried to flee the carnage, scrambling over upturned chairs and bullet-riddled bodies. Some of Sadat's bodyguards began firing wildly, others hid for their own safety. Amidst all this, the president lay mortally wounded; he was dead before the day was out. There was panic in Washington – was Egypt poised to go the same way as Iran and become a West-hating Islamic theocracy? And there was concern in Exeter for the students who had been sent out to study in this apparently unstable country. Should the course be stopped and the students repatriated?

In fact there was a surprisingly smooth transition of power to Hosni Mubarak, who was seen at the time as a bland and unexciting choice after the flamboyance of Sadat. Some speculated that he did not have the political nous to stay in power for long and predicted he would be ousted within five years. But by the time I interviewed Mubarak in 2001 he had held down the top job for twenty years and was showing no sign of slowing down – or giving up power. The Exeter Arabic course continued to send its students abroad to Egypt, and on a warm evening in September 1982 our class converged at Heathrow for our bargain-basement flight to Cairo.

My father came to see me off. If he had any misgivings about letting his only child go off to live in the Middle East for a year he hid them well. My parents both knew that going to live in Cairo was something I was passionately keen about and they had given me every encouragement. But that summer my approaching departure had cast a shadow over an otherwise perfect walking holiday we spent in Provence. As the Kenya Airlines Boeing 707 roared down the runway we were all immersed in our own thoughts about the year ahead, except perhaps for Peregrine, who was concentrating on guzzling a large bunch of white grapes on take-off.

Some time after midnight we landed at Cairo airport. Even before the doors opened we could see there was so much dust in the atmosphere that the lights of the terminal building were giving off a mournful yellow glow. I recognized the building, which I had passed through in transit two years previously; on that occasion I had foolishly downed a glass of airport tap water, then spent the rest of the flight to Manila commuting from my seat to the loo and back.

As soon as the aircraft hatch swung open and we descended on to the tarmac a strange new smell greeted us. It was a subtle blend of car fumes, overripe fruit, dust, heat and just a hint of sewage, and I will never forget it. It did not strike me as unpleasant; in fact if anything it spelled adventure.

Once inside the tomb-like terminal building, processing our passports took an age. They would be examined in minute detail – and sometimes upside-down – by a succession of police officers in ill-fitting white tunics held together by black leather belts and cross-straps. Ensconced inside their tiny glass booths, chain-smoking cheap Kilopatra [sic] cigarettes and muttering gravely to each other, they would look up occasionally at us, as if to check we hadn't run away. Tired to the point of being silly, we made up imaginary conversations between them. 'This one is definitely a spy, what do you think, ya Hamdi? Deportation or jail? How about this one, claims she's a student, I think she's bluffing. Hey, look, this one looks like Princess Diana.' Since most of our class were girls there was definitely an element of self-importance here, with senior officers striding on to the scene to give the all-important entry stamp with a flourish.

Outside in the car park we loaded ourselves into a convoy of orange taxis and drove through the empty streets of Heliopolis, a Cairo suburb, with the taxi's cassette blaring 'Get Down On It' and the warm night air rushing past. We could hardly believe our eyes: it was now about three o'clock in the morning yet here were whole fifty-strong crews of labourers working through the night to put up new blocks of flats. Skinny men in overflowing turbans carried pails of liquid concrete up rickety ladders; it reminded me of an engraving of the building of the Pyramids. Later we learned that modern Egyptian architecture is not quite what it was at the time of the Pharaohs. In Cairo's sprawling slums – and even sometimes in upmarket Heliopolis – shoddily built apartment blocks occasionally collapse on top of their tenants. Most often it is a case of a greedy landlord building yet another storey on top of an already shaky edifice, skimping on the reinforced concrete and rewarding a contractor for finishing ahead of schedule. But frequently it is a case of desperation; Cairo is one of the most overcrowded cities on earth and living space is at a premium.

In Egypt, we learned, it is all too common for a newly married couple to have to wait years before they can afford to live in a flat of their own. In the meantime they move in with the in-laws, sharing a cramped apartment with Magdi the father-in-law, Zubaida his oversized wife, Ahmed the school-age son and Salwa and Nashwa, the two unmarried daughters now in their twenties. Once the excitement of the wedding is over family nerves can soon fray. Hamdi and his new wife are painfully aware of the pressure on them to start a family, yet they struggle to find the privacy to get the job done. Before long there is talk of building a vertical extension to accommodate the new couple, and so on. Once, after we had been living in Cairo for a few months, we were sitting in a café in the poor quarter of Imbaba when I noticed clouds of dust falling inexplicably from the ceiling. The next thing I knew there was a hoof protruding through a hole, then another one, and suddenly half the ceiling gave way and a sheep fell through the roof and on to the floor of the café. Amazingly, it was unhurt. It picked itself up, shook its fleece a couple of times, nodded as if to say 'beat that' and wandered off into the street. Café conversation paused for about five seconds to take this in, then resumed as if nothing had happened. Cairo.

The apartment that the university first put us up in was a shambles. It was only half finished, there were no sinks, and workmen wandered in and out with pharaonic-looking tools giving everyone very little privacy. It was all very different from the cool white lines and cleanliness of Tunisia, which Peregrine and I had travelled around that spring. We were soon introduced to the joys of the Egyptian lavatory. From a distance it looked familiar, but lift up the lid and you were confronted by a curious metal spout poking towards you. This, we learned, was meant to be turned on or off with a tap beside the cistern, the idea being to clean your backside with the help of your left hand. (In Arab society the left hand is traditionally considered 'unclean' for this reason, hence the offence given by Westerners who touch food with it, and the punishment meted out to thieves in Saudi Arabia and Iran of lopping off the right hand so the amputee can no longer feed from the communal platter.) The Egyptian lavatorial spouts had an obvious design flaw: one look at them betrayed the pieces of excrement lodged in there. Left in, these formed a hard pellet. When one of the Couch People turned on the tap thinking it was the flush, the pellet shot out and hit her in the chest. She took it quite well, as I remember.

Outside on the street, Cairo was still sizzling in the late-summer heat. We walked past fruit stalls where the owners had carefully and artistically stacked their colourful produce into little pyramids beneath tattered canvas awnings. Here were fruits none of us had ever tried before: mangos, guavas and pomegranates (this was the early eighties, remember). We had been warned that since watermelons were sold by weight, stall owners sometimes dipped them in Nile water to make them heavier, but nothing could keep us away from the delicious juice drinks and milkshakes on sale at every street corner. We were in Zamalek, the embassy quarter, and down almost every street stood whitewashed embassies guarded by truckfuls of soldiers with helmets, Kalashnikovs and fixed bayonets. They were from the *Amn Al-Markazi*, 'Central Security', and although at first they looked forbidding we soon learned they were mostly illiterate country farmers' boys serving out their lowly paid conscription. One soldier outside the Chinese embassy used to sing to himself in a high-pitched voice, and once we saw another one crawling on hands and knees at night to steal a mango from a grocery stall. A couple of years later it all turned nasty when thousands of these Central Security troops rioted over poor pay. They set fire to hotels and various belly-dancing clubs along the Giza road and had to be quelled by the regular army in what was the first major challenge to President Mubarak's rule.

Zamalek is part of an island that forces the Nile to divide briefly as it flows serenely through Cairo on its way to the Mediterranean. One morning Peregrine and I took a tiny rowing-boat taxi across the river to the neighbouring quarter of Imbaba. We were suddenly in a different world. Skeins of sand blew across the street and built up on the ragged pavement in drifts; a bent set of traffic lights shone red, amber and green all at the same time for a whole minute, then went blank. The traffic ignored them anyway and hurtled along the Nile road regardless. Men came out of their doorways dressed in pyjamas and slippers and argued melodramatically with their neighbours, then promptly hugged each other. Rotund women swathed completely in black *milaya* gowns squatted beside baskets of red dates. A small flock of sheep with fat, uncut tails dozed on the pavement, while one of them wandered over to a café and dumped a load of dung in the doorway. A weary donkey stood ankle-deep in its own filth, and a child wearing nothing but a grubby T-shirt urinated beside a pile of guavas for sale. A boy in a pair of oversized trousers held up with string came running past us, wheeling a hubcap like a hoop, bouncing it through stinking puddles and over crushed tin cans. Looking up at us he lost his concentration and fell amidst the rubbish, but he did not cry, he just stood up, brushed off the pieces of rotting vegetables that had stuck to him, and ran on. Round a corner we came across a seemingly untended herd of thin white camels that picked and nibbled their way over a pile of rubble. Despite the squalor, this was a far more authentic Cairo than the one we were temporarily lodging in and we longed to explore it further. Over the coming months we went there often, getting to know some of the regulars in the cafés, exercising our new-found Arabic and losing badly at dominoes and backgammon. Years later, during the violent Islamist insurgency of the mid-nineties, I was saddened to hear that Imbaba had become a no-go zone for Westerners, a place where the police fought running gun battles with Islamists trying to topple the secular government of Husni Mubarak.

But now, fresh off the plane from London, we were told we still had a few more days of liberty before the start of the academic course. Why not escape the last of the summer heat and take the train up to Alexandria, Egypt's second city? suggested the Egyptian teachers. Unfortunately, half the city seemed to have had the same idea and as the train pulled slowly out of Cairo's Ramses station it was a shock to see hundreds, perhaps thousands, of young men clinging to the sides of trains and clustering together on the roof. But Egyptian trains move at such a sedate pace that we decided it would probably be hard to fall off, and even if you did you could probably pick yourself up and catch up with the train again. Inside our second-class compartment we met Marwan, a burly Special Forces captain going home on leave. On his combat fatigues he wore a little gold octopus – 'for scuba dive', he told us – and a pair of parachute jump wings. Another badge said 'Ranger'. He had trained with the Americans, he said, at Fort Bragg in Carolina, and for the entire journey he kept us entertained with stories of how tough his training had been. 'What an interesting guy,' we all said as we parted company at Alexandria station. We thought we were saying goodbye, but Marwan had other ideas. Every day that week he would come round to the rented flat we had found; day or night, it didn't matter to him, he seemed to have unlimited time on his hands. It was our first encounter with the sometimes suffocating embrace of Egyptian hospitality and we were forced to develop elaborate ruses to shake him off. 'Just off for a haircut,' one of us would lie. 'OK, my friend, I come with you,' Marwan would reply. 'Er, we're really too tired to come out.' 'No problem, I come sit with you.'

But despite Marwan's over-eager attempts at friendship, I liked Egyptians immediately. They have a tremendous sense of humour, a winning way with words, and an ability to see the funny side of themselves and their situation that is sorely lacking in much of the rest of the Arab world. Every day I would learn new phrases, picked up in conversation or overheard at a bus stop. '*Haasib walla'l-arabiyaat ha taklak!*' I once heard a mother shout to her young son as they were crossing the road. 'Be careful or else the cars will eat you up!' Perhaps it is because Egypt is the Bollywood of Arab cinema that I found people were prone to melodrama, with arguments quickly escalating into harmless shouting matches. One of the greatest insults was to be called '*gazma!*', a shoe. Only one thing could top that and that was to be called '*sitteen gazma!*', 'sixty shoes!'

Egyptians share the British love of irony: a junior and impoverished civil servant sitting in a café will often be addressed as '*ya ustaaz*', 'oh professor'. Taxi-drivers might call each other '*muhandis*' ('engineer') and almost everyone is called '*ya rayyis*' ('oh President'). We found that many Egyptians had a strong sense of fatalism, with a popular expression being 'If it is written upon the forehead then the eyes must see it.' The answer to almost any problem was '*ma aleysh*' – 'it doesn't matter' – which could be maddening when the person saying it had just trodden on your toe. Once, when we were invited to a rooftop wedding party in the Cairo slum of Bulaq, the host welcomed us with the customary greeting '*Nawwartina!*', meaning 'Your presence has lit us up.' Hours later, at the precise moment we left the party, there was an unexpected power cut, plunging the festivities into darkness. The Egyptians found this hysterical.

Alexandria had a wonderful, open, maritime feel to it. Running along the length of the city was the corniche, a great sweeping thoroughfare that hugged the Mediterranean shore, flanked by a broad pavement and low harbour wall. The Nobel prize-winning Egyptian novelist Naguib Mahfouz wrote evocatively about the corniche in his 1960s book *Miramar*: he described his main character roaring along it at night in an open-topped sports car, feeling the wind in his hair and the city as his. Now fishermen sat all day in the balmy September heat, casting their lines into the clear water of the bay. Men in aprons wheeled brightly painted trolleys up and down, selling strange yellow beans soaked in brine called *termees*, wrapped in cones of newspaper. They were eaten by nibbling the top of the bean then squeezing it out of its skin into your mouth with thumb and forefinger, one of many Egyptian skills we had yet to perfect. Just before sunset young Alexandrians would come out in their best clothes to eat ice cream and eye each other up. Peregrine and I, as rare Europeans, would inevitably attract a good deal of attention from some of the girls, especially as Peregrine had got a local tailor to run him up a pair of white Egyptian naval officer's trousers. We would notice girls walking past us in pairs, flashing us long looks, sometimes whispering a silky 'Good evening, how are you?' But that was as far as things went. Alexandria may have had a corniche, but this was not Rio.

This city had a reputation for being a lot more liberated than Cairo, partly due to the cosmopolitan mix of Greeks, Italians and Jews who had settled here decades ago. But most of them left after the 1967 war and longtime residents told us that Alexandria was rapidly becoming like every other over-crowded Egyptian city. Certainly there was no sign of bikinis on the public beaches. In scenes repeated all over the Arab world, whole families would take to the water, the women completely clothed. Mothers veiled in headscarves and wearing several layers of all-enveloping garments would wade stolidly into the waves, holding on to their struggling children, while the men of the family always seemed to get away with the most contour-hugging swimming trunks to go with their swaying neck medallions. Once, with Peppy and Rosemary, who were dressed in conservative one-piece bathing suits, we made the mistake of spreading our towels too close to the city centre and almost immediately two young gigolos descended on us, their eyes feasting on the girls' cleavages. The girls tried hard to be polite without encouraging them, and when eventually they left one of them whispered a parting shot to Rosemary: 'Later I make love to you, Miss.'

Yet the very next day we experienced the full warmth of selfless Egyptian hospitality. After a day's swimming off the white sand beach at Agami, we were invited into the Police Naval Club by Muhammad, a genial police sergeant in white duck khaki. He spread out a rush mat for the girls to sit on, keeping a respectful distance, then fetched us bread and goat's cheese wrapped in police documents. He even dispatched two policemen to fetch us ice-cold bottles of Fanta and offered us police transport back into Alexandria if we wanted. Muhammad had no ulterior motive other than to see us enjoy ourselves in his country and for us to think well of Egyptians, which we did.

No sooner had we rushed back to Cairo for the start of term and the first of our lectures than we were told they were postponed for a week. Some of my fellow students were clearly disappointed. The Couch People, now reduced to the two quietest and cleverest girls in the class, Janet and Jane, made a bee line for the nearest library. Another shy pair, Julia and Yolanda, had by now been corrupted by Peregrine's and my disdain for homework and were like birds released from a cage. Together, the four of us lost no time in boarding an already overcrowded bus for the long journey south along the Red Sea coast to Hurghada, then a little-known fishing village but one popular with backpackers. South of Suez the road became rutted and potholed, requiring all the driver's skill as he threw the bus around the bends. We passed the beach at Ain Sukhna, nicknamed 'Mine Sukhna' on account of the number of landmines left over from the 1973 Arab–Israeli war. A story doing the rounds in Cairo had it that an American family had chosen a fatal spot to pitch their parasol on the beach, with the father driving the spike of the parasol straight on to a buried mine. It was a long journey and as the afternoon sun sank lower it was easy to see how the Red Sea had got its name, from the reflected colour of the great sandstone crags that rose up inland.

On the bus we met two young holidaying Egyptians who were to become close friends all year. Haitham was a large jovial police cadet, a self-declared arm-wrestling champion and spear-fishing enthusiast. Wael's father was some top general and although he did not appear to have any profession himself he was never short of money, jokes and enthusiasm for adventure. While we checked into a guesthouse they put up a tent, but the next day we hired a boat to stay out overnight on the Red Sea. I knew nothing about sailing, nor did the girls, but Peregrine and the Egyptians seemed to and soon we were pulling away from the coastline, moving into deeper water where a procession of huge black manta rays flapped slowly past beneath the boat. Terns hovered and screamed above the mast and skeins of flying fish flew across the shallow waves. After a few hours we moored up at a completely barren and uninhabited island – the classic desert island, in fact. If we had not brought boxes of flat Egyptian bread, fresh water, fruit and other supplies we might have had to turn our hand to some Ray Mears survival techniques, but Haitham and Wael were soon casting lines into the sea and that night we feasted on fresh fish cooked in oil with rice and mint tea. Later we lay on our backs on deck, gazing up at one shooting star after another, lulled to sleep by the warm breeze blowing in from the Sinai, the gentle rolling motion of the boat at anchor and the soft slapping of the waves against her hull. In such a perfect place even Haitham's snoring was forgiven.

Back in Cairo, the main aim was to learn to speak colloquial Egyptian Arabic. This was really what I had taken this whole degree course for; I wanted more than anything to converse with Arabs in their own language. But some of the students who had excelled at the more academic work back in Exeter found Cairo initially overwhelming and disorienting. This was, after all, the biggest city in Africa and the Middle East, a teeming, overcrowded, polluted metropolis of over ten million people. In the first week one girl burst into tears when a taxi-driver leered at her, another hit a young man full in the face when he tried to touch her breasts. Some people had to be talked out of jacking it in and going home. The course itself was anything but demanding. The previous year the students had been sent up to Alexandria and given so much homework they saw nothing of Egyptian life. There had been complaints, no doubt exacerbated by the country's president getting assassinated two months into the course. So we were given an easy ride: just two hours of lectures a day, four days a week, with no homework and no exams. All we had to do was stroll down to a dusty schoolhouse where our lecturers came to teach us from two of Cairo's best-known universities, Ain Shams and the American University in Cairo, known as the AUC.

By the time lectures began four of us had found a landlady from Egypt's 10 per cent minority of Coptic Christians. Not being Muslim, she had no religious scruples about lending out her flat to a mixed group of male and female students, just as long as we paid the rent on time. Julia and Yolanda shared one bedroom, I shared the other with Peregrine. Naively, he and I decided we should find ourselves Egyptian girlfriends;

we had no idea how we were going to go about this but it gave us plenty to talk about as we sat in cafés admiring the scenery. In this part of Cairo, girls were used to seeing Westerners and our burgeoning knowledge of Arabic soon melted the ice when we met them in shops and patisseries. Yet even here, in the so-called 'diplomatic quarter', there was an unmistakable stigma attached to being seen getting too close to a foreigner. In this predominantly Islamic society the general assumption was that if an Egyptian girl dated a Westerner then she must be sleeping with him, and only marriage to him could save her honour. On the few occasions that I managed to secure a date, the girl in question would turn up chaperoned by her mother, who would treat me politely but with understandable suspicion. Why on earth was her daughter wasting time with this Christian 'khawaaga' (foreigner) when she should be saving her attentions for a good Egyptian fiancé, chosen by her family?

In our student flat we revelled in the enormous balcony that overlooked the Chinese embassy, at which we occasionally threw paper darts that never landed anywhere near it. But we had no air-conditioning and the temperature often stayed up in the thirties all through the night, leaving us gasping for air on sweat-soaked sheets. We soon decided there must be some sort of pact going on in the insect community. At night the mosquitoes would dive-bomb us constantly, forcing us to hide under the covers until we could stand the heat no longer. Then at dawn, as if changing shifts, the mosquitoes would stop work and hand over to the flies. Egyptian flies were a novel experience for us all: they were small and silent but they were oblivious to the wave of a hand. With no warning they would settle on our eyelids, lips or nostrils and we would virtually have to swat them to move them on. On later trips into rural villages we saw children who had clearly given up trying to wave them off, with moving black clusters around their eyes and nostrils. We also encountered men with glaucoma, a fly-borne disease that turns the eyes grey and sightless. It is easily treatable, but not out there in the sticks.

In Cairo every apartment block has a *bawwab*, a concierge. Usually a proud Nubian from the south of Egypt, he knows everybody in the building and everything that is going on. I quickly got on the right side of Ahmed in our block by learning a handful of words in Nubian, a separate language from Arabic, but Peregrine ran into a misunderstanding almost immediately. He put his shoes outside our door in the hope that Ahmed would polish them for a small tip. Ahmed duly took them away, but after two days had still not returned them. Peregrine went downstairs to investigate, only to find Ahmed happily wearing them. The *bawwab*'s smile faded a few days later, however, when we held our first party on the landlady's enormous roof terrace. Several of our new-found Egyptian friends had too much to drink and Ahmed scolded us the next day with the words: 'Too much noise last night. Water – and other liquids – came crashing down from your balcony.'

Egypt was an incredibly cheap place to live, ideally suited for impoverished students. Our rent was just fifteen pounds a week each and our staple food was the *ta'miya* sandwich, a round wedge of pitta bread stuffed with deep-fried falafel (ground chickpeas), salad and sesame-seed sauce. It cost about two pence. The important thing was to remember to say 'without salad, please', as we never knew what microscopic beasties lurked within. Sometimes, of course, we forgot and would spend the next twenty-four hours lying on our beds feeling wretched, although Peregrine offered another explanation: 'I'm feeling quite sick tonight,' he'd say. 'I think it must be the lack of alcohol.' But by 1982 Cairo tap water was so heavily chlorinated you could drink it happily if you could stand the taste of swimming pool. To get round this we bought jugs of the fresh fruit juice at which Egypt excels; in the autumn it would be mangoes, then there would be strawberries, guavas and bananas. Our local juice-vendor would see me coming down the street and he would set about preparing my favourite cocktail with a huge smile. Again, a mouth-watering glass of chilled mango juice cost all of five pence. Egyptians often tried to make us accept drinks for free as a reward for speaking Arabic, and for them it would turn into a battle of honour to make us accept their hospitality when we of all people could afford to pay.

One of the things we most enjoyed doing was riding up at the Pyramids. There were few things better than getting up to Giza early in the morning before the tourist coaches arrived. We would check in at our favourite stables, saddle up and canter across the sand, up over the crest of a dune to watch the sun's rays lighting up the three pyramids against a sky of pure pale blue. Because the Pyramids of Giza are built on a slight plateau they overlook the whole of Cairo. On the one hand, this gives you fresh air and a great view over the nearby date palms to a million rooftops, then all the way to the Citadel and the Muqattam hills. On the other hand, one look at the brown layer of smog that hangs over the city tells you that what you are breathing every day is probably not what the doctor ordered.

Not long after our arrival in Cairo, Peregrine and I joined a group of diplomats from the British Embassy for a gallop over the sands. After skirting the Pyramids our horses sensed we were heading back towards the stables and nothing I could do would either slow my horse down or get it to change course. We entered a narrow track beside a cemetery and I rounded a bend to see a riderless horse galloping straight at us. There was just time to swerve abruptly and I was thrown clear, landing unharmed with a bump on the sand. As I was picking myself up and dusting off the sand, I was introduced to one of the better horsemen in our party, a young First Secretary (a middle rank in the Foreign Office) who was said to be going places fast. He was Sherard Cowper-Coles, the man who was to save my life twenty-two years later in Riyadh with his swift and decisive action there as ambassador in June 2004.

Meanwhile, Peregrine had been keeping quiet about his impending twenty-first birthday, confiding it only in me for some obscure reason. We decided to celebrate it at the Sahara City nightclub up near the Pyramids, a sprawling encampment of brightly coloured tents that has long since been dismantled. The place stayed open until three in the morning and as soon as the waiters learned it was Peregrine's birthday they ushered us to prime seats near the stage usually reserved for big-spending Egyptian guests. After the acrobatics and the singing came the pièce de résistance: *Al-Raqs Al-Sharqi* or 'Oriental dance', otherwise known as belly dancing. Neither of us had ever seen this before and we were mesmerized. A full Arab orchestra took their seats, warming up with the melancholy half-tones so typical of Arab music. There followed a pause of no more than a second, then the drums began, the musicians strumming the taut goat-skins of their earthenware *tabla* drums with their thumbs and fingers, holding the drums sideways across their knees and beating out an exhilarating rhythm. With all eyes now on the stage, the dancer burst through a parted curtain to huge applause, twirling around with her skirts swirling after her. Peregrine and I exchanged glances. Her midriff was encased in a sort of curious, see-through gauze that looked as if it had been lifted from a hospital A&E department. We were told that Egypt's first president, Gamal Abdel Nasser, had issued a decree in the 1950s ordering the skin to be covered and this netting was the most that dancers could get away with. So what was the point of belly dancing, we thought, if you could not see the belly? But the dancer's skill soon became apparent as she sidestepped nimbly across the stage, arching her body backwards and from side to side, then curling her arms above her head with fingers crooked, allowing her black tresses to tumble down the top of her back. As the drumming slowed to a deliberate, rhythmic beat, she placed her hands on her hips and expertly gyrated her belly in time to the music, catching men's eyes in the audience as if to say 'Yes, I know exactly what you are thinking.' The few women in the tent looked distinctly uncomfortable but the men wore expressions of glazed satisfaction. This was what they had come to see, and now we too could appreciate what all the fuss was about. Twenty years later, when I became the BBC's Middle East Correspondent in Cairo, I went on one of the more enjoyable assignments of my career, covering the first international belly-dancing contest to be held in Cairo. Despite the enthusiasm and dedication of the various Japanese, American and German contestants I interviewed, nothing could match the passion and drama of that first performance we watched in Giza as impressionable twenty-one-year-olds.

It was all very well carousing into the small hours at Sahara City, but our student grants were not going to last the year if we went on like this. So to make a bit of money I decided to try my hand at teaching in the mornings before our lectures started, enrolling on the staff of the imperiously named Sadat Academy for Management Sciences. As far as I could tell, they just taught English, so that was what I offered, despite having no qualifications or training whatsoever. The pay was generous for Egypt: £5.50 an hour, tax-free. But I was soon to discover that teaching English to Egyptian undergraduates, some of whom were older than I was, was no pushover.

Two of them were particularly bright and particularly lazy. In a college for the children of the privileged elite they reckoned their futures were assured. Mustafa was the son of a famous general, a hero of the Sinai tank battles, Hamdi the son of a politician. Their progression into the ranks of the political or commercial über-class seemed inevitable. At first I politely refused their invitations to dinner, not wishing to be accused of favouritism in a town that can keep no secrets.

Eventually I went along, taking Yolanda and Julia along with me. Mustafa, our host, gave us an exaggerated welcome then ran back into the smoking kitchen. He had burned the dinner to a crisp. 'Mustafa, he can cook,' said Hamdi, 'but it is nothing like foods.' While we waited for a takeaway to arrive we sat out on his crumbling balcony, listening to the two boys trading slang.

'*W'illahi! Inti gayya min 'ailat bani sadr walla eh?*' shouted Mustafa at a big-chested woman going past in the street below. 'By God, do you come from the Tribe of Big Chests or what?' ''*Arba' dur!*' – this to a very tall woman – 'Four storeys!'

After the remains of the takeaway had been scraped into the bin, Mustafa brought out his pièce de résistance, a treat he had secured through his father's connections which he thought we would appreciate. It was a German porn video. We all squirmed in embarrassment: Mustafa had made a bad error of judgement and we left to the sound of simulated groans and gasps.

Years later – ten, to be precise – I came across Mustafa and Hamdi working at the reception of a smart hotel in the Saudi Gulf town of Al-Khobar. They seemed embarrassed to be found working there, but it spoke volumes about the lack of opportunities in Egypt at the time. With all their connections and expensive education they were still better off financially at the bottom end of the hotel-management scale in Saudi Arabia than trying to forge a career in their own country. I thought that was terribly sad.

At about the time I started teaching, Egypt became gripped by a fever of patriotic excitement. It was late 1982 and the Sinai Peninsula, that triangle of desert and mountain that sits on the map like a wedge between Africa and Asia, was coming home. According to the Camp David Treaty, Israel was due to hand it back to Egypt in stages. The western section had already been returned, and now Egypt was poised to regain control of the rest of the peninsula. Billboards were going up all over Cairo with the words ''*Audat Sinaa*' – 'The Return of the Sinai'. Peregrine and I decided it was time to give lectures a break and go and take a look at this much-fought-over piece of real estate.

From Cairo we took a bus eastwards to Suez, where several of the buildings were still pockmarked with bullet and shell holes from the fighting in 1973. It was the first time either of us had seen a ship pass through the Suez Canal and it was an awesome sight. From a hundred yards away all you could see was flat desert, then an enormous freighter would slide majestically forwards, seemingly cutting right through the sand, steaming southwards towards the Red Sea and the Indian Ocean. Looking up we could see the ship's crew lining the decks high above us, waving before they vanished into the heat haze. An Egyptian captain, immaculate in naval whites, could just be seen stepping down from each ship, having piloted her safely through to the open sea from Port Said in the north.

In those days there was no car tunnel under the Suez Canal as there is today, so we took the ferry, chugging across the blue waters from the African to the Asian shore. There we joined a group of Egyptian labourers and managed to hitch a lift on the back of a military truck that happened to be heading all the way down the Sinai coast to Sharm El Sheikh. At first, things did not go well. The truck stopped in the middle of nowhere and an army officer came round the back to order everybody off.

'Why?' protested all the labourers in the back.

'Because there is no driver.' Strangely, we could hear the sound of someone revving up the engine in the cab.

'He is an idiot,' said a worker, pointing at the officer.

'Who's an idiot?' countered the officer.

'You are! There is a vehicle and a driver but still you tell us to get off.'

'It is forbidden.'

Nobody moved, so the officer sighed, shrugged and the truck proceeded south.

It was not exactly comfortable rattling around in the open back of a lorry for ten hours between a consignment of heavy tyres and barrels of DDT insecticide. For all we knew, this truck was heading for a chemical-warfare unit, but the ride was free and we had an all-round view as night began to descend over the Sinai. In the gathering gloom we passed the shattered hulks of Russian-built tanks and anti-aircraft guns left over from the Yom Kippur War, their barrels jutting towards Israel like accusing fingers. Rusting signs in Arabic and English warned people not to leave the road for danger of mines. As we passed through the mountains a full moon rose, casting this biblical landscape in a ghostly silver light. We could see the recently vacated Israeli trenches clearly, which the Egyptian army was starting to occupy. Already somebody had laid out white stones to spell the Arabic words *'Da'iman Misr'*, 'Always Egypt'. And then we came to our first checkpoint manned by US paratroopers. As part of the handover agreement an international monitoring force was put in place called the MFO, the Multinational Force and Observers. It consisted of nearly three thousand troops from the USA, UK, Australia, New Zealand and a handful of other nations, but the bulk of the manpower came from the US Army's 101st Airborne Paratroopers. And here they were in sand goggles and desert camouflage, essentially on traffic duty. It was the first time I had ever seen US troops in the Middle East, although the US military was just months away from getting a very bloody nose in Lebanon with the suicide bombing of their Marine Corps barracks at Beirut airport.

Sharm El Sheikh in 1982 could not have been more different from the popular winter-sun package-holiday destination it is today. There was just one hotel and it was way beyond our budget, but arriving as we did after midnight we were allowed to sleep in the garden of a little mosque. We were woken when the first rays of a fierce desert sun crept over the blue ridge of mountains and lit up our faces. As we strolled into town and queued at the bakery for loaves of hot, flat bread, we heard a strange sound, a sort of chant that came welling up from the other side of a ridge.

> 'I don't know but it's been said
> Navy boots are made of lead.
> Sound off! One two! Break it on down . . .'

Hoving into view came a squad of sweating, shaven-headed, sunburned American paratroopers, out for their morning run, their voices echoing off the rocks, the mountains of the Sinai rising up behind them. One of them wore a T-shirt with the logo 'Pure Pain'. It was an incongruous sight in the land where Moses once walked.

Despite its majestic setting, the tiny beach resort of Sharm El Sheikh was not a pretty sight back then. The withdrawing Israelis had executed something of a scorched-earth policy, taking with them whatever they could and leaving the place ankle-deep in rubbish. Almost the only things left intact were the signposts calling it by its Hebrew name, 'Ofira', and signs printed in English, Hebrew and Arabic saying, 'Security Forces in operation to detect any suspicious objects'. There were several deep security wells dug by the Israelis for the disposal of suspicious packages but these were now filling up fast with Egyptian litter. The only locals around were not ethnic Egyptians at all, they were lean-faced Arabs, Sinai Bedu from one of two distinct tribal groupings that live on the peninsula. Unlike the well-fed, round-faced Egyptians from Cairo, these men had strikingly sharp, hawk-like features and they spoke a much purer, classical Arabic. We befriended some of them and they gave us a lift on their pick-up truck, out to one of their encampments in the mountain valleys.

It was my first sight of a Bedu camp and it was not very inspiring. Instead of the black goats'-hair tents I had expected, there were scruffy corrugated-tin shacks, surrounded by coils of chicken wire. But the Bedu were hospitality personified, plying us with tea from pots that bubbled constantly on the glowing coals of a rudimentary fire. We sat on rugs in the shade, trying to follow their Arabic and sneaking glimpses at the gorgeous embroidered dresses and elaborate gold jewellery worn by their women, even as they went to milk their camels. We were allowed to watch one of them making gourds from goatskins. First a dye was boiled in a cauldron, using slivers of a reddish bark. The skins were thoroughly soaked in this to make them water-proof, then they were left in the sun to dry. We were told that the gourds would be used to carry water on the camels' backs when the camp moved on. Like Wilfred Thesiger, I felt privi-leged to have had a glimpse of the south Sinai Bedu way of life before it disappeared and the character of this coast changed for ever. The Bedu spoke no English and they were completely unprepared for the wave of mass tourism that was about to sweep over their ancestral land. In the space of two decades the indigenous Sinai Bedu have been all but driven out from where they used to fish and graze their camels along the coast. In their place has come an army of Egyptian labour-ers, hoteliers and shopkeepers selling gawdy souvenirs from Cairo. Nearly a quarter of a century later these Egyptians bore the brunt of the casualties when Islamist terrorists drove their truck bombs into Sharm El Sheikh on 21 July 2005.

One weekend in November we decided to do something different. 'Let's go overland to Jerusalem,' suggested Peregrine. 'Good idea,' I replied. Egypt was still the only Arab country to have signed a peace deal with Israel, and at the expense of being briefly ostracized by the rest of the Arab world Cairo now had a regular bus service to Tel Aviv. Off we set, inching our way through the suburbs of Cairo then eastwards across the top of the Sinai Peninsula, until we found ourselves, several hours later, at the Israeli border-crossing point at Rafah. A spotless blue-and-white Israeli flag flew above a sandbagged watchtower whose occupants studied us closely. We were almost the last people to cross over that day, but the Israelis were certainly not going to let down their guard for us. The questions came thick and fast from a steely-eyed female lieutenant. 'Who are you visiting in Israel?' 'Who sent you?' 'Do you know any Palestinians here?' 'Who packed your bag?' Just in time we stopped the passport clerk from marking our passports with an Israeli stamp, which would have prevented us from getting into any Arab country apart from Egypt.

By the time we got up to Jerusalem it was dark, bitterly cold and had started to snow. We walked through one of the many massive stone gateways that perforate the walls of the Old City and looked for a place to sleep. We knew from our guidebook that the walled city was divided into four quarters based on ethnicity: Arab, Christian, Jewish and Armenian. We plumped for the Arab quarter and a backstreet hostel popular with backpackers called the Lemon Tree Hostel. The place was friendly and had a warm glow about it and I was only mildly embarrassed when Peregrine saw fit to change into a pair of pressed English pyjamas, much to the amusement of the bearded Australians in this laid-back travellers' crashpad.

We were within walking distance of the Wailing Wall, where black-clad Orthodox Jews intoned their prayers and nodded their heads back and forth; the Haram Al-Sharif, the third-holiest shrine in Islam and site of the famous gold-plated Dome of the Rock; and the Via Dolorosa, the street walked along by Jesus as he dragged his massive cross up to his own crucifixion. Here we could hear both the rich peel of Christian church bells and the Muslim call to prayer, and we breathed it all in as we strolled to and from our hostel. Jerusalem was a city that exuded religious history and for Peregrine, a devout Catholic, it was a moving experience. Never normally more than a few seconds away from a pithy witticism, he now fell silent and contemplative in the hushed reverence of the Church of the Holy Sepulchre.

Over the course of that long weekend we met silent, Trappist monks in the monastery of Latroun, friendly Palestinian shopkeepers in Jericho and a Russian Jewish couple who had just immigrated from Moscow. On a whim, we hiked south from Jericho into the dried-up ravines and riverbeds or *wadis*, in search of the cave where the Dead Sea Scrolls had recently been discovered. Dwarfed by the great rocks that reared up around us, Peregrine and I got chatting about our respective families. His story was rather more interesting than mine: having sired several children, Peregrine's father had then abandoned the family and never returned. He had an uncle who had behaved equally badly, amusing himself by taking potshots with an air rifle at his wife's backside as she was gardening in a particularly thick leather skirt. I was just digesting this piece of information when we came across a Bedu shepherd, who was surprised to see us in the desert *wadis* so close to dusk. 'Watch out for the *nimr*,' he told us in Arabic before moving on. *Nimr?* The word sounded familiar but we just could not place it. Then we remembered it. 'Leopards! Hell, let's get out of here!' In our panic we even flagged down a lift along the Dead Sea road with a heavily armed patrol from the IDF, the Israeli Defence Force, otherwise known as the Israeli Army.

We had only been away from Cairo for three days but on our return we found two things had changed. Leonid Brezhnev, the ursine Soviet leader, had died, and the long Egyptian summer was well and truly finished. Rain was emptying out of a leaden sky and not draining very successfully from the waterlogged streets. The city's millions of pedestrians were trying to avoid walking under the filthy girder bridges where six months' worth of summer grime was splashing down on to their crumpled suits and nylon dresses. One girl in high heels and smart stockings just managed to negotiate a street crossing without getting her feet wet when a bus roared past, drenching her in mud from the waist downwards. Cairo's ubiquitous traffic policemen had changed out of their white cotton uniforms to dark bristly woollen ones. Bus conductors were now doing the rounds in bulbous, hairy jackets and heavy, clumpy shoes, giving everything an air of the 1950s.

Before long we began to miss the balmy heat we had grown so accustomed to, and when the Christmas break came round we decided to head south. We had friends out from Exeter: John, who never lost a game of backgammon provided we were playing for money, Emma, and Hamish, who frequently overdid it on the hubble-bubble and would sit up on his bed half the night, burping uncontrollably. Together with Peregrine and Peppy we all took the overnight train for Luxor and the far south. Riding donkeys and bicycles, we explored the pharaonic temples and tombs of Thebes, on one occasion coming across a recently excavated tomb where workmen proudly displayed an ancient skull that was quite probably several thousand years old. Christmas Day in Aswan was a memorable shambles. We stocked up with provisions then piled into a felucca, one of those graceful, tall-masted sailing boats that have been plying the Nile for centuries. Unfortunately Ali, our Nubian boatman, helped himself rather too liberally to our supplies of local Omar Khayyam wine, and before long we became wedged intractably between two huge boulders just south of the Old Cataract Hotel. We were there for hours until the currents moved round but it didn't bother us – we just sat on the side of the boat, dangling our bare feet into the swirling waters of the Nile and singing out to every passing boat a recently learned Egyptian phrase: 'Boolak eh . . . walla haaga!', meaning 'I tell you what . . . nothing at all!' We were young, drunk and extremely happy to be living in Egypt.

Back in Cairo I found it hard to concentrate on our lectures when I felt there were so many places to explore. The trip to the south had whetted my appetite, and with the spring break approaching I wanted to press on further into Sudan. I was keen to see what lay beyond the great Aswan High Dam, built with Russian help in the 1960s to stop the annual Nile floods and harness the power of this awesome river to hydroelectric turbines. I knew that to the south of the dam – upstream, in fact – were crocodiles and enormous Nile perch, the Nubian desert and the largest country in Africa: Sudan. In short, it was a place that smacked of untamed wilderness and adventure and I yearned to visit it. Peregrine was not remotely tempted; he announced he would be spending the holiday in the local patisserie in Cairo, where a Coptic Christian girl had taken a shine to him and was sneaking him free cakes when her boss wasn't looking. So, armed with a tiny rucksack and a hard-won Sudanese visa, I set out alone to travel overland to Khartoum. It was to be one of the best journeys I have ever embarked on.

At six p.m. precisely the overnight train to Aswan slid slowly out of Cairo's Ramses station and crossed the girder bridge of Imbaba with a long and mournful blast on its horn before turning south towards the moonlit villages of southern Egypt. The carriage was crowded with rural families returning home, all of whom had brought their own packed suppers, and within minutes the floor was carpeted with the broken shells of monkey nuts and pumpkin seeds and the discarded stalks of spring onions. The amiable chatter of Egyptian conversation rose and fell, then eventually subsided as the night wore on, lulled into silence by the rhythmic sway of the train. I settled as best I could into my bolt-upright seat with a copy of Alan Moorehead's *The White Nile*, an account of a nineteenth-century journey of exploration that I could hardly hope to emulate in three weeks but which helped remind me which continent I was on.

I awoke to see verdant fields of green sugarcane drifting past the window, the brilliant blue waters of the Nile beyond, and then, with a frightening inevitability, the Sahara desert. A decade later these sugarcane fields would provide cover for Islamist gunmen waiting to ambush police patrols during the anti-government insurgency of the 1990s. But now they were empty and harmless, and I sat on my rucksack in the open doorway of the train, taking in the scenery. Farm workers in pale-blue *gellabiya* robes and tight-wrapped turbans looked up from the cane fields and waved, black-swathed women tottered along village paths with three-foot jars balanced on their heads, and bands of laughing, barefoot children fell over each other trying to keep pace with the train, calling out to me 'Hello Miss You', meaning 'Hello Monsieur'. I wondered idly if their ancestors had greeted the French writer Gustave Flaubert the same way when he passed through on his own libidinous journey of exploration a century ago.

In Aswan I stayed on the floor of a hut belonging to a family of grocers I had met on our earlier trip at Christmas. The eldest son was nicknamed Ahmed El Fil, Ahmed the Elephant, because he was vast. But he seemed quite comfortable with both his size and his moniker, and whenever there was a lull in the conversation his brothers would nudge him in his well-covered ribs and shout 'El Fil! El Fil!' The place smelled strongly of overripe fruit but I was just glad of a roof over my head.

In the morning I went down to the dock on the shores of Lake Nasser, the huge artificial lake created by the High Dam which straddles the border between Egypt and Sudan. There was the boat – in reality three barges lashed together – that was to make the twenty-four-hour crossing to the

Sudanese dock at Wadi Halfa. There was pandemonium as hundreds pushed and jostled to get on. Returning Sudanese families and visiting Egyptian teachers alike struggled with baggage gathered up with flimsy netting. Several people were clutching an *'oud*, a traditional Arab instrument similar to a lute, and every single adult male was chain-smoking, which only bothered me when I got to my cabin later on. The fare was so cheap I had thought I might as well do this in style and go first class, but I found myself sharing with three Egyptian teachers who devoted their evening to generating an acrid blue fug in the tiny enclosed space. Too tired to speak Arabic I muttered some whinge about their incessant smoking. They looked at me blankly, then one said to the others, '*Al-Ustaaz mish kwayyis*', literally 'the professor is no good'. I could not resist letting him know I understood by replying in Arabic that 'the professor' didn't smoke. He was mortified and after that the cigarettes were put away and we all became friends.

Up on deck it was party time. A group of Sudanese men were clustered round an *'oud* player who managed to strum, sing and smoke all at the same time. There was a soft lilting rhythm to the music and his admirers were clapping hands and nodding in time. At the other end of the deck several Sudanese women were holding their own party, dressed in their brilliantly patterned all-encompassing shrouds and painting each other's hands and feet with henna, delicately applying the black paste in intricate patterns and swirls. When the paste dries it comes off, leaving a temporary brown tattoo effect that lasts several days. Henna is used by both men and women in the Arab world, with some older men – especially in the mountains – using it to dye their beards orange, while women hold henna parties as part of the wedding celebrations for the bride. Here on deck I was surprised at how open and friendly the Sudanese women were, inviting me to sit with them and watch. It had only been three years since I had first set foot on Arab soil but I had long ago learned that mixing between the sexes outside marriage or family is generally taboo. So I was doubly surprised when one of the girls began flirting with me in Arabic.

'How long will you spend in Sudan?' she asked, fixing me with her soft brown eyes that sparkled below the veil draped loosely over her hair.

'About three weeks,' I replied.

'And then what?'

'Well, back to Cairo, I suppose – then eventually back to England,' I added.

'Hah! Me too!' she exclaimed with a mischievous expression.

'Really? How come?' I asked naively.

'Because I will be going back with you!'

Her teasing was innocent and playful, and I admit I was flattered by her attention. But that was the last I saw of her. She rejoined the conversation around the henna and I went off to the bridge to chat to the captain. For a while he let me steer, putting me in charge of his precious cargo of over three hundred passengers, but it was hardly rocket science. The great lake was still as a millpond, broken only by the odd mysterious ripple that I liked to imagine was a crocodile breaking the surface. On either side, the arid, barren hills of the Nubian desert lay all around, so low that when the sun set in a fiery ball the waters of the lake almost kissed the sky.

About a year later, when I was back in Exeter, I read that this same vessel met with disaster. Someone had been using a cooking stove too close to the fuel tanks, and there had been a huge explosion that destroyed the ferry. The survivors tried to swim to the shore but the report said many drowned or were taken by Nile crocodiles. Apparently even the lucky few who reached the shore had to contend with venomous snakes and scorpions. But I was in happy ignorance of this as I returned to my bunk, safe in the knowledge that I would wake up the next morning in a new and different country.

Wadi Halfa was a charmless entrypoint to Sudan, little more than a boat and railway terminal. Incredibly tall, dark and skinny customs men in green fatigues bossed everyone around while money-changers and porters did their best to rip off the few Western backpackers disembarking from Aswan. It was dawn when we arrived and the train to Khartoum did not leave until the evening, so I filled the day by drinking cinnamon tea with the local Nubians and watching scrawny vultures tug at the garbage on a tip. Nowadays I suppose travellers would probably pass the time by sending text messages or tackling a Sudoku puzzle, but there were no such distractions in 1983.

The Khartoum train had three classes of ticket. First was fully booked, second was inexplicably sealed off, so that left me in third. The bare, wooden-slatted compartment was so overcrowded and hot that the only sensible place to be was up on the roof, and this was where the few Western travellers soon congregated. Squatting on the flat, rough surface we had an unobstructed, all-round view as we rattled slowly southwards through the great Nubian desert. The banks of the White Nile alongside us were dotted with thorn bushes where emerald-green birds flitted and swooped. We passed a flock of hundreds of storks on migration, following the river north on their way to Europe. The few houses we saw were not square, stone and whitewashed, but were conical thatched huts. The men we encountered at station halts did not have short black hair, but wild Afros with three-pronged combs stuck in the top. We were seeing the Middle East slowly turn into Africa.

After thirty hours on the train roof and 550 miles of desert we drew into Khartoum at midnight. There was a delicious, overpowering scent coming from the blossom of the *neem* trees that grew around the station, but I had a pressing issue to worry about: where to sleep. The streets were deserted; the capital had gone to sleep. All the cheap hostels were closed up for the night and I could not afford anything bigger, so desperate measures were called for. On impulse, I knocked on the gates of a grand colonial building bearing the sign 'Khartoum General Hospital'. After a few seconds a sleepy night-watchman appeared with a lantern.

'Are you a doctor?' he asked in Arabic.

'Of course,' I bluffed.

'Then please come in.'

Exhausted from the train ride, I slept like a log on a concrete slab. In the morning I woke up next to a motionless body in a blood-soaked shroud; I had been sleeping next to a corpse. Outside in the courtyard a boy was spraying insecticide against the mosquitoes, the sky was full of wheeling vultures and the hospital was stirring to life. It was time to go before I was asked to perform an autopsy.

Sudan was the wildest, most exotic country I had ever been to. In the market stalls of Omdurman animal hides, horns and skulls hung out in the sun for sale, probably illegally. Here I met Dinka and Nuer, tribesmen from the equatorial south, incredibly tall and with their faces ritually scarred with pin-prick patterns. In a dusty square not far from the tomb of the so-called 'Mad Mahdi' who fought Lord Kitchener's troops in 1898 there were whirling dervishes who danced themselves into a hypnotic trance, flinging their shoulder-length hair from side to side. But I had little time to explore the country, as I had promised Cairo's Sadat Academy where I was teaching that I would be back in time for the start of their summer term. Frustratingly, I had to decline an invitation to join a jeep safari into big-game country in the south, travelling east instead by bus to Kassala, nine hours away on the Ethiopian border. Here, the baking landscape trembled in the heat haze and as I scanned the horizon a line of camels materialized, blurred at first and then clearly defined, the tribesmen riding them with one leg cocked up on the saddle, cantering across the flat valley floor then vanishing once more into the mirage.

This region was home to some of Sudan's most war-like tribes, with wild-haired tribesmen from the Hoddendowa and Baggara strolling through Kassala market with metre-long swords draped across their backs. (I managed to get one of these magnificent specimens out of Sudan and back to Britain, carrying it on to the plane in a less paranoid, pre-9/11 age, and it eventually saw service cutting the first slice of our wedding cake.) Kassala market was like a microcosm of the tribes of the Horn of Africa, the very people whom Wilfred Thesiger had travelled amongst when he led a Royal Geographical Society expedition into Danakil country in Abyssinia in 1933, aged just twenty-three. Here too were the Rashaida, an Arab race that had migrated across the Red Sea from the Arabian Peninsula, their sharp-featured faces visible beneath their head veils, the hair at the sides of their heads shaved off in traditional fashion. Eritrean women were also here, wearing vertical nose rings through the thickest, fleshiest part at the tip of the nose that must have been incredibly painful to put in. I noticed they wore their hair plaited at the front into three strands, all emanating from a gold ring above the forehead. They were refugees from the low-level guerrilla war going on just across the border, where Eritrean independence fighters were battling it out with the Ethiopian army. One afternoon I visited a Sudanese army border post where their dinner consisted of a gazelle, shot with an AK-47 and now strung upside-down from a Russian tank barrel with its guts hanging out.

I stayed in a border village on the outskirts of Kassala with a kind Sudanese family. The father, Sayyid Ahmed, was the sheikh of the village and the moment I stepped off the bus he insisted I be his guest. Ahmed had ten children and they lived in a round, mud-walled thatched hut surrounded by a defensive hedge of interwoven thorn bushes to keep out the wild animals. Once again I thought of Thesiger: when he was working for the Sudan colonial service in Kordofan province in the 1930s he had lived exactly like this, and the villagers had often begged him to ride out on horseback and hunt down the lions that were marauding their livestock. When he wrote about this in his memoirs half a century later he was criticized by some people in Britain, who accused him of depleting Africa's big game. But Thesiger always maintained that back in the Sudan of the thirties lions were so plentiful they had become a public menace and he would never have hunted them nowadays.

In the afternoon, as the temperature hovered around 45 degrees (113°F) in the shade, we ate lunch of flappy un-leavened bread dipped in the communal bowl of spicy meat casserole, washed down with cool water from the family well, poured from a stone jug with a horsehair stopper, followed by cups of scalding cinnamon tea. Sayyid Ahmed bounced one of his many small children on his knee, but when I asked him her name he had trouble remembering it and had to call out to his wife to be reminded. He was a fan of the BBC World Service, he told me, and he proudly produced an old radio that hissed and crackled like wet firewood. This meant nothing to me at the time – it was to be another twelve years before I worked for the BBC – but I now realize it is exactly remote communities like these that depend so heavily on the World Service for impartial news. At night I found it too hot inside the hut so I slept beneath the stars, lulled by the warm breeze that brushed my face and the melodic chirring of the cicadas that sounded in the darkness from beyond the thicket of thorns. I felt deeply content.

By day I went walking in the Toteel hills on the Sudanese side of the border, trekking up a steep track marked with the spore of wild baboons. A few hundred yards above the valley floor I watched as a *haboob*, a travelling squall of a dust storm, marched inexorably towards a cluster of thatched huts, enveloping them and flinging their flimsy roofs high into the sky. Up in the treeless hills, I reached a plateau where something large suddenly rushed towards me from above, narrowly missing my head. It was a vulture, one of a flock of hundreds that had risen on the thermals and was now scouring the rocks for anything to eat. I thought vultures were supposed to eat only carrion, but up here, exposed and out-numbered, I was not about to put this to the test and I scrambled back down the hill extremely quickly.

That night I was given a rare privilege: I was invited to attend a *zarr*, a secret exorcism in a private house. I stumbled across it by chance, drawn by the sound of drumming, chant-ing and clapping coming from a backstreet courtyard. When I peeked through a half-open gate I was ushered quickly inside and the gate was slammed behind me as I was guided over to a corner, where veiled girls with flashing eyes hand-fed me a local dish called *lugma*. I was the only male present. This was the *zarr reehat ahmar*, they explained, 'the exorcism of the red wind', for the benefit of a woman supposedly possessed of an evil jinni. I looked over to see a woman groan-ing and rocking backwards and forwards, clutching her sides. All around her, seated on rush mats, were about a hundred young women, watching while four older women, their faces lined and tribally scarred, performed a bizarre ritual in the middle of the courtyard. They rolled around on the ground like seals, beating the earth with their fists in time to the drumming. Things then took a strange and alarming turn as the elders began whipping themselves and flinging small battleaxes into wooden posts. The aim, said the girls, was to draw out the evil jinni and banish it from the afflicted woman's body, but when one of the axes landed with a thunk in a post close to my head I decided it was time to make my excuses and leave.

I returned to Cairo vowing to come back and explore

Sudan further but I never did. Two years after my trip there the country's leader, President Numeiri, was overthrown by Islamists. Government officials made a great show of pouring bottles of alcohol away into the Nile and it was announced that Islamic *shari'ah* law would now be strictly enforced. Relations with the West and with moderate Arab countries plummeted, Western travellers were viewed with suspicion and by the early 1990s Sudan had become home to Osama Bin Laden, his bodyguards and his contracting business. Although he personally invested millions in the country, Sudan grew steadily poorer, and nowadays when I tell Sudanese I went there in '83 they sometimes smile wistfully and say, 'Ah, those were the golden days.'

Now back in Cairo I had to concentrate on the business of learning colloquial Arabic, the whole raison d'être for this year in Egypt. By chance I met up with an Egyptian family that completely changed my time there. I had student friends out from Exeter and I was showing them round the bazaars of Khan El-Khalili, part of the historic quarter known as medieval or Islamic Cairo. It is a misnomer, really – rather like saying 'British London' – since nine out of ten Cairenes are Muslim anyway, but it alludes to the concentration of surviving Islamic architecture here. Suddenly bored by the endless displays of tourist tat in the bazaar, the plastic sphinxes and the bogus papyrus, I took a turn down a tiny backstreet alleyway and walked up a flight of dimly lit steps in a district called Gamaliya. Although this was effectively a slum quarter, it was a place still dominated by eight-hundred-year-old mosques and other buildings from the greatest era of Islamic architecture. On impulse, I knocked on a door and it opened immediately. A large-chested woman in traditional dress, the all-encompassing black *milaaya laff*, stood in the doorway, a hint of curiosity playing across her face. Mustering my best colloquial Egyptian Arabic, I explained that we had never seen the inside of a house here. Immediately she beckoned us in. Stooping to get through the doorway, we entered a dirt-poor living room where a family of about a dozen was squatted on mats, eating the communal supper. There were crumpled piles of blankets and bedclothes and I was pretty sure this was where they slept as well as spent most of the day. '*Itfaddal!*' she commanded, 'please join us'. I felt guilty at interrupting their meal, but they were so welcoming it was hard to leave. Within minutes we were cracking jokes, with Umm Layla, the big-chested mother, pretending to be an expert in karate and her children pretending to cower in fear. '*Baytna baytak,*' said Ahmed the father, a taxi-driver, 'our house is your house'. It was a happy place, despite the squalor, and I was invited to return whenever I wanted, so I did.

On a cold afternoon in January I told Peregrine and the rest of the students that I was transplanting myself to Gamaliya to stay with my Egyptian family for a few days. Ahmed's family had no telephone so I had no means of warning them; I just turned up and they seemed to accept this as the most natural thing in the world. Egyptians can be famously kind and hospitable, so this open invitation did not strike me as unusual, but if I had not spoken Arabic it would have been unworkable. I was given a space on a narrow shelf just under the roof and next to the dovecote on which to lay out my sleeping bag and we all shared the communal footprint loo. Umm Layla lit a fire in the battered, portable grate and we snuggled round it, watching Egyptian soap operas on their fuzzy black-and-white TV and eating *lib*, cracknuts, which to my mind do not repay the considerable effort needed to split them open without spilling the contents all over your lap. As the rain pelted the corrugated roof we shared a meal of black olives, hard cheese, flaps of unleavened bread, tomatoes, spring onions, peppers, honey and tangerines. Layla, the eldest daughter, bombarded me with questions about England. Was London like Cairo? Did my parents live like this? Had I met the Queen? Her younger sister Seneyya found it endlessly fascinating to comb my hair, while Hamdi, one of the sons, who was studying engineering, sat silently watching TV. From the glowing embers of the fire Ahmed ignited his *shisha*, his waterpipe or hubble-bubble, smoking it contentedly while surveying his family then handing me the pipe for a puff. I have never been a smoker so I was not keen. Perhaps luckily for me, a couple of illicit drags on a cigarette at the age of twelve were enough to put me off for life and even persuade me to make both my parents give up. But the whole idea of a waterpipe is that the smoke actually passes through the water, cooling and filtering it so that what you inhale is so light that cigarette smokers say they cannot even taste tobacco. I was converted, and have since brought back *shishas* from as far away as Basra to smoke in our back garden in London.

That night I drew up my sleeping bag tightly around my neck, partly from the cold, partly to keep out any vermin. I awoke with a start when something ran across my sleeping bag, assuming it to be a mouse or even a rat. But in the morning, over breakfast of hot, deep-fried falafel, the family laughed when I told them. It was a stoat, they said, there were many of them here, attracted by the pigeons, and I was not to worry. Outside, the sounds of the bazaar coming to life drifted up like woodsmoke and a peek through a crack in the wall revealed Egyptians muffled in grey tasselled scarves and big crumpled overcoats. I turned my attention back to the family. Umm Layla was wearing a bright-blue gown that could barely contain her bulging arms. Now she was asking me about England: did we live like this over there? Like the Norwegian author of *The Bookseller of Kabul* I was accepted by this family with no preconditions. I chipped in a few well-worn banknotes towards the groceries and taught the children as much English as I could, and in turn I was free to come and go as I liked. On the morning after my arrival I wrote in my diary:

January 15th 1983. How I love Cairo, especially now that I am at last living in the medieval Islamic quarter. Immersed in this teeming environment and surrounded by friendly, witty people whose ways and language I am beginning to understand, right now I have no desire to ever leave this place.

On our Arabic literature course at university we had been taught that the story of The Thousand and One Nights was actually written about medieval Cairo, but that to conceal his identity and protect himself from the possible wrath of the caliph the author had pretended it was set in Baghdad. With all these teeming medieval backstreets and Islamic monuments on my doorstep it was easy to picture life as it would have been here eight hundred years ago. Many aspects, I felt sure, had probably not changed that much, like the *makwagis*, the laundrymen whom I saw taking a swig of water from a jug then spraying it out through their teeth to dampen the clothes before ironing them. In the historic district of Ghouriya which I now explored, most of the houses were so old they would probably have collapsed long ago if they had not been held up by each other. Many still had wooden lattice harem windows protruding out above the street. Known as *mashrubiya*, these intricately carved constructions were designed to let the women of the house look out on to the world without being seen themselves, a sort of architectural version of the *burqa*. More than once I caught a fleeting glimpse of a face peering at me from behind one of these lattice windows, dappled for a moment by the sun and shadow, then gone, vanished into the dark interior of a private house.

I drifted aimlessly through the spice bazaar, past vivid cones of aromatic powder, then into a side street where crates of live ducks and geese were being weighed on antique bronze scales suspended from ceilings. Everywhere I went I was invited to sit down for tea, not the English milky variety but a strong dark liquid, heavily sugared and sipped from a glass with a thick sediment of tea-leaves swilling around inside. In the shadow of the massive medieval gateway of Bab Zuweila I settled down on a three-legged stool to sketch the architecture, periodically blowing the fine dust and grit off the pages of my diary. All around me Cairo street life flowed past without pause: I felt like a small rock in the middle of a fast stream. A high-pitched whistling sound would herald the baker's boy, weaving his way through the crowd on his bicycle with one hand on the handlebars, the other balancing a wooden tray of a hundred loaves on his head. A frantic clucking would give away a chicken that had strayed into the tailors' and was now being chased out with a broom. And always on the same street corner, Fawzi the beggar, his skinny arm outstretched in supplication, pathetically grateful for the few piastres someone might drop into his tin.

That winter was so unusually cold that one afternoon it even hailed, which was a novel experience for most Cairenes. But within weeks spring had returned, marked by a vicious *khamseen* storm. The *khamseen*, meaning 'fifty', can blow any time during the fifty days of spring, and is essentially an international dust storm. Building speed and strength across the Sahara, it picks up several tons of dust, sand and donkey dung from the Sahel and Nile villages in the south, then carries it north and dumps it on Cairo. Shutting all the doors and windows in our student flat was not enough to keep out the sand, which blew in through the cracks and quickly found its way to the back of our throats. Given the often unsanitary origins of this grit it is not surprising that a lot of people fall ill during the *khamseen*.

By the time the summer heat returned I was thoroughly immersed in Cairo life and I didn't want this year to end, yet each time the temperature notched up a few degrees we knew that our return to Britain was drawing closer. By now I had arranged to spend a few days at a time with my Egyptian family and the rest based in the flat with the other students. I had an Egyptian girlfriend, although by Western standards it was a very chaste relationship. She lived with her parents in the flat across the street from ours and Peregrine used to go out on to our balcony and make a point of observing her through a naval telescope. She found this very amusing and one day we arranged by sign language to meet downstairs at the grocer's. Asmaa, as she was called, had dark, beguiling eyes which she used to great effect. She was studying literature at Cairo University, where she complained that the classes were hopelessly oversized – her eyes widened with envy when I told her there were just fourteen in our class of undergraduates. She was fascinated to have met a *khawaaga*, a foreigner, who spoke Arabic and together we began to take long walks around Zamalek. Coming from a traditional family, even this was risqué for her; various brothers would trail us at a discreet distance and on the few occasions when I tried to take her hand she would chastise me with a flirtatious smile, whispering, '*Eedak gambak, ya Frank!*' meaning 'keep your hands to yourself'. I gave Asmaa a book about England and she gave me a fake blue pharaonic sphinx; it was well-meant but, to be honest, quite hideous and I resolved to get rid of it without giving offence. None of my flatmates would take it and I had visions of our doorman triumphantly and publicly rescuing it from the dustbin if I disposed of it in our neighbourhood. So to be absolutely certain it would never be discovered I packed the offending sphinx in my rucksack and took it with me on a trip I made with Mustafa, an Egyptian friend, deep into the Western Desert. Up on a windswept crag above the remote oasis of Dakhla, about ten hours' bus ride from Cairo, I buried the blue sphinx where no one would find it. Afterwards I wondered if Asmaa had had to go to similar lengths to dispose of my coffee-table book about English heritage.

Peregrine, meanwhile, had made himself very comfortable

in Zamalek, where he was an habitué of several patisseries, and I never managed to persuade him to cross the Nile and meet my adopted family in Islamic Cairo. But we had a lot of fun with other young Egyptian friends, racing in convoy up to the Pyramids at four in the morning and sitting on the 4,500-year-old blocks singing in Arabic, or trying to. Even Julia and Yolanda were missing England less and liking Cairo more. We went to a lot of parties, including a fancy-dress one where I narrowly avoided being arrested for flagging down a taxi in drag. In our final month we went to an embassy bash, and it was there that I realized how far the local culture had seeped into my bones. A female diplomat whom I knew vaguely loomed towards me, offering me her cheek to kiss. I recoiled instinctively, having been conditioned to avoid any public display of affection with the opposite sex.

I spent the last few days of my Cairo year with my Egyptian family. It was Ramadan, the Muslim holy month of fasting and other abstentions, and I switched over to their timetable. We would wake up late and listless, then eat nothing till sundown, when Umm Layla would prepare a huge spread of food on tattered rush mats on the floor. Friends and relatives would crowd into their tiny hovel, helping themselves from the cauldrons of soup, trays of roast chicken and rice and an inexplicably popular dish called *mulukhiyya*. Made from some aquatic vegetable, it looked like green saliva and dribbled off the spoon in sticky, gelatinous globules. I managed to escape being made to try it right to the last.

After all these months Ahmed decided he could now trust me enough to take me off after the meal to one of his favourite haunts: the seedy backstreet quarter known as Batniyya, the hashish capital of Egypt. In dingy and dimly lit cafés we passed men puffing desperately on improvised bongs made out of jam jars and two protruding bamboo tubes, one for inhaling, the other to support the tobacco, hash and burning charcoal. Ahmed found us a couple of chairs and explained how it worked. It was up to the customers, he said, to bring their own lumps of hash with them. When the waiter came he brought a rack holding a dozen clay pots stuffed with sweetened tobacco, which were then fitted on to the bamboo ready for inhaling. With a mischievous expression on his face, Ahmed inserted his fingers into the back of his mouth and retrieved his personal lump of hash, hidden behind his teeth, bit off a chunk and placed it on top of the tobacco. As the charcoal burned and he began to inhale, the effect was a sweet smell and a profound coughing fit from Ahmed. Tears welled in his eyes but he attacked the hash pipe with renewed vigour, pausing only to hawk up some phlegm on to the pavement. It was not the most enchanting way of spending my last night in Cairo and I worried that if this was how the head of the family spent his taxi fares then this family was going to fall on even harder times.

Years later, on a BBC trip to Cairo in 1998, I took an Egyptian banker friend Ossama with me to find the family. He thought I was winding him up as I led him through the dim, narrow backstreets and up the grimy steps to their home. As a well-educated, well-travelled international businessman he had never darkened the doors of a place like this, and when the door opened I think he expected me to make my excuses and leave. But instead it revealed Umm Layla, the karate-chopping mother, and it was as if nothing had changed. She embraced me in her ample bosom, sweeping me up in that same tidal wave of Egyptian hospitality I had so cherished as a student. Ossama was stunned; it was the only time I have seen him lost for words. I suppose it would be the equivalent of an Egyptian taking me to see his English friends on a tough estate in south London, except that instead of the latent threat of a mugging, here in Islamic Cairo I had found only kindness, security and generosity.

That year in Cairo affected me deeply, giving me a lasting love of the Arab world that has survived many of its less pleasant aspects, not least getting shot by people who called themselves Muslims. My experiences in Cairo formed a bedrock for all I learned later about the Middle East and Arab culture. It was a gentle introduction, in a way, since Egyptians are generally very tolerant of Westerners and, unlike the more conservative Arab societies of the Gulf, the friends I made in Cairo were of both sexes. Time and again I found that speaking Arabic was the ice-breaker, the lubricant for every friendship and the key to understanding the rich Egyptian sense of humour. For a student of Arabic eager to learn about the Middle East, a university year spent in Egypt was the perfect grounding.

4

From Bedouin to Bahrain

النخيل في الرمال

THE CAIRO YEAR OVER, I NOW HAD TO THINK ABOUT PASSING
the final exams for my degree. My approach to cramming
at Exeter University was to spend an afternoon swotting up
in the library, putter home through the country lanes on my
motorbike to our shared student cottage, go on a really
pounding run over the red clay hills of Devon, then meet up
with friends in the local village pub. I knew I was never really
going to impress the examiners with my grasp of early Arabic
poetry, and my hopes of redemption through my reasonable
fluency in spoken Arabic were dashed when we learned that
the verbal exam consisted of reciting . . . early Arabic poetry
again. What was wrong with these academics? Didn't they
know there was a thriving, cosmopolitan Middle East out
there? But my salvation lay in the dissertations. These were
two eight-thousand-word essays we were instructed to write
on just about any Middle Eastern topic of our choice, as long
as it had some scholarly merit. I chose the Islamic
Architecture of the Maghreb (North Africa), and Egyptian
Women, not because I had recently had an Egyptian girlfriend
but because I was genuinely interested in how their role in

society was changing. My research included reading works by the controversial Egyptian female writer Dr Nawal El Saadawi, who recalled in agonizing detail the horrors of being held down on a bathroom floor at the age of six and forcibly circumcised by a bunch of old women. Incredibly, this barbaric practice still occurs in parts of rural Egypt, and is perpetuated by the older women of the village in many of the countries of Saharan Africa under the pretence that it 'conforms with tradition', in spite of Muslim scholars insisting it has nothing to do with Islam. I finally got to meet Dr El Saadawi nearly twenty years later when I interviewed her for BBC World. Still a strikingly good-looking woman in her seventies, she was as outspoken as ever, telling me how wrong she thought it was for impoverished Egyptian farmers to be blowing their family finances on sending themselves off on pilgrimmage to Mecca. 'The Prophet Mohammed never wanted this sort of sacrifice,' she said. She had recently been declared 'an apostate' by some of Egypt's more radical preachers and was contesting a bizarre lawsuit that was trying to separate her from her beloved husband of over forty years on the grounds that she was no longer a good enough Muslim to be married to a Muslim.

Rather to our surprise, we all achieved our degrees – in my case an unremarkable 2.2, known as a 'Bishop Desmond' (as in Tutu). Now that we were graduates in Arabic and Islamic Studies, our lecturers brightly informed us that the world was our oyster. This was not quite true, since unless we were planning to go into academia – a temptation I somehow managed to resist – a degree in Arabic was practically useless on its own. It needed to be combined with an actual profession, such as, well, journalism, but I hadn't worked that out yet. I took a rather casual approach to job hunting, in fact I even omitted to draw up a CV. I did go to one interview before I graduated, though, which was for MI6, the Secret Intelligence Service (SIS). In the small community of Western expatriates living in Cairo I had come across a British diplomat who turned out to be an SIS officer there. I had no idea of this when I took him on a tour of my favourite back-streets, nor that he was assessing me for possible recruitment, but some time later he asked if I would be interested in being put in touch with 'the right people' in London. Why not? I thought, this could be fun. But once I had signed a copy of the Official Secrets Act, the initial interview turned into something of a disappointment and it successfully put me off a career in the espionage business. 'I should warn you now,' said the man in the grey suit behind the desk, 'that if you choose this career you will never be able to tell your friends about it, you will have to lie continually about what you do and,' here he leaned closer towards me as if letting me into a great secret, 'you will be unlikely ever to get any public recognition for your achievements.' Well, that rules me out, I thought, I'm much too vain for this outfit. If I achieved something I wanted to see it recognized, so a career of tight-lipped modesty in the world of spooks simply did not appeal, either then or since.

The trouble was that, like most twenty-two-year-olds, I hadn't a clue what I wanted to do. Because of my love of running and keeping fit I had made some enquiries about taking a short service commission in the Parachute Regiment, but my parents sensibly persuaded me this would be a waste of four years of Arabic studies. There was one potential employer who took an interest in me at a campus job fair, a firm that manufactured police and military uniforms for export to the Middle East. Not quite the life of glamour I had in mind but it would do for a start, I thought, and assuming I had the job I promptly headed off round the Mediterranean for an extended backpacking trip with Carrie, my first serious girlfriend. After all that time in Egypt it felt strange to be amidst topless sunbathers on sybaritic Greek islands, or plied with wine and spirits by Italian villagers near Pompeii. We had a great time, but when I returned in the autumn I was surprised to find there was no job offer. This was getting serious. Graduates from my year at Exeter had already landed lucrative jobs in the City; one had even wangled a position with a high-octane firm of City money-brokers after scoring a third in Zoology. It was like being the only person at a party without a partner.

In desperation I ran my finger down the London phone directory looking under 'M' for Middle East. I then rang up every organization that looked as if it might be a prospective employer and invited myself round for interview with anyone who would see me, wearing one of my father's hairy old suits and carrying an empty briefcase for added effect. I accepted the first offer I got, joining a tiny firm that exported chocolates and perfume to the Arab world, on a starting salary of £6,000 a year. The kindly Egyptian boss, Sharif, had made his fortune in Kuwait and he still had many connections in the Gulf. I yearned to be sent out there to haggle with his clients, but he rightly judged me to be far too inexperienced. Instead, I got assigned to the firm's perfumery division and soon found myself learning the distinction between the top, middle and base notes of a scent. Before long I was required to put this into practice when the firm launched a new 'gentlemen's fragrance'; I had to spend several weeks behind the counter at Selfridges flogging it to potential customers. It taught me how surprisingly tiring it can be, standing up all day with a false smile on your face. Word of my deployment to a perfumery counter in Oxford Street soon got out to my friends and they took it in turns to come and have a good giggle, assuring me that I had really found my niche in life. At first, the mostly Iranian female sales assistants all assumed I was gay, since the only other two male assistants in perfumery were very much an item. When the girls discovered I wasn't they made a big fuss of me, teaching me choice and un-repeatable expressions in Farsi in between reminiscing about the days of bikini pool parties in Iran under the Shah. But I could only take so much of squirting stuff on to the hands of ungrateful customers before I was begging to be allowed back to head office. All the new-found eighties hype about 'male grooming' made me think of Churchill's pithy quote: 'A man should damn well smell of himself.'

Working for Sharif was both amusing and infuriating. With his residual Egyptian accent he would often mispronounce words. His lunchtime seafood takeaway order from the Regent Street deli, for example, came out as 'Bring me a crap sandwich,' something we all tried very hard not to envisage.

As an antidote to London office life, I persuaded Carrie that we should spend our summer holidays somewhere really wild and adventurous, like Yemen. I went off to see Wilfred Thesiger again in his Chelsea flat, to ask his advice. Now in his mid-seventies, he greeted me at the top of the stairs in an immaculate three-piece suit, his handshake as powerful as ever. 'Don't drink the water there,' he said, as we sat down in his rather gloomy living room and his ageing housekeeper brought us tea, 'or else you risk catching guinea worm.' Thesiger, who had worn out two kneecaps exploring Yemen's mountains and who once complained that a near miss by a rebel bullet during the civil war there in the sixties had wrecked his cigar case, went on to describe how he had seen people infected by this worm have it come crawling out of their necks or even, if they were very unlucky, out through their eyes. It was probably the best advice he gave me; we drank 7-Up and Coca Cola for two weeks.

Yemen wasn't quite the holiday Carrie had had in mind – she'd packed for the Bahamas, I'd packed for the desert – but she coped stoically with having to be almost fully covered up in the August heat, having conservative Yemenis avoid all eye contact with her, and, at one point, getting chased out of a mosque by an angry imam. On the day we arrived in the ancient mud-walled capital, Sana'a, a man in the street gripped my arm and cautioned me: 'Be careful, my friend, for there are many wizards here.' And it was true: ten thousand feet up on the terraced hills of Hajjah we watched a man blow coins out of his nose and perform other inexplicable tricks to an audience of grinning, heavily armed tribesmen.

Yemen was a little-known country of extraordinary contrasts: one day we would be swimming in the Red Sea amongst the pelicans of Khokha, the next we would be reclining on padded benches in the port of Hodeida, smoking metre-high hubble-bubble waterpipes beneath slowly turning ceiling fans. In the sand dunes of the Empty Quarter we traipsed round the pre-Islamic Sabaean Dam and the Temple of Marib, gasping in the 45-degree heat. In the northern town of Sa'ada we awoke to the sound of gunfire: happy shooting by local tribesmen, we learned. There, two young Yemenis befriended us and took us for a drive in the hills, where we took turns at target practice with their Kalashnikovs and pistols until an irate farmer came out and complained that bullets were ricocheting around his sheep.

When we returned to London I resolved to do something about using my Arabic, which had been idling away in neutral at the back of my brain for a year now, waiting in vain to be called on. A friend of a friend passed my CV to Sir James Craig, a former British ambassador to Saudi Arabia and now head of the Middle East Association. His Arabic was so flawless that he could hardly have been impressed by mine, but the following week I was summoned for an interview in the City at Saudi International Bank (SIB), a joint venture between the Saudi government and a handful of Western banks. I tried to make it clear that I had no grounding in finance or economics, but the interviewer droned on about interest rates, leverage and product placement. I had no idea what he was talking about and was about to write off the interview as an afternoon wasted when they offered me a job on double my present salary. Hell, I thought, even if they kick me out after six months' probation it will have been worth it financially. I fixed my starting date to allow a generous three months' travelling and set my sights on the Middle East. If I had been hired for my Arabic and familiarity with Arab culture then I had better deliver and brush up on it fast. It was time to pick a country.

The early summer of 1986 was not a good time to be a Westerner in the Middle East. Hijackings and kidnappings in Lebanon were all the rage, while Arab tempers had been raised by events in Libya. In retaliation for Colonel Gaddafi's suspected role in the bombing of a Berlin disco frequented by US servicemen, the US Airforce had carried out a bombing raid on several targets in Libya on 15 April. One of Gaddafi's many homes, his barracks in Tripoli, had been hit and his adopted daughter killed. The colonel had escaped unharmed but severely rattled. Meanwhile the world's TV screens were filled with the sight of angry fist-shaking crowds on Arab streets. Robert Fisk of the *Independent* pronounced that the Arab world had changed irrevocably and that the US had blown for ever its chances of making friends in the region. There would be reprisals, he warned. Sure enough, there were more kidnappings in Lebanon and a Western hostage was executed. But the violence seemed largely confined to that country, which was anyway in the grip of an eleven-year-old civil war, with various factions shelling and shooting each other from the pockmarked husks of ruined houses.

So where to visit to brush up my rusty Arabic? I ruled out the Gulf – too expensive and I didn't know anyone there yet. Yemen, North Africa and Egypt I had been to fairly recently. Syria would be fascinating, but Anglo-Syrian relations were at a low ebb after a Syrian intelligence plot to put a bomb on board an El Al Israeli airliner flying out of Heathrow had just been foiled. (The Palestinian perpetrator, Nizar Al-Hindawi, had tried to put his pregnant Irish girlfriend on the flight, who was unaware that she was carrying 1.5 kg of Semtex high explosive in her luggage – if this had not been discovered at Heathrow the bomb would have killed all 375 passengers on board.) It's worth remembering these things when we think the 2000s are dangerous – there was plenty of terrorism around in the 1980s too, it just wasn't in the name of Al-Qaeda and was not quite so apocalyptic in intent.

Jordan looked like a good bet for a visit, though. It had a stable monarchy under the charismatic King Hussein, its people spoke some of the purest classical Arabic in the Middle East, and I knew it to be rich in culture and heritage. As a schoolboy I had been intrigued by pictures I had seen in a travel brochure of bandoliered border police patrolling the red sand dunes of Wadi Rumm. Altogether it seemed the right place in which to re-immerse myself in the Arab world, so I bought a ticket and took off on Air France.

In my pocket I carried a letter of introduction from *Time Out* magazine commissioning me to write a travel piece on Jordan. Even though I was soon to begin a career in investment banking I had an irrepressible urge to write. I had managed to get my first article published the previous year – on life as a student in Cairo – in a magazine put out by the Egyptian embassy, and I used that as a stepping stone, sending off the published article, with accompanying glossy photos, to the editor of *Midweek* magazine, a freebie handed out to commuters at London Tube stations every Thursday morning. *Midweek* agreed to take a piece I wrote on Yemen – they paid £150 a time and it was a great thrill to see my byline in print. I then showed the article to *Time Out*, and so on, until eventually I built up a stable of newspapers and magazines that took my work, even squeezing an account of a Bulgarian train ride into *The Best of Sunday Times Travel Writing 1987*. It was nearly all travel writing or the occasional think piece about security in the Middle East, and for a while I was content just to write on a freelance basis while using my banking salary to pay the rent.

The flight to Amman was almost empty; nobody was going to the Middle East. The French flight attendants had plenty of time to chat to me, so I asked them if they had received any special training for hijacks and hostage-taking.

'Sure,' said one of the cabin crew, 'they issue us with these special loose-fitting jackets.'

'Really?' I replied. 'How do they help?'

'They allow us to raise our arms in surrender even quicker!'

In Amman I stayed with a university friend, Nigel, who was out there working for a British bank and living in a pale-stoned villa where purple bougainvillea tumbled down the walls. Nigel was playing with fire. He had started an affair with a Jordanian girl from a well-known family, and although they were Christians, not Muslims, any hint of pre-marital sex was considered a grave insult to the family's honour. The girl's brothers had learnt of the affair and had sent him a death threat. In a country notorious for its so-called 'honour killings' this was not to be taken lightly, so Nigel was now contemplating leaving Jordan rather sooner than he had intended.

I found Amman to be a pleasant but unexciting city, built on the rolling, boulder-strewn hills of the biblical Middle East. I was eager to get out to the desert, so I lost no time in walking into a small building marked Ministry of Tourism, clutching my letter from *Time Out* magazine. The place was as quiet as a grave and my arrival caused quite a stir amongst the bored officials behind their desks.

'You're a tourist? You want to write about our country?' Pause, quick exchange of glances, then big smiles. 'Yes, of course! How can we help you?'

The Jordanians could not have been more helpful. They assigned me a driver/guide and put a jeep at my disposal to go anywhere in the country for as long as I wanted. I could hardly believe my luck. Feeling as if I was the only tourist in the country, we ranged eastwards towards Iraq, exploring the castles and forts where T. E. Lawrence had rested and regrouped before attacking the Turkish Army in the First World War. We went north to Ajlun, where I spent a sun-drenched afternoon wandering over the fantastically preserved Roman forum with only basking lizards for company. Then we turned south, down the King's Highway, one of the two arteries that connect the country.

My guide was Jamal (pronounced *juh-mairl*, not *jummal*, which means 'camel' in Arabic). He told me he had previously worked as a security guard at the Jordanian embassy in London, and it wasn't long before he was showing off the automatic pistol he carried. On a high plateau in the hills north of Aqaba we set up a line of cans and blatted away at them, sending them spinning into the clear blue air, the gunshots echoing around the empty landscape.

The ancient city of Petra took my breath away. Built in the third century BC by the Nabataeans, this once-rich trading settlement lay hidden away in the wind-blasted canyons of south Jordan until it was 'discovered' in the nineteenth century by a European explorer. The Nabataeans derived their income from taxing local caravans, then spent the money on building whole streets, temples and baths out of the sheer rock face. It was easy to see how explorers failed to find this place for so long. A mile away we had been walking through the gentle, grassy hills of Wadi Musa; now we found ourselves in an almost labyrinthine world, shut in by towering red cliffs hundreds of feet high with only a ten-foot gap in between. The clichéd words 'a rose-red city half as old as time' kept repeating themselves in my head; I just wished I had thought of them myself.

That night I wrote in my diary:

Jamal and I dismounted from the jeep and rented a pair of white horses to take us through the narrow, mile-long canyon known as the Seeq. Powder-fine dust hung around us, kicked up by the animals' hoofs and we raced the final few yards, pulling up breathless and coated in sweat just in front of the Khaznat Faron, the Pharaoh's Treasury, the first building you come to in ancient Petra. Its stone columns rose several storeys high, built into the red rock, topped by a carved capitol. Dwarfed by its shadow, languid Bedu lay at its base, twirling their sticks in the sand and pulling their chequered head-scarves closer around their faces to keep out the summer flies. Aside from them, there was no one around, no sound but for the wind whispering in the flowering bushes of oleander.

All day I roamed around Petra, climbing two-thousand-year-old steps that had been chiselled into the rockface, trying to imagine what must have happened at the High Place of Sacrifice, picturing the great trading caravans that passed nearby on their way up from Oman to Syria, bearing sacks of frankincense. In the noonday heat the air was rent by the scream of swifts wheeling through the blue void, and my path was crossed often by the skitter of a heavy lizard. The force of the sun rebounded off the rocks like an echo; they were like nothing I had ever seen before. Eroded and mutated by wind and water, they resembled treacle poured over a cake and then frozen, so that the rock appeared to drip down from the peaks. Shepherds and their goats emerged from tiny caves that festooned the mountainside, then vanished back into the cool shadows. The colours, too, were extraordinary. In places the rock had formed itself into an intricate kaleidoscope of reds, yellows, browns and purples, stretching one's belief in its natural formation.

There was an overpowering feeling of history here, but I was sad to learn that the local Bedu families who had lived for centuries in these caves with their sheep and goats were now being moved out in a government drive to smarten the place up for tourists. I mentioned to Jamal that I was keen to meet the Bedu as I wanted to experience a life as close as possible to that lived by the nomadic tribes that had long roamed the Middle East. 'Right,' said Jamal, 'but not here. I know just the people for you.'

We drove east, past Ras Al Naqab, an abandoned station on the old Hijaz Railway that T. E. Lawrence attacked during the First World War. The railway lines remained, overgrown now by purple thistles and littered with the detritus of seventy years. Some villagers, seeing a vehicle with the official markings of the Ministry of Tourism, came forward eagerly to ask if there was to be a project here with work for them all. But Jamal shook his head and they turned away sadly. We gave a lift to a cloudy-eyed sheikh with a gold-trimmed robe, and then we entered the broad desert valley known as Wadi Rumm. Great golden rock massifs rose up hundreds of metres high on either side of us, split by purple-shadowed crevices and flanked by red dunes. In his book *Seven Pillars of Wisdom*, T. E. Lawrence wrote that 'a whole squadron of aeroplanes could have wheeled in formation within its walls'. He was probably thinking of tiny Sopwith Camel biplanes, but I have since seen modern footage of RAF Tornado jets flying through just this sort of terrain across the border in Saudi Arabia.

Wadi Rumm was huge and majestic; dwarfed by this setting, the tiny settlement of Rumm was a scruffy, un-imposing place. Rusting corrugated-iron shacks stood surrounded by chicken-wire fences, hemming in the odd camel or a couple of goats. Here and there was the occasional black goats'-hair tent, giving a tantalizing glimpse of nomadic desert life. We drew up at the police post, a surreal Beau Geste fort with crenellated battlements and a Jordanian flag flutter-ing from the top. The national guardsmen were dressed in long khaki-coloured robes, criss-crossed with leather bandoliers, beneath red-and-white chequered headdresses encircled by the royal Hashemite crest. They offered us coffee from brass pots with curved spouts that simmered in the hot ashes from a dying fire. It was my first taste of Arabian coffee, and it took me by surprise. Instead of the sweet bland flavour of instant coffee that I had grown up with in school bedsits and dormitories, or the sugary, grainy texture of Turkish coffee served in thimble-sized cups that I had become used to in Cairo, this was a thin, green and bitter liquid flavoured with cardamom seeds. It was clearly an acquired taste and I had difficulty in not spitting the first mouthful on to the sand. (I have later come to love it, finding it goes down especially well with sweet Hassa dates from Saudi Arabia.)

Jamal disappeared off into the village of Rumm, leaving me to chat to the border police. They still patrolled the southern border with Saudi Arabia by camel, they said, mainly to stop smugglers. Sometimes they found it more efficient to travel by jeep, but there were still places only a camel could reach. I was about to ask them what happened to the people they caught when Jamal reappeared, his bearded face beaming with excitement. 'You're in luck,' he announced. 'One of the most respected sheikhs in the whole area just happens to be visiting Rumm today, and if he likes you then you can stay with his family out in the desert. They are from the Bani Howaitat tribe. How does that sound?'

We found Sheikh Hajji Attayig sitting bolt upright and cross-legged in the tent his family used when they came into Rumm. He was scanning the sides of the canyon with an old pair of binoculars, his gnarled fingers working the focus, his lined face squinting in concentration. We exchanged courtesies in Arabic and then I noticed Jamal withdrawing to the corner of the tent, watching to see how I got on. Despite his tough, hawk-like features, Sheikh Attayig was kind and hospitable. I was welcome to stay with him and his extended family, he said, for as long as I wished. Tomorrow we would be moving out deep into the desert. Jamal was satisfied I was in good hands. 'I'll come back for you in a month,' he said and drove off in a cloud of dust, leaving us in the stillness of this desert valley.

The sheikh pointed to a magnificent curved sword in a silver sheath that dangled from the roof of the tent behind his head. 'Do you know who that sword belonged to?' he asked with a look of pride on his face. I did not. 'It belonged to Auda Bin Abi Tayyi. Have you heard of him?' I most certainly had. He was a famous warrior chieftain of the Howaitat tribe who had fought alongside T. E. Lawrence against the Turks in the Arab Revolt of 1916. In David Lean's film *Lawrence of Arabia*, Auda's part had been played by Anthony Quinn, whose stentorian voice uttered that memorable curse, 'My mother mated with a scorpion!' I am quite sure the real Auda Bin Abi Tayyi said no such thing, but that did nothing to lessen the drama of the moment. I was sitting with a sheikh from one of the most famous tribes in Arabia. At that point a vile-smelling goat poked its head round the tent flap, as if asking to come in. The sheikh hissed at it and shooed it away by tossing a pebble at its hoofs.

Sheikh Hajji Attayig passed me his binoculars. They were old, made entirely of metal, with tiny cracked lenses and none of the black rubber coating found on modern versions. 'They belonged to Glubb Pasha,' said the sheikh. 'I was his scout and he gave them to me as a farewell present.' The sheikh then fished into a pocket and pulled out a worn piece of paper. Sure enough, it was his discharge papers from Glubb Pasha's Camel Corps; I was impressed. Glubb Pasha was an honorary title bestowed on John Glubb, a former British Army officer given the job of raising an army of Bedu tribesmen to keep order in what was known in the 1950s as Transjordan. Called The Arab Legion, it had a reputation as the best-run force in the region, but when the teenaged King Hussein ascended the throne after the assassination of his father in Jerusalem, he decided he would rather not have his army run by a foreigner and he dismissed Glubb

Pasha. But sitting in his tent that afternoon, Sheikh Attayig was happy to meet someone from Britain – Glubb Pasha's 'tribe' – and he talked at length about his service with the Camel Corps. When he first joined, he said, his marksmanship was already so good that the sergeant asked him where he had acquired his experience. Just here in the desert, he had replied truthfully, and the sergeant had hit him twice in the face for being a liar.

In the mid-afternoon the sheikh rose for prayer, muttering the verses softly under his breath, while Gaudaan, his camel, stirred in the dust and frisked at the occasional fly. Later he went over to her and removed the annual crop of camel fluff for his pillows, taken from the worn patches on the animal's back. That night, my first in the desert, there was an *ihtifaal*, a celebration, in a relative's tent. In the fading light of day the sheikh's sons led me to a large black goats'-hair tent that was pitched in the soft sand. Seated inside, on coarse but richly coloured rugs, were about forty Jordanian Bedu in various states of repose. Each wore the traditional red-and-white headcloth above a neatly trimmed moustache and pointed beard. A fire crackled noisily in their midst while old and encrusted kettles stood by. The Bedu rose to greet us in turn, their formal movements following a prescribed pattern. To me, a stranger brought in by a guest, they were courteous and welcoming, shaking my hand firmly. But with those that they knew they would bow slightly, grasp hands and make a strange kissing sound, their lips sometimes touching the other's cheeks. Then they would flick their right hands briskly up to their hearts, to signify that, praise be to God, their hearts were happy.

The greetings were a welcome distraction from the fact that we were all ravenously hungry and thirsty. Since this was Ramadan, the month of fasting, I had decided that afternoon that I must fast with my hosts. They had not insisted on this, in fact they had said from the outset that they quite understood if as a Christian I wanted to break the fast during the day, but if so, could I please do it discreetly behind a rock somewhere. But I felt it would be impossible for them to accept me if I started sneaking off behind rocks: it would throw up a barrier between us and I would never know what it was like to fast in the desert in the height of summer. So now, as the last light vanished from the gathering, I could sense the tension in the air as an exercise in forbearance began. Brimming bowls of cool water and apricot juice were placed before us on the sand, but no one could touch them until the words '*Allahu Akbar!*', 'God is the greatest!' were uttered by the muezzin of the Al Husseini Mosque in Amman, broadcast over the radio to a nation of very hungry Muslims. I could see that to these desert Bedu such discipline and self-restraint were second nature, and they talked and joked to speed the dragging minutes. Water was poured over our hands in preparation for the feast by silent, veiled women while Sulaiman, the host, strode amongst the seated guests, his silver inlaid dagger flashing from the hip.

At last the moment came and giant trays were brought in laden with a dish called *mansaf*. Each was so heavy it took two men to carry it. *Mansaf* is a traditional Jordanian Bedu feast consisting of chunks of mutton scattered over a huge pile of rice and unleavened bread, then drenched in scalding hot milk and fat; it tastes better than it sounds. The food was divided into four trays, with about ten of us feeding from each communal tray. I rolled up my sleeves and ploughed in with the right hand but it was now so dark it was almost impossible to see what I was eating. My greasy fingers searched the tray for meat, but things kept slipping, squid-like, from my grasp. The man next to me was offering me various parts of the sheep's anatomy, and although I think I was spared the testicles it did feel rather like a practical class in biology.

No one spoke until they were sated. Then, as abruptly as

they had scrambled to the loaded trays, everyone left off eating and rose, muttering their thanks to God, and went outside the tent to rinse their hands. Collective prayer followed, the final one of the day, with the Bedu all facing due south to Mecca. Now began the ceremony of the tea and coffee. First the tea was poured into tiny glasses with handles. It was so tooth-rottingly sweet it made my teeth grate, but I was glad of the liquid since my mouth was gritty with sand from the unleavened bread. Then a handful of Yemeni coffee beans was brought out from a bag and emptied into a flat, long-handled pan. These were roasted over the fire until they turned a rich, dark brown and then placed in a heavy brass mortar, where they were pounded with a pestle until they were crushed to a powder, which was mixed with boiling water. The coffee, once brewed, was poured in a thin stream from a curved Oriental pot into golfball-sized cups. This pouring is an art and undertaken with some panache, I noticed. It is acceptable to drink anything from one to three cups of this thin, bitter-tasting Bedu coffee. When the drinker has finished he lets the pourer know by shaking the cup vigorously from side to side with his right hand.

While some of the guests returned to their tents or drove off into the night in their battered pickup trucks, the rest of us stayed up chatting around the fire. The Bedu had an inexhaustible supply of questions to ask about my country, but eventually I could stay awake no longer. One of the last things I remember thinking was how at home Thesiger would have felt here and how I would enjoy recounting it to him when I got back to London. (When we next met up he was duly delighted to hear that this Bedu life still survived, largely as it had for centuries, in the deserts of Jordan.)

I awoke just before sunrise to find I had been covered with a blanket where I lay, full and contented after last night's feast. I was now being tended to, as if convalescing, by the daughters of the family, who brought me glasses of sweet tea. I had expected Bedu women to be shy and withdrawn with strangers – certainly those I had seen in the Sinai had barely uttered a word in front of me – but the sheikh's svelte grand-daughter was openly friendly without being flirtatious. Her dark eyes shone with each smile and her hair fell down to her waist in two separate plaits, joined together at the ends.

In the late afternoon we set off for Baarda, another encampment, set amidst the ever-changing patterns of this intensely beautiful desert. It had rained in April and Wadi Rumm's pink sands were sprinkled with green bushes and short tufts of yellow grass known as *sif souf*, so that from a distance the valley floor looked almost verdant. Tonight was another feast and once again I felt privileged to be amongst these hardy desert people. I recognized some familiar faces from last night: Hammad, the tracker with Jordanian Special Forces; Sabah, the kindly elder son of the sheikh; and Farid, who was both deaf and dumb yet whose face somehow bore strength and nobility. I greeted them in turn then took my place on the rug beside the fire, glancing around me at the rows of lean, hawk-like faces turned chestnut brown by the desert sun, the glint of teeth both white and gold, listen-ing to the crackle of twigs on an improvised hearth and the bleat of goats outside the tent, scolded by black-shrouded women. I took in the quick flash of an upturned hand, questioning, voices raised, squinting eyes reflecting the flickering light of the fire, hardened feet drawn up under white robes and tucked into coarse woven rugs. Feeling totally at ease here, I tuned in and out of conversations, try-ing to keep up with this very pure, classical Arabic, perhaps one of the closest forms there is to the language spoken at the time of the Prophet Muhammad 1,400 years ago.

We ate well that night, feasting on lamb cooked in milk and spices. But twenty minutes after the dish was served I found the rice still too hot to touch with my fingers due to the scalding juice poured over it. The Bedu had no such worries and most of them finished long before I did. In the sated aftermath of dinner I asked them about the Abu Tayi, the traditional enemies of these Bani Zallabiya of the Howaitat tribe. A few decades ago these blood feuds would have led to raids, reprisals and wars, but now, God be praised, they said, such times were over. I asked if anyone could recite *qaseed*, verses of ancient Arabic poetry passed down by word of mouth from one generation to the next. Faces cracked into broad grins and gnarled fingers pointed at a man called Sheikh Ali. But Sheikh Ali, it seemed, would not be drawn. Tonight he was *hirdaan*, angry with his wife, and not interested in entertaining anyone.

At Sabah's suggestion we climbed into the pickup truck and went in search of livelier company. Pale jerboas (long-tailed jumping mice) bounced across our track at intervals, frozen for an instant in the headlights. Sabah was perplexed. We had reached the campsite where he had expected to find friends, but instead there were just traces of habitation. I spotted a distant light on the horizon; Sabah said it was a star; I disagreed. We drove towards it and it disappeared. Sabah said that it had never existed and we disputed again, good-naturedly. It turned out to be a small encampment at the foot of a mountain, Jebel Sirdaan. A shepherd named Shayih and his wife Umm Sheeha welcomed us and we joined them round their fire on a soft carpet of compressed goat dung. Shayih was very unhappy; at dawn that morning a wolf had come and taken one of his sheep. We were now deep in the desert, close to the borders of Saudi, and such predators were common here. I could see how hard it would be to sell the idea of wildlife conservation to the people who eke out a living in these tough conditions. Years later, when we were in Dubai, someone spotted a rare Arabian leopard up in the mountains on the Omani border. The villagers immediately put together a hunting party and went and shot it.

As we sat chatting beneath the stars, Umm Sheeha caught a huge and harmless beetle – nicknamed *Abu Gasim* – between her fingers, while her husband played the *rababa*, a basic stringed instrument, singing in a thin and plaintive voice of love and marriage amongst the Bedu. We lay in the open on the sand, staring up at the vast and awe-inspiring panoply of stars, listening to the wind sighing in the bushes. Every so often shooting stars would arc above us, sometimes fast and bright, extinguishing themselves in less than a second, and sometimes travelling slowly and deliberately across the galaxy, as if choosing their course with care.

That night I dreamed of wolves. In fact I slept little as it was cold and I was glad of the *suhur*, the second meal of the night during Ramadan, eaten at three in the morning. We drank glasses of tea flavoured with fresh goat's milk and ate fluffy cakes from a nearby market across the border in Saudi Arabia.

In the morning I proposed we climb Jebel Sirdaan, and when I found my worn boots slipping on the rock I discarded them and climbed as the Bedu did, barefoot. (For the record, I could not conceive of ever emulating T. E. Lawrence and walking barefoot on the burning sands in summer. The pain must have been unbearable.) From the top, the desert had a freshness and purity that would later be erased by the overwhelming blaze of heat and light. Illuminated by the still slanting rays of the fast-rising sun, sandy trails snaked away across the valley floor from Shayih's encampment, reaching distant black tents that sheltered beneath rose-coloured mountains. On the way back down I caught sight of something that surely did not belong here. It was a lizard of dazzling blue, about a foot long and moving quickly over the rocks. Nicknamed *Ibn Akhu*, meaning 'His Nephew', its scales were such an unnatural, almost chemical blue that it was as if someone had caught and spray-painted it for a joke.

Back in Shayih's tent we were all parched with thirst, and

since he and his wife could not make up their minds whether they were fasting or not they insisted we drank some water. A tin bowl was fetched, filled with greenish water, with a couple of small bugs swimming contentedly in its midst. '*Ishrib! Ishrib!*' implored Shayih. 'Drink!' Was this a test? I wondered. But Sabah was drinking deeply and it would have been rude to refuse, so I swallowed my misgivings along with the brackish liquid. Umm Sheeha invited us to share their flabby bread dipped in a bowl of melted goat's butter. This too was a challenge, as the flies gathered in swarms, commuting between the sticky bread, our faces and the surrounding goat dung. We talked of fidelity and trust, both qualities the Bedu value highly. In their tough, desert world there has never been any place for dishonesty, something which always attracted Wilfred Thesiger to their company.

Sabah needed to make a trip through the hills to distant Aqaba, so he handed me over to his father's family, camped in their tents in a nearby *wadi*. I asked to fit in with whatever the family were doing and they obliged, assigning me to shepherding duties. The first day did not go so well. A goat trod on my face before dawn and I found it hard to get back to sleep after that. Ayd, Sabah's younger brother, roused me at six thirty and scolded me good-naturedly for 'lounging in bed so long'. At seven we moved out with the flock, about eighty sheep and goats, taking them to graze in the shadows of cliffs and small mountains. There were four of us: Ayd, his sister Hilal, his younger brother Muhammad, and me. There was also a donkey for carrying water and Shauhaan, a fast Saluki hunting bitch, in case we came across any rabbits.

For thirteen hours we wandered in the stifling heat through a landscape straight out of the Twenty-Third Psalm, drifting with the animals over the pink and yellow sands, winding through gorges where the dust kicked up by over three hundred cloven hoofs made our teeth grind and scrape. Sometimes Hilal would reach into the saddle pack and take out a *shabaaba*, a flute, and play Bedu shepherd songs as she sat side-saddle on the donkey with her embroidered dress swaying in the hot breeze. I never tired of looking at the desert here in Wadi Rumm. Always there were stupendous crags, pitted with cavities like rotten teeth, always the sand was criss-crossed with innumerable tracks, of lizard, beetle, lark, snake, jerboa and goat. Whenever I have spent time in deserts I am always amazed at the abundance of life they support; it just takes time to find out where to look.

In mid-morning we watered the herd at a tiny dam of rain-water collected in the shaded crevice of a mountainside. Getting up there from the valley floor was, I detected, something of a test of agility for the Bedu. Ayd, who was just nineteen, took off his shoes and said with a rather superior smile that I was not to worry, he would not be long. To his dismay, I followed him up there, barefoot after his example. But my turn to worry came when I was put in charge of shepherding the animals into the narrow watering hole. Two of them escaped and – horror of horrors – reappeared on a precipitous ledge about forty feet above me. I had visions of them tumbling to their deaths and my returning in disgrace to explain myself to the venerable Sheikh Hajji Attayig who had been so good to me. In the end we got the goats down by scaring them off the ledge with a shower of small stones.

The plan was to sleep off the hottest part of the afternoon beneath a rock ledge, but this was impossible due to the persistent maniacal bleating of one hoary old billy goat called Tees. (They were all named after the sheikh's children.) Instead we sat on the ruined wall of a Roman castle that was stuck out there in the desert, and excluded from any guide-book I have ever seen. We returned just in time for *Iftar*, the breaking of the fast, with my clicking and scolding the animals in the Bedu way, much to everyone's approval. The story of my irritation with the goat Tees had got around, and again and again I was asked to imitate it, describing in ever greater detail how we had all craved sleep and how this infernal animal had denied it to us. Each time a new guest joined the circle I was called on to entertain him. I was happy to oblige because the Bedu set great store by the way in which someone presents himself at these fireside gatherings. Storytelling could make or break a man's reputation here: if he was dull he would be ignored and not asked for his opinion, but if he was lively and entertaining then his reputation preceded him wherever he went and he would become a frequent guest at the *ihtifaal*.

The Bedu placed a surprising amount of trust in me. After a few days I was sent off shepherding with just Hilal, the sheikh's teenage daughter, for company, with no male chaperone. We soon developed an easy rapport, ambling along through this biblical scenery, chatting, with Hilal sometimes playing her flute. Perpetually short of sleep, we each took it in turns to watch the sheep and goats while the other slept. Shauhaan, the Saluki hunting dog, often slept beside me, and I was so incredibly comfortable embedded there in the warm sand that when I woke up it would take me a while to remember where I was. I knew that the desert was probably crawling with snakes and scorpions – I had once found a large black scorpion, fortunately dead, near where I slept – but I had yet to encounter a live one and I really did not worry about them much. That was about to change.

On my final night with the Bedu of Wadi Rumm there was a large gathering at a specially erected goats'-hair tent. It was the Eid feast to celebrate the end of Ramadan and everyone was in high spirits. Someone hooked up a lightbulb to the battery in their Toyota pickup truck, flooding the campsite with unnatural light. Unfortunately this also had the effect of attracting every bug for miles around, so that the sand was literally crawling with the things. Most were harmless and the Bedu seemed to have nicknames for each species. Then there were the *shabat*, the camel spiders, big, hairy, yellow things with massive jaws. They ran very fast, sometimes coming into our circle by the fire where the Bedu would lash out at them with their sandals. But the only time I saw the Bedu break into a sweat was over the snake. Ayd was padding barefoot around the edge of the tent, serving coffee to the guests, when he noticed its tracks in the sand. A frantic search ensued as we followed the snake's trail around the camp, beating the ground with sticks. Then I spotted it coiling away into the bushes several yards to our right. The Bedu killed it swiftly in a flurry of flailing branches. Lying there limp and dead, it looked so small and innocuous that I questioned if it was even dangerous. The Bedu looked at me with grave faces.

'We call it *Abu 'Ashara Daqiqa*, "The One Who Gives You Ten Minutes". After that . . .' They made a gesture of finality, brushing the palm of one hand against the other and looking up to heaven. I later found out it was a Horned Viper.

Despite our close encounter with The One Who Gives You Ten Minutes, I was sad to leave the desert. When the time came I said goodbye to the sheikh's camp and caught a lift with some relatives to another Bedu tent halfway back to Rumm. There I spent the afternoon in the shade, playing games with the children while the bangled old women sat around talking, their heavily tattooed faces puffing on two-inch silver pipes. The children would try to bury my feet in the hot sand until I winced with pain and they would get a mild scolding from the women, which of course made it all the more fun. 'Now you are a real Bedu like us!' said one of the breast-feeding mothers proudly.

In the relatively short time I was with them the Bedu had accepted me without question, and with the generosity of a people who have little to share but share it anyway. Their lives may have been totally different from mine back in Britain, but we were never short of conversation or humour. For a people who lived in such majestic surroundings they derived a lot of amusement from them, laughing without malice when I tripped over a pile of goat dung or when one of their more independent-minded sheep went off on a little mission of its own. Most of all, I was impressed that they had deliberately chosen this hard life over a softer one in the towns of southern Jordan. The Bedu were not poor. Their many head of livestock made them comparatively rich and they could have sold up and lived in a comfortable flat in Aqaba any time they chose. 'But,' said Sheikh Hajji Attayig, when I asked him why he did not do just that, 'what would be the point? Out here we are free to live our lives the way we always have. There is peace here in the desert.' For me, the Bedu will always be a special people; despite the rigours of their daily existence, my weeks with them in Jordan were some of the happiest and most carefree of my life.

Still mentally back in Wadi Rumm, I turned up for my first day at work at Saudi International Bank in the City a week before my twenty-fifth birthday. I was assigned to the 'dealing room', a long, low-ceilinged, neon-lit broiler house of a place on the twenty-third floor of a tower block in Bishopsgate. Everyone seemed to be talking at once on the telephone, sometimes into two phones at once, while staring at coloured numbers on screens, then standing up to shout at each other. I was completely bewildered. Between coming back from the desert and reporting for duty I had been given a hefty booklet to read entitled 'The Floating Rate Note in the Eurodollar Market'. Most of it was gobbledegook to me, but I understood the broad idea: when a government or a company wanted to borrow money it issued a sort of international IOU. Anyone buying this IOU not only got their money back after a set period of time but they also received regular interest payments which could go up or down according to what prevailing bank interest rates were doing (hence they were called Floating Rate Notes or FRNs). Investment banks like Saudi International Bank then traded these FRNs between themselves, buying and selling them at a discount or premium to their original value. Since they dealt in millions of dollars' worth at a time, the tiniest fluctuation in price could mean large sums gained or lost. As well as trading them for profit, banks also sold them to investors, who built up a portfolio with the aim of getting a better return on their money than they would by simply sticking it on deposit. Because of my Arabic I had been hired to join the sales force that sold FRNs to the bank's Middle East clientbase. Unfortunately, the week I started witnessed the collapse of a large part of the global FRN market. 'Perps' stood for 'perpetuals', meaning FRNs that never actually 'matured', i.e., paid the investors their money back. The lay observer might think that paying over the odds for a piece of paper that effectively said 'Yes, I do indeed owe you x sum of money but I have no intention of ever paying it back' made these investments a bit of a bum deal, and they would be right. Someone had finally realized that these things were overpriced and had started selling. The mood caught on and the market nose-dived in the space of twenty-four hours and then flat-lined. Suddenly, the ready-made clientbase I was about to be given had evaporated. Somehow I managed to hang on to my job and develop a new clientbase of my own, conveniently situated in places like Bermuda and the Bahamas, that just had to be visited.

A rebel against this corporate world was Andrew, a graduate fluent in several languages who joined at the same time as me and who never missed an opportunity to avoid working. When he was assigned to the Syndicated Deals desk, I found him photocopying the next hundred pages of a Russian novel on to A4 paper so he could read it at his desk while appearing to be poring over the finer details of some financial document. He developed the knack of leaving his suit jacket draped over his chair as if he had just gone off to the loo, when in fact he had left the bank for the afternoon to have tea with friends in St Katharine's Dock. He even got hold of the key to the chief executive's suite on the top floor, where he conducted a torrid affair with a girl from Corporate Banking and never quite got caught. Andrew had pithy nicknames for everyone he met, including a stubbornly unhelpful facilities manager whom he dubbed Arthur C. Clarke, because, as Andrew maintained, 'It's one of the world's last great unsolved mysteries what that guy actually does for a living.'

There was also Stevie B. from Huddersfield. When asked on the graduate induction course what he hoped to get out of his first few weeks at the bank, he replied, 'To learn a bit o'protocol, mate.' But once he took up his job on the money-broking desk he discovered to his delight that this was not necessary, and his was soon a familiar voice on the trading-room floor, yelling, 'Gimme a price for First Chicago cable in ten, ya fat bastad!', meaning 'Quote me an exchange rate for another bank wanting to trade US$10 million into sterling.' If you asked Stevie what he had got up to the previous evening the reply was usually the same: 'Pavement pizza, mate,' meaning an excess of Beck's beer had eventually parted him from the last meal he had eaten, which he had liberally distributed outside a bar in Bishopsgate. Stevie certainly put his soul into whatever he was doing; when someone cleared out his desk a few weeks after he eventually left the bank, there, nestling in a bottom drawer, was one of his dealing-room shirts, still damp with sweat.

There were several Saudis dotted around the dealing room, over on secondment from Riyadh, and while some people at first mistook their shyness for arrogance, they often proved to have a good sense of humour. One young Saudi used to stare down the cheekiest cockney in the room, claiming he was so rich he might just buy up the Brit's favourite corner-shop to deny him his daily packet of fags. Another, a girl from a wealthy Jeddah family, used to banter with me in Arabic. When I complained one morning that I was '*tafshaan*' (worn out) after a late night clubbing, she replied briskly, '*Tafshaan inta? Tayyib. Fassikh wa ijri aryaan!*' meaning 'Tired? Fine. Then tear your clothes off and run around naked!'

Although I was a couple of years older than most of the graduate intake, I managed to get myself sent to New York for the coveted four-month J P Morgan graduate-training course on Wall Street. It was an eye-opener. American bankers, I realized, worked crazy hours and took almost no holiday. In between lectures on global derivatives, stock options and corporate finance, we were shown a film of *A Day in the Life of a Treasury Bond Salesman*. To use the American vernacular, it sucked. Here were these exhausted-looking young men, in the office by six a.m., identical in their white Brooks Brothers shirts with the button-down collars, biting their fingernails while staring at a screen. Again, there was a lot of talking on phones and calling out numbers to each other; I never once saw anybody take a break for lunch.

But in a way, we had the best of both worlds. As graduates on the Wall Street course we were being paid as bankers and living as students. On Friday nights we would descend on Lucy's, a bar on the Upper West Side where people often ended up dancing on the bar with the bar staff. Peer pressure dictated that everyone had to try and 'shoot the worm' – to slug down a shot of tequila with a fat, mescal-saturated maggot at the bottom, in order to be awarded a T-shirt reading 'Official Danger Ranger Surfworm Shooter of New York City' or some such nonsense. There were ugly rumours that the worm would sometimes wake up in your stomach and start squirming around; I must admit I always tucked mine behind my teeth then quietly removed it when no one was looking. My flatmate in New York was the cynical Andrew, the Russian-novel photocopier, whose refined tastes meant he was more interested in going to the opera than shooting the worm, let alone labouring through the reams of corporate-finance case studies we were expected to take home each night. He even failed to stay very long at his own party.

Having suggested we throw one for the whole course, he lost interest halfway through and drifted off into Manhattan for a burger.

After a month or so we were all bussed out to a campsite in the Pennsylvania woodlands for 'Executive Challenge', one of these corporate touchy-feely team-building experiences. The MBAs, who were joining the course halfway through, all wore gut-churning sweatshirts that read 'MBA – the Chosen Few'. It was October and the trees were a kaleidoscope of golds and reds, the air was sharp with the nip of impending winter and the wildlife was entertaining: at one point we managed to coax a skunk into one of the MBAs' tents. The American instructors were well-meaning but humourless. 'Today we're discussing kinship and kinfolk,' said one of them, turning to Stevie B. from Huddersfield. 'Stephen, perhaps you can give us an example of kinship from where you're from?' 'Sure, mate,' came the reply. 'In Yorkshire we say it's 'kin cold.'

On our last night in the Pennsylvania woods there was a sing-song round the campfire. The night air resounded to the hiss of ring pulls on Budweiser cans and the mournful verses of 'American Pie' when suddenly there was a cry of alarm. Someone had been listening to the radio and it seemed that Wall Street had crashed. Badly. It was Black Monday in October 1987 and the New York we had left a few days ago was now in shock. There were reports of ruined investors throwing themselves off skyscraper window ledges, and many of the Americans on the course wondered openly if they would still have a job when they got back to the city. At least one was in tears.

But the course ploughed on and I took the opportunity to write some racy dispatches for *Midweek* magazine in London, still indulging my journalistic cravings a good eight years before I left banking. I befriended Manhattan's Puerto Rican doormen, got them to recommend the best salsa music joints, then liked the music so much I went down to Latin America three times before the course was up.

Back in London, two summers later I was introduced at a drinks party to Rupert Wise, who was also an Arabist and a banker. 'You'll have so much in common,' said our mutual friend, leaving us to circle each other like wary sharks. It reminded me of when I was about five years old and was being nudged by my parents to 'Go and make friends with those children over there.' Rupert was short, fit and tanned, with a boxer's build and a steely glint in his eyes (he turned out to have been a boxing blue at Cambridge). He now launched into a stream of flawless Gulf Arabic; I replied in backstreet Egyptian. At the time I thought it was a pointless pissing contest to see who could speak the best Arabic, but in fact he was checking me out as his possible successor to run the Bahrain office of Flemings, a small but successful Scottish investment bank named after its nineteenth-century founder, Robert Fleming.

A few weeks later I was summoned for an interview at the bank's elegant head office in the City, which was decorated with the world's finest collection of Scottish paintings. I was quite happy where I was at Saudi International Bank, and Flemings were not even offering much of a pay rise, but Rupert took me aside and told me this was an opportunity of a lifetime and I would be a fool not to take it. He proved to be right. I signed on the dotted line, then worked out my notice at SIB. I had saved up a bit of money so I took three months off to go round Eastern Europe, where the Berlin Wall had just come down, followed by a trip round Brazil and Chile. I was in my twenties and had an incurable itch to go travelling. I sent back an article for *Midweek* magazine which resulted in a cover photo of a sequinned girl at the Rio Carnival with the caption: 'Sex, Samba and Soccer. Frank Gardner in Rio', a byline I have never quite been able to match since.

When I turned up for my first day of work at Flemings I was put under the wing of my new mentor, Mark Bullough, who immediately took me out for a champagne lunch. 'Let's get one thing straight,' he said as the waiter discreetly popped a Bollinger cork into a crisp white napkin, 'holidays take precedence over everything.' I wasn't sure if he was being serious, but as I was just back from the Amazon jungle this was music to my ears. Mark was tall, bald and very entertaining; he looked like a benign version of John Malkovitch. He wore bow ties with collars and studs and rode everywhere on his motorbike, including to post-Velvet Revolution Prague and back for the weekend with a girlfriend on the back. He spoke almost no Arabic, but told me how what little he knew had sometimes caused misunderstandings. In Oman, he told me, a meeting with a prospective client had turned to farce when the host asked him which angle he wished him to face. Perplexed, Mark replied that he was there to talk about Jardine Fleming Unit Trusts. 'Oh,' said the client, 'I thought you were from *Filmings*, not Flemings.' (When printed in Arabic the two words are indistinguishable.) But the biggest gaff had taken place in Saudi Arabia. Mark described how he had been invited to a banquet in the oil-rich Eastern Province. At the end of the meal the sheikh had called out to Mark at the other end of the table to ask him whether he was full or would he like anything else. Summoning his meagre reserves of Arabic, Mark had tried to ask for a coffee, but had confused the Arabic word for coffee, *qahwa*, with *qahba*, meaning prostitute. When he asked in all innocence for a *qahba* the table apparently collapsed with laughter, but the sheikh had replied with a straight face. 'Of course, Mark . . . but would you like black or white?'

Flemings sent me round three continents to familiarize myself with its global network of offices. But I had not been with them long before something happened which profoundly affected both the Middle East and our business there. On the morning of 2 August 1990, a friend woke me early with the news that Iraq had invaded Kuwait. Setting out before dawn, Saddam Hussein's massed tanks had simply rolled across the border and driven down the main Basra Highway to the capital, Kuwait City, meeting little resistance. Iraqi paratroopers also landed in the city by helicopter and quickly secured the key points. Much of the country and its ruling family were away for the annual summer holidays; those who had stayed behind could hardly believe this was happening.

Yet the warning signs for the invasion had all been there. Iraq had been grumbling that Kuwaiti oil wells were drilling diagonally across and under its border, and that Kuwait was exceeding its OPEC quota, thereby depressing the oil price. Saddam's regime also resented the suggestion that it should one day pay back some of the billions of dollars loaned by its neighbours Kuwait and Saudi Arabia while it was fighting Iran in the 1980s. Saddam had taken to seeing himself as the champion of the Arab world against non-Arab Iran (Iranians are Persians, not Arabs), and he felt his neighbours owed him a debt of gratitude for stopping the encroachment of the Iranian Islamic Revolution at the Iran–Iraq border. In short, he did not feel that Iraq's 'sacrifices' during that war were sufficiently appreciated.

Iraq had been a rich country when Saddam attacked Iran in 1980. Now it was exhausted by eight years of war and the coffers badly needed replenishing. Kuwait must have presented a tempting prize: it sat on close to 10 per cent of the world's proven oil reserves, and with only a tiny population to provide for it was rich beyond belief. Iraq had made a grab for Kuwait before, in 1961, when its forces were repelled by British troops. Now Saddam set his sights on swallowing up his southern neighbour, looting its treasury and renaming it 'the nineteenth province of Iraq'. In the summer of 1990, Iraq's Republican Guard divisions moved south from their bases and began to stage manoeuvres close to the Kuwaiti border. The world wondered if Iraq would really invade Kuwait, but the experts came to the wrong conclusion. By the time everyone realized what was going on, Iraqi forces were in effective control of Kuwait.

For my employers Robert Fleming, the Iraqi invasion presented both a crisis and an opportunity. We had a large clientbase in the Gulf and a small office in Bahrain. Because of my Arabic coupled with my basic banking experience I had been hired to join the bank's Middle East marketing team, the plan being for me to go out and run the Bahrain office the following year. Now, with war looming, our clients and local staff would need reassuring immediately, while there might be some new business to pick up from other banks, which were hastily cutting credit lines and abandoning the region to its fate.

'It's quite clear,' said Mark Bullough. 'You'll have to go out there at once for a couple of weeks to look after the Bahrain office.'

I had just returned from an extensive tour of the bank's Far East offices and knew this news would go down badly with Carrie, who had seen very little of me this year.

'Why can't *you* go?' I ventured.

'Sorry, old bean. Holiday in Scotland already booked. Besides, you're the most junior member of the team. Oh, and you'll need to take respirators [gas masks]. You never know what Saddam might have up his sleeve. Good luck.'

To be fair to Mark, soon after that he did drive alone through the US front line in Saudi and over the border into Iraq-occupied Khafji to meet a Kuwaiti client, still wearing, he claimed, a stiff collar, bulled shoes and a pinstripe suit.

I was told to report to the Scots Guards barracks in Hounslow, where a favour had been called in by one of the regiment's former officers who was now working in the bank. A gruff Scots quartermaster handed me a cardboard box packed with respirators, NBC (Nuclear, Biological and

On a cold North Sea beach in Holland, aged eight.

School races: I loved the freedom of cross-country running.

With my parents, Grace and Neil – both keen walkers right into their eighties – in the Dordogne in 1987.

left: In Manama for my first business trip to the Middle East, 1989.
below, left: With Saudi friends Tareq and Omar in Jeddah.
OPPOSITE PAGE
top: In my beloved Mustang in Bahrain: it eventually overheated and caught fire.
middle: Beach life in Bahrain, 1993. Peter, Disco Ron, me, Tracy, Samantha, Julius and James (my best man).
bottom: Disco Ron sampling Lebanon's militarized ski pistes, 1992.

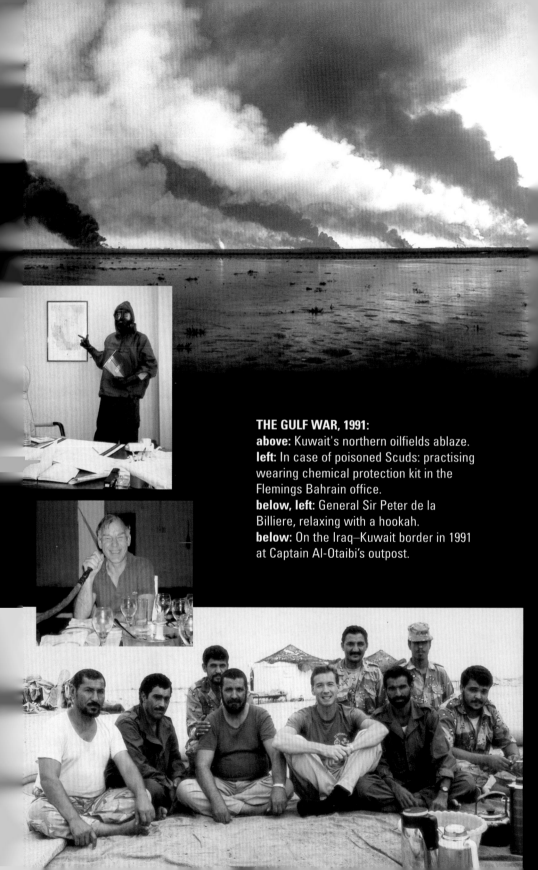

THE GULF WAR, 1991:
above: Kuwait's northern oilfields ablaze.
left: In case of poisoned Scuds: practising wearing chemical protection kit in the Flemings Bahrain office.
below, left: General Sir Peter de la Billiere, relaxing with a hookah.
below: On the Iraq–Kuwait border in 1991 at Captain Al-Otaibi's outpost.

Chemical warfare) suits, rubber overboots and several decontamination kits, enough to protect me and the staff of the Bahrain office from Saddam's chemically tipped Scuds.

Within forty-eight hours of the Iraqi invasion I was on a plane for the Gulf. When the BA flight stopped off in Bahrain, I noticed I was almost the only person getting off. At the time nobody knew whether Saddam's tanks were simply going to roll on southward, invading Saudi Arabia and Bahrain, so the eyes of a lot of passengers were following me when I got off that plane. In the airport terminal a large poster advertised the services of a certain Japanese bank, calling it 'your friend in the Middle East'. Yet beneath the poster stretched a long line of Japanese bankers who couldn't wait to get the next plane out. All over the Middle East credit lines to Arab clients were being cut, a move that was to cost our competitors dearly.

For Bahrain's ruling family, the Al-Khalifas, the invasion and occupation of their close ally Kuwait was a disaster; Kuwait's ruling Al-Sabah family were their friends and they worried they could be next. A joke was already doing the rounds in expat circles that had Saddam boasting he took Kuwait in a day, Saudi Arabia in twelve hours, and Bahrain by fax. One British banker got into big trouble for leaving a message on his answerphone that said, 'This building has now been taken over by the Iraqi Revolutionary Guard.' When the authorities found out they failed to share his sense of humour and he was questioned exhaustively, eventually even moving to Cyprus as a result. Employees of Gulf Air began to get bizarre notices posted under their doors advising them what to do in the event of a chemical (poison gas) attack. The advice included taping up the cracks in doorways and lying submerged in a bath and breathing through a straw. A similar official leaflet that later did the rounds in Saudi Arabia warned citizens that if they saw birds falling from the skies they should take cover indoors. 'However,' it said, 'if

117

you are caught in the open without cover then you must consign your fate to Allah.'

But for most expatriate Westerners in Bahrain that summer it was a case of crisis, what crisis? The pool parties and the barbecues at the rugby club continued, infused with a new spirit of defiance. T-shirts appeared, emblazoned with cartoons of a British boot kicking Saddam out of Kuwait. Isobel, our office manager, a hard-bitten Scottish divorcée, announced that if Bahrain got invaded she would be locking herself in her flat with a bottle of whisky.

Once the immediate fear was over I was allowed to return to London, but my boss, Rupert Wise, was keen that I move myself permanently out to Bahrain before war began. 'Clients will be impressed you made the effort,' he advised.

But I was in no hurry to leave London. I was twenty-nine and had just mortgaged myself to the hilt to buy a flat in Covent Garden's Floral Street, home to The Royal Opera House, Paul Smith and the women-only health spa, The Sanctuary. My tiny, top-floor flat above that pretty cobbled street became the starting point for every evening out my friends and I embarked on. Carrie had by now pressed the ejector seat on our relationship after six years, complaining that she was hardly seeing anything of me these days. She was right. I was bitten by the travel bug: I had been to twenty-six countries that year and I couldn't put all the blame on business trips. Understandably, Carrie was not prepared to jack in her life in London to come and live with me in Bahrain when our lives had already grown apart.

The gathering storm in the Gulf seemed a world away from my hedonistic existence in the bars and clubs of Soho. I won a reprieve when Bahrain airport was closed to civilian flights during the early stages of Desert Storm. But when flights resumed I could delay my departure no longer and boarded a flight to Bahrain, this time for three years.

*

By now the Gulf War was well under way and my Gulf Air flight gave Iraq a wide berth, skirting far to the east over Iran. I arrived to find the inhabitants of Bahrain's capital, Manama, breathing a collective sigh of relief. The windows were all still taped up with white crosses to prevent shattering, but the Iraqi Scud missiles that had rained down on Tel Aviv and Riyadh had largely ignored Bahrain. Of Saddam's dreaded Scuds tipped with chemical weapons there was not a whiff; he had plenty of chemical warfare stocks at the time, but it was made very clear to him through his then spokesman, Tariq Aziz, that if he deployed any such unconventional weapons against Coalition troops the retaliation would be colossal. Nevertheless, one of my first duties was to go to the British Embassy for chemical-protection training, practising how to put on a gas mask in a hurry. That evening, while Rupert Wise and I were out jogging near the prime minister's palace on the west of the island, we heard and felt a massive explosion just across the water that separated Bahrain from the Saudi mainland. In the dying days of the war the Iraqi Army had scored a lucky hit, a direct missile strike on a warehouse in Dhahran where dozens of US Army servicemen had been assembling before heading home. Over twenty were killed that night, one of the worst blows sustained by the Coalition in the Gulf War, although of course it paled compared with the losses sustained by the frontline Iraqi troops.

The Gulf War ended with the routing of the Iraqi Army and the headlong dash northwards of the retreating invaders with their convoy of looted Kuwaiti vehicles, resulting in their destruction from the air along the Basra Highway. Over the next days and weeks reminders of the war were all around. The sky was a heavy leaden grey from the seven hundred oil fires that Saddam's forces had lit as a parting gift to their Kuwaiti hosts. Even this far down the Gulf the oil smoke blotted out the sun, and when it rained the drops left oily black smudges.

British soldiers and airmen were a common sight in Bahrain in the spring of 1991. I used to play backgammon with some of the RAF Tornado pilots round the swimming pool at the Sheraton once they'd come back from their sorties over Iraq. It must have been bizarre for them: a couple of hours of sheer adrenaline over enemy territory, followed by lunch in swimming shorts surrounded by off-duty air stewardesses in bikinis. A few days after the end of the Gulf War I bumped into a bevy of Royal Scots officers I remembered from a friend's wedding. They had been training hard in the Saudi desert for six months before seeing some of the most ferocious hand-to-hand infantry action of the war. They had not had a drink in all this time and now they were looking for fun. I volunteered to show them round, so we started with some fiery Thai green curries washed down with ice-cold beer, then went on to the island's most popular bar, Henry's. Undaunted by their six months in the desert, they kept drinking into the small hours before crashing out on my floor, apparently no worse for wear, while I was finished. I made a mental note to never, ever go drinking with Scottish soldiers again.

The short war over, Rupert Wise set out to teach me the ropes before handing the office over to me and returning to London. Impeccably proper in front of his staff, he only once looked a bit rattled. Isobel, the Scottish office manager, rang him one day on the intercom to tell him, 'Rupert, it's a hoor on the line fer ya.' 'A what?!' snorted Rupert. 'A whore? Impossible!' 'No!' she protested. 'It's Zuhour from Sheikh so-and-so's office, he wants to go over the contract.' Rupert was an incredibly focused and driven individual, having worked in several Gulf capitals, and I had much to learn from him. He had memorized a number of classical Arabic proverbs, which always brought a smile to people's faces and could defuse almost any situation. Rupert knew how much personal relationships mattered to Arabs and he rightly guessed that our clients would be impressed at our visiting them in these dark days of war and uncertainty.

'By God, you have come all this way to see us? Then you must really be hungry for business!' exclaimed one client in Jeddah, laughing as he strode across the thick pile carpet of his office to welcome us.

I loved these meetings. We hardly ever did business at them, it was all just getting-to-know-you stuff. Business may or may not flow at a later date. We would settle back into expensive leather armchairs, while a smiling Sudanese would bring us steaming glasses of lemon tea, or tiny cups of bitter Arab coffee. The conversation would range everywhere. What did we think of the war? Was Saddam finished now? Why weren't the Americans pressing on to Baghdad? How is life amongst all those Gulf Air stewardesses in Bahrain? Why did Britain force *Al-Sitt Al-Hadeed* – meaning the Iron Lady, Margaret Thatcher – out of office?

But getting to see these movers and shakers of the merchant world was far from easy. Often it was the end product of months of trying to outmanoeuvre 'the blocker', a mid-level employee whose prime role seemed to be to test the perseverance of Western bankers in netting an audience with Mr Big.

'You see, Mr Gudnerr,' he would say with what he assumed to be a disarming smile, 'the sheikh is very busy these days, he is not really investing, you understand.'

Sometimes we would give up on the middleman and look for another approach; the ideal was always to get on good terms with the sheikh himself. One of the delightful things about doing business in the Gulf is that so much of it is based on personal friendships. It must be one of the last places in the business world where the art of good conversation really counts. If the client likes you and trusts you, he will eventually do business with you. If you try to talk business too soon into the relationship he will make sure he is unavailable next time you are in town.

One of the tricks I picked up from Rupert Wise was to visit Saudi clients during the month of Ramadan, and after he left I did this often. Most Western bankers in Bahrain thought I was mad. Ramadan was a month to be avoided, they reckoned, a time when business slows to a crawl, when tempers can be frayed by a whole day of fasting, and when anyone caught breaking the fast in public risks going to prison. But Ramadan is a very special time for Muslims and I found it a wonderful opportunity to get to know Saudis at their most relaxed after dark. As one of the five pillars of the Islamic faith, Ramadan forbids all eating, drinking (even water) and smoking between the hours of dawn and dusk. Slander and sexual intercourse are also proscribed, making this a time to test one's faith, rather as Lent is for some practising Christians. But in the Middle East Ramadan is an experience shared by the whole of society, with families donating gifts and food to the poor, adults offering up special prayers in the mosques, and families holding vast nightly banquets to break the fast at dusk.

I usually chose Jeddah for Ramadan, it being the friendliest city in Saudi Arabia. I would let people know I was coming, then on arrival I would just switch over to a Ramadan timetable, sleeping till late in the morning, then holding a few desultory meetings before heading back to the hotel for a siesta. The hotel concierge would hand me a phone message: 'Sheikh Saleh's office called. They will send a driver to collect you for *Iftar* at six p.m.'

To be invited to share *Iftar*, the Ramadan banquet, is a happy privilege. There I would sit, awkwardly cross-legged, the only non-Saudi in the room, my shoes discarded at the door amongst the pile of patterned sandals. Nobody would even think of touching the food until the muezzin gave the dusk call to prayer, the all-clear to pile in to the banquet. On a low table would be arranged over thirty dishes, loaded with food. Stuffed vine leaves, deep-fried cones of spicy mince, a subtle paste made from pulverized aubergines, all competing for space with an Arabian speciality called *ouzi*. This was a whole stewed sheep, served at the table skull and all, on a bed of flavoured rice. After gorging ourselves silly, men would burp, rinse their hands in a bowl of lemon water, rise from the table and file into a room strewn with cushions and couches. There the sheikh, or whoever had invited me, would always try to draw me into the conversation in Arabic. Now was the time to socialize, with everyone staying up well into the small hours. But when I returned later in the year, it would be remembered that I had made the effort during Ramadan and doors would open that might otherwise have remained closed.

Back in Bahrain I realized how lucky I was. I was not yet thirty years old and I had been given all the trappings of a playboy prince. I drove a five-litre Mustang convertible sports car that growled like a tiger whenever I turned the key in the ignition; I lived in a traditional white-walled Bahraini villa, with slowly turning ceiling fans, its own private swimming pool, all utilities paid for and a houseboy who looked after it. I had a tax-free salary with nothing to spend it on, and I had first use of the company speedboat, which I had chosen then kitted out with a two hundred hp outboard engine, enough to lift even corpulent bankers from London up out of the water on skis.

Despite all these material comforts, I was decidedly lonely at first. While embarking on an endless circuit of client visits around the Gulf, I was all too aware that I had left my friends and parents behind me, and I missed having a girlfriend. University friends now working in the Far East socialized freely with Singaporean, Thai and Japanese girls, but in the conservative Gulf any contact with local women seemed out of the question – or so I thought.

One evening I was taking the shuttle flight from Riyadh to Jeddah, a journey of about ninety minutes. I settled into my spacious window seat and helped myself to the sweet Hassa dates and bitter cardamom coffee that were being offered round. Shortly before take-off a billowing black shape descended on to the seat next to me and fastened the seatbelt. All adult Saudi women are obliged by custom to cover themselves in public with the *abaya*, an amorphous, all-enveloping black cloak designed to disguise their figures. Some go further, covering their hands with black gloves and their faces with sheer black veils through which they can see out but no one can see in. Contrary to what many in the West think, most Saudi women welcome this anonymity, which protects them from unwanted attentions.

I had no idea whether the woman sitting next to me was an eighty-year-old grandmother or a teenager. It didn't matter; I played by the rules and modestly averted my eyes. Once airborne, I pretended to doze. There are many conservative Saudis who would be outraged just at the thought of one of their women sitting next to a foreign stranger, but this woman appeared to have no male chaperone. Suddenly she turned to me and asked if I could reach down and retrieve her boarding pass, which she had dropped to the floor. Her voice was soft and silky – this was no grandmother.

'There you go, you're welcome,' I said in Arabic, handing her the ticket stub.

'Ah, but you speak Arabic!' she exclaimed, clearly delighted. 'Then we can talk.'

She then did one of the most sensual things I have ever seen in Arabia. Slowly she lifted the veil from her face so that only I could see it, a sort of private viewing for one. She was young and breathtakingly beautiful. Her eyes shone beneath immaculately groomed eyebrows, her lips were wet with gloss, revealing perfect white teeth. A few minutes into our conversation it emerged that she was royal by marriage. As a princess – of which there are several thousand in Saudi – she told me she enjoyed a privileged life, but she was bored.

'I am just twenty-four years old, ya Frank,' she purred, 'but already I have been a widow for many years. I was married when I was a very young girl to a prince, but he was old and soon he died.'

'So what now?' I asked. 'How do you fill your time?'

'I want to start a gym for women. We need this here in my country. Too many women just grow old and fat as soon as they marry. Now,' said the princess, changing the subject and shifting subtly closer, 'I would like to ask you a favour.'

'Er, certainly,' I replied, feeling very far from certain as to what I might be letting myself in for.

'You live in Bahrain. It is easy to buy music there. Could you get me some tapes of romantic music?'

'Sure, I can send them to you.'

'No,' she replied firmly, displaying for the first time the signs of someone who is not used to being refused. 'I will give you my number and I will come to your hotel room tonight in Jeddah.'

There must have been a long pause during which I said nothing. I was speechless. I was remembering what a friend had told me, that in this highly conservative society it is automatically assumed that if two young and unrelated people of the opposite sex are left alone in a room they must be having sex. The princess raised an eyebrow at me and a dozen thoughts crowded into my mind. I was young and single and she was beautiful . . . Wait a minute, I thought, are you mad? Sex outside marriage is totally taboo in this country. All it would take was a sharp-eyed concierge, a phone call, then a rap on my hotel-room door from the religious police and that would be it. I would be carted off to jail to face a hefty lashing, and heaven knows what would happen to her.

'OK,' I said, taking her neatly folded phone number, 'I'll call you tonight.'

When the plane landed we acted as if we had never met. I headed for the taxi rank, she for her chauffeur-driven limo.

By the time I reached my hotel I had made up my mind. In the privacy of the hotel bathroom I carefully tore the princess's phone number to shreds and flushed it down the loo. This was one Saudi experience I was going to give a very wide berth.

But I did make some excellent platonic Arab friendships. The all-male Bahraini crowd I fell in with were kind, hospitable, amusing. They welcomed me into their circle without judgement, pleased that I spoke Arabic although they frequently broke into Farsi, the language of Iran which is spoken by so many in Bahrain. My Bahraini friends, who were all on the cusp of thirty, knew that their families would soon be steering them towards a selection of possible brides from suitable local families, and they were determined to have fun while they could.

The driving force behind Bahrain's social life in this circle was Gulf Air and its 1,500 foreign stewardesses all based on the island. While those recruited in Asian countries tended to keep their heads down and stay out of trouble, the British and Irish girls knew how to party hard. Their 'Wings' parties on completing their training courses were legendary for getting out of hand. Inevitably, some of them fell in love with their Arab boyfriends, believing they were destined for marriage and a life of leisure in some white-walled villa. For a very, very few this actually happened, but many of their boyfriends simply played the field as soon as Sharon or Siobhan had flown down-route to Bombay for a few days.

One thing I learned early on in the Gulf was that you must have *wasita*, meaning influence or connections. Technically, nobody but the ruler was above the law, but in practice any-one from the ruling family was highly unlikely to fall foul of the police. The closer you were to senior members of the ruling family the more the magical *wasita* rubbed off on you. Certain Gulf Air flight attendants from England loved to boast that they knew Sheikh so-and-so, 'And he can have you thrown off the island, so there.'

The ultimate *wasita* was knowing the ruler and his immediate circle. In Bahrain this was the diminutive and affable Emir, Sheikh Isa Al-Khalifa, who must have been the friendliest monarch in the world. On Fridays, Jack, as he was known to the British expats, would stroll around outside his beach palace, where he would invite picnicking Westerners to join him for tea. The first time I met him he was in his full robes of state and I was in my surf shorts, but Jack was used to this. 'I don't like London,' he said to me with a twinkle in his eye as a servant poured out the tea. 'You don't?' I asked, surprised. 'No,' said the ruler of Bahrain. 'London's too full of Arabs these days!' I had the impression he had made this joke before, but it certainly broke the ice.

After I had been in Bahrain a few years I got an invitation to spend the day on board the crown prince's yacht, along with the British ambassador, his wife, the defence attaché, and General Sir Peter de la Billiere, who had left the army after commanding British forces in Desert Storm and joined the bank I worked for. The yacht belonging to Crown Prince Hamad (now King Hamad) was an enormous floating gin palace that was moored on the exclusive west coast of the island; in fact it was so big that we were not going anywhere in it. Instead we were shown downstairs into our state rooms to change while the crown prince performed aerobatics in a helicopter above us and a speedboat was prepared for our amusement. An Egyptian boatman, Hani, was at the wheel, but he was somewhat distracted by the ambassador's wife, who had changed into a bikini for waterskiing, and he kept leering round over his shoulder. Suddenly I noticed we were heading at speed straight for a huge metal pole. 'Look out!' Sir Peter and I shouted in unison, and at the same moment I jumped ship, preferring self-preservation to valour, expecting to resurface a few yards short of a fireball. At the last minute the boatman had swerved, aided perhaps by my leap overboard, and disaster was averted. Hani was quite unrepentant, thinking this a huge joke, and once ashore he clowned around with a venomous sea snake he had just fished out, waving it perilously close to the ambassadorial swimming trunks until the Bahraini sheikhs intervened and dismissed him for the afternoon. The Bahrainis were perfect hosts, but it was a glimpse into a rarefied, privileged world that belied the tensions building in their island nation. Within a year there were to be violent clashes between the police and some of the restless Shi'ite majority, who were demanding better job opportunities and a return to parliamentary democracy. The clashes continued for several years, taking over thirty lives and shaking Bahrain's reputation as a peaceful island state.

In the early 1990s Dubai had yet to take off and Bahrain was still debatably the most popular posting in the Gulf for white-collar British expats, mostly bankers, brokers, lawyers and insurance types. The Hong Kong airline Cathay Pacific made this their regional hub and the manager was an old school friend of mine. 'Disco' Ron Mathison had made a name for himself at Marlborough in the late seventies, organizing summer dances with girls' schools and reproducing John Travolta's *Saturday Night Fever* moves on polished school floors, in assembly halls where the curtains were drawn at seven p.m. because there was still another three hours of daylight and the dance had to end at ten. Ron had grown up in Colombia and was widely reputed to have escaped a mugging by dancing sideways down a street in Bogota. Now he was in Bahrain, living in a big villa where he sensibly sneaked off for 'power naps' in the dead hours between finishing work and going out clubbing, emerging full of beans and outlasting all of us into the small hours, like some premium AA battery.

One morning he rang me in my tinted-plate-glass office overlooking Manama. 'How do you fancy skiing in Lebanon this weekend?' It was more of a challenge than a question. Bahrain was safe, Lebanon was probably not. The Lebanese civil war had more or less petered out since the recent peace accord brokered in Saudi Arabia, but the country still bristled with armed factions and memories were fresh of Westerners being kidnapped and held for years in the southern suburbs of Beirut. Skiing in war-ravaged Lebanon sounded dodgy, but Ron had connections and he assured my friend Mark and me that they would meet us at the airport and chaperone us.

From the moment we landed in Beirut's dusty airport in that spring of 1992 it was obvious who was in charge of this country: the Syrians. Their uniformed soldiers hung around the terminal building, their shifty-looking intelligence agents stood behind the passport kiosks, watching everyone who flew in. That week there had been a gun battle on the road from the airport into Beirut between Syrian troops and the local Lebanese gendarmes. The gendarmes had set up their own checkpoints, the Syrians wanted them removed. The Syrians won: the checkpoints were gone. As we drove through the southern slum of Bourj Al-Barajneh, where Terry Waite had been held hostage chained to a radiator by his Lebanese captors, we passed giant posters of Shi'ite religious leaders in turbans and sunglasses. 'Rock 'n' roll,' said Disco Ron.

Coming from tranquil, conformist Bahrain, everything surprised us. It was supposed to be the holy month of Ramadan. Yet here we were, sitting out at a seafront café in Muslim West Beirut in the middle of the day, and not only were people breaking the fast all around us, they were drinking beer in public! Nothing prepared us for the sight of the buildings on either side of the Green Line, the street that divided East from West Beirut. Every possible surface of the once elegant French-built houses was pockmarked with bullet-holes. It was like walking through a village made of Swiss cheese. Even the small bronze statue in the middle of Martyrs' Square, once a famous tourist landmark in the 1960s, was riddled with bullet-holes. The roads were in a dreadful state, full of potholes, and one plate-glass bank building had still not been repaired after having had every window blown out. The former US embassy was like a collapsed house of cards, its concrete storeys all slumped one on top of the other where they had been blown up by a suicide bomber nine years previously.

As we drove up into the mountains we passed men with rocket-propelled grenade launchers perched on their shoulders, standing guard at each hairpin bend. Once above the snowline this obsession with weaponry became frankly ridiculous. We checked into an alpine chalet in the resort of Faraya and trudged off to the ski slopes. Yet even here we found the ski queues patrolled by uniformed Lebanese soldiers cradling M16s. I have to say it was the most orderly ski queue I have ever seen. 'I dare you to throw a snowball at one of them,' said Mark. I declined, but Ron rose to the challenge, then left me to do the explaining. Lebanon is the only place I can think of where you can see the sea while you are on the ski piste, and the Lebanese told us with some pride that in happier days they would spend the morning skiing and the afternoon water-skiing. This winter the snow-fall had been particularly heavy, cutting off whole villages that then had to be rescued with helicopter food-drops. But word of the ski conditions had spread to the young, rich and beautiful of Beirut, and on the day we left we passed convoys of luxury four-wheel-drive jeeps heading up the mountain, their roof-racks laden with skis.

Driving back past Beirut's Green Line I stuck the video camera out of the window to film the shattered buildings. But as we passed the St Georges Yacht Club there was a coarse shout from the side of the road. '*Waqaf!*' It was a Syrian soldier ordering us to stop the car. I glanced at Ali, our Lebanese driver, who looked absolutely terrified and brought the car to an abrupt halt. Had I known that I had inadvertently filmed Syria's Military Intelligence HQ in Beirut

I would have shared Ali's concern, but as it was, when the Syrian conscript thrust out his hand to demand the tape I shook it warmly, gave him a huge smile and a traditional Arabic greeting. This took him aback at first, but he soon recovered his scowl and demanded the tape again. Unwilling to hand over all the footage we had shot up on the ski slopes, I reached into the car and handed him Dire Straits' Greatest Hits. I was sorry to see that go too ('Brothers In Arms' hit the spot for Beirut), but it did the trick. My next encounter with an armed Syrian security man was to be rather more serious.

If skiing in Lebanon in the early nineties had sounded a little unhinged, then the offer of travelling round Syria with two Swedish girls was irresistible. I had yet to meet my wife and I had an unrequited interest in one of the Scandinavians. Christina was tall, blonde and slim, with a slightly aloof air that earned her the nickname the Ice Maiden. Inge was the opposite: short and hearty with a smoker's laugh and an infectious sense of humour. Syria was a country I had always wanted to go to and they seemed to have the itinerary all worked out, so I jumped at the offer.

Stepping out of Damascus's ageing airport was like walking back into the 1970s. Dilapidated Citroëns and other clapped-out French cars puttered along beneath ubiquitous posters of the absolute ruler, President Hafez Al-Assad. A crudely painted canvas banner was strung up outside the terminal, reading: 'The Syrian people have an eternal well of love that gushes for their country and their leader and which cannot be extinguished.' I thought, who dreams up these slogans?

In Damascus, Christina and Inge stayed in the only 'luxury' hotel, an overpriced and soulless tower block, while I found an attractive little pension in the old quarter where vines grew on the roof terrace. I would sit out chatting with the affable owner in the evening as the sky grew pink over the Golan Heights, the dusk call to prayer reverberated over the rooftops and the swifts wheeled and screeched above us in the gathering twilight. I treasured moments like these in the Middle East.

Despite Syria's oppressive political atmosphere – this was, after all, a place where ten years earlier the president had crushed an Islamist uprising by ordering his army to shell the town of Hama indiscriminately, killing an estimated twenty thousand people – I liked this country. Syria had few Western visitors and the people were courteous, kind and friendly. In the backstreets off the fabulous Hamadiya Souk I tracked down the brother of my Arabic teacher in Bahrain. He was a traditional barber and I watched in awe as his nimble fingers worked a taut string into constricting triangles to pluck the hairs from his customers' cheeks. He took the Swedes and me to his favourite restaurant above the bazaar, where tables groaned with food at ridiculously low prices. A man played the 'oud and sang in exquisite Arabic as we reclined on cushions, eating iced grapes and sipping mint tea. Then the spell was broken as a posse of several well-built men in leather jackets sat down nearby. 'Secret police,' whispered my barber friend. Conversation dried up all round; it was time to pay up and leave.

Thanks to Christina and Inge's punishing itinerary, we did see a lot of the country. We hired a driver and a battered limousine and headed east across the desert to Tadmur, otherwise known as Palmyra, one of the best-preserved Roman ruins in the eastern empire. On the roads we passed convoys of Syrian tanks and Russian-made anti-aircraft missile batteries, giving the impression that the whole country had been mobilized. While most other Arab countries had moved on from the era of the Arab–Israeli wars, Syria seemed to be stuck in 1973, profoundly militaristic, its whole outlook on the world seen through the prism of hostility to Israel. Later, as a journalist, I found that many Arabs see this enduring hostility as a point in Syria's favour, a mark of pride, but it has cost this country dear. While Jordan and Egypt – which both made controversial peace deals with Israel – are in the mainstream of international trade and politics, Syria has long been isolated, the grumpy uncle of the Arab world. For decades now, Syria has been riddled with cronyism and corruption, its centrally planned economy weighed down with the outdated baggage of a one-party state. One day, I felt sure, the full potential of this culturally rich country would be released, but not under this regime.

Palmyra was amazing, and there was no one else there. For hours we wandered undisturbed through its spectacular Roman colonnades, arches and forum. Of all the Roman ruins in the Middle East I have been lucky enough to visit – Leptis Magna in Libya, Ajlun in Jordan, and El Djem in Tunisia – Palmyra must rate as one of the best. To the bemusement of the Swedish girls, I set up my video camera on a tripod with the forum behind me and gave an impromptu piece-to-camera on the history of the place. I was still three years away from switching careers from banking to broadcasting but I was already fascinated by filming. To make my films more watchable for friends back in Bahrain, I attached the headphones of my Walkman to the video camera's microphone and played lilting Arabic music as the camera panned slowly over this ruined desert city. I had done the same in Damascus by playing excerpts from the soundtrack of *Lawrence of Arabia*.

From Palmyra we drove north, skirting the snow-capped mountains of Lebanon where I had gone skiing the previous month and moving on to the lush fields of the Mediterranean coast. Krak des Chevaliers, or *Qala't Al-Husn* in Arabic, was a perfectly preserved Crusader castle – you could even see the grooves above the drawbridge where boiling oil was poured on to invaders if they got that far. I would have liked to go on to Aleppo, with its famous waterwheels and café culture, but we were running out of time. The Swedes had an appointment with a diving instructor in Aqaba; I had an office to run in Bahrain. We had a last night out in Damascus and went our separate ways. And that was when I ran into trouble.

Heading to the airport in a taxi the next morning, I found the whole thirty-kilometre-long airport road had been blocked off to traffic. President Assad was going to the airport to greet Sudan's president, El Bashir. Paranoid about assassination attempts, his guards lined the road at intervals, standing around smoking beneath the trees and turning back civilian cars. 'Do not worry,' said my laid-back driver, 'I know another route. You will catch your plane.' He weaved his way through a crowded Shi'ite suburb of the capital, where black-turbanned mullahs in Iranian-style cloaks emerged from a blue-tiled mosque with twin minarets. The road became a track that led through the trees fringing the airport road, and sure enough, we emerged back on to the airport road. Almost immediately an angry-looking presidential guard blocked our path. He was very young, perhaps about twenty, almost European-looking and dressed in jeans and T-shirt with a bandolier and a short, paratroopers' version of the AK-47 assault rifle. He was pointing it right at us. 'Move back!' he shouted. But my driver had other ideas. He started to argue with him, speaking in the peculiar Syrian drawl that ends each sentence on an upnote, as if asking a question. 'Hey, my brother,' he said, 'keep calm, we'll just wait here till the president passes.' Bad idea. One of the most terrifying sounds in the world has to be that of someone cocking a Kalashnikov machine gun, especially if it is being pointed at you. *Tshick tshick.* 'I mean it!' screamed the guard. His hands were shaking and I could see the whites of his knuckles on the AK's pistol grip. 'I'm going to shoot you if you don't move back!' The trembling barrel was pointed directly at the windscreen and while his target was the driver I doubted I would escape a burst once he squeezed the trigger. Yet my driver seemed transfixed; he said nothing, did nothing. I heard a cracked voice calling out in Arabic, 'It's all right, we're moving back. Don't shoot!' The voice was my own and I gripped the driver by his lapels and shook him. 'Do what he wants, for God's sake!' I screamed at him. Painfully slowly, the driver jiggled the gearstick into reverse, looked over his shoulder and drove backwards down the track. Needless to say, I missed my plane.

Six months later I met Amanda, my future wife. Every year a group of us – both Arabs and expats – held a black-tie ball for three hundred people at my Bahraini villa. The tradition of the Jasra Ball had been started by Mark Bullough in the eighties, when he had used a stepladder to climb up on the roof and leaped long-legged and fully clothed into the pool. It had been held every year since, except 1990 out of respect for Iraqi-occupied Kuwait. There was a jazz band, a DJ, balloons in the swimming pool, waiters, white table-cloths, a hot buffet from the Sheraton, a dance floor on the tiny lawn and a barrel-chested Sikh security guard manning the door. The guest list was eclectic: Bahraini sheikhs and merchants, British bankers, diplomats and lawyers, Indian entrepreneurs, Lebanese advertising executives, the occasional royal from Oman, Kuwait or Saudi. My Bahraini friends would arrive with their Western girlfriends in tiny, shimmering cocktail dresses and we could always rely on the Irish air stewardesses to be the first to hit the dance floor and the last to leave. British expats based across the water in Saudi Arabia would plan their weekend round the ball, and often friends would breeze in on their way from London to Hong Kong. Writing this now, it seems like another world, a lost society from the 1920s, but for most people there, living in Bahrain really was the lotus life.

At my second Jasra Ball I noticed a blonde, Scandinavian-looking girl in a short black dress, appearing through the throng and then vanishing. She had a magical smile, bright-blue eyes and everything about her spelled fun. 'Now why do I never meet anybody like that?' I complained to a Bahraini friend. 'Who is she?'

'I don't know but I'm going to find out,' he replied.

The mystery girl was Amanda, a New Zealander living in Bahrain with her parents and working at the Gulf's largest advertising agency, where someone had invited her along tonight. By the end of the evening my Bahraini friend had secured a date with her, but at my suggestion we agreed to a double dinner. He would bring her and I would bring an Egyptian girl I knew.

So there we sat, in Cicco's, Bahrain's most popular Italian restaurant, clustered round a candlelit table, and I felt sure there was an electric current flowing between me and Amanda. I wheeled out my best jokes and more than once she caught my eye. Weeks later, when my Bahraini friend had given up on her, I asked him if he would mind if I asked her out. 'Go ahead,' he said. 'She'll just say no.'

But Amanda said yes, and the following month we headed off to one of the most romantic hotels in the Middle East, the Al Bustan Palace in Muscat. Built specially for a Gulf summit of monastic rulers, it overlooked a white sand beach, bracketed by jagged, black, volcanic mountains. A small grove of coconut palms shaded a lawn where exotic coloured birds perched amongst the fronds. In the vast hotel atrium an elderly Omani villager squatted on cushions beside the embers of an ever-burning fire. He was the incense man, placing sticky globules of Omani frankincense from Dhofar on to the hot coals, wafting the sweet smoke towards guests and nodding a wordless greeting. As a Gulf resident who had stayed there before, I managed to get us upgraded to a suite on the seventh floor, an 'Islamic' room with a sea view. 'Islamic' in this case meant the walls were decorated with an exquisite frieze of tiny tiles arranged in a North African mosaic reminiscent of the mosques and *madrasa*s of Fez. Our balcony looked out over the Indian Ocean, where a warm breeze blew, a welcome change from Bahrain in winter, which could be surprisingly cold and dank. All in all it was a heady package and a wonderful place to get to know each other.

When Flemings recalled me to London after three and a half years in Bahrain, it never occurred to me not to invite Amanda to come too. We had become inseparable and I revelled in her fresh, breezy approach to life; she was always thinking up new things to do, whether it was smuggling a bottle of champagne past the guard at Bahrain Fort and out on to the ramparts at sunset, or going indoor ice-skating while the temperature soared outside. We had a brilliant time in the Gulf, taking holidays in nearby Sri Lanka and Goa and taking the Flemings speedboat out to sea at weekends. Amanda even forgave me for nearly drowning us when I discovered, some miles offshore, that I had forgotten to put the bung in (a sort of nautical bathplug used to drain the water out when the boat is on dry land). Only frantic bailing by her and her friend Pippa saved us from slowly sinking as I steered us heavily back to the marina in shame. When a dozen of us went camping in the Wahiba Sands of Oman, Amanda overcame her phobia of snakes to sleep beside me on a rug beneath the stars. But the biggest tests were yet to come. Neither of us were to know that within two years her well-paid boyfriend would become a freelance journalist, nor that the broadcaster she then married would one day lie bullet-ridden and close to death in a city he once breezed in and out of as a besuited banker.

5

Journalism pre 9/11

B Y THE AGE OF THIRTY-THREE I HAD BECOME SEDUCED BY THE perks of the banking industry, if not by the job itself. I had grown used to flying everywhere in first or business class, staying in five-star hotels, eating good food and even having my suits run up by a Savile Row tailor. After three years in Bahrain I had paid off my London mortgage, learned to waterski and scuba dive, and, quite incidentally, met the girl of my dreams. The fact that the underlying industry of marketing investment management – essentially persuading other people to let us invest their money on their behalf for a fee – did not set me on fire did worry me, but I told myself it was too late to switch careers. Young journalists in their twenties were already making a name for themselves, and I must admit I didn't fancy the idea of giving up a six-figure income for a dogsbody job on a provincial newspaper.

But I yearned to do something more exciting, like reporting for TV news. I could not remember the last time I had experienced adrenaline on the job, and so to compensate, on visits to war-ravaged Kuwait I would pack a video camera and practise pieces-to-camera in front of abandoned Iraqi sandbags. Amanda thought this was ridiculous. 'You're a banker,' she reminded me. 'Get over it.' But I was not necessarily in charge of my own destiny.

After running the Flemings Bahrain office, I was rewarded for my efforts by promotion to Director. It had been a spectacularly successful period for our little Middle East office and all my client visits and socializing in Arabic had helped win the bank over US$2 billion of new Arab funds under management. Now I was being brought back to London to 'drive' the Middle East business from head office. Frankly, I was rubbish at it. Out in the Gulf I had been able to convince myself I was doing something interesting, holding late-night meetings with charismatic sheikhs and merchants, then tacking on extra days to business trips to go exploring in the mountains of southwest Saudi Arabia. But commuting into the City of London every day and holding budget meetings with heads of departments just didn't do it for me. I was suddenly surrounded by people who were genuinely interested in accounting and I was a fish out of water. My lack of enthusiasm showed in my work and I was given a gentle warning. General Sir Peter de la Billiere, who had joined the bank as a non-executive director in 1992, pulled me aside a few months after my return from Bahrain and told me to 'buck my ideas up'. I was impressed that after spending most of his forty-year military career in the dangerous world of Special Operations he had adapted so well to corporate life, but then I was only half his age. By May 1995 I had lost all interest in banking and the feeling was mutual. I was summoned upstairs to a meeting room where my boss, John Drysdale, a kind-hearted and genial man, sat stern-faced next to a girl from Personnel (in the days before this term became Americanized to Human Resources). 'I'm here to tell you there is no longer a job for you,' he said. It was just over five years since he had said the exact opposite – 'I'm here to tell you we'd like to offer you a job' – and I think he probably found this more painful than I did. I mumbled a half-hearted protest, but actually it was a relief, the executioner's bullet after a sleepless night in the cell. Flemings were generous and we parted on good terms, like a couple who realize they are really better off just as good friends. That night Amanda and I celebrated with a bottle of champagne. 'Now you can do anything you want,' she said, her face as radiant as the day I first met her.

After nine years in investment banking I had been given precisely the kick up the backside I needed to throw myself into a career in journalism. I even resisted temptation in the form of a head-hunter who pounced on me the day I left Flemings, trying to convince me I would be perfect for a £200,000 a year (plus guaranteed bonus) Middle East financial marketing job he needed to fill. General Sir Peter de la Billiere showed a paternal concern for what was to become of me. The man who had commanded 45,000 British troops in the Desert Storm campaign of 1991 seemed genuinely worried that my departure from Flemings was going to lead to a tailspin of unemployment and self-doubt. He took me to lunch at his club, the Special Forces Club in Knightsbridge, where portraits hung of various SAS characters included one of Sir Wilfred Thesiger. Thesiger had joined David Stirling's band of marauders in the Second World War to go raiding German airfields deep in the Western Desert, and his weathered features now stared down at me as if willing me to take a chance. I told Sir Peter that my mind was made up – although it had nothing to do with Thesiger's portrait – I was determined to get into the news business. I was not a complete stranger to journalism, having written articles for

140

the print media for the past ten years; I had even written a piece on Middle East security and terrorism for *Executive Travel* magazine at the height of the hijacking and hostage-taking scares in 1986, never imagining I would one day become the BBC's Security Correspondent. But these had been freelance efforts, a bit of pocket money on top of my banking salary; now I needed to earn a living and get myself on to a very steep learning curve.

I went into overdrive, researching courses, reading manuals, phoning contacts. I went on an excellent radio-production course run by Morley College, where they sent us out into the streets around Victoria Station to make a radio feature report about rollerblading. The rather nasal radio presenter running the course decided I was too posh for his liking. 'There's only one place for your sort of voice,' he sneered in front of the class. 'Radio 4's *Today Programme*. In fact your homework can be to record it tomorrow morning, bring it in and we'll dissect it.' He was not impressed when I overslept and only managed to switch on the tape recorder in time to hear John Humphreys thanking his producers and saying goodbye.

I attended another good, hands-on course on TV production run by ex-BBC people at Thames Valley University. We all took turns at being studio floor manager, director, cameraman and presenter. I quickly learned that I was happiest in front of the camera, but it gave me a useful grounding in how the all-important technical parts of a TV studio fit together. I also completed a diploma course in General Journalism at the London School of Journalism, just in case anyone asked me to produce a qualification. Which they never have. I bought a Hi-8 video camera and tripod, then practised filming tourists in Covent Garden and an anti-nuclear protest outside the French embassy. (It was the summer of 1995 and the French government was annoying the world by irradiating Moorea Atoll with underground nuclear explosions.) I took the camera to Latvia that summer and made an amateur tourism promotion film, which I sold – at a loss – to a Baltic travel company in London. I even managed to wangle permission to be the first to film inside a women's prison there on the outskirts of Riga.

But what really counted was getting a foot in the door at the BBC, and here my Middle East experience came in useful in exploiting contacts. I cold-called executives, got them to tell me who was the right person to speak to, phoned them, implored them to see me, then turned up, overdressed in a suit. One manager who had already sent me a letter politely asking me not to bother him again was surprised to see me going into the office of his colleague across the corridor. This time I got a toe-hold.

'Would you be interested in a two-week work experience on BBC World?' asked Daniel Dodd, adding quickly, 'It's unpaid, of course.'

I leaped at the chance. BBC World is the BBC's satellite news channel, almost unknown in the UK but watched by hundreds of millions around the world. In Bahrain this had been our staple source of news, long before I got interested in how it was made. This was my first break, my first time inside a newsroom, and I was willing to make the tea if that's what it took. The head of the team I was assigned to took a long cool look at me. Ann McGuire was a slim, elegantly poised woman with a sharp mind and – I don't know why I remember this – curious pointed green-suede shoes.

'Normally we get eighteen-year-old school leavers in here on work experience, but you're obviously a bit older,' she said. She was right there, I was thirty-four, a rather ripe age to be embarking on a full-time career in news journalism. 'So, do you want to just look around or do you want to actually do something useful?' She guessed my answer before I gave it and immediately sent me downstairs to a planning meeting. The following day was the fifth anniversary of Iraq's invasion of Kuwait and they were discussing how to mark this. 'Has anyone here been to Kuwait?' asked the person in charge of the next day's programme. I waited a few seconds, then put up my hand as if I were at school. A roomful of seasoned hacks turned to look at me; until then no one had noticed me come in. 'All right,' he said, wanting sorely to add 'smartass', I'm sure, 'any ideas, then?' I suggested interviewing the Kuwaiti ambassador, Khaled Al-Duwaisan, so off we went to see him in his South Kensington embassy. I was allowed to accompany the duty reporter, Peter Biles, as long as I did not get in his way. I asked him how he had got to where he was and he sketched out an already impressive career as a foreign correspondent in East Africa. It was clear I had a lot of catching up to do if I was going to get taken seriously in the newsroom.

Fortunately for me, Ann McGuire did take me seriously. Both she and Daniel Dodd stood up to the naysayers who huffed and puffed that there was surely no place in a cash-strapped newsroom for an ex-banker with zero television experience. When my unpaid work experience came to an end I was asked to come back as a freelance assistant producer to do shift work. Often this meant thirteen-hour night shifts, which were exhausting and thoroughly destructive to one's social life, but once inside TV Centre I loved the feeling of being at the centre of this big rolling news machine, taking in satellite feeds of events as they unfolded on the other side of the world, going off to the graphics department to help organize an animated map of the Middle East, sorting through the next morning's papers to find stories for the presenters to talk about, or just going down to Reception to meet and greet the early-morning studio guests.

Since in these early months there was almost no chance of being on TV myself I saw no reason to dress up. On one overnight shift I was wearing a particularly baggy jumper that had seen better days when I bumped into Eddie O'Sullivan, the tough-talking editor of a business magazine called *Middle East Economic Digest* (*MEED*). The last time he had seen me was at an Arab finance forum in a five-star hotel in Knightsbridge, when I was a besuited banker. He recoiled in horror. 'Bloody hell, Frank,' he said. 'What's happened to you? Are you all right?' He found it hard to believe I was happier now as a lowly paid journo than I had been as a high-flying banker, but by then I had worked out that, for me at least, job satisfaction was measured in something less tangible than money.

Amanda too was happier. In the first months after our return from Bahrain neither of us had enjoyed London much. While I had been working hard in the City, coming home at night tired and disgruntled, Amanda had found it hard to get interesting work. In Bahrain she had been used to giving high-powered advertising presentations to clients; now, a New Zealander on a two-year 'working-holiday' visa, she was being asked by employment agencies for qualifications she didn't have, then being told to apply for jobs she didn't want. Having been used to living in sunny places like New Zealand, Hong Kong and Bahrain, Amanda also found England hard to adjust to at first. But now we were both doing jobs we enjoyed – she'd started working for a slick American PR company – and in the evenings we made the most of living amidst the buzz and bustle of Covent Garden. One evening I took Amanda out to dinner at her favourite restaurant, Le Palais du Jardin, with something very much on my mind. I had woken up that morning and suddenly known, with the utmost certainty, that she was the girl I wanted to marry. In my lunch-break I had gone straight to Hatton Garden and bought an engagement ring. Now, with coffee and desserts on the table, I was struggling to extract it from my jacket pocket. Apparently I looked so flushed she thought I was having a heart attack. But when she heard me propose her face shone as she accepted, and she added mischievously, 'Now you'd better call my father!'

*

I had only been at BBC World for a few weeks when I heard someone say, 'Hey, does anybody here know anything about this Egyptian guy convicted in New York?' The Egyptian guy was Sheikh Omar Abdurrahman, a blind Muslim cleric on the run from the Egyptian authorities. He had been part of an extremist group based around a mosque in Brooklyn, and in 1995 he was convicted of playing a part in the 1993 attempt to blow up the World Trade Center in New York. It was quite late in the evening in the BBC studio and the chances of booking a studio guest to comment on this conviction at short notice were slim. I stuck my hand up again. 'OK, we'll tell you if we need you, but you'd better get some make-up on just in case. Sorry, what did you say your name was?' My heart leaped. What had I gone and done? What if I froze up and couldn't remember what I wanted to say? A number of people looked at me in disbelief. I was a complete newcomer to broadcasting, and to be honest, I did not even know a great deal about this blind Egyptian cleric. But I was the only person in the newsroom who could pronounce his name, and after an agonizing two-hour wait, wondering if they would need me on air or not, I was summoned to the studio. To someone who had never before done live television, 'You're on in five' were some of the most frightening words in the English language.

I was ushered into the revered set during a commercial break (unlike domestic BBC, the international channel runs advertisements) and a studio manager clipped a pin microphone on to my lapel. 'Remember,' she said, noticing I was white with nerves, 'three minutes all up and you must stop talking after the presenter waves his hand for you to stop.' The presenter was Alastair Yates, whose kind and calming personality put me instantly at ease, despite his strange penchant for green and lilac jackets. The lights came up, Alastair did a short intro into the camera then swivelled round to face me. 'And with me here to discuss this is our

Middle East analyst Frank Gardner. Frank, what do you make of this?' Middle East analyst! That had a nice ring to it, I thought. It felt as if I had barely opened my mouth before the interview was over, but I was on a high for the rest of the night. I went to join Amanda and Brad, an Australian friend, in a Covent Garden bar. Brad looked at me incredulously and said, 'Strewth, I don't believe it, you're wearing make-up!' He then examined my glass, 'To check yer not wearing lipstick as well, ya ponce.'

The next day the Head of BBC News, Chris Cramer, brought me back down to earth. 'Get a haircut' was his only comment, a fair one since I did have a rather un-newslike boy-band fop hanging over my forehead at the time.

Before long Ann McGuire gave me my second break, putting me in charge of producing BBC World's weekly news feature films – we're talking three minutes here, not a Hollywood epic. The topics were varied, to say the least. One week we would be filming an ostrich farm in Oxfordshire, the next a university debate with O. J. Simpson. It was a case of the blind leading the blind, since the reporter was always a radio hack out of Bush House who was almost as new to TV as I was. The only person who knew what he was doing was the cameraman, who was more often than not the huge, imposing Kiwi, Adam Kelliher. Adam had been a stringer for *The Times* in Beirut in the worst days of the civil war in the eighties; he had also seen up close the recent horrors of war in the Balkans. He needed regular feeding and refreshment or he would turn grizzly, but he bore our ignorance with patience and good humour and we were to become lifelong friends. It was also useful to keep in his slipstream whenever there was a press scrum.

One of these occasions was when Yasser Arafat, the chairman of the Palestinian Authority, or the 'President', as he liked to be called, came to give an address at the Oxford Union. Before he spoke to the assembled undergraduates he was introduced to the press upstairs in a wood-panelled chamber. When it was my turn Arafat gripped my hand and looked imploringly into my eyes, almost certainly mistaking me for someone else. It was summer 1996 and Arafat was still in shock. His great friend and peace partner Shimon Peres, who had become prime minister following the assassination of Yitzhak Rabin by a right-wing Israeli, had just lost the Israeli election to the arch-hawk Binyamin Netanyahu. Arafat's dream of the early achievement of Palestinian statehood had been shattered and he simply did not appear to have a Plan B. George Galloway was there too, puffing on a cigar, oozing bonhomie and calling me by my first name, although I suspect that he could not have known me from Adam.

When Yasser Arafat strode into the debating chamber of the Oxford Union on that warm summer evening he got a standing ovation. Fresh-faced and idealistic students cheered him to the rafters, perhaps seeing him as a sort of Middle Eastern Mandela. But then it all went wrong. Arafat started well enough, although his English was sometimes hard to follow. But when it came to questions from the floor someone touched a raw nerve. Arafat was asked why he had imprisoned the Palestinian human-rights campaigner Iyad Sarraj for apparently saying Gazans had more freedom under Israeli occupation than they did under Palestinian rule. Quite simply, Arafat lost it. He banged his mottled fist down hard on the table, shouting over and over: 'I will not allow it! I will not allow it! How dare anyone say this?' There was a gasp from the audience, who suddenly realized that far from being a champion of freedom and justice they were actually looking at an authoritarian dictator who could not tolerate criticism, especially from a fellow Palestinian.

The following year, I got the chance to meet both Netanyahu and Arafat on their home turf. Ann McGuire, the BBC World programme editor who had taken an inexplicable liking to me, had a new project. She had been spearheading a half-hour interview programme called *HardTalk*, where the veteran reporter and presenter Tim Sebastian would put world leaders and news-makers under the spotlight. I had been there when the programme was just beginning, at a rather difficult interview with a cantankerous Ted Heath in his house by Salisbury Cathedral, still under police protection even though he had stopped being prime minister over twenty years ago. Now *HardTalk* was to head to the Middle East in the hope of interviewing as many leading Israelis and Palestinians as possible, and it was my job to help set up the interviews and accompany the team out there.

Pinning down the Israelis for interview was easy. They understood the value of the media and knew exactly how to turn it to their advantage. They spoke perfect English, albeit with American accents, and they made every effort to provide facilities to make our job easier. With very little work we secured an interview with the Israeli prime minister, Binyamin Netanyahu. We were advised to turn up two hours in advance to be cleared by security and not to ask him about his brother Jonaton, a Special Forces officer killed in the raid on Entebbe in 1977. Netanyahu insisted on having his own favourite make-up girl – at the BBC's expense – which struck me as faintly ridiculous. Here was this strapping former Israeli commando who prided himself on his tough stance on terrorism, and now he was coming over all choosy about cosmetics. Whether or not the make-up was to blame, once the interview got under way a solitary fly kept circling the PM's head, alighting again and again on his immaculately combed grey hair. But Netanyahu was a consummate performer in front of the camera. When Tim Sebastian thought he had him cornered with a killer question about how almost the whole world had condemned the Israeli shelling of a UN base in South Lebanon in 1996, Netanyahu turned on the theatrics.

'Whoa! Whoa! Whoa!' he boomed, leaning forward

towards the BBC man. 'Back up here a minute.' And by the time he had said his piece most viewers would probably have forgotten Sebastian's original question.

By contrast, getting Yasser Arafat to commit to interview was a nightmare. It was not that his people said no, they were just incapable of reaching a decision. I spent night after night down in his Gaza headquarters, then another night at his base in Ramallah, trying to persuade the *Rayyes*, the 'President', to appear on *HardTalk*. For every two minutes of conversation snatched with the Palestinian leader as his entourage swept in and out of the building I spent hours waiting in his kitchen, chatting away in Arabic to his chainsmoking guards. We would sit round a Formica table late into the night, munching falafel sandwiches with a small armoury of assault rifles piled up to one side. It made no difference: Arafat never did the interview with us anyway.

We did, however, secure a lengthy and colourful interview with Iyad Sarraj, the Palestinian human-rights campaigner who had so infuriated Arafat by being quoted as saying there had been more freedom under the Israelis than under the new rule of the Palestinian Authority. We interviewed him up on a rooftop in Gaza's teeming and squalid Al-Shati refugee camp. Filthy children ran barefoot in the street below while Israeli Air Force F-16s screamed through the sky just offshore. You did not even have to listen to the interview to know that life down here in this slum camp was grim and largely devoid of hope.

Someone who had been watching the misfortunes of Palestinians and other Muslims was as yet largely unknown to the West, but he would one day become a household name. The Saudi businessman-turned-holy-warrior Osama Bin Laden had returned home to Saudi Arabia after years of helping the Afghans drive out the Soviet Army. Unhappy with the Saudi government's alliance with Washington, he moved to Sudan, then fled to Afghanistan in 1996 when the Sudanese came under US pressure to expel him. Bin Laden took a keen interest in the media; his message to the world was that Muslims were oppressed and the United States and Israel were to blame. In London he had a front organization to distribute his communiqués, the Advice and Reformation Committee, headed by a man called Khalid Al-Fawaz. On a muggy August afternoon in 1996 I went to meet Al-Fawaz in the tearoom of London's Waldorf Astoria hotel, close to the BBC World Service in Bush House. A tall, imposing Saudi in a long white robe, Khaled Al-Fawaz was in constant contact with Bin Laden in Afghanistan. He strode purposefully towards me, past the Waldorf's potted palms and the bare-armed girl playing the harp, to take his seat at our table. I exchanged glances with my BBC colleague, Nick Pelham, who had arranged the meeting. This devout Saudi looked a little out of place here in London's theatreland. His long, untrimmed beard marked him out as a fundamentalist Muslim, while his forehead bore a smooth brown mark where he had touched it to the ground in frequent prayer. He cut straight to the chase.

'Sheikh Osama is ready to give his first TV interview,' said Al-Fawaz, scowling briefly at a woman at a nearby table who was throwing her head back, laughing too loudly. 'And he has chosen to give that interview to the BBC.' Although few people had heard of Bin Laden back then, to those of us who followed events in the Middle East he was already a familiar figure. The son of a wealthy Saudi construction magnate of Yemeni origin, Osama Bin Laden had used his wealth and engineering know-how to help the *mujahideen* (Islamic fighters) battle the Soviets in Afghanistan throughout the 1980s. Tens of thousands of young, idealistic Saudis, Yemenis and other Arabs from all over the Middle East had flocked to join his cause, seeing it as a sacred duty to help drive out the 'infidel' Russians from Muslim land. They became known as the Arab Afghans, even though many of these volunteers never got further than Pakistan. To them Bin Laden was a hero, who commanded both their respect and their loyalty.

Although the US government was starting to view him as a dangerous enemy, Bin Laden was not considered too dangerous to interview in 1996, even by Western correspondents. The print journalists Robert Fisk from the *Independent* and Scott Macloud from *Time* magazine had both interviewed him in Sudan, but this scourge of the Saudi royal family had yet to appear in a TV interview. All right, we said, we were definitely interested, but we did have some concerns. What about this declaration of war Bin Laden had just issued, announcing that all Americans, whether military or civilian, were fair targets for attack? It sounded like an anti-Western *fatwa* to us, so how did we know that as Britons we would be safe in Bin Laden's company? Al-Fawaz looked rather embarrassed at this point. 'Ah yes, the declaration. Well, I disagreed with Sheikh Osama on this, I told him it was not the right time to issue it, but it is done now. But you can be assured it does not apply to journalists. The Sheikh values the media and wants the world to understand his message.'

My BBC colleague and I accepted the invitation to go to Afghanistan, trusting in the Arab code of honour of hospitality and protection for invited guests – which in twenty-four years, up until the Riyadh attack, never let me down. Despite the carnage and bloodshed that Bin Laden has inspired and sanctioned, to my knowledge he has never harmed an invited journalist. We now got down to working out the logistics; the invitation to interview Osama Bin Laden came with certain stipulations. 'Sheikh Osama does not want you to come through Pakistan,' said Al-Fawaz, who said he feared we would be trailed by agents from ISI, Pakistani military intelligence. Bin Laden clearly did not want people knowing who he was seeing, or even, perhaps, where he was based. 'So you must fly via Delhi to Jalalabad in Afghanistan, where you will be met by a guide who will take you to Sheikh Osama's camp.' I have to say that at first my masters in the BBC were less than enthusiastic, and for quite the wrong reasons. 'Sorry,' said one manager, 'no one's heard of this guy, so we're not interested.' But with a little pressing and a strong endorsement from the Cairo bureau we were back in business. I went round to the sleepy Afghan embassy in London's Prince's Gate and procured visas for Afghanistan and then transit ones for India, worked out a budget, booked flights and arranged for a translator to meet us in Jalalabad with jeeps, water and spare fuel.

And then, forty-eight hours before our departure, the unexpected happened. The Taliban's army of bearded, black-turbanned warriors, who had been spreading slowly out through the country from their Kandahar base in the south, suddenly made a dash for the capital, Kabul, putting the government to flight. Sitting in Nangahar province, Osama Bin Laden was initially unsure of what this would mean for him and his Arab Afghans, so he sent us an urgent message through his man in London asking us to wait until things settled down in Afghanistan. But it was too late. In the renewed flurry of interest in that country other networks soon grabbed the first TV interviews with Bin Laden. Even the US networks got in on the act, and sure enough, their American reporters ventured right into the lion's den and emerged unscathed. Khaled Al-Fawaz, who so nearly delivered us what would have been a scoop, was arrested in London soon afterwards and was held pending extradition to the US on charges of terrorism, which he denied. We had missed our chance.

But this narrowly missed scoop redoubled my determination to go and report from the Middle East. The BBC's response was lukewarm. I was told that since I hadn't come in on the news-trainee scheme, nor did I have a proven track record of reporting from abroad, my chances were slim. So I set out to rectify this. Soon after I started those night shifts at BBC World, I managed to secure a lucrative weekly live-interview slot with Canada's state broadcaster, CBC, and this time it was me in front of the camera. Every Monday evening a limousine would take me to their studios in Bloomsbury, where a laid-back technician would hook me up to an earpiece and a microphone. When the live countdown played in my ear I had seven minutes to talk Canada's viewers through three Middle Eastern topics of the week. It was unscripted, with no autocue, and at first it was terrifying, but I always got to agree the questions in advance with the presenter in Calgary, who was only too happy to let me run the show. It made him look knowledgeable about the Middle East and it gave me the perfect grounding in live television. If I ever made any career-threatening blunders on Canadian television my colleagues at the BBC were unlikely to hear of them.

At the same time, since no one was sending me abroad to report I started to send myself. When Amanda and I went on holiday to Queensland I took my Hi-8 video and made a film about the increasing threat to swimmers from lethal box jellyfish that were straying ever further south from their breeding grounds. All right, so the self-filmed reporter's piece-to-camera in a mangrove swamp was so bad it was unusable, and there was the small problem that I didn't actually have any footage of live box jellyfish. But we salvaged the project in London with natural-history archive and my first film made it to air in less than a year of my leaving banking.

In early 1996 I took the camera with me on a gruelling South American jungle trek with James Maughan, my future best man, up to the Lost City in Colombia's Sierra Nevada mountains, dodging the snake known as *la pudidora*, 'the putrefyer', so called because a victim's flesh becomes necrotic around the site of the bite. At night we slept in hammocks while the rain fell in sheets and howler monkeys emitted blood-curdling screams in the foliage above us. It was a magical trip. This time I framed the piece-to-camera properly with a line of ancient, moss-covered steps trailing away over my shoulder, and I tried to deliver my lines as casually as I could whilst clouds of malarial mosquitoes dived around my head. I also did my best to construct a 'sequence' of a river crossing. This is a cinematic device which entails filming the same scene several times from different angles. So if you have two Colombian porters wading across a boulder-strewn torrent with tottering backpacks, you film it wide from a distance, then up close and low so their boots nearly bump the camera lens, and then perhaps once more for luck at head height, concentrating this time on their faces. It did not exactly endear me to the porters, but back in London the videotape editor was delighted to have a variety of shots to play with, and he cut them together into a watchable sequence.

In terms of the Middle East and my grand plan to go out and report from there, this newly acquired skill meant I could now be bi-medial, meaning I could make my own news reports for both radio and TV. Looking at a map of the region I reckoned I had spotted a gap in the BBC's coverage. They had a bureau in Cairo and another in Amman, but nobody in the Gulf. 'Well, that's because there's no news there,' said Kevin, a rather unimaginative World Service manager, when I put this to him. 'There's no news there because you've got no one reporting it!' I countered. Having lived there for three years, I was confident there would be plenty to report on. Already, Islamist militants had blown the side off a US Air Force accommodation block in Dhahran in Saudi Arabia, killing nineteen US airmen. There were other stirrings of discontent in that closed country, but almost no Western journalists were getting in to report on what was happening there.

To test the BBC's appetite for stories from the Gulf I embarked on a series of self-funded reconnaissance trips around the region, armed with my new digital video camera. I filmed reports in Iran, Oman, Bahrain and the UAE, bringing back slightly off-the-wall business stories from countries where there was no BBC bureau at the time. The presenter of a BBC1 business programme said almost apologetically after one of my films, 'Well, I expect it will be some time before we hear again from the dagger-makers of Oman.' The trips barely broke even, but I was getting myself on air and I found it a huge thrill to be the only Westerner on the twenty-four-hour train journey across the length of Iran, for example, from Tehran to the Gulf coast, filming children outside in dusty villages as they cheerfully stoned the train. From each film I would make a radio version and then write a piece for *The Times* or *The Economist*; there was no question about it, there was a market for these stories, but I would have to move quickly before somebody better known than I was jumped in and set themselves up in Dubai. 'All right,' conceded Kevin, that unimaginative BBC manager, 'we'll give you accreditation, but you're on your own. We'll only pay you for the stories you get on air. Personally, I think you'll starve.'

Poor Amanda. When I first left banking she had implored me to find a job in Dubai, but now, just as she was starting to enjoy London, here I was proposing we up sticks again and move back to the Middle East. We had just had a gorgeous, sunlit spring wedding in the country, she was pregnant with our first child and halfway through a degree course in computer studies. In short, we were happily settled. But after we had talked it through, Amanda agreed that moving to Dubai would be the right thing not just for my career, but also for us as a family. She supported me unequivocally.

Wilfred Thesiger was less encouraging. 'Ghastly place, Dubai. Completely ruined,' he huffed when I went round for lunch in his Chelsea flat. As we cooked up omelettes and the old explorer offered me some very stale white wine that he kept for visitors (he didn't drink), he reminisced about the Dubai he had known in the 1950s. His black-and-white photos showed a sleepy trading port of barefoot smugglers and pearl-divers squinting suspiciously at the camera, a world of labyrinthine backstreets and intrigue, where cars were rare and tower blocks unheard of. But I was able to assure him that beyond the plate-glass sheen of modern Dubai, much of the spirit of that old world still lived on, and he conceded that it would be an excellent base for exploring the region. In his day, half a century ago, he had the Desert Locust Control Organisation to fund his trips, while I now had the BBC.

Shortly before midnight on 23 September 1997, Amanda and I wheeled our luggage out of Dubai's airport terminal into the dripping heat of late summer. We had packed up our flat, said goodbye to our friends and were embarking on a major gamble. Amanda was six months pregnant, I had no guarantee of income, and we had no one to help us set up in the Gulf. Outside the terminal we were greeted by a chaotic scene, with scores of Asian guest workers all shouting at each other in a dozen languages. At this time of year the Indian Ocean monsoon passed close to the southern Gulf, raising the humidity to almost unbearable levels. We were coated in sweat before we had even flagged down a taxi. Slumped in the back seat, on the way to our temporary home in Golden Sands rented apartments, I switched on my mobile phone. There was a message from Radio 4's *Today* programme: they wanted to do a live radio interview with me the very next morning about two British nurses facing possible flogging and execution in Saudi Arabia. At that moment, as we pulled up at the nondescript block of flats that was to be our home for the next few weeks, I realized I had become what I had always wanted to be: a foreign reporter in the Middle East.

Over the next few weeks, as we struggled with the local bureaucracy, found a place to live and implored the phone company to hurry up and put in a line, my mobile phone became our lifeline. We were so tight for money that at first we could not afford a second mobile phone, so Amanda was left with no means of communication while I was off reporting. Given that she was expecting a baby within eight weeks, this was a testing time for her, but living within five minutes of the beach had its compensations: floating with friends in the sea allowed her to feel mercifully weightless for a while.

One call I always welcomed was from the BBC's foreign assignments editor, Malcolm Downing. If he had been around in the Second World War he would have doubtless been one of those people shuffling wooden ships across maps and marking up friendly troop deployments on a blackboard. His job was to ring up stringers and correspondents in far-flung postings and send them to places where a story was brewing. He always asked nicely and said 'Good man' if you accepted, but you knew it would not be a good career move to say no. Malcolm could make or break a foreign correspondent's career.

In October 1997 he asked me to go up the coast to Bahrain to see if I could interview the team of UN inspectors as they flew in from Iraq. Tensions were mounting between the UN and Iraq over Saddam's refusal to give the inspectors un-fettered access to suspected WMD sites, and if I could grab a soundbite from them in Bahrain it would put us well ahead of the competition. It was a classic piece of forward thinking by Malcolm, but it began to go wrong from the start. As I was a journalist, the Bahrainis at first refused to let me through Immigration without a visa acquired in advance. They only relented when they were satisfied I had not come to report on Bahrain's rumbling anti-government insurgency by the country's Shi'ite majority. I hired a car and drove round to the field office of UNSCOM, the original UN weapon inspectors' organization. Yes, they said, they were expecting a flight in that afternoon from Iraq's Habbaniya airfield, but no one could give any interviews without authorization from a Scotsman called Euan Buchanan at UN HQ in New York. I called up Euan Buchanan and he laughed in my ear.

'You're wasting yer time, laddie. Bahrain's just a support office, it's where we come to buy our light bulbs and loo roll. And noo, I'm not going to authorize any interviews, so yer best off going back to Dùbai.'

Great. My first foreign news-gathering assignment in the Gulf and I had blown it. But just then I saw a white-painted C-130 with UN markings banking in the sky in preparation for landing. I got back into my hire car and raced round the perimeter fence to confirm it was landing with a manifest of UN weapons inspectors. As I called up the news desk in London to give them the news, I suddenly found myself surrounded by police cars. I was placed under arrest on suspicion of spying and taken off to Muharraq police station. The arresting officers were crude and aggressive, probably congratulating themselves on breaking up some imagined foreign conspiracy, but the police chief was plainly em-barrassed. He could see at once that I was who I said I was and he even allowed me to do a live interview with News 24 on my mobile as I sat in his office, still technically under arrest. 'I understand you're doing this interview under rather difficult conditions,' said the presenter, safe in her studio in London. Like a naughty schoolboy being fetched by his parents, I had to wait until someone from the Ministry of Information came to vouch for me and then took me straight to the airport.

The rest of 1997 passed in a blur of assignments. The stand-off between Iraq on the one hand and the UN and US on the other grew worse, and as the BBC's stringer in the Gulf I was the easiest – and cheapest – person to deploy on to a US Navy aircraft carrier to report on the US military build-up in the Gulf, something I did a number of times. This meant tip-toeing back into Bahrain again, waiting in a hotel for the call from Navcent, the headquarters of the US Navy's Fifth Fleet, then racing out to the airport to board a Navy flight out to sea. For reasons I resented at the time, the American media always seemed to be offered the soft option, flying out in big, comfortable CH-53 helicopters, while the rest of us were corralled on to a diabolical invention called the COD. This stood for Carrier On-board Delivery, meaning a stubby-winged propeller plane almost certainly invented by a direct descendant of the Marquis de Sade. The metal seats faced backwards, there were almost no windows to see out of, and it felt like a giant, airborne coffin. The turboprop engines were so incredibly noisy that after the initial safety briefing on the runway we all had to clamp ear-defenders on our heads, wondering why smoke was filling the cabin (it turned out to be dust). A shout bordering on panic would then go up from the Navy Flight Supervisor and we would be off, pitching and rolling high above the Gulf. When it came to landing on the deck of the aircraft carrier it felt like we were literally dropping out of the sky, hitting the floating runway with a heavy thump then screeching to a halt within seconds. The ramp would go down at the rear of the plane and we would be marshalled into a world straight out of Hollywood's *Topgun*.

Apart from Tom Cruise, all the other details were the same: the screaming jets, the drifting steam from the catapults, the towering superstructure, the helmeted bomb-loaders pushing their lethal trolleys. Within seconds of landing on the USS *Nimitz*, a massive 95,000-ton leviathan with 5,500 people on board and a small, floating air force of attack jets, I witnessed my first air launch. One after another, F/A-18 Hornet jets would taxi up on deck a few feet away from me, the names, nicknames and ranks of their pilots stencilled on to the fuselages below the cockpit canopies. The red-jacketed flight-deck crew would crouch down by the front wheel to check the plane's attachment to the steam catapult, then step back to signal to the pilot, who would give them a thumbs-up. A moment later and several tons of hi-tech weaponry would be catapulted off the deck and there would be a massive roar as the jet's afterburners kicked in, two blazing rings of orange fire that rose like a comet into the clear Arabian sky before the jet turned north and headed for Iraq. 'Phooar! That's the lot, boys!' went a voice on the ship's tannoy that turned out to come from a man called the Air Boss.

The US was not actually at war with Iraq in late 1997, but on that testosterone-packed warship it certainly felt that way. The aircraft carrier was a hive of constant activity, with jets being raised up to the deck on hydraulic lifts then armed with enormous, laser-guided 'smart bombs'. 'What you are seeing here, gentlemen,' said the admiral up on his surprisingly cramped bridge, 'is Operation Southern Watch in action.' Southern Watch was an Anglo–US–French coalition operation set up after the Gulf War in 1991 to prevent Iraq's air force from taking to the skies in the southern third of the country, which, along with the northern Kurdish part, had been designated a 'no-fly zone'. The aircraft were flying CAPs – Combat Air Patrols – but were carrying enough armament to destroy Iraq's anti-aircraft installations the moment some hapless Iraqi operator on the ground was ordered to switch on the radar to illuminate the aircraft and thereby effectively sign his own death warrant. By the time the US and Britain formally went to war with Iraq in 2003 their air forces had had twelve years of flying missions over the country.

I was on and off US Navy aircraft carriers as tensions built further with Iraq, delivering one inaudible piece-to-camera in goggles and helmet on the crowded flightdeck as F-14 Tomcat jets screamed past me down the runway and up into the air.

Back on dry land, I went up to the tiny UAE emirate of Umm Al-Qaiwain to report on an oil spill that turned out to have come from a sunken fuel barge that had been smuggled out of Iraq and which now wrecked the emirate's entire coastline. I got the full story about a corrupt local importer from an oil official, who misheard me saying I was from the BBC and thought I had said 'BPC' – British Petroleum Company. There were limits, though, and I was not willing to overstep them at the risk of being deported. In the Gulf, it seemed, you could criticize government but not individuals, especially members of the ruling families. Any journalist breaking that rule did not stay long in the country.

On 15 December 1997 Amanda announced, 'Get the car, the contractions have started.' Our first child was preparing to greet the world. We had Amanda's mother Jennie staying with us, and when the BBC rang to ask if I could cover a plane crash that had just happened in Sharjah she nearly snatched the phone and spoke to them herself. Mobile switched off, we raced to Dubai's American Hospital, where some hours later Melissa was born. I will never forget that wonderful smell of a newborn baby, our own kin, cradled in my arms when she was not yet five minutes old.

Like most first-time parents we were beside ourselves with excitement, and bringing Melissa home to our little villa near Jumeirah Beach made life complete. We had had to put down a whole year's rent on the place in advance, such was the power Dubai landlords could exercise over expatriate tenants, but we were blissfully happy. We had planted our tiny walled garden with jasmine and bougainvillea, and we hired a talented Pakistani gardener who would occasionally produce in triumph a plastic bag into which he had stuffed the nest of a venomous redback spider. From out of our window we could see the outline taking shape of the Burj Al-Arab, what was to become the world's most expensive hotel, with a top suite costing close to ten thousand pounds a night at the time of opening. But there was still enough open desert outside our front door for me to go running at night with a diplomat friend from Exeter University days. There was almost no crime – we often left our doors unlocked – and we had the warm waters of the Arabian Gulf to swim in just a few hundred metres away. In short, life was very sweet.

If I had stayed put in Dubai all year we would have very quickly run out of money; there simply weren't enough big stories here to fight for a place on the BBC news programmes. Instead, the country that put me squarely on the map in news terms was Yemen. The poorest country on the Arabian Peninsula, it has arguably the best scenery, the richest culture, the worst food and the most guns. Yemen was awash with weapons. In fact it has long been said (but never proven) that the country has over fifty million guns in private hands, nearly three per capita. Outside the big cities few men would be seen dead without their trusty AK-47; I have known taxi-drivers to keep loaded pistols sliding around their dashboards, and almost every Yemeni male past puberty wears the *jambiya*, a huge curved dagger tucked into a broad waistband.

And if Yemen did not have enough on its hands with its surfeit of weapons, it also had a drugs problem. Not the pill-popping or hypodermic-needle sort, but a narcotic leaf called *qat*. Yemenis chew it by the bundle, sending them into a sort of hallucinogenic torpor by five in the afternoon. Personally, I could not see the attraction: it looked and tasted like a privet hedge. But a lot of Yemenis swore by it, blowing their house-hold budget on the leaf and doing very little from noon until dusk. The president had publicly condemned the practice and tried to stop government employees from chewing the leaf, but with limited success. But one Western diplomat told me he believed *qat* got an unfairly bad press. 'If people were not getting together to chew *qat* every afternoon,' he said, 'there would probably be a lot more arguments and a lot more bloodshed.'

To complete the picture, Yemen in the late 1990s was start-ing to get a reputation for kidnapping. At first, it was all pretty benign. A tribe would seize a Western hostage, often an oil worker but occasionally a tourist or two, and use them as bargaining chips to demand economic concessions from the government. The hostages would be treated as honoured guests, lavished with plates of mutton and rice and generally made as comfortable as possible while negotiations went on nearby. What usually happened was that the Interior Ministry would quickly encircle the tribe with the hostage, sending in tanks and troops, but not too close. Someone from Yemen's capital, Sana'a, would then be dispatched to open negotiations with the tribal chief or his representative. These would drag on for days, extended by lengthy *qat* sessions in the afternoons. The tribe would demand a new road, a school or a greater share of the oil that was being piped across its land. Eventually a deal would be struck, the hostages would say their goodbyes and be taken to a waiting helicopter for the flight back to the capital, a public thank-you to the Yemeni government and a final car journey to their country's embassy. Often the newly released hostages would be given parting gifts by their captors and one British couple was even presented – with no hint of irony – with a pair of hand-crafted shotguns.

But of course nobody ever knew for certain how the kidnappings would be resolved, and in April 1998 the Mitchell family from Britain became the latest victims. It takes about six hours to drive from mountainous Sana'a to the steamy Indian Ocean port of Aden. The road they were on begins in the dusty suburbs of the capital, where the city's ancient white mud and stucco walls give way to a barren black landscape of laval hills. One hour out of Sana'a the road is bisected by a scruffy military checkpoint manned by wary soldiers in a variety of uniforms, their lone sentry hut standing beside concrete-filled oil drums and home-made 'stingers', a row of spikes that can be dragged across the tarmac in a hurry to stop a speeding car. Beyond the checkpoint the road starts to descend sharply through a mountain pass, down to a hazy, sun-baked valley. Just before the town of Ma'abar the road curves sharply between two rocky promontories and levels out. There is little traffic; this part of the road is often deserted. It was here that the Mitchells were attacked by the Bani Dabyan tribe as they drove north from Aden, about to go on leave.

As their car emerged from the mountain pass, the family noticed a four-wheel-drive jeep suddenly swerve across the road in front of them, blocking their path. A Yemeni man got out carrying an AK-47 assault rifle and fired it in the air. It was obvious he wanted them to stop. When the Mitchells got out, another gunman struck David Mitchell, the forty-eight-year-old father, with the butt of his gun as they bundled him, his wife Carolyn and their fourteen-year-old son Ben into their vehicle. The Yemenis then drove off the road, bouncing over the rough ground, taking them eastwards into the law-less land of the Bani Dabyan tribe.

In fact it was a case of mistaken identity: the kidnappers had been after the British Consul in Aden, David Pearce, and had been confused by Mr Mitchell working for the British Council (the two English words would have sounded identical to a Yemeni). A few days earlier the gunmen had tried to seize David Pearce on the outskirts of the capital by forcing him off the road and into their car, but he had simply driven his jeep straight at their car, hitting one of their passenger doors. One of his would-be kidnappers had leapt on to the back of Pearce's jeep and hung on until Pearce managed to throw him off by swerving; in the meantime this conveniently prevented his fellow tribesmen from opening fire on the British diplomat as he drove off to safety.

In the summer of 1998 Britons could still get a visa on arrival in Yemen, so after suggesting to the BBC that this was a story worth covering I flew down to Sana'a, bought my visa for thirty pounds and, since no one asked, neglected to tell anyone I was a journalist. I had my own digital-camera kit, purchased from London's Tottenham Court Road the year before, since I was not yet grand enough to merit my own cameraman. While the negotiations for the Mitchells' release dragged on, I decided to film as much as I could to explain the phenomenon of kidnapping in Yemen. In fact what I really needed was an interview with a kidnapper – but without being kidnapped myself. With the help of a friend at the embassy I hired the most ideal fixer any journalist could wish for. She was a former TV presenter with a face that opened doors wherever she went, she was the second wife of someone important in the government and hence well connected, and she had time on her hands and was bored out of her mind in Sana'a, so was keen for some adventure. She was also rich enough to refuse payment. I trusted her immediately. I will call her Lubna.

With Lubna in the back seat of the taxi and me in the front (it was emphatically not the done thing to sit together unless you were married or related), we charmed our way through the government checkpoint on the outskirts of the capital with my camera kit stowed beneath the seat. We then filmed the exact point on the road where the Mitchells had been kidnapped, taking advice from local Yemenis. In the town of Ma'abar we did not have to look far to find a shop selling machine guns by the van load. To illustrate the poor state of the local infrastructure I only had to point the camera at the street, which was a river of shallow mud after a recent cloudburst. The drains had overflowed and there was a foul stench in the air.

We then had to choose our *rafiq*, our companion from a local tribe who would vouch on his honour to protect us. Lubna was suspicious of the first two we talked to. 'Why?' I asked. 'Because I can see it in the way they are looking at you, ya Frank. They would sell you to the kidnappers the first chance they get.' Lubna went through Ma'abar marketplace like a housewife selecting ripe fruit, eyeing up, evaluating and dismissing possible guides for our trip. Eventually we chose two honest-looking men and we set off eastwards in their Toyota Land Cruiser, their Kalashnikov rifles resting between their knees.

Within minutes we had left the relative civilization of Ma'abar behind; the going grew progressively rougher, the stony scenery ever bleaker and the skies darker. Eventually we pulled up at a mud-walled fortress-like building surrounded by a grove of fruit trees. Our guides went in to investigate, then came out with the owner. He was a young man dressed immaculately in the Yemeni style, with clean shirt, jacket, black-and-white chequered scarf draped around his shoulders and a wraparound embroidered *futa* (lunghi) above an expensive-looking pair of leather sandals.

'Welcome, welcome, I am Faris. I am so sorry that my father cannot be here to welcome you as our guest,' said the young man in Arabic, 'but please, I hope you will accept some fresh oranges from our family orchard.' The pleasantries over, I set up the camera and tripod and got down to asking him about kidnapping. Our two guides had hinted at his possible involvement in this murky business.

'Well, yes,' said Faris, stroking his close-cropped beard. 'I myself kidnapped some tourists last year. I think they were Belgian – or were they Italian? I forget. The government promised us a new road and some money so I released the tourists. But . . .' he sighed and picked up an orange, turning it in his hand '. . . the government never delivered on its promise and so now I am looking to kidnap again.' Faris looked up with a grin like the wolf from Little Red Riding Hood and added, 'In fact I would happily kidnap you now, only I see you are well protected!' Only then did I notice that our two guides/protectors had manoeuvred themselves ever so subtly into positions where they had a clear field of fire towards Faris while avoiding Lubna and me. Their fingers rested lightly on their Kalashnikovs and their faces betrayed no emotion. This, I thought, must be daily fare for the people who live out here.

We parted with smiles and drove quickly back to the main Aden–Sana'a road, passing fields of *qat* bushes on the way. It was typical of Yemeni hospitality that our guides would accept no payment other than for the petrol. We stopped at a roadside café to make a call to Sana'a, and learned that after seventeen days in captivity the Mitchell family had been released unharmed and were on their way back by helicopter. We raced back to the capital, arriving just in time for me to film their convoy of cars sweeping through the gates of the British ambassador's residence after dark. Exhausted as they must have been, they were kind enough to give me and Channel 4 an impromptu interview. I passed the footage I had shot to a woman from the Consulate who was accompanying the Mitchells back home on the morning flight. We celebrated that night in the embassy bar, downing steak, chips and lager behind the high walls of the compound. The next day I had the pleasure of sitting back in my hotel room and watching my footage go out at the top of each hour on BBC World.

The next kidnapping in Yemen was to be a very different affair. In December 1998 a party of nineteen Western tourists, mostly from Britain, set off on a package-holiday tour of Yemen, run by the company Explore Worldwide. They were cultural tourists, mainly middle-aged men and women who were prepared to pay good money – £1,300 a head – for a well-organized fifteen-day excursion round remote sites in an unusual destination. But what should have been the holiday of a lifetime turned into a truly terrifying ordeal. Yemen is not a rich country and outside the main cities the roads are often dirt tracks navigable only by sturdy four-wheel-drive jeeps. So the Explore party left Sana'a in a convoy of five four-wheel-drive jeeps driven by men who knew the country well. They visited the pre-Islamic Sabaean temple of Mar'ib, where legend has it that King Solomon met the Queen of Sheba, then headed south towards Aden. Along the way, the convoy passed through a wild and lonely corner of the province of Abyan and it was there that their ambushers lay in wait.

At around eleven o'clock on the morning of 28 December, as the convoy of tourists descended a gentle dip in the road, the driver of the lead jeep saw several vehicles stopped up ahead. The next thing he and his passengers heard was shots ringing out over their heads. They were being ordered to stop by a group of around twenty men armed with machine guns and rocket-propelled grenades; the kidnappers had blocked the convoy and were now forcing it off the road and into the mountains. Once again, Western tourists were being kidnapped in Yemen. But this time was different. The kidnappers were not hospitable tribesmen with an economic grudge against the government. They were Islamist rebels, part of a banned organization calling itself the Aden-Abyan Islamic Army, and unlike most Yemenis they had a violent hatred of Westerners.

The leader of the organization was also running the kidnap. He was a small, wiry man called Abu'l Hassan Al-Mihdar. (Three years later a distant relative of his became one of the nineteen suicide hijackers who flew planes at US cities on 11 September 2001.) Al-Mihdar and his men forced the tourists off the road and drove them deep into the black, volcanic landscape, trying to put as much distance as possible between them and the road, from where government troops would surely come looking for them. In fact the lead vehicle in the tourists' convoy, containing the Explore guide and two tourists, had managed to break away and they raised the alarm in Aden. As the kidnapped tourists spent their first night in captivity, eating a meagre meal beneath the stars, the lead kidnapper, Al-Mihdar, phoned Abu Hamza, the imam of Finsbury Park Mosque in London, to say that he had 'captured some infidels' and he needed to discuss what to do with them. They had no idea that every word of their conversation was being recorded by GCHQ, the British government's secret listening station.

Since most of the captives were British, the Ambassador, Vic Henderson, went to see the notoriously hardline Yemeni Interior Minister, Mohammed Al Arab, in Sana'a to re-emphasize the Foreign Office's request that the situation be resolved peacefully, by negotiation, and not by a shoot-out. The safety of the hostages had to come first. 'Ah,' said the Interior Minister. 'Well, in fact I have some news for you. There has been some shooting and there have been some casualties.'

It was a bloodbath. Once the Yemeni security forces had located the terrorists' hideout they became convinced that the hostages were about to be executed, so they went in guns blazing. Accounts differ over who fired first. Yemen says the terrorists started the gun battle, but the hostages later told me it was their 'rescuers', the Yemeni army. The net result was that out of sixteen Western tourists, four were killed, while another, an American woman, was shot in the thigh, according to the hospital in Aden. A policeman and two of the kidnappers were also killed and the remainder arrested, including their ringleader, Al-Mihdar.

While the survivors were being flown westwards by helicopter to Aden I was touching down in the same city on a flight from Dubai, dispatched there once again by the BBC's tireless Malcolm Downing, the Foreign Assignments Editor, although since I was a humble stringer I was still on my own without producer or BBC camera crew.

Driving into Aden past the old Russian apartment blocks, I braced myself for one of the hardest assignments of my career. I now had to interview the British survivors of this ordeal, some of whom had lost loved ones, and play the interview back to London over the phone in time to make the six o'clock news. How would they react? What if the last thing they wanted right now was to talk to some reporter? As I walked into the lobby of the Aden Movenpick hotel I had my answer. The survivors were huddled in a corner of the adjacent bar, nursing beers and strong drinks, giving me wary looks. One of them even told me to go away. I could hardly blame them, but what I did not know was that earlier that afternoon a TV crew from Lebanon had gone round shoving a camera in their faces and saying they were from the BBC. I was starting from a disadvantage here. Just then a well-built man in their group spoke up. 'I'll talk to you,' he said. 'I want people to know what happened to me and my wife.'

Lawrence Whitehouse was a schoolteacher from Hampshire. He and his wife Margaret had come on this trip to see something of another culture, to broaden their horizons. They had left the Christmas tree and the presents at home and flown to Yemen with Explore Worldwide. Everything had been going well, he said as we sat in a dark corner of the bar, speaking into my digital minidisk, and they had been looking forward to visiting more of this historically rich country. But then of course it had turned into an ordeal. Their kidnappers were horrible, horrible men, he said, who showed no interest in talking to their captives. One of the tourists had brought with him an English translation of the Koran in an attempt to learn more about Islam, but Al-Mihdar had refused to enter into a discussion with him, treating him and his fellow captives as infidels worthy of contempt. When the botched rescue attempt began, Lawrence Whitehouse said the terrorist guarding him and his wife had tried to use them as human shields. Margaret had been hit by gunfire. Outnumbered, the terrorists tried to escape, but by then it was too late for Margaret. She had died in Lawrence's arms.

At that moment there was a commotion in the lobby: the tour group's suitcases had arrived and were being unloaded. 'That's my wife's suitcase,' said Lawrence, who knew he would be returning home to an empty house and all those unwrapped Christmas presents.

That night, upstairs in the privacy of my hotel room, I cried and cried. I did not usually allow myself to get emotionally involved in the stories I was covering but I think everyone has their breaking point. Why would anyone want to hurt innocent cultural tourists this way? I asked myself. It was my first brush with Islamist terrorism and an introduction to the sheer ruthlessness of those who commit murder in God's name.

The Yemeni authorities wanted the freed hostages to stay and give detailed statements, but the British Consul-General, David Pearce, worked tirelessly to get them repatriated as fast as possible. I flew with the survivors up to Sana'a, where I spent the last night of 1998 on the phone in my hotel room doing 'two-ways', down-the-line interviews for various BBC programmes, though I did wonder who would be listening at that time of year. Marooned in the Yemeni capital on New Year's Day, I spent the morning in the old town listening to Yemenis wringing their hands in apology over what had happened. They were appalled at what their fellow country-men had done to these tourists, they said. It had brought 'ayb, shame, upon their country.

Meanwhile, David Pearce had been negotiating to get the bodies of the dead Britons flown back to Britain, but the Yemeni authorities would only agree to release them if an autopsy was carried out on their soil, the bullets were all extracted and if he was present to watch. Pearce described it as the most gruesome moment of his diplomatic career. 'I had to go to the mortuary, where I was surrounded by dead bodies,' he told me. 'There were about fourteen corpses in all. Some of them had been there for ages and were all inter-twined, with leathery skin, but one was of a recently killed Yemeni man who was missing half his head and whose eyes were staring out at me. There was this horrible smell. When the doctor strolled in, dressed in a *futa* and open shirt, he used a coat hanger and his bare hands – no gloves – to remove the bullets. Some of the bullet tracks ran upwards through the bodies, implying that at least some had been fired by the terrorists as they cowered on the ground, shooting upwards at their hostages who they were using as human shields. But other bullets had hit from other directions, suggesting they could have been fired by the advancing Yemeni security forces. After this,' said Pearce, 'I was diagnosed with post-traumatic stress disorder when I returned to the UK.'

But there turned out to be yet another twist to this tale. Unknown to the Foreign Office, the police in Aden had arrested several British Muslims of Asian origin and two Algerians a few days earlier on suspicion of terrorism. Several other wanted men, including three Britons, were said to be on the run in the wilds of Abyan province. Yemen claimed that the arrested men had been caught red-handed with explosives and firearms, plotting to blow up three Western targets in Aden. According to the authorities, these targets included the British Consulate (where David Pearce was staying with his family), the Anglican church and the Aden Movenpick hotel, where I was now staying. The men insisted they were tourists, not terrorists, although they were having difficulty explaining why they reportedly had a Global Positioning System with them, as well as *jihadi* films showing four of them holding automatic weapons in Albania the previous year. The Yemen authorities said they had arrested them after they crashed a police checkpoint at midnight on 23 December with weapons and explosives in the boot of their car, and following police raids on two hotels and a villa. The Yemeni government went further, asserting that these mostly British Muslims had been sent to Yemen to wage violent *jihad* by a man named Abu Hamza Al-Masri, the now infamous hook-handed imam of Finsbury Park mosque in north London, and that Al-Mihdar and his group had carried out the kidnapping to put pressure on the Yemeni government to release the British Muslims.

Back in London, Abu Hamza Al-Masri did not deny that he

had been in contact by satellite phone with the lead kidnapper, Al-Mihdar. Nor did he deny that one of those on the run from the Yemeni authorities was his son, Mohammed Kamel, and another his stepson, Mohsen Ghailan, but he dismissed having anything to do with terrorism. The Finsbury Park imam did, however, issue a communiqué on 30 December on behalf of Al-Mihdar's Aden-Abyan Islamic Army, and his organization The Supporters of Shari'ah had advertised what it called 'military training for brothers', featuring a picture of a hand grenade. Three weeks later Abu Hamza held a press conference in London warning all Westerners to leave Yemen and calling for the overthrow of the Yemeni government. Doubtless he would have thought twice about doing all this in the more draconian atmosphere of Britain after the London bombings of July 2005, but by then he was in Belmarsh prison awaiting trial and extradition to the US.

Britain's multi-cultural society was no doubt an alien concept to the jailers of Aden Central Police Station in December 1998. Yes, the men they had in custody claimed they were British, but they looked like Pakistanis so surely they were Pakistanis. At first, the local police chief, General Muhammad Turaik, insisted his captives were carrying forged British passports and he asked the British embassy to check them out. A few urgent calls to London established that they were British and it suddenly became a huge story. In London journalists swarmed round Finsbury Park mosque, where Abu Hamza Al-Masri started to become a media personality.

I was immediately ordered back to Aden from Dubai, but since there were no connecting flights that day I had to disembark in Sana'a at dawn then hire a taxi for the scenic but nerve-racking six-hour drive across the country to Aden. It had been less than a year since the Mitchell family had been kidnapped on this road and less than a month since the murderous kidnapping of the tourists, so I spent an uneasy journey, hunkered down in the back seat with my Arab *shemagh* headscarf concealing my face in the hope that anyone looking in would assume I was a Yemeni passenger. My one consolation was the sight of some exotic Rift Valley birds in the south: hornbills and hamerkops that lived here, close to the Red Sea and the coast of Africa.

There was no media access to the Britons in Aden, but through diplomats and their lawyers we learned that the men claimed to have been mistreated in prison and were protesting their innocence. The British government was now in an awkward position. If the Yemeni government's accusations were true then here were several dangerous British terrorists, bent on killing Westerners in Yemen, dispatched on their mission by a London imam. But according to British detectives sent by the Anti-Terrorist Branch, the Yemeni authorities had made almost every mistake in the book. They said no forensic or fibre analysis had been done at the scene of arrest, the men had been physically abused in custody, and the prosecution's case seemed to rest largely on confessions made under duress. In other words, whatever the men had or had not been doing in Yemen, this case would not have stood up in a British court of law. There was a brief outcry about this in Britain, but the trial went ahead and in August 1999 a panel of three judges in Aden convicted the men, including Abu Hamza Al-Masri's son-in-law Mohammed Kamel, of participation in acts of terrorism. Kamel was sentenced to three years in prison, Ghailan to seven years, while the others also got varying jail terms.

As for the lead kidnapper, Abu'l Hassan Al-Mihdar, he was completely unrepentant. On 13 January 1999 I attended his first appearance in court in the exotically named fishing port of Zinjibar, down on Yemen's steamy Indian Ocean coast. Guarded by nervous soldiers manning heavy machine guns mounted on pick-up trucks, he emerged in handcuffs and a clean shirt from a windowless police van. I called out to him in Arabic to ask if he considered himself innocent or guilty – a dumb question, I know, but it would add a little colour to my next radio broadcast. He replied that only God could judge him.

Inside the courthouse he was charged with kidnapping, highway robbery, premeditated murder, sabotage and forming an armed group – the Aden-Abyan Islamic Army – but in fact he dominated proceedings, telling the rather timid judge that he should be ashamed of himself and that God had guided him on this righteous path to kidnapping. 'God sent them to us,' he shouted, referring to the Western tourists, 'these sons of pigs and monkeys. We fought in Afghanistan and Chechnya and we will continue the struggle until the establishment of an Islamic state in Yemen.' But his prowess in court did not impress the Yemeni government. Al-Mihdar was sentenced to death and executed that October, along with three of his accomplices, while a fourth member of his gang was given a twenty-year jail sentence. Yemen continued to demand in vain the extradition from Britain of the Finsbury Park imam, Abu Hamza Al-Masri, even though there was no extradition treaty between the two countries. Fed up with the kidnappings that had given his country such a bad reputation, President Saleh decreed that from now on anyone committing armed kidnap would automatically be executed, without any negotiation. Kidnapping in Yemen dropped off dramatically: between 1996 and 1999 a total of 140 foreigners had been seized, an average of thirty-five a year, but by 2000 that annual figure dropped to just eight. At the peak of the phenomenon in 1997 a total of forty-three foreign tourists were kidnapped; in 2001 just two were taken and then released.

All this may have been taking place on the same Arabian Peninsula as Dubai, but it was a world away from our cosy life in the villa. While I was away on these trips, Amanda was adapting quickly to life as an expat mother and had been getting to know our neighbours. There were Tim and Sian, both accountants from Surrey; Birgit, a timid German married to a devout Tunisian; and Marco, an Italian newly married to a taciturn German girl. Marco told us proudly about his fantastic banking salary, his bright-red Mercedes sat gleaming outside their villa and their dining table was always set perfectly for guests. Then one day, seemingly without warning, his wife left him and he was devastated.

By early 1999 Amanda was eight months pregnant with our second child, and I was recalled from Aden for duties closer to home. On the day before Sasha was born we strolled between Dubai's Jumeirah Beach Hotel and the soon-to-be-opened Burj Al-Arab Hotel. The latter was designed to resemble a billowing Arab sail, but when Amanda stood in front of it the similarity was striking: it mirrored her pregnant contours perfectly.

Once again, we pulled up at the doors of the hospital in a hurry. 'The anaesthetist will be with you soon, he's just busy with someone right now,' we were told. But the anaesthetist never showed up and Amanda gave birth without an epidural. One of the most frighteningly impotent moments of my life was being shouted at by the midwife to hold Amanda down as she screamed and writhed on the bed and the South African nurses yelled into the corridor, 'Where's that bloody anaesthetist!' Sasha was born a perfectly healthy baby, although not a day too soon. Having run out of food in the womb she had started trying to nibble her own arms.

In the early summer of 1999 I got a call from the United Arab Emirates Ministry of Information up the coast in Abu Dhabi. Would I like to visit the UAE's humanitarian mission in the Balkans? I jumped at the chance. I had been to Yugoslavia a few times in the eighties, but it was a very different picture in the Balkans now. Slovenia had slunk quietly off to its own sovereignty before anyone noticed,

Croatia had fought for its independence from Belgrade and there had been carnage in Bosnia-Herzegovina in the mid-nineties. Now the Serbs of Kosovo seemed to have embarked on wholesale ethnic cleansing to drive out the Kosovars, the ethnic Albanians, from their homes. This time the West appeared determined to intervene before it was too late. Serb convoys were bombed by NATO planes, while refugee camps were set up just across the border in Albania. But since the Kosovars were Muslims their plight struck a chord with Arabs, especially in the Gulf where vast sums are donated in charity to Islamic causes. The UAE had gone one step further, setting up its own refugee camp, run, protected and patrolled by the UAE Army.

I was not the only Gulf-based journalist going on this trip. About a dozen others had been rounded up, mostly Indian expatriates working as staff writers on local newspapers. They looked very apprehensive as we boarded an ageing Russian Ilyushin jet for the flight up to the Balkans. This was not at all what they had signed up for, accustomed as they were to writing cosy articles about local news in Abu Dhabi, where danger is almost unheard of. Sure enough, the runway at Tirana airport was like a scene from the film *Apocalypse Now*, with US Army Apache helicopter gunships clattering through the sky, and military transport aircraft disgorging soldiers and pallets of ammunition. The journalists' faces fell even further when, on arriving in the Balkans, it was announced that due to bandits it was too dangerous to reach the refugee camp by road, so we would now be boarding two UAE Air Force Puma helicopters for the flight up to Kukes in northeast Albania. It was a breathtaking, stomach-turning forty-five-minute flight through narrow alpine ravines and up over craggy ridges, and the Emirati pilots were superb.

Down on the ground, the UAE camp was very impressive. Not for nothing was it known amongst the journalists as 'the Gucci camp'. It had everything: clean, comfortable tents, three meals a day – including crates of fresh chickens prepared and cooked by legions of Indian workers flown up from the Gulf. I particularly enjoyed telling my BBC colleagues this when I visited them in their spartan lodgings by the lake, where I found veteran correspondent Feargal Keane boiling up some starchy spag bol for the nth day in a row. 'Must dash,' I said. 'It's roast lamb tonight. Can't be late.'

So organized was the UAE camp that it even had a telephone mast erected by engineers from Abu Dhabi so we could all use our UAE mobile phones in Albania for the cost of a local call. In the First Aid section refugees were lining up to be treated by army medics, some of whom were Arab women in camouflage uniform and headscarves. I was told they would soon be introducing 'telemedicine', whereby doctors back in Abu Dhabi would perform operations by remote-control video link. The camp also had a makeshift mosque, complete with long-bearded imam who oversaw the slitting of sheep's throats to ensure it was done according to Islamic tradition and the meat was halal. Supplies and workers were flown in regularly by C-130 transport plane to the nearby Sheikh Zayed airstrip, built by UAE engineers on almost the only flat bit of land. But above all, the camp had good security. The local Albanian bandits, all armed with AK-47s, had a fearsome reputation for armed robbery and rape. A story was doing the rounds of how a group had broken into the nearby Italian camp and successfully abducted a Kosovan girl at gunpoint. When bandits tried it on at the UAE camp while I was there they were vigorously rebuffed; an army patrol scrambled immediately and caught them just outside the fence. I was told they handed the men over to the local Albanian police, who promptly let them go.

But I was only at the UAE camp long enough to get a flavour of the whole operation. I would have liked to stay on to see the end of the story, to see the Kosovar refugees getting repatriated and returning to the homes they had been driven out of across the border. But, as I almost forgot, I was supposed to be covering the Gulf for BBC News and already an interesting story beckoned, one which I had more than a passing interest in.

At eighty-nine years of age, Wilfred Thesiger was coming back to the Gulf for what could be his final visit. The man who had first inspired me to come to this region, over tea with my mother in his Chelsea flat twenty-two years earlier, was coming to the UAE to promote a newly published book of his photographs of a vanished Arabia. Remarkably, Bin Kabina and Bin Ghabaisha, the men who had travelled with Thesiger on his gruelling treks across the Empty Quarter of Arabia half a century ago, were still around. I found them sprawled on sofas in the air-conditioned lobby of a five-star hotel in Dubai, beneath Thesiger's black-and-white portrait photos of them as the young boys they once were. It was an extraordinary juxtaposition of two worlds. In a photo above them stood a dark-skinned Arab boy, his long unkempt black hair falling over his shoulders and his eyes glowering at the camera. He was dressed in rags but was naked from the waist up, his sinewy arm clutching an ancient rifle, while a line of empty dunes stretched infinitely past him. And now, on the cusp of the Millennium, that same person sat on the couch, a venerable old man with grey beard, turban and black kohl antimony painted around his eyes in the manner of some desert traditionalists. Thesiger sat between his two old companions, his eyesight, his hearing and his Arabic all failing now, but still able to trade stories of their harsh times on those great desert crossings in the forties and fifties.

Thesiger appeared rather bewildered by all the people who milled around him and I could not be certain that he remembered who I was. For such an accomplished photographer he seemed surprisingly disconcerted by the flash of cameras going off around him and I remembered how, when I first went to see him on my own, he had said, 'If we're going to have a decent conversation you're going to have to put that camera down and stop taking my photograph!' Heaven knows what he thought now of my digital video camera and tripod for the mini-documentary I was making about him for BBC News.

But when the then ruler of UAE, Sheikh Zayed Al-Nahyan, invited Thesiger to visit him in his palace in Abu Dhabi, I was allowed to accompany him, along with his publisher, Iain Fairservice. We drove in a convoy of air-conditioned limos from his hotel to the palace gates, but at the first security checkpoint there was a problem. Men with walkie-talkies waved their arms and wore troubled expressions. The sheikh was not yet ready to receive him, so would we please return to our hotel and wait for the summons. Thesiger, who had spent a lifetime railing against almost every mechanical invention, was already complaining about the car's air-conditioning. 'Can't we switch that infernal thing off?' he demanded. It was June and 45°C in the shade outside so the driver thought he was insane. Thesiger refused to go back to his hotel, demanding to be allowed to sit beneath a date palm instead. This sent the sheikh's protocol people into a complete flap; they had never seen a guest get out of a car at the gates.

Eventually our convoy was waved through and we trooped into a large ornate reception room to meet the oldest living ruler in the Middle East, and Thesiger cheered up. Sheikh Zayed was almost the same age as him and they had hunted together in the desert in the 1940s when Abu Dhabi was part of what was known as 'the Trucial States'. Dirt poor then, with nothing but a mud-walled fort and a jumble of fisher-men's huts, it was incredible to think that since the discovery of oil and independence from Britain in 1971, Abu Dhabi had morphed into one of the richest places in the world.

Thesiger and the sheikh quickly began to reminisce about old times. Sheikh Zayed, who had been ruler of Abu Dhabi for thirty-eight years, reminded his guest of the time they had gone hunting together and shot a rabbit, which the sheikh then threw to his dogs as a reward. But in those lean times, he said that Thesiger had been so hungry that he had snatched it back and eaten it himself. The whole room laughed at this, then Sheikh Zayed caught my eye and his son Sheikh Mohammed, then the UAE Chief of Defence Staff, introduced me (we had shared a washbasin at the UAE's 'Gucci camp' in the Balkans only the month before). When I told Sheikh Zayed that both my daughters had been born in Dubai he declared they should be given UAE nationality. With his heavily hooded eyes and craggy desert features, it was hard to tell if the old sheikh was being serious or not; I decided he was joking. Since then I have often wondered if I should not perhaps have taken him up on the offer and given Melissa and Sasha a headstart in life with a prime piece of real estate on the fastest developing stretch of coastline in the Middle East.

There was one last duty to perform with Thesiger in order to complete the film: I needed to interview him in his favourite milieu, the desert. This was no easy task in the sweltering heat of June, but the old explorer was more than up to it. Driven out to the dunes by his indefatigable publisher, we marched up the nearest sand dune in the full hammer heat of midday. Thesiger was dressed in a three-piece woollen English suit but he refused to make any concessions to the weather, remaining buttoned up all the way as he strode with the aid of a stick up through the soft red sand. His refrain was the same as it had been when I first met him all those years ago in 1977: the desert Bedu were a great and noble people ruined by oil; the world he had once known was gone for ever. It made for a sad and poignant interview, all the more so since not long afterwards he died in a Surrey nursing home, far from the deserts of Arabia or the dry bushland of northern Kenya where he made his home for so many years.

I have the greatest respect for Thesiger's skills in exploration, narrative description and photography, and, above all, his endurance in appalling conditions. I was lucky to have known him and am grateful that he gave me so much time, but I never found him a particularly warm personality and had he not done the journeys he did I doubt we would have been friends. In fact we did argue once, about Oman. He was critical of the transformation of a backward sultanate into a relatively modern, peaceful country with schools, roads and hospitals. I said I was convinced that most Omanis were happier now than before; Thesiger, I suspected, would have preferred them to remain in picturesque poverty. But beneath his gruff exterior he did have a sense of humour. When I took him to tea at the Royal Overseas League in London in the 1980s he asked me to open one of those tiny, fiddly UHT milk cartons. After wrestling with the seal for some minutes it finally burst all over my lap. I cursed, then apologized, but Thesiger smiled knowingly and said, 'It's all right, I knew that would happen. That's why I passed it to you.'

At the end of 1999 the job of BBC Middle East Correspondent in Cairo came up for grabs, and Amanda suggested I should go for it. Although our life in the Gulf was idyllic it was far from secure financially, and we had two very small children to support – Sasha and Melissa were born just fourteen months apart. The only guaranteed income I had was a small monthly stipend from *The Economist*, which I occasionally wrote for. If I went on holiday – or more worryingly, if stories simply dried up – I did not get paid. I was thirty-eight years old, and after five years of freelancing we decided it was time I grew up and got a salaried job with the BBC. An Egyptian friend, Ossama Nasser, warned me that Cairo was no place for a young family, especially after the soft life in Dubai, but we were deaf to his advice. I flew to London and waltzed through the interview. 'What would you do,' asked one of the interviewers, 'if you got a call saying you could do any story anywhere in the Middle East and you had an unlimited budget?' 'I would assume it was a wrong number,' I replied. Perhaps because I had taken such a big gamble in going out to Dubai in the first place and then watched it pay off, I now had a new-found confidence. I came out of the interview and went off to the cinema in the West End, but my mobile rang before I had even bought the ticket: the Cairo job was mine.

Down in Dubai, there was one final story to report before we packed up and moved to Egypt. On Christmas Eve 1999 a hijacked Indian passenger plane landed at a UAE military airfield in the desert outside Dubai. There were over a hundred terrified passengers on board and at first no one was quite sure who the terrorists were or what they wanted. For me, as the Gulf correspondent there on the spot, it was a stringer's dream: riding the wave of a fast-moving story and getting paid for every single interview I did on air. But it was also a struggle to manage on my own, relying on my mobile phone to gather the latest news from my sources in the UAE government and then immediately calling London to do the next interview. By midnight I had tracked down the airfield, talked my way through security and was camped out on a sand dune, watching the plane on the tarmac through binoculars with one hand while giving a live commentary for BBC World on my mobile. If anyone had seen me there it would have looked as if I was calling in an air strike. I could see a set of mobile steps being brought up to the plane and some passengers getting off; the UAE Ministry of Information initially thought the hijackers were Sikhs, but in fact it was a complex tale with connections to Al-Qaeda. It turned out that the hijackers were demanding the release of several Islamist prisoners in Indian jails, including one Omar Said Shaikh, a graduate of the London School of Economics. The plane was allowed to fly on to Afghanistan, where negotiations with the Indian government resulted in the release of Shaikh. Within three years he had gone on to lure the

Wall Street Journal reporter Daniel Pearl into being kidnapped by Al-Qaeda supporters in Pakistan, where a grisly video showed him being held in an orange Guantanamo Bay-style jumpsuit then beheaded on camera. It was to set a hideous precedent for future kidnappings by Islamists of Western contractors in Iraq.

After Dubai, Cairo was a shock. To go from a squeaky-clean emirate of 700,000 people to the largest city in Africa and the Middle East was never going to be easy, but we managed to pick the worst day to travel. Our Egyptair flight coincided with the day expatriate Egyptian teachers in the Gulf were returning home for their holidays. The plane was crammed to the brim with electrical goods, all heading for the kitchens and living rooms of Cairo and beyond. Customs at the other end was a vision of hell, with chain-smoking passengers and customs officers shouting at each other at the tops of their voices. Our exhausted little family joined a queue that seemed to be funnelling towards an exit gate, only to find it peter out as the immigration official went off on a break and we had to start all over again. Already we could taste the dust in our lungs.

But just as it all seemed too much, a balding man in seventies retro sunglasses came to our aid. It was Raouf (pronounced like a dog barking), the BBC Cairo office driver. He had been an Egyptian army driver in the 1973 October war in the Sinai and was completely unfazed by the chaos all around us. Throughout our years in Cairo he proved to be a godsend for our family and the friends who came to stay, fetching people from the airport at all hours, even driving us through the night all the way down to Sharm El Sheikh on an assignment, without ever once complaining. For me, Raouf typified the good soul and big heart that so many Egyptians have, with their innate desire to help and their profound need to see a guest in their country be truly happy. I am ashamed to say that when the pressures of work piled up I was often unable to match Raouf's boundless reserves of patience and good humour.

Everything about Cairo was different for me this time round. When I had lived there in the early eighties I had been a carefree undergraduate with no responsibilities, flat-sharing with friends, partying, flirting, exploring and sketching; Cairo had been one big wonderful playground. Since then the country's population had virtually doubled in size, going from forty-two to seventy million people in under twenty years, and I was back with a young family, with the added onus of running a BBC office, under the faintly pompous title of Cairo Bureau Chief. In practice this meant managing the half-dozen local Egyptian staff who, although all charming, gave me two weeks' grace then queued up to present me with their problems. One tendered her resignation because she was unhappy with her contract, another wanted better overtime pay, several wanted to be paid in hard currency, preferably dollars, instead of wobbly Egyptian pounds, while the Nubian messengers wanted the TV in their staffroom to show local soap operas instead of BBC World, of which they could not understand a word. Dealing with management issues like these was anathema to me and I could hardly wait to get going on my first assignment.

This loomed within days and it was to cover the visit of Pope John Paul II to Egypt in February 2000. It was to be a historic visit, taking in St Catherine's Monastery in the Sinai Peninsula, and it coincided with his papal drive to heal the differences between the world's three great monotheistic religions: Christianity, Islam and Judaism. Since the Polish pontiff was by now frail and in declining health there was much speculation about whether this trip would be his last, or even – hold the front page – if he would survive the trip at all.

Egypt has a sizeable minority of Coptic Christians numbering around 10 per cent of the population and in Cairo the streets to the airport were lined with flag-waving children chanting, 'John Paul Two! We love you!' The foreign press corps dutifully gathered at the airport to see him kiss the ground, at which point I was supposed to be giving a live, running commentary for BBC World TV. Unfortunately, the over-zealous security people had corralled us into an area from which we could see precisely nothing, so we had to be inventive. Egyptian state television was broadcasting the event live, so we got someone to watch it back in the office and give a running commentary on the phone to our producer beside me, who in turn whispered her commentary in my ear. By the time I told the viewers of the world what the Pope was doing they were hearing it third or fourth hand, but I hope they got the general idea.

From Cairo we all flew down to St Catherine's Monastery, a Greek Orthodox Christian retreat built into the mountains around what is believed to be the original burning bush of Moses fame. In the cool of the winter afternoon a hush descended on the assembled press corps as we waited in the orchard for the Pope to appear alongside the monastery's chief monk. It was to be a deeply spiritual moment and there was no sound except for the soft cooing of the palm doves. Suddenly the silence was broken by a very English public-school voice.

'All right, I admit it, I've cocked it up! Happy now?'

It was Julian Manion, the larger-than-life ITN reporter, arguing with his veteran and fearless cameraman, John Steele. 'Those two are like a married couple,' remarked a nearby journalist. 'They're inseparable and yet they never stop bickering.' It turned out that John had gone to great lengths to secure the best vantage point in the orchard, only to have Julian insist on relocating at the last minute. Having moved the camera, tripod and all their gear, they were promptly turfed out of their new position by an Egyptian security guard. The spiritual moment had most definitely passed.

Back in Cairo, all was not well on the home front. Amanda and I had chosen our flat when we came up from Dubai on a recce the previous year, and although it was luxurious by local standards its walls concealed a shambolic wiring system. We returned one afternoon and turned on the lights only to see the wall burst into flame. The prospect of a full-scale fire in our building terrified us since we lived on the eighteenth floor and once we had extinguished the flames we investigated a number of emergency plans, including buying three hundred feet of rope with which to lower ourselves down to the street far, far below. Another option was to phone our friends the Bin Ladens for a helicopter – I am being serious here, since one of Osama's entirely law-abiding and peaceful brothers lived in Cairo and his step-daughter went to the same nursery as our children; I enjoyed saying to Raouf on the school run, 'Do you see that girl over there getting out of the Land Cruiser? Well, guess who her uncle is!'

On top of the dodgy wiring, our daughters were struggling to cope with the local food. Both Melissa and Sasha, who at the time were aged just two and one, were at times very ill with food poisoning, which nearly scared Amanda into booking the three of them one-way fares back to London. For a while, though, we had the benefit of the Cairo branches of Sainsbury's, which everyone pronounced as 'San Zubairi's'. Although the produce on sale was very different from the diverse and squeaky-clean fare in the supermarkets of Dubai, it still offered Cairenes more choice than they had ever known, and cheaply too. But the project was doomed. Egyptian wholesalers were not happy about being undercut and rumours began to circulate that there was an Israeli connection; noisy protests were organized and soon someone issued an unofficial street *fatwa* that anyone buying food from Sainsbury's would be condemned to hell. Meanwhile food began disappearing out of the back door of outlets; the chain was haemorrhaging money. Before long the pride of

British retailing was admitting defeat and the young managers who had come out to Cairo to 'show Egyptians how it was done' were returning home under a cloud: Sainsbury's Egyptian venture had collapsed, reportedly costing the company close to £100 million.

There were, however, a lot of pleasant aspects about living in Cairo that offset the unhealthy pollution, perpetual noise and questionable food. The Egyptians were every bit as friendly and welcoming as I remembered them from my student days, the sun shone for most of the year, albeit through a haze of smog, and we had the gardens of the Marriott hotel just a short stroll away. The Marriott was a converted nineteenth-century Khedive's palace and one of our favourite pastimes was to spend an evening in its outdoor café, reclining on padded couches beneath palm trees decked in fairy lights, puffing on a *shisha*, sipping mint tea and savouring the warm night air and the ebb and flow of Arabic conversation. At times like this Amanda and I would congratulate ourselves on living here, but then all too soon I would be off on assignment again and she would be left to bring up these two blonde daughters of ours in a city that reverted to being strange and frustrating the moment I left for the airport. The life of a foreign correspondent can be very rewarding, but it is often not a lot of fun for the partner left behind.

My experience of most Arab governments is that they have often employed all the available machinery of state in an effort to put a positive spin on any bad news about what is going on in their countries. But a noble exception to this rule is Kuwait. Its highly efficient Ministry of Information actually invited me over to cover a bad news story. For me, this was unprecedented.

In early 2000, Kuwait had a serious drugs problem. In fact it probably still does, because the underlying causes have not changed: too much money chasing too little recreation, and an irresistible proximity to the smuggling routes from

Afghanistan, Iran and Pakistan in the East and the dealers and users of Europe in the West. According to official statistics there were at least 26,000 known drug-users in Kuwait, out of a population of less than two million. The government decided something must be done and in February of that year it started running a nationwide anti-narcotics campaign, which included posters everywhere of a popular Arab singer accompanied by the rather meaningless phrase, 'I too am with you.'

As part of the TV report I was making about the problem, I interviewed a jovial police brigadier who proudly displayed some of the objects used to conceal drugs – a radio, a pile of newspapers, an old shoe – all laid out on his enormous desk for my benefit. That night I went out on police patrol, filming the officers as they stopped and searched young Pakistani expatriates in a suburb of Kuwait City notorious for drug-dealing. They found nothing, but we arrived back at the police station just as a very stressed young man was being brought in. He was completely strung out on something and was lashing out with his feet at whoever came near him. 'We know him,' said one of the Kuwaiti officers. 'His father is some big shot in the government, but that's not going to stop us booking him!'

The next morning I was allowed to conduct the first interview by a Western journalist with an inmate of Kuwait's Central Prison. It was certainly a filming challenge as most of the prisoners did not want their faces shown. Since my film was going to be broadcast internationally on BBC World, anonymity was especially important for the foreign prisoners, most of whose families did not even know they were in jail and would be consumed with grief and shame if they found out from watching the evening news. In practice, this meant setting up the camera at knee height so the uniformed convicts could be seen milling around without us showing their faces. One exception was a twenty-something Kuwaiti heroin addict, who seemed happy to be interviewed in his cell, describing to me on camera how he had descended into addiction then a life of crime to support his habit. I could quite see how the government had no objection to this being broadcast as it was certainly a cautionary tale. There was nothing shocking about his prison conditions – he was probably better off here than on the street – but his windowless cell stank and there was an air of hopelessness about him. Yet this was nothing compared with what was to come.

As night fell I was driven down to the far south of Kuwait, past the oil fields and close to the Saudi border at Khafji. Here, in a rather basic villa by the sea, I was to witness a gathering of one of Kuwait's most secretive organizations: Narcotics Anonymous. There were about a dozen men of various ages, all Kuwaitis, wrapped up in scarves against the chill of the northern Gulf winter. One had an 'oud, an Arabian lute, which he strummed while he sang a mournful tune that they all joined in. They were very reluctant to be filmed, telling me I could only record the sound, but once I switched the camera off they queued up to tell me their stories. One had gone over to Iran and picked up an opium addiction there (over 3,500 Iranian border guards have lost their lives trying to stop drugs being smuggled in from Afghanistan and Pakistan). Another had become an addict in Riyadh, Saudi Arabia, of all places. In both cases it was boredom, just not having enough to do to fill the long, empty, bachelor evenings. But another addict, who spoke perfect English, told me how he had been completely 'clean' until he had gone to Cambridge to study. There, he said, he had tried hashish, but friends had persuaded him to experiment with harder drugs and by the time he came back to Kuwait he was addicted to heroin. He seemed to hold a grudge against Britain as a result. As I filmed him talking, his red-and-white chequered headscarf concealing his haggard face, it occurred to me that I could not see any rehabilitation or counselling taking place here. Still, I thought, as I left them to their mournful songs and the salty breeze that blew off the waters of the Gulf, at least they could console themselves with each other's company. In this intensely traditional, tribal society these were members of a secret, taboo tribe that could never show its face in public.

In the early summer of 2000 I flew down to the Asir mountains of southwest Saudi Arabia to make one of my more enjoyable films for BBC World: on Saudi tourism. For ten years I had been going to this region to explore the hill villages, with their fortress-like architecture and colonies of wild baboons. Now I was here to film French mountaineers from Chamonix setting up rock-climbing courses for Saudi teenagers, and I even tried out paragliding myself, jumping off a nine-thousand-foot ridge and doing a piece-to-camera as I soared amongst the eagles. I could hardly believe I was being paid to have so much fun.

From there I crossed over into Yemen to tackle a rather more sensitive story. The year 2000 was the tenth anniversary of unification between the old North and South Yemen and it had not been an entirely happy marriage. The two partners bickered over oil revenues and in 1994 they nearly tore each other apart in a short and nasty civil war, even trading Scud missiles with each other. But with the North victorious, the past was being put behind and I flew into Sana'a to find banners and bunting hanging from the ancient city walls. Men gathered in groups dancing the *bara'*, a traditional Yemeni dance that involves stamping the feet to the rapid beat of a drum while waving a curved dagger in the air and twirling around in the centre of an admiring, clapping circle. The best performers tend to be old men who learned it from their fathers and grandfathers.

I had been granted an interview with the president in his fortified palace on the outskirts of town. It was nearly a disaster. President Saleh insisted the interview would be conducted in Arabic and enquired if I needed an interpreter. Partly as a matter of personal pride and partly because I prefer to ask the questions myself, I replied that no, I would speak in Arabic. I knew that unification between North and South was the president's pet project, something he was very proud of, so to get him warmed up I decided to open by asking him what he thought was the main benefit of this unification. By the look that suddenly appeared on his moustachioed features, I might as well have asked him if he often wore girl's clothes as a child. 'What?!' he demanded, turning for an explanation to his official interpreter who had been retained for just such an emergency. It turned out that while the Arabic word I had used for 'benefit' was only slightly out, my question had come out as: 'So, what's the point of all this unification then?'

After that, I thought it best not to take any chances with a man who had not hung on to power in one of the more violent countries of the world by being nice to his enemies. The interpreter, Muhammed Sudam, was pressed into service and the rest of the interview was conducted through him.

But President Saleh was soon to have rather more important things to worry about than the subtle nuances of a BBC interview. Yemen and the US were forging an increasingly close military partnership, building on the low-key deployment of US military engineers to carry out de-mining projects in southern Yemen. The Commander of Centcom (US Central Command, based in Tampa, Florida), General Anthony Zinni, was keen to build on this relationship, and two months after my awkward interview with President Saleh one of the most modern ships in the US Navy steamed into Aden harbour for refuelling. The USS *Cole* was a guided missile destroyer with state-of-the-art communications equipment and it had berthed in what was supposed to be a friendly port. When sailors on deck noticed a small speedboat coming out towards them they at first assumed it was local traders hoping to sell some fresh produce – after all, the three men in the dinghy were waving up in greeting. Some of the Americans waved back. But the boat was packed with high explosives and was driven by fanatical suicide bombers directed by Al-Qaeda. When it came alongside the US warship it blew a hole so huge the ship nearly sank. Seventeen US sailors died that day, thirty were injured and the USS *Cole* had to be loaded ignominiously on to a Norwegian transport ship for the slow voyage round the Cape of Good Hope and back across the Atlantic to its US home port for major repairs. Washington demanded a full-scale investigation and full-scale cooperation, yet so murky was the plot that five years later there were still no full answers as to exactly who had hatched it and how.

Meanwhile we had been back in England for the summer holidays, spending an idyllic few days on the Isle of Wight with my parents, who had seen all too little of their new grandchildren. Coming from Cairo, we could not get over how green the landscape was, and the weeks away from the dust and smog of the Egyptian capital did wonders for our lungs. But up in London on a visit, a friend told me that there was a whispering campaign going on against me at Bush House, home of the BBC World Service. 'Frank Gardner's missing the big story in the Middle East. He's off doing films about drug addicts in Kuwait and tourism in Saudi Arabia when the real story is the Palestinians versus the Israelis.' This was quite true, but I had deliberately left that to our very well-staffed Jerusalem bureau, figuring that as the Cairo-based Middle East Correspondent I had a duty to bring our audience news and features from the rest of the Arab world that they would not otherwise get to see. No sooner had I decided to rectify this than events on the ground propelled half the world's press corps towards Jerusalem, including me. On 27 September 2000, the former Israeli defence minister (and later prime minister) Ariel Sharon decided to go walkabout on one of the most sensitive and controversial patches of land in the Middle East: the *Haram Al-Sharif*, the Noble Sanctuary, site of the third-holiest shrine in Islam. Sharon was reviled by Arabs and blamed by them for the massacre of hundreds of Palestinians in Beirut in 1982, so he must have known how provocative his visit would be, and he took no chances, surrounding himself with a hefty phalanx of security guards. The Palestinians went berserk. Within hours clashes had escalated into open gun battles between Palestinians and Israelis. The second *Intifada*, or Palestinian Uprising, had begun.

Everyone feared the worst, a war between Arabs and Jews that could suck in even the moderate neighbouring states of Jordan and Egypt, which had already signed a peace treaty with Israel, as well as militaristic Syria with its rusting arsenal of chemically tipped Scud missiles. Like many big news networks, the BBC immediately began twenty-four-hour news coverage, sending reporters to the region who were expected to talk meaningfully on air within hours of arriving for the first time in the region. I was soon assigned to our Jerusalem bureau to help with the coverage; I took the short flight from Cairo to Tel Aviv, then made the one-hour drive east to the heart of the Holy Land. I had been given the dawn reporting shift, so I went to bed early in a soulless Israeli hotel overlooking a park (in my experience Israeli hotel staff vie with Saudi consular officials for being the most unhelpful people in the Middle East). I had barely got to sleep when I was woken up by a rhythmic thumping in the middle distance. Heavy machine-gun fire, I told myself knowingly: someone must be getting a pasting. But the thumping continued unabated and when I peered out of my cell-like window I could see no sign of tracer fire lighting up the hills. I decided to get dressed and go outside to investigate. To my amazement I found a full-blown open-air rock concert getting under way in the park a few hundred yards away; the rhythmic beat was coming from a pair of giant speakers. Young Israelis were drifting up in twos and threes, smoking dope and swigging from bottles of Maccabee beer. This was no war zone, here were no politics: this was a slice of normal Western life and I had to pinch myself to remember I was in the Middle East. After three years of living continuously in the Arab world I found the contrast strangely refreshing, so I thought 'What the hell,' and I sat down on a grassy bank and watched the whole thing.

That short, bizarre interlude gave me a precious breathing space before launching into the maelstrom of *Intifada* coverage. In the next few weeks I interviewed hapless Palestinians who had got a rocket through their kitchen because someone had used a nearby orchard as cover to fire on an Israeli road. I met terrified Israeli civilians in south Jerusalem who went to bed each night in fear of the next attack on their houses. I strolled amongst the Arab market-traders in the old walled city to hear their views and took a drink with Christian bar-owners. I listened bleary-eyed as my taxi-drivers, alternately Palestinian and Israeli, gave me their world view of events, forever blaming the other side for today's sorry state of affairs. I tried hard to learn how to interpret the stilted language of press announcements put out by each side. Even months later, when I thought I was getting the hang of it, I nearly got the BBC into big trouble.

I had spent a long day up on the northern border with Lebanon on a press facility organized by the Israeli Defence Force's Northern Command, who wanted to show how they were countering the threat of rocket attack from Hizbollah's guerrillas just across the border. My cameraman and I had got back to Jerusalem shortly before midnight and we popped briefly into the office to return equipment. The phone rang as I was going out of the door. I hesitated, then answered it. It was a captain from the IDF press office. In heavily accented English she told me that Israel was 'mobilizing' to move into several Palestinian-controlled areas of the West Bank. I asked her to repeat what she'd said, then put down the phone and looked at my watch. It was seven minutes to midnight. There was no time to warn the news desk, I would just have to write and file by satellite a thirty-second voice piece and get it on air in time for our radio bulletins at the top of the hour. The dramatic wording had every on-air news programme queueing up to interview me. Was this the big one? I kept being asked by presenters in London. Was Israel calling up its reserves to reoccupy the whole of the West Bank? I couldn't answer that because I really didn't know who to call in the Israeli hierarchy at one o'clock in the morning. But as soon as I drew breath from the first wave of broadcasting I sat down with the bureau producer, Keren Pekes, to decipher what the IDF announcement really meant. Keren had high-level contacts in Tel Aviv that a non-Israeli like me could not possibly have and she had rushed into the office as soon as she heard the news. Back came the answer from her sources. Yes, the army was going into several Palestinian-held areas, but by 'mobilizing' the spokeswoman who'd called me had meant 'moving' its forces, a very different meaning to the English concept of 'calling up' reserves or civilians. We decided that my broadcasts had been ambiguous enough for me to have got away with it. Just.

The *Intifada* presented the Arab and Islamic world with one of its many crises. During the last *Intifada* of 1987–93 people read about what was happening in the newspapers and watched the occasional report on government-controlled TV. But this time round there was Arab satellite TV, most notably Al-Jazeera, and live reports were being beamed into living rooms from Gaza and the West Bank. Day in, day out, people watched clashes between mostly stone-throwing Palestinian protesters and heavily armed Israeli soldiers. One particular scene became the enduring, iconic image of the *Intifada*. An unarmed Palestinian man and his ten-year-old son got inadvertently caught up in a confrontation in the Gaza Strip. A cameraman filmed them as they crouched terrified against a low wall, the father trying desperately to shield his son from the bullets. But then the footage showed the boy's body go limp: he had been shot dead and the Arab world was in no doubt the Israelis were to blame. The boy was called Mohammed Al-Durra and it became a household name all over the Arab world. Photographs of this tragic scene were reproduced on posters, car stickers and inflammatory leaflets, demonstrators in Arab capitals chanted his name and broadcasters referred to it almost every day.

In one way it suited certain Arab governments to have the *Intifada* draw popular anger away from the many causes of domestic discontent at home. Military-political elites may have grabbed all the power, corruption have been endemic and human rights as rare as freedom of the press, but hey, this was nothing compared with what the Zionist entity was doing to Palestinians. In Cairo I went to interview the Israeli ambassador, Zvi Mazel, in his heavily guarded villa in a southern suburb. He complained that every day he and his staff counted dozens of anti-Israeli cartoons and other references in the state-controlled press. He said his complaints to the Egyptian government fell on deaf ears.

But before long, Arab governments realized there was a risk that this popular anger could get out of hand. One Friday afternoon after prayers I went up to Cairo's Al-Azhar Mosque to cover a small but noisy demonstration where rabble-rousers with megaphones were whipping up the crowd. One man held his baby son in my face and screamed that Israel was butchering Arab babies. 'Egypt is the strongest country in the world!' shouted another. 'Israel can't touch her!' And then the slogans turned political, mocking and insulting President Mubarak and his government, which had long sought to mediate between Israel and the Arabs but which seemed incapable of delivering a homeland to the Palestinians. At a given signal, the riot police moved in, blocking off the street with their serried ranks of helmeted troops, and the demonstration dispersed. Similar protests were happening outside Cairo Zoo, where rioters advanced on the office block that contained the discreet Israeli embassy, but they were stopped and dispersed by the riot police.

Still, Arab and Muslim governments all agreed that the *Intifada* was a crisis that had to be addressed, and it became the top priority at an Islamic summit in Qatar that autumn. I suspected there would be lots of talking, a worthy closing statement and not a great deal else achieved, but it was a great opportunity to meet people and enlarge my contacts book. Events such as these presented the best chance of getting impromptu interviews with people like the Saudi foreign minister or the Yemeni prime minister. A lot of Western journalists, I have found, take a sort of perverse pride in dressing down, as if looking shabby somehow implies a dedication to exposing the inequities of the world – or perhaps it is simply a case of not being very well paid. Luckily, I still had two tailored suits from my banking days, and although in London double-breasted suits were becoming the preserve of gentlemen's clubs and heirs to the throne, in the Middle East I could still get away with wearing one. It came in handy.

Halfway through the Islamic summit there was a photocall for all fifty-six Islamic leaders. A roped-off area and tiered stage had been prepared for the kings, presidents, sheikhs and prime ministers. A Qatari official with a clipboard ushered the dignitaries through like a maitre d' at an exclusive restaurant. Suddenly I found myself being guided into the roped-off area, and the next thing I knew I was standing between Yasser Arafat, King Abdullah of Jordan, Crown Prince Abdullah of Saudi Arabia and President Khatami of Iran. I knew it would only be a matter of seconds before I was rumbled – or even arrested as a security risk – so if

I was going to seize the opportunity and talk to any of these leaders I needed to choose one fast. Well, I've met Arafat already, I thought, Iran is off my patch, the Saudi leader will probably call for security, so that leaves King Abdullah.

'Your Majesty,' I turned to the Jordanian monarch and introduced myself, 'hello, I'm Frank Gardner.'

'Oh yes, hi, Frank. I've seen you on BBC World lots of times. How are you doing?'

King Abdullah could not have been friendlier. A small, well-built ex-paratrooper who had graduated from Britain's Royal Military Academy at Sandhurst, he had a firm handshake and a winning smile. His accent was mid-Atlantic. We talked about the Dubai Desert Endurance Marathon, which his Special Forces had competed in two years ago. (Embarrassingly for them, they forgot to bring any puncture-repair kits for the mountain-bike phase so they ended up having to carry their bikes over fifty kilometres.) The king had been so intrigued by the BBC film I had made about the race that he had wanted the next one to be held in Jordan, running from Aqaba to Petra. But then his father King Hussein had died in 1999 and Abdullah had been thrust unexpectedly on to the throne. This conference was important for him, since most of Jordan's inhabitants were Palestinians, and I left him before I was evicted by security, the king having readily agreed to an interview next time I was in Amman. But I did not have the same cachet as CNN's Christiane Amanpour or the BBC's John Simpson and I could never quite get through the layers of court protocol to secure the king's time.

Instead, I headed for Riyadh, where an international oil conference coincided with the start of a low-level terrorist campaign that was to be the harbinger of far worse things to come. The afternoon of 17 November 2000 was unseasonably wet for Saudi Arabia. The rain swept across the bleak desert landscape of the central Nejd plateau on the drive into

Riyadh from the airport; winter had come early to the Saudi capital. I was in a taxi heading into town when something on the radio caught my attention. I asked the driver to turn it up. I could barely believe the news bulletin: a British expatriate, Christopher Rodway, had been killed by a car bomb in central Riyadh. Such things were unheard of in a country that made internal security one of its highest priorities.

Rodway, a forty-seven-year-old hospital technician from Salisbury in Wiltshire, had been driving his car with his wife in the Olaya shopping district when the bomb exploded beneath his seat. The police duly threw a cordon round the wreckage, allowed the news agencies to publish a photo of the rain-soaked scene and began their own investigation. All sorts of spurious theories were doing the rounds but the interior minister, Prince Nayef bin Abdelaziz, who had been Mr Internal Security for over thirty years, was quick to offer an explanation: he was quoted in the official press two days later as placing the blame squarely on 'a turf war amongst Western bootleggers in alcohol'.

I was doubly surprised: firstly that his investigators seemed to have solved the murder so promptly, and secondly that Britons or other Westerners were being blamed for such a dramatic act of terrorism. Drinking or dealing in alcohol is strictly forbidden in Saudi Arabia, yet despite the mandatory penalty of multiple public lashings most Western expatriates do drink alcohol from time to time and a handful even make some money on the side by dealing in it wholesale. But there is a wealth of difference between greasing a few palms to take delivery of half a dozen crates of Johnny Walker round the back door, and acquiring, then planting, explosives beneath someone's car. Something did not feel right here. In fact it smelled strongly of sweeping trouble under the carpet. Back in London, the Saudi opposition figure, Dr Saad Al-Fagih, had his own theory. His numerous contacts inside Saudi Arabia – including some individuals even inside the security forces – were telling him that the bombing was the work of a small group of violent Islamists. Before long, the Foreign Office was drawing the same conclusion.

Discussing the bombing and the investigation live on air from Riyadh that week, I pointed out to BBC audiences that any Western expatriate would have to be insane to dabble in terrorism in a country that beheads criminals for less. The rewards were simply not worth the risk. And what exactly were the rewards for dealing in bootleg alcohol? I subsequently did some research into this, interviewing, amongst others, a Yorkshireman who proudly called himself 'a barman in Saudi Arabia', which is about as ironic a title as 'a diabolist in the Vatican'. Westerners did not on the whole, he said, get involved in the importing of alcohol. That was too risky and was left to middlemen, usually Arab expatriates, who in turn had to pay a cut to certain Saudis to get the stuff into the country. Where the Brits and the Irish made their money, he claimed, was in selling the alcohol in illegal 'pubs', usually converted games rooms on housing compounds full of expatriates. In a good year, the Yorkshireman said, he would make close to £50,000 on top of the salary he earned for his day job. A nice little earner, but was it worth committing murder for?

Expatriates I interviewed scoffed at the notion of a turf war amongst them. This was not Chicago in the 1920s, they said, this was Saudi Arabia, where Western expats all got along with each other, united by the shared pressures of living in a country where alcohol and all forms of public entertainment were banned. For years the Saudi authorities had largely turned a blind eye to what went on behind the walls of expatriate compounds. It was an open secret that Westerners brewed and distilled their own home-made wine and beer. As long as their 'decadent' habits did not spill over into the wider community, even the *mutawa* – the religious police, responsible for upholding morality in public places – did not usually venture into the compounds for fear of starting a diplomatic incident. When it came to the alcohol business everyone got their cut and everyone was happy, which was why the killing of Christopher Rodway came as such a shock and why the sizeable expat community did not believe the official explanation.

Within six months of Rodway's death there had been several more bombings, several more Westerners had been injured, and the Saudi police had rounded up and incarcerated half a dozen Britons and a Canadian as the prime suspects. The men were initially put in holding cells, deprived of sleep and, according to them, brutally beaten by their interrogators. Again and again, they said, the Saudis kept asking them, 'Who ordered you to place these bombs?' Under pressure, one of the Britons gave the most unexpected answer. He told the detectives he was acting on orders from none other than the British Consul at the embassy in Riyadh. It seemed an absurd suggestion but the Saudi Interior Ministry took it seriously and demanded the British government order a full-scale investigation. So serious was this allegation that the demand went right up to Number Ten, Downing Street. Special Branch was duly asked to conduct a painstaking investigation, but they found nothing to substantiate the accusation. The British Consul was in the clear; almost. The Saudi Interior Ministry did not accept Special Branch's findings and demanded the expulsion of the consul. Well before his tour of duty in Saudi Arabia was up, the hapless consul found himself being quietly shipped off to a posting in China. It was a dark chapter in Anglo-Saudi relations.

Matters came to a head in 2001 when suddenly, without warning, the Saudi authorities put the imprisoned Britons on television to broadcast their 'confessions'. Dressed in identical shirts, one by one the men told how they were ordered to place bombs in various places around Riyadh. They were even given little batons with which to point at a street map of Riyadh, while Arabic subtitles ran at the bottom of the screen, translating their confessions for the benefit of the Saudi audience.

It was an appalling piece of theatre, intended to ringfence the bombings as something expatriates did to each other, rather than admitting them to be a symptom of a wider, growing malaise within the Saudi population. Certainly the men's Saudi lawyers did not believe their confessions and nor did the British Foreign Office. Again and again, Tony Blair sent Baroness Amos to Riyadh to press for the Britons' release. The Saudi Foreign Ministry was sympathetic, the Interior Ministry was not. A small coterie of advisers round Prince Nayef, the interior minister, had convinced him that these men were convicted criminals, terrorists even. The fact that the bombings continued after their imprisonment did not seem to sway him. Rumours began circulating that two of the men had been tried in secret and sentenced to death by execution. When Tony Blair held an impromptu press conference in a Riyadh palace after meeting the king and crown prince in October 2001, we asked him what progress he had made on the release of the Britons. The question clearly irked him. Yes, he had raised the subject with his Saudi hosts, but this was not the right forum to discuss it. Next question, please.

A few months later, in the spring of 2002, I flew to Geneva for *Newsnight* to interview the Britons' Saudi lawyers, Sheikh Salah Al-Hejailan and Tariq Al-Tuwaijiri, who were on a brief visit to Switzerland. Sheikh Salah had already made a name for himself as the lawyer who had successfully defended the two British nurses accused of murdering an Australian nurse in Saudi Arabia in 1997. When I had spoken to the two Saudi lawyers in Riyadh they had been tight-lipped about the case of the imprisoned Britons. This was hardly surprising, since their phones were almost certainly being tapped. But in the relatively liberal atmosphere of Switzerland they felt able to speak freely, and confirmed what I had long suspected. Yes, the Britons had been coerced into making those confessions. In fact, when they had been filmed with the map of Riyadh the prisoners had had no idea they were going to be on TV. But coercion can take many forms, they said. It does not have to mean torture in the classic sense of thumb-screws and electric cattle prods. It can be psychological, and this was the primary means used by the Saudi interrogators to get the Britons to confess to bombings they had nothing to do with. After a lengthy period in a cell with little or no sleep it must have been hard to resist the temptations of a man waving the prospect of a flight to London, saying, 'Look, this is your ticket out of here. All we need is for you to own up to what you did and you can leave.'

In August 2003 all six were pardoned and released by King Fahd. By then Saudi Arabia was waging a full-scale counter-terrorism campaign that had nothing to do with boozed-up British expatriates. In the three years since Christopher Rodway had been killed by that first bomb beneath his car seat, Britain had quietly sent over sixty delegations at ministerial level or above to Saudi Arabia to plead for the men's release. One of the most strained periods in Anglo-Saudi relations since the screening in Britain of the film *Death of a Princess* could now draw to a close.

Saudi Arabia was not the only Arab country with an image problem over terrorism. The Great Socialist People's Libyan Arab Jamahiriya – or just 'Libya' to you and me – was in the dock, literally, over Lockerbie. When a bomb on a PanAm jumbo jet exploded in December 1988 over the Scottish village of Lockerbie, killing 270 people in the air and on the ground, the finger of blame pointed towards Tripoli. It was surely revenge, it was argued, for America's bombing raids on Libya in 1986. The West demanded that Libya hand over two men suspected of putting the bomb on board in

Frankfurt, and when the country's leader, Colonel Gaddafi, refused to comply the UN slapped on sanctions and Libya was isolated by an air embargo. The sanctions were only lifted in 1999 when Libya agreed to hand over the suspects to a Scottish court specially convened at Camp Zeist in the Netherlands.

I made my first visit to Libya in the spring of 2000 under the pretext of reporting an Arab–African NGO conference in Tripoli. My first impression was a pleasant surprise. Despite the years of sanctions the airport was clean and efficient, the road into town went past sunlit groves of olives and fields of wheat, and the Libyans seemed polite if a little reserved. Wearing a mixture of Western suits, loose white robes, waist-coats and small black felt berets, they looked like no other Arab race I had ever encountered. Their faces were sharp-featured and clean shaven but their hair was often frizzy – rather like a cross between Tom Jones and Lionel Richie.

The Sahara desert may well have been just over the horizon, but the immediate view along the coast was pleasantly Mediterranean and old Tripoli was a gem. Overlooking the harbour was a magnificent castle that backed on to a bustling souk, where coppersmiths beat out giant pans and traders sold old swords from the oases far to the south. Outside the walls of the old city there were neat rows of date palms and whitewashed colonnades where men sipped espresso coffee and stole sideways glances at the women, a legacy, perhaps, of all those years of Italian rule.

There was no question of choosing a hotel. The Al-Kabir ('The Big One') was chosen for us by the Ministry of Information, so we had to assume that all our phone calls were bugged, if not the rooms themselves. Neither I nor our audience was interested in the NGO conference going on in some vast Hall of the People, but we were interested in the Lockerbie trials and how Libya was coping under years of UN sanctions.

To do this story properly I had to play a ridiculous game of cat-and-mouse with our designated minder, who never wanted to let me and my digital camera out of his sight. His name was Miftah, which in Arabic means 'key' or 'something that opens things up', but he was quite the opposite, and proved so irritatingly obstructive that my Egyptian colleagues from the Cairo bureau soon dubbed him Ifl, meaning 'lock'. I learned later that only a few months before my visit, the Metropolitan Police team sent out from London to interview Libyan intelligence officials in the Lockerbie investigation had had similar trouble with Miftah. To try to wear down the British investigators from Scotland Yard's Anti-Terrorist Branch, Miftah and his stooges had arranged for their hotel-room doors to be knocked on at intervals all through the night.

To get away from Miftah and visit the British Embassy in Tripoli for an impromptu interview with the British ambassador, Richard Dalton, I had to let Miftah see me go into our hotel and get into the lift – apparently to my room – but in fact I went down to the garden, climbed through a gap in the fence and out into the street, and quickly flagged down a taxi. I had to employ similar ruses to talk to ordinary Libyans about the sanctions and Lockerbie, as no one was going to speak their mind with some shifty-eyed minder glaring at them from behind my shoulder. Libyans, I found, were equivocal. They liked Britain and wanted to rejoin the world and be friends with the West. But the sanctions were surely unfair; why, they argued, should Libya be punished for failing to hand over two suspects when it was obvious to them that another country had done it?

The Scottish court in the Netherlands had other ideas and in January 2001 the international press were invited to Tripoli to be on hand when the verdict was announced. So confident was the Libyan regime that the court would acquit both their suspects, the Libyan intelligence officer Abdelbaset Al-Megrahi and his co-defendant Al-Amin Fahima, that it let a substantial press pack into the country. Anticipation was written all over the faces of the Libyan airport baggage-handlers as our chartered flight from Cairo (via Milan, of all places) disgorged huge metal boxes containing satellite broadcasting equipment. For a people who had just spent seven years as international pariahs, this was welcome attention at last. One man was particularly pleased to see us. As the BBC team checked into the designated hotel, he came sidling up with a look of triumph on his face. In his hand he clutched a yellowed bill, unpaid, apparently, since Kate Adie's reporting visit on the US Air Force's bombing of Tripoli and Benghazi in 1986.

Bill paid and check-in completed, we milled around the lobby of the large, charmless hotel. But Libyan media minders were quick to seize the opportunity to 'educate' some of us on how things worked there.

'You see, Mr Gudner, we have no government here in Libya.'

'Really?'

'That is correct. The country is ruled by the people through the People's Revolutionary Committees.'

'I see. And where does the Brother Leader [Colonel Gaddafi] fit into this?'

'The Brother Leader is there to advise and guide us, but he does not rule. Nobody rules here. You will see.'

Given that Libya had long had the reputation of being a police state ruled by an unelected clique of tribal and military men close to Gaddafi, it was hard to tell if my minder was being serious. But he was. My Egyptian producer told me afterwards that these Libyan minders have very difficult jobs, trying to keep up with the ever-changing official line on how the country's system is supposed to work. For years they were told to welcome all Arab visitors, but when a disillusioned Gaddafi turned his back on the Arab world and looked to Africa instead, his minions had to adjust accordingly.

In the tense days before the Lockerbie verdict I went to see a Libyan lawyer in the backstreets of Tripoli who had worked on this case since day one, and he showed me piles of papers which he said proved that the men were innocent. And then, on 31 January, nine months after it started, the Lockerbie trial ended with a verdict. The news from Europe came like a bombshell. The Scottish court in the Netherlands had found one man – Fahima – innocent and the other – Al-Megrahi – guilty. He was sentenced to life imprisonment in Glasgow's notoriously tough Barlinnie jail.

Putting a brave face on the verdict, the next day the Libyans bussed us all out to a former US airbase east of Tripoli to watch the homecoming of the acquitted man. What began as a distant speck over the Gulf of Sirte soon materialized into a C-130 military transport plane of the Royal Netherlands Air Force. I struggled to make myself heard over the roar of its four turboprop engines as I tried to give a live commentary for News 24 back home. The plane taxied to a halt, a door slid open, a ramp extended to the tarmac, and down stepped the VIP passenger, Al-Amin Fahima. A small crowd had been permitted to gather on the runway and Fahima was now swept up by his fans, who chanted while he flashed victory signs to the assembled cameras. Then suddenly the word went up: we were going to be taken to see the Brother Leader.

Off we roared in a convoy of honking cars, escorted by green-uniformed militiamen who leaned out of the windows brandishing machine guns, frantically waving traffic out of the way, until we reached the Bab El-Aziziya barracks. Gates swung open to let the convoy pass, incredibly scruffy soldiers eyeing the Western press pack as if we were from another planet. More imposing were Gaddafi's female body-guards, glimpsed briefly through a chain-link fence. Trained in martial arts and a variety of weapons, they looked a tough bunch.

Bab El-Aziziya had special significance for Gaddafi. This was the barracks that the US Air Force bombed in 1986, killing his adopted daughter but missing the man himself. A team of government artists had been busy since then, turning one pockmarked wall into a gaudy mural: there were America's F-15 warplanes, fleeing before the defiant might of the Popular Resistance Committees who chased them off with missiles and clenched fists.

We disembarked from our bus to find a well-orchestrated uproar. A group of unshaven green-uniformed soldiers was gathered around two men, chanting and thrusting their machine guns in the air. 'We've got back Al-Amin!' they cried in Arabic. 'Now give us Abdelbaset!' At the centre of this mêlée was the newly acquitted Al-Amin Fahima, fresh off his flight from the Netherlands; he looked completely bemused. Next to him was Colonel Gaddafi. Dressed in a cream-coloured robe, he smiled enigmatically in silent approval of this demonstration of Libyan patriotism. I sidled up to him with my minidisc recorder, ready for any eccentric pearls of wisdom that might spill from his lips. He did not disappoint. 'I hereby announce', said the good colonel, 'that in four days' time I will reveal fresh evidence that will prove to the world that Abdelbaset Al-Megrahi is innocent of the Lockerbie bombing. We have the evidence and I will reveal it to you. You must be here then.'

You could almost hear the press corps groan. Another four days stuck in Tripoli with no bars, no entertainment, no nightlife. One or two of the less well-funded TV networks pulled out that afternoon, but the rest of us felt obliged to stay, knowing that if we left now we would never get visas in time to return for this great revelation. Personally, I was rather glad of this hiatus. It allowed me time to wander un-disturbed over the fantastic Roman ruins of Sabrata, exploring the ancient theatre and the temple that overlooked the azure waters of the Mediterranean. One day, I thought,

Libya will have a thriving tourist industry, but that day I felt as though I had some of its best treasures all to myself.

Finally, the time came for us to return to Gaddafi's bombed-out barracks and hear what he had to say. Hundreds of chairs had been set out before a lectern, and a solitary camel was tethered nearby, but there was no sign of the colonel. He was still in his tent, conferring with his advisers, we were told. Eventually a limousine made the two-hundred-yard journey from the tent to the open-air auditorium and out stepped Gaddafi. He certainly made an entrance. Dressed in dazzling cobalt-blue robes, he wore a matching blue hat and retro seventies sunglasses. He had definitely gone for the African look, leaving behind all vestiges of Arab conservatism, but unfortunately the effect was wasted by a false start. Gaddafi decided he did not like the height of the lectern so he stood off to one side while another one was fetched. Alone and, I think, a little self-conscious, he did not seem to know what or who to look at, and was visibly relieved when the new and approved lectern was installed.

We waited, pens, microphones and TV cameras poised, as the Libyan leader cleared his throat to begin. What could this new evidence be? Was it a secret tape recording? Was he going to embarrass another country by proving that their agents were behind Lockerbie after all? Some of us journos had been chewing over the possibilities that morning at breakfast. We had decided that to make any positive impact on world opinion the evidence would have to be both tangible and convincing. But Gaddafi's mind did not work like ours, and within minutes our worst suspicions were confirmed: Colonel Gaddafi had almost nothing new to say, he was just objecting to the decision of the Scottish court and he spent the next few hours railing against the Scottish judges and their judgement. Those journalists who had gone home a week earlier must have been chuckling with delight; we had, on the surface of it, wasted our time. But it was a wonderful piece of Gaddafi theatre, an illustration of how far out of touch with international thinking this man was. Clearly no one had dared tell him that for a government – sorry, 'Brother Leader' – to disprove the findings of a reputable court he would need real evidence, not words. Anything less would make him look foolish, which is exactly what happened.

I did feel sorry, though, for the ordinary Libyans, who must have been expecting their leader to have something more impressive up his sleeve than just his own opinions. To this day there are many who still doubt that Libya was really behind the Lockerbie bombing. There is a well-argued school of thought that says Iran was the real culprit, seeking revenge for the shooting down in error of one of its IranAir Airbus passenger jets by the USS *Vincennes* in the Gulf in summer 1988. Despite the US apology, the Iranians had, after all, promised retribution. Another school of thought maintains it was a three-way conspiracy between Libya, Iran and a radical Palestinian group. The one thing that is clear is that by the turn of this century Libya had had quite enough of being an international pariah and was prepared to pay almost any price, however humiliating, however costly, to get sanctions lifted and the country back on the map. It is an indication of how much things have changed since September 2001 that, after decades of conspiring against the West, Libyan intelligence has since been working in close cooperation with the CIA and MI6 against Al-Qaeda.

'What were you doing on 11 September 2001?' has become one of those oft-asked questions, in the way my parents' generation would ask each other what they were doing on the day John F. Kennedy was shot. I was in Jerusalem, finishing up a stint of *Intifada* coverage in our bureau before heading home to Cairo. While New Yorkers began their daily commute into Manhattan and Mohammed Atta and his team were preparing to hijack four US airliners, I was packing up my room at Jerusalem's American Colony hotel. I had one last cup of coffee in its elegant tiled courtyard, then hired one of the hotel's garrulous Palestinian taxi-drivers to take me to Tel Aviv's Ben Gurion airport. He knew a back route that avoided the traffic on the main motorway that connects Jerusalem to Israel's Mediterranean coast, and I settled back in my seat to enjoy the scenery. But my driver was listening to the BBC World Service in Arabic, and suddenly he slowed the car and turned up the volume. The news was too shocking to take in: New York's twin towers attacked and destroyed, the Pentagon attacked too and a fourth aircraft hijacked over Pennsylvania. My God, I thought, where will this end? I suspected immediately the hand of Al-Qaeda – who else had the motivation and the capability to carry off something like this? But when I got to Ben Gurion airport and asked an El Al airline official if anyone had claimed responsibility, he replied with a mixture of disgust and self-satisfaction, 'The Palestinians did it!' (In fact there were no Palestinians amongst the 9/11 hijackers, and although one of the chief Al-Qaeda planners behind the attack, Khaled Shaikh Mohammed, is originally Palestinian, he is thought to have long ago signed up with Bin Laden rather than with any militant Palestinian groups.) Israel's primary airport was in the throes of an alert; it was natural to assume that whoever hated America enough to attack it this way would want to hit Israel too. The Israeli Air Force was said to be scrambling into the skies ready to shoot down any unidentified aircraft approaching their country's airspace. When I finally boarded my plane back to Cairo, I was told it was the last to take off that night before the airport was closed to civilian traffic.

And so began a course of events that was to turn me away from mainstream reporting and into the specialist field of investigating the whole Al-Qaeda phenomenon. It was to be another six months before I was appointed as the BBC's first Security Correspondent, but already, as news networks around the world scrambled to find Arabic speakers and Middle East hands, I found I was in the right place at the right time. In the immediate twenty-four hours after the attacks I sounded out the opinions of ordinary people in the backstreets and cafés of Cairo. Most felt sorry for America, some said, 'Yes, but . . .' and then went into a diatribe about US support for Israel, and many insisted that Israel was behind the attacks. 'We Arabs are not sophisticated enough to carry out such a well-coordinated attack' was a refrain I often heard.

Not long afterwards I got a call from the Egyptian Ministry of Information.

'We have some good news for you, Mr Gardner. The president has agreed to your request for an interview.'

'Oh, that's great,' I replied. Like many foreign correspondents in Cairo, I had put in a bid to interview Mubarak from almost the day I arrived. 'So when will this be?'

'Don't worry, you will be informed.' And that was the end of the phone call. It felt like a secret mission.

A few days later I was told to report to a high-security military airbase on the outskirts of Cairo that I had never even known existed. I got Raouf, the ever-dependable office driver, to take me there, and his eyes widened as the gates swung open and a pair of blue-bereted Presidential Guards stood to attention. Of President Mubarak there was no sign, but I was immediately ushered into a VIP departure lounge and then out on to the tarmac. I was to board a plane to the Sinai resort of Sharm El Sheikh, accompanied by the two most powerful men in Egypt's extensive media machinery: Safwat Sharif, the longstanding Information Minister, and Nabil Osman, the smooth-talking head of the State Information Service. The plane was so small that when I stood up in the aisle and stretched my arms out I could touch both walls with my fingertips.

We cruised in comfort over the wrinkled mountains and

*wadi*s of the Sinai Peninsula, flying over a route that I had hitch-hiked along as a student nearly twenty years earlier. In Sharm El Sheikh we were taken swiftly to President Mubarak's guest palace, where a room was allocated to us to set up in, complete with the gilt-painted 'Louis Farouk' furniture so enduringly popular in Egypt. The president was in the mood for giving interviews and this worked to my advantage. While we were setting up, adjusting lights and chair angles and I was rehearsing in my head the questions I would ask him, Mubarak was upstairs doing a live interview by satellite link with CNN's Larry King. By the time he came downstairs he was in a jovial, expansive mood. Dressed in a well-cut suit tailored to his wrestler's physique, this air-force officer-turned-president gripped my hand tightly. He may have been over seventy years old but he had the strength of a bull. I did my best to show off my Arabic, sending his eyes skyward when I told him I had learned my colloquial Egyptian in the overcrowded and impoverished slum quarter of Gamaliya.

With the attacks on New York and Washington still fresh in everyone's minds, our interview inevitably focused on Al-Qaeda. President Mubarak talked of the need to resolve the Palestinian issue which was stirring up considerable anti-Western feeling in the region. I then turned to a subject closer to home.

'President Mubarak,' I began, 'your government overcame a violent Islamist insurgency in the mid-1990s. What advice would you give now to Western leaders in tackling the phenomenon of Al-Qaeda?'

The Egyptian leader leaned forward, his square-jawed features breaking into an all-knowing smile. 'Tell me why they persist in harbouring these Islamic dissidents?' he asked rhetorically, turning up his palms in that universal Arab gesture that means 'surely this is a reasonable question to ask'. The Egyptian government was particularly irked by the

London-based activities of Yasser El-Sirri, whom it accused of being behind the murder attempt on one of its ministers some years previously. But Arab Islamist dissidents are a wily lot and up until the London bombings of July 2005 they had managed to continue their campaigns against their countries' secular, West-leaning governments while staying above the UK law: one analyst had cynically nicknamed the capital 'Londonistan'. 'I warned Britain ten years ago about this matter!' Mubarak said to me. 'I told your government that these people were dangerous and no one would listen to me. Now look what has happened!'

But in fact Egypt's most dangerous exile had set up rather further afield, in Afghanistan. Dr Ayman Al-Zawahiri, the former head of the radical terrorist group Egyptian Islamic Jihad, had become the close confidant of Osama Bin Laden. In fact, that very month they appeared side-by-side in a video-tape smuggled out from their Afghan hideout. Many observers believe it was the Egyptian doctor who was responsible for broadening Bin Laden's horizons and turning Al-Qaeda into a truly global terrorist network.

Back in Sharm El Sheikh, the interview over, we stood up and shook hands while a state photographer snapped away for the picture that would appear in the next day's paper. Mubarak retired to his suite, sending down a messenger to enquire what time that evening the interview would be shown on BBC World. Unfortunately the local Egyptian company we had hired to provide the satellite uplink to London developed a technical hitch, and as each hour went by the messages coming down from the president's suite grew frostier and frostier. 'Why have you not shown the interview yet? The president watched in vain at eight o'clock and again at nine and he is very upset. Why are you doing this?' Since I knew nothing about how satellite links work I could only stand there in bovine ignorance, offering empty reassurances while the technicians wrestled with the equipment. Eventually, we got our interview on air, and I think he probably quite enjoyed it as three years later when he passed through London he asked for me again, like a sultan summoning his favourite minstrel.

As Afghanistan and its Taliban rulers became the likely target for America's wrath, there was suddenly a flurry of interest in a big British military exercise about to take place in Oman. A total of 23,000 British servicemen and women were taking part in Exercise Saif Sareea; would they simply move on to Afghanistan when it was over? The Royal Navy was sending submarines and an aircraft carrier, and the dust of the Omani desert would soon be kicked up by British Challenger 2 tanks. With all the talk of an Afghan war, the prospect of filming British troops in the desert was too good to be missed. The Omani Ministry of Information, which had been expecting a trickle of defence journalists from London, found itself deluged with visa applications. Whereas it would normally vet foreign journalists carefully, now it just threw up its hands and let everyone in.

In the capital, Muscat, I joined up with Kate Adie, the veteran BBC war correspondent, and her good-natured cameraman, a young Irishman called Simon Cumbers. He had a ready smile, and whenever you caught his eye it was as if you were both sharing a private joke. Kate had not been on the mainstream news bulletins as much as she used to be, but when we all walked into the bar of the Muscat Intercontinental a cheer went up from the squaddies. 'Bloody 'ell, it's Kate Adie!' said someone. 'Things must be getting serious!'

In fact Oman in October 2001 was a bit of a holiday camp. We all moved down to Salalah in the southwest where most of the troops were concentrated, basing ourselves in a newly built five-star hotel, then making occasional forays up on to the desert plateau to see what the troops were up to and braving the ugly but harmless camel spiders to sleep under canvas. Exercise Saif Sareea got plenty of high-profile visitors that autumn. Tony Blair swung through on his mission to forge an international coalition against terrorism. The British band Steps arrived at Salalah airport, where I recorded the one and only interview I have ever done for Radio 1 and sent it by satellite to London two minutes later, such are the wonders of modern journalism. And former Spice Girl Geri Halliwell flew in to 'raise morale', according to her PR people. In preparation for her concert the Royal Engineers constructed an artificial sand mound known as 'Halliwell Hill'. Down in the bar at the Salalah Hilton the troops were mimicking her songs, clamping two beer glasses to their eyes like binoculars and singing, 'Come on look at me!'

In London the Ministry of Defence kept reminding journalists until it was blue in the face that Saif Sareea was not an 'operation' but an 'exercise', and that any idea that troops would fly on to Afghanistan was pure speculation. But speculate the media did, with the result that the poor squaddies had to use up most of their precious phone time to the UK reassuring worried spouses and families that they were not about to go into a war zone. But quietly, behind the scenes, preparations for action were under way, and British Special Forces had already been warned to expect deployment to Afghanistan. Although Oman's ruler, Sultan Qaboos, had placated the Muslim world by saying he would not allow any attack to be launched from Omani soil, this did not apply to the Royal Navy submarines, which simply steamed further offshore into the international waters of the Arabian Sea when the time came to launch their cruise missiles at the Taliban.

Oman was delightful, but it was time to move on. President Bush's newly declared War on Terror was about to grind into action and as Middle East Correspondent I had an awful lot of ground to cover in the region, not to mention trying to get some time back home with my family in Cairo – always a difficult balance to strike for a foreign correspondent. On the evening of 12 October, I set out for Muscat airport to head for home when my mobile buzzed into life. 'It's started,' said the duty news editor in London. 'They're attacking the Taliban.' Operation 'Enduring Freedom' had begun. This meant doing an abrupt U-turn and going straight back to the hotel, where Simon Cumbers was only too happy to help me get rigged up to broadcast live. Of course I had absolutely nothing to report, being two countries and a small ocean away from Afghanistan, but BBC World were commendably interested in knowing what the Arab reaction was likely to be.

I had spent the previous few days canvassing opinion on just this subject in the decorative souk of Mattrah, strolling around its labyrinth of covered stalls, where shafts of sunlight illuminated great skeins of Indian brocade or steeply piled cones of pungent spices. I had also checked out what young Arabs were saying to each other in internet chatrooms. The answer was, broadly, that although nobody liked the Taliban, nobody thought an attack on Afghanistan, another Muslim country, was justified. 'What about the Al-Qaeda camps and the attacks on New York and Washington?' I would ask Omanis in the souk. 'They didn't do it,' was the usual response. Some said the Taliban should be allowed more time to give up Bin Laden, but the mullahs of Afghanistan had already ruled out handing him over for trial in the West. If he was guilty of any crime, they said, then he should be judged by a *shari'ah* court in Afghanistan. The Americans were not convinced, and by the end of the year, the Taliban were out of a job and Osama Bin Laden was on the run.

6

Arabia
post 9/11

THE ATTACKS OF 9/11 WERE A body blow not just to America, but to the entire Arab and Muslim world. As it became increasingly apparent that the attackers had carried out their 'blessed raids' (as Al-Qaeda later called them) in the name of Islam, I watched the Middle East move on to the defensive. A chasm of mutual suspicion opened up between the Arab and Western worlds, just as Bin Laden and his followers had hoped. Every Arab leader condemned the attacks, except for Saddam Hussein, but some were still in denial that Muslims could have been behind them. One country that found itself in a particularly uncomfortable spotlight was Saudi Arabia.

Even after it transpired that fifteen out of the nineteen suicide hijackers were Saudi nationals, certain Saudi princes found this hard to accept, insisting for months that there must have been some sort of 'third force' involved, i.e., Israel. The US press turned its full wrath on Saudi Arabia, accusing it of nurturing and supporting the monster that Al-Qaeda had become. The Saudi state-controlled press responded by accusing the US and Western media of being controlled by Zionists. A country that had long been prone to xenophobia now regarded Western journalists with even greater suspicion. It was amid this atmosphere that I flew into Riyadh in October 2001.

I travelled out from London with the Westminster press pack on 'Blairforce One', the plane chartered for the prime minister's whirlwind Middle East tour. President George W. Bush had given a defiant speech from the White House, and the military campaign to oust the Taliban from Afghanistan was two weeks under way. But when it came to international diplomacy, the US president seemed happy to leave the leg-work to Tony Blair, who quickly grasped the need to bring other countries on board in a broad-based coalition against terrorism.

At first the trip went badly. In Damascus we all cringed at that awkward press conference where Mr Blair shared a podium with Syria's President Bashar Al-Assad. The idea had been for them to present a united front against terrorism, but the host refused to play ball, defending instead the radical Palestinian groups based in his country. 'What you call terrorists,' declared the Syrian leader, 'we call freedom fighters. What about your French resistance against the Nazis? Do you call them terrorists?' Tony Blair shifted uneasily and looked as if he would much rather be some-where else.

In Riyadh he had an altogether smoother reception. In the warm glow of an autumn afternoon our plane drew up along-side a red carpet and a band played the national anthem. Crown Prince Abdullah, the effective ruler, was there to greet him, and various flunkies with colourful bandoliers and curved daggers looked on, beaming, before he was whisked off to a palace for an audience with the ailing King Fahd.

Saudi Arabia was still hard to get into as a broadcast journalist and none of us had visas to stay on after Blair's plane departed the next day. But at this point I saw my opportunity and pounced. As the welcome ceremony wound down I spotted a prince I knew vaguely and greeted him. 'Your Royal Highness, I wonder if we could do an interview tomorrow. I'll still be in Riyadh.'

'Of course, with pleasure. Just call my office manager to fix a time,' replied the prince, who, like many well-travelled Saudis, had a reputation for shifting effortlessly between his own culture and that of the West. This was perfect: now I had both an official reason for staying on in the country and the prospect of a useful interview. To the amazement of the Westminster press pack I produced a miniature digital camera and telescopic tripod from my bag, my tools for going solo here for the next few weeks. I also had the latest radio broadcasting pack, known as an M4. Andrew Marr, the BBC's recently appointed political correspondent, was not impressed. 'The M4's a motorway to Bristol, isn't it?'

Twenty-four hours later, as Blairforce One took off for Tel Aviv and the next leg of the prime minister's Middle East tour, I embarked on a journey into what some were calling 'the spiritual heartland of Al-Qaeda'. The town of Buraida lies about two hundred miles north of Riyadh and is not a place used to seeing Westerners. With 9/11 still fresh in everyone's minds and Osama Bin Laden's latest anti-Western diatribes pouring into Arab living rooms via the Al-Jazeera TV channel, I wanted to assess how much support his movement really enjoyed in this most conservative corner of the country. I had the pseudonym and phone number of a local Saudi who was willing to show me around, whom I had arranged to meet beside a certain mosque at a prearranged time.

To avoid any awkward official questions as to why I was going to Buraida I decided to travel at night, in the back of a taxi, dressed as a Saudi to get through the police checkpoints. I wore a red-and-white chequered headcloth neatly creased in the middle above the forehead, capped by an *aqaal*, the woven black rope that keeps it in place. I also wore the full-length white *thaub* shirt dress, like all Saudis, above a pair of plain sandals. I am not normally a fan of local disguise – this is the one and only time I have employed it – believing that in broad daylight a Westerner still stands out a mile just from the way he walks, compared with the graceful, loose-limbed gait of a Saudi. But that night it worked fine and we sailed through the checkpoints on the lonely desert road.

In the darkened streets of Buraida, a flash of headlights beside the mosque told me we were in the right place and I swiftly changed cars. 'Abdullah', who never did tell me his real name, was immediately welcoming. Young and intelligent, with dark, thoughtful eyes, he seemed surprised and pleased that a British journalist should want to come all this way to visit his town. Was I hungry? he asked. I was, so we drove to a late-night fast-food joint, one of thousands that have sprung up all over the country since the nineties.

While Abdullah went up to order a snack I sat at the Formica table and looked around. The clientele here looked very different from those in Riyadh. They were all men, which is not unusual since men and women are not allowed to eat together in public unless they are from the same family, in which case they must sit in a screened-off section. But all of these men sported lavish, unkempt beards and their white *thaub* robes were cut short above the ankle, in accordance with the style at the time of the Prophet Muhammad 1,400 years ago. There are two other distinguishing features that identify a deeply religious or fundamentalist Muslim, and many of these men had them. They wore their headcloths without the black rope coil, showing that they spent so much time bent over in prayer that it was impractical as it might fall off. They also had what Egyptians irreverently call the *zabeeb*, the 'raisin', meaning a dark, worn spot on the fore-head where they had touched the ground so often in prayer. There was no question about it, this was the fundamentalist heartland of Saudi Arabia. I would have to tread carefully to avoid upsetting any sensibilities.

Abdullah had taken a risk in letting me stay in his family's house. Foreigners are supposed to stay in hotels, where the authorities can keep track of them. I soon learned that he had had some trouble persuading his family to let a Western journalist stay under their roof. It turned out that Abdullah's brother had recently left for Afghanistan to 'wage jihad' against the infidel Americans and others. But nobody was up when we arrived at his house, a typical dust-coloured, high-walled villa tucked away down a leafy backstreet. I slept on a mattress on the floor, then awoke to Abdullah performing his dawn prayers.

Breakfast was hard-boiled eggs, black olives and flat, round loaves of bread. I was then introduced to Abdullah's parents. Arab custom demands that the elders of the household be treated with great respect and dignity, even if you disagree with their views. So that morning I nodded politely and kept my views to myself.

'What happened on September the eleventh was the work of the Jews,' said the old man, an opinion I have heard count-less times since all over the Arab world. 'It was the Israelis who did it and then blamed it on the Arabs. Why? To make President Bush wage war on the Muslims, and now look, he is attacking defenceless women and children in Afghanistan, bombing them in their homes. Bush is a war criminal!'

I asked if they had heard from their other son.

'No, but God give him strength,' chipped in the mother. 'May he achieve his wish and die a martyr fighting for Islam.'

It struck me then how extraordinary such words would sound coming from a Western, non-Muslim mother – and there, I realized, was one of the advantages Al-Qaeda had over its enemies. Most of its followers were not afraid to die; in fact they relished the prospect, convinced that if they died in the cause of their religion they would be guaranteed a place in paradise. 'We love death just as you love life,' boasted Osama Bin Laden in one of his many audio broadcasts.

It was Friday and most of Buraida was preparing to head for the mosque for the midday prayers. Abdullah offered to show me round town, so together we set off in his car. There appeared to be only two colours here: desert brown, as all the buildings took on the colour of the desert that surrounded them, and dusty green, from the date palms that fringed the city. In contrast to the ornate architecture of mosques in Egypt, Morocco or Syria, Buraida's houses of worship were especially austere. The minarets were modern, with square outlines and no hint of decoration. This was the Wahhabi style, the prevailing brand of Islam in Saudi Arabia. Derived from the teachings of an eighteenth-century cleric, Muhammad Bin Abdul Wahhab, it allows for few earthly pleasures. It urges its followers to reject many of the trappings of the modern world and emulate instead the simple lifestyles of the Prophet Muhammad and his early followers.

Within thirty minutes we encountered three police check-points. These were more than just a couple of squad cars with flashing blue lights. Saudi checkpoints often involve a soldier in a flak jacket sitting on top of a pickup truck and manning a heavy machine gun. The police have lists and photographs of wanted suspects, but Abdullah showed me how easy it was to evade them, taking shortcuts through groves of young palm trees to emerge on the other side.

'This town has become a security nightmare for everyone,' said Abdullah, as he swerved to avoid a dozing camel beside a bush. 'Always they are searching people, looking for weapons, but this way they are making many enemies. Even the mosques are full of informers, they are listening to see if anyone supports Al-Qaeda then they report them to the *Mabahith*.' These are the 'Investigators', the secret police, a rather more feared version of Britain's Special Branch. Some

Saudis claimed that their methods of interrogation were brutal but the government denied any use of torture. I certainly had no wish to come across them, but I had a film to make for BBC2's *Newsnight* so Abdullah took a considerable risk in letting me film the checkpoints discreetly through the window of his car. He wanted the outside world to see how nervous the Saudi authorities had become. 'Perhaps,' he said, 'it would not be like this if we had democracy.'

After prayers I went down to the market on my own. It was a colourful place, but as a Westerner I was not welcome. 'What's that bloody American doing here? Get him out of here,' screamed an old woman from behind a spice stall. Giving them what I hoped was a disarming smile and announcing I was British, not American, made no difference. In their eyes my country's government was the enemy. Like others in the Arab world, many Saudis had been watching the war in Afghanistan unfold on Al-Jazeera. What they saw was not so much a campaign to dislodge a brutal, repressive regime that nurtured terrorist training camps, but an unjustified aerial bombardment of defenceless Afghan civilians. Al-Jazeera had a good working relationship with the Taliban, so they were able to get access quickly to some of the places that had been bombed, showing close up the horrific results when bombs hit civilian instead of military targets. (This later became a feature of many Arab TV networks during the Iraq conflict of 2003.) For a while Al-Jazeera played a short promotional video montage between its news bulletins, showing first an American B-52 bomber flying overhead and then an Afghan child in tears beside a ruined house. The message was clear: 'US warplanes bomb innocent Muslims.' Images like this undoubtedly helped galvanize Arab opinion against the war in Afghanistan. The net result for me was that Buraida spice market was not a sensible place to get out the camera.

Back inside Abdullah's house we logged on to the internet, where he was an avid contributor to a chatroom run by

Palnet. The internet was, and still is, an ideal mechanism for information-hungry Saudis to discuss events and express views anonymously or under pseudonyms, in case the *Mabahith* are monitoring the website. Ordinary people tend to use playful names like 'khalilhero2'. Those who are closer to Al-Qaeda adopt nicknames taken from historic Muslim victories and campaigns, or names that refer to their geographic origins, such as Al-Zarqawi ('the one from Zarqa in Jordan') or Abu Mus'ab Al-Suri ('father of Mus'ab, the Syrian').

Abdullah and his internet chat mates were not close to Al-Qaeda. But when he switched on the computer's speakers it was fascinating to hear some of the pro-Al-Qaeda opinions bouncing around in cyberspace.

'Here,' said Abdullah, 'why don't you join in?' He introduced me to the online forum and two of the contributors abruptly logged off. But from those who stayed I learned more about why Osama Bin Laden's enmity for America and the West was finding a ready audience amongst certain Arabs and Muslims. They may not have agreed with his methods, but they admired anyone who could stand up to the most powerful country in the world and still remain at large. (Bin Laden has enjoyed a fugitive 'survivor' status ever since President Clinton ordered a cruise-missile strike on his camp in 1998 and failed to get him.)

'We admire Osama Bin Laden because he's our hero,' said one contributor. 'He tells the truth about what's happening in Palestine, Iraq, Chechnya, Kashmir and all the places where Muslims are being persecuted. He stands up for us.'

'So do you think he was behind the attacks of 9/11?' I asked.

There was a long pause.

'Maybe, but I don't think so. Arabs don't have the technology to do something like this. It was most likely the Israelis.'

By then it was two in the morning and even the tireless Abdullah was yawning. The next day he drove me to a taxi company he knew and haggled the fare back to Riyadh for me. We said goodbye and I never saw him again. A few weeks later I learned through a mutual acquaintance that he had been picked up and questioned, although not about my visit. He vanished from the internet chatrooms for some time before making a cautious return. He is one of thousands of young men to be picked up and interrogated in the wake of September 11th. The authorities were belatedly waking up to the problem of the 'Afghan Arabs' – all those volunteer fighters, including Saudis, who took off for training camps in Afghanistan, where they learned to combine their contempt for the West and their own government with the sort of crude military skills perfectly suited to an armed insurrection.

I know that there are some in the Saudi establishment, including in the *Mabahith*, who think I had the Riyadh attack coming to me because, in trying to get a true picture of what was going on in their country, I had ventured up to conservative strongholds like Buraida and Sakaka without a government escort. But the irony is that I was never in danger on these solo trips; it was only when Simon Cumbers and I put our safety in the hands of Saudi Information Ministry minders that we came horribly unstuck.

In 2003 the Saudi security situation changed dramatically. Intercepted phone calls in January between Al-Qaeda's fugitive leadership hiding out in Waziristan and their followers in Saudi had revealed an order for the Saudi-based militants to begin their insurgency against the government and Westerners in the kingdom. The militants were reluctant, protesting that they were not yet sufficiently organized and saying they feared they would take huge losses if they began the insurgency too early. But Bin Laden and his deputy, Al-Zawahiri, were adamant; they needed to show that they were still a force to be reckoned with after being driven out from their Afghan bases. So in May 2003, their Saudi adherents launched a devastating triple-suicide-bomb attack on housing compounds in Riyadh where Western expatriates were known to be living.

One of those expats, David Budge from Wiltshire, survived the attack on Al-Hamra compound where his family were living and he later told me how it was carried out. 'There were seven *jihadi* militants and they drove straight through the main gate into the walled compound with no difficulty. Dressed in black, they just tailgated behind a Briton in his car. They shot up the gatehouse, wounding the unarmed security people who all then fled. The militants then split up and fanned out along the streets between the villas, firing their guns into the air. That brought a lot of people to the windows and one Jordanian girl mistook them for policemen so she called out for help. They shot her.' When Al-Qaeda exploded their truck bomb, David recalled: 'The blast came down the compound and hit like an express train. I was blown out of bed but saved by the curtains, which stopped the flying glass and metal window-frame from tearing through the room.' He was quite certain that Al-Qaeda had done a thorough reconnaissance: at least one *jihadi* had been seen on the compound and a safehouse was subsequently discovered near by. One of the most chilling things he remembers about the attack was the *jihadi* militants calling out as they dismounted their vehicles. 'You infidels! We've come here to kill you.'

Over thirty people died in the Riyadh attacks of May 2003 in the space of a few hours. It was a tremendous shock for most Saudis, who had never imagined that Al-Qaeda would wage war on holy Arabian soil. Only a few weeks earlier the Saudi Interior Minister had boasted, 'We have no Al-Qaeda sleeper cells here. If we did we would have woken them up long ago.' Saudis now called the bombings of May 2003 'Saudi Arabia's 9/11'. The attacks shook the ruling Al-Saud family to the core, but also allowed them to say to their detractors in the West, 'Look, you see? Terrorism is our common enemy, we are fighting it just as much as you are.'

Soon after the Riyadh attacks I secured a Saudi visa to go and report on how the government was conducting its counter-terrorism campaign there, but at first things did not go according to plan. Arriving at Jeddah airport I could see no sign of the Ministry of Information officials who were supposed to be meeting me. When I phoned them the next day they said rather crossly they knew nothing about my visit and that I should call them back next week. Fortunately, I managed to obtain the number of the private office of the prince in charge of Saudi Arabia's counter-terrorism efforts, and a midnight meeting was arranged. As one of the militants' most prized targets, the prince was well protected: there were armed guards everywhere and his office in Jeddah was half palace, half fortress.

'I don't normally meet journalists,' he said with a smile. 'I do not believe that intelligence and the media go very well together.' He was referring, I could tell, to the whole Iraq WMD/MI6/David Kelly/Andrew Gilligan saga which had been brewing in Britain that summer. 'However,' he continued, 'I have been told you are a sincere journalist, so how can I help?'

I explained that most of the world had no idea how Saudi Arabia was going about fighting terrorism, or whether it even had a counter-terrorism effort at all, so here was an opportunity to show what it was doing. It was as if a curtain had been lifted: I was to be given an unprecedented insight into how this secretive Arab country was battling its Al-Qaeda-inspired insurgency.

The sun was barely up the next morning before I was boarding the early flight to Riyadh and the headquarters of the Interior Ministry's Special Security Force, the unit tasked with confronting the country's Al-Qaeda terror cells. The investigators showed me evidence gathered from the scene of the Riyadh suicide bombings two months earlier, spread out on a long low table. There were fire-blackened Kalashnikovs, twisted and buckled magazine clips and other objects blasted and burned almost beyond recognition. Shortly before the bombings the Saudi authorities had issued the names and photographs of two dozen most-wanted militants, a controversial move at the time since it was highly embarrassing for the militants' families. The police discovered a massive cache of arms and explosives in a Riyadh safehouse and they began to close in on the wanted men. Then suddenly, mysteriously, they escaped, and days later they drove their deadly cargo into those housing compounds.

Over at a row of desks a team of technicians was studying a set of monochrome images on computer screens; these were the marks made by the 'lands', the rifling grooves inside the barrel of a firearm. Every weapon leaves a microscopically different pattern and from this it is possible to identify which gun has been used; another method is to study the marks on the ejected cartridge case. I had no idea, as I crouched there with my camera looking for the best filming angles, that one year later this would be exactly how the Saudi forensic people would identify my own armed attackers. Now I was being shown the DNA labs, where senior police officers explained how they would take samples recovered from Al-Qaeda safehouses, such as a toothbrush or strand of human hair, then build up what they called a 'DNA map' of where a suspect had been staying around the country and whom he had met. The technology, I was told, was quite new and they were receiving a lot of technical help from the Americans and to a lesser extent the British.

By now the sun was high in the white sky, blazing down from a point almost directly overhead, but it was time to film a black-clad Saudi SWAT team as they blasted their way with blanks through a hollow house, abseiled down vertical walls and lobbed stun grenades into imaginary terrorist lairs. A series of demonstrations was set up, firstly of a rescue operation to intercept a hijacked school bus, then of EOD, Explosive Ordnance Disposal. The Saudis showed me a robotic device that could open car doors, set off booby traps and blow up briefcases. It all looked very impressive but I was dripping with sweat, dashing around trying to film all this entirely on my own, in a shade temperature of around 45 degrees. And then, as if this was not enough, my mobile rang and someone on the BBC news desk in London announced that there had been a raid just north of Riyadh on a suspected Al-Qaeda hideout, resulting in several casualties. I had to break off filming to gather the details of this operation as best I could, with my mobile buzzing constantly with requests from programmes in London for live interviews. The net result, though, was a highly productive visit, with the films running as exclusive reports on *Newsnight* and the ten o'clock news. It was exactly this sort of access that Simon and I were hoping to get when we came to Riyadh a year later on our fateful visit in June 2004.

By then, Al-Qaeda's militants in Saudi Arabia had struck again and again, scoring an own goal in November 2003 when they blew up the Muhaya housing compound in Riyadh – most of the victims were expatriate Arabs and Muslims from countries like Lebanon. In April 2004 they set off a bomb at a police headquarters, where I had once been allowed to film the surveillance cameras that monitored every passenger movement in and out of Riyadh airport; that explosion killed five, all Saudis, a fact which lost the *jihadi*s further public support. On 1 May 2004 Al-Qaeda targeted Western expatriates working at a petrochemical facility in Yanbu on the Red Sea coast, killing five of them, including two Britons, and reportedly dragging their victims' bodies around town from the bumpers of their pickup trucks, seemingly impervious to the risk of arrest or execution. And in the same month they executed the murderous raid in Al-Khobar that left twenty-two people dead. The Al-Qaeda franchise in Saudi

Arabia now had a self-appointed title, Al-Qaeda in the Arabian Peninsula, or AQAP, and they had an online magazine, *Al-Batar*, which included biographies of men they called heroes and holy warriors, men whom the Saudi authorities referred to as deviants and terrorists.

On 1 June 2004, immediately after the Al-Khobar raid, a credible Islamist website posted the biography of AQAP's leader, a thirty-two-year-old fanatic named Abdulaziz Al-Muqrin. Since March, when his Yemeni predecessor Khalid Bin Al-Hajj had been killed in a shoot-out with police in Riyadh, Al-Muqrin had been heading Al-Qaeda's operations in Saudi Arabia. Al-Muqrin used the nom de guerre Abu Hajar and his CV gives an intriguing insight into the short, violent lives of international *jihadi*s.

Al-Muqrin reportedly left school at seventeen to wage *jihad* in Afghanistan. This would have been the same year that the Soviet Army withdrew, a retreat hailed across the Muslim world as a massive victory for Islam. According to his internet biography, he spent much of the next four years at training camps in Afghanistan, where he was 'promoted from trainee to instructor' and took part in a 'battle' near the town of Khost in the early 1990s, presumably fighting the remnants of the communist government in Kabul.

Still only in his early twenties, Al-Muqrin was then said to have moved to Algeria, a country in the grip of a brutal civil war that eventually claimed well over 100,000 lives. His biography records him as training Islamist rebels who were fighting the secular government, instructing them on 'weapons and equipment bought in Spain and smuggled through Morocco to Algeria'. Al-Muqrin appears to have had a narrow escape from the Algerian security forces, getting out of the country with the help of his fellow *jihadi*s. After a brief spell training militants and fighting in Bosnia-Herzegovina, Al-Muqrin reportedly moved to Somalia, another lawless failed state like Afghanistan. There, it is claimed that 'He fought against Ethiopia in the Ogaden battles'. (By that time Somalia had been abandoned by the US and the international community, which had tried in vain to restore order from anarchy there in 1993. Somalia's Islamists were riding high after the humiliating loss of nineteen US servicemen in Mogadishu, a day immortalized by the Hollywood block-buster *Blackhawk Down*.)

In Somalia Al-Muqrin's luck appears to have run out. The biography reports him as getting arrested and spending over two years in jail before being extradited home to Saudi Arabia. There he faced trial by *shari'ah* court on a number of charges and was sentenced to another four years in jail. 'However,' says his biography, 'his good manners and his ability to memorize the entire Holy Koran made the competent authorities at the Interior Ministry reduce his sentence by half.' You might think that after two and a half years in a Somali jail, followed by a further two years in a Saudi one, he would have been tempted to throw in the towel and opt for an easy life, becoming an accountant, perhaps, or a curator in some quiet library. But it seems Al-Muqrin was not to be deterred. After a further stint in Afghanistan in 2001 he made his way back to his native Saudi Arabia, where he went into hiding and took up the *jihadi* cause once more. At secret desert camps in the west and centre of the country he reportedly trained fresh recruits to Al-Qaeda in prepar-ation for its armed insurgency.

Reading all this on the plane as I headed for Saudi in June 2004, I remember thinking, 'Crikey, I hope I don't run into this guy.' And yet our paths were destined to cross within a week: Al-Muqrin was to direct the murderous attack on us in Riyadh.

But Saudi Arabia has been by no means the only country on the Arabian Peninsula fighting a campaign against Al-Qaeda militants. When the Pentagon and World Trade Center were attacked on 11 September 2001, America, not surprisingly, went looking for revenge. With Al-Qaeda's leaders being the prime suspects, it was always inevitable that their Taliban hosts in Afghanistan would top the target list. But where else would be in the Pentagon's sights? Iraq was one candidate, but in the Yemeni presidential palace there was deep concern. Would the Pentagon launch some sort of pre-emptive strike on suspected terrorist training camps in the interior, or, worse still, invade this ancestral homeland of the Bin Laden family? President Saleh had no wish to wait and find out. He wasted no time in flying to Washington, where he offered President Bush his country's full cooperation in the newly minted 'War on Terror'. 'Great,' said the Americans, 'we'd like to see real cooperation between your people and our FBI and CIA, we want proper maritime patrols of your coastline, which we'll help you with, and we want real-time intelligence on the movements of Al-Qaeda suspects. Oh, and we want them caught or killed. Please do whatever it takes.'

The Pentagon sent an extremely low-profile team of Special Forces trainers to help the Yemenis form their own counter-terrorist capability. The State Department sent Ed Hull as ambassador to Yemen, a tough, hands-on Arabic speaker with a counter-terrorist background. He was cautious in his assessment of Yemen's efforts to combat terrorism. The will was there, he told me, but too often the security forces failed to act quickly enough on intelligence they were given. I wondered whether the unspoken implication was that some-body on the inside was tipping off the terrorists when an operation was about to be mounted in their area.

There were three people who particularly concerned the CIA and Britain's MI6, where Yemen was concerned. A key member of the Hamburg cell that prepared for the 9/11 hijackings was a Yemeni national, Ramzi Bin Al-Shibh. He had hoped to become one of the suicide pilots by training with the others at a US flying school, but his visa application was turned down no less than four times. After attending Al-Qaeda's final pre-9/11 summit in Spain in July 2001, Al-Shibh disappeared before being finally captured in Karachi in September 2002 after a fierce gun battle.

The other two were Muhammed Al-Ahdal and Qa'id Sunyan Ali Al-Harithi, thought to be Al-Qaeda's most dangerous operatives in the Arabian Peninsula. In December 2001 the Yemeni security forces thought they had Al-Harithi pinned down in the village of Al-Husun in Marib province, but their operation was a disaster. The villagers turned out to be heavily armed, and assuming they were under attack they let rip with everything they had, killing at least twenty government troops. The security forces retreated and Al-Harithi remained at large.

'We think they're both still hiding out somewhere in Yemen's Empty Quarter,' said a Western counter-terrorist official in the summer of 2002, 'and we think they're planning something big.'

That summer I managed to negotiate a tribal escort deep into Marib province to that same village of Al-Husun. My personal experience is that if a respected tribesman on the Arabian Peninsula gives you his word of honour that he will vouch for your safety, you are better off with him than with any number of government minders. The further we drove from Sana'a the more glad I was of this escort. As we approached Al-Husun I noticed that all the local tribesmen had Kalashnikov machine guns slung casually over their shoulders, which they are forbidden to do in the main cities. The desert village was built of sun-baked mud, nestling in a valley beneath imposing purple mountains. A camel walked in endless circles, yoked to a grindstone, while goats foraged amongst the bitter-leafed bushes known as Sodom's Apple. An elderly villager told me what had happened a few months earlier when the Interior Ministry troops came looking for their suspected terrorist.

'We had never heard of this terrorist,' he said, 'but the army attacked us anyway. Their planes flew over very low and we thought we were being bombed so we fought back. Look! They destroyed half my house!' The old man pointed to a gutted room and to the tail fin of an unexploded missile that poked out from his living-room wall. I edged away from the house fairly quickly after that.

It was impossible to tell if Al-Harithi and other Al-Qaeda suspects were really using Marib province as a base or not, but I thought it only fair to go and hear what the governor had to say, although I already suspected what he would tell me.

'We have no Al-Qaeda terrorists here,' he said, patting the magnificent silver dagger in his waistband and sipping sugary tea from a tiny tulip-shaped glass. 'Believe me, my friend, this whole area is under control.' As if to reinforce this point, he arranged for me to be taken to a remote army outpost in the desert.

But if it was meant to impress me, it had the opposite effect. We arrived in the hottest part of the afternoon, bang in the middle of siesta time, and it was hard to find any soldier with his boots on, let alone doing anything worth filming. The camp was a picture of somnolent inactivity, yet Marib province was about to witness one of the most dramatic events in the so-called War on Terror.

On the morning of Sunday 3 November 2002, President Saleh was enjoying the fresh sea breeze that blew off the coast of Aden. Being on a yacht in the Arabian Sea must have made a pleasant change for Yemen's strongman. For most of the year, ensconced inside his fortress palace in the mountain capital of Sana'a, Saleh juggled power between his country's heavily armed tribes, the Islamists and the Parliamentarians. But that day was no holiday for the president: he was about to authorize a landmark action in counter-terrorism. When the call from Washington came through to his yacht, the caller had only one question: 'Can we go ahead?' President Saleh's answer was abrupt: 'Do it, but make it unattributable.'

A short distance away across the Bab El-Mandeb Strait, an unmanned aerial vehicle (UAV), a drone known as the Predator, lifted clear of a desert runway in the Republic of Djibouti, climbed to cruise height above the Horn of Africa and headed east. The Predator looks a bit like a giant white cigar with wings. It was designed initially for surveillance, being able to stay in the air for up to twenty-four hours and send back live footage of its target area while still airborne. It had been used in the Balkans, and soon after the 9/11 attacks was adapted to carry anti-tank missiles. The Predator that took off from Djibouti that day bore no markings, but it carried a brace of lethal Hellfire missiles. It belonged to the CIA, and thousands of miles away at the CIA headquarters in Langley, Virginia, its flight was being steered with minute precision by operators staring at TV monitors that gave them instant 'real-time' information.

Their target was one of the most wanted men in the Middle East: the same Mr Al-Harithi whom Western intelligence was convinced was lurking in Marib province, plotting death and destruction. The Americans in particular had a score to settle with him over his suspected role in the bombing of their warship the USS *Cole* two years previously.

That Sunday, Al-Harithi left his latest hideout in Marib province and set off across the desert in a four-wheel-drive jeep. He had five companions with him and they were heading in the direction of the Indian Ocean port of Mukalla. His departure did not go unnoticed. A Yemeni informer, working for his government's intelligence service and, indirectly, for the CIA, contacted his masters as soon as Al-Harithi set off. After several previous unsuccessful attempts to capture him alive, US and Yemeni intelligence quickly decided they could not afford to pass up this opportunity: they had to act now or risk losing Al-Harithi for years. But they had a problem.

Using the Predator drone might be the surest way to kill Al-Harithi, but public opinion in Yemen would never stomach the killing of Yemeni citizens by the US government. It had to be made to look like an accident.

When the news broke the next day that Yemen's most-wanted terrorist had died when his car exploded east of Marib town, the government was vague about the details. Yemeni officials implied that the car had been carrying explosives and that its occupants had been on their way to attack a shipping target off Mukalla. It was suggested that perhaps the explosives had gone off as the car had driven over a bump, à la *Pulp Fiction*. Locally filmed footage showed a couple of Yemeni men in traditional dress lifting up pieces of charred wreckage from the car against the backdrop of a sand dune. There was no sign of the bodies. But cracks began to appear in the story when Yemeni journalists interviewed local tribesmen who reported seeing an object in the air just before the explosion.

The truth might still have been buried with Al-Harithi had it not been for some loose tongues wagging in Washington. Officials there could not resist crowing to journalists in private about this apparent success in the War on Terror. A top terrorist was dead and without the loss of a single American life. The US Defense Secretary Donald Rumsfeld was clearly delighted. 'He's been an individual that has been sought after as an Al-Qaeda member as well as a suspected terrorist connected to the USS *Cole*,' he commented to reporters, 'so it would be a very good thing if he were out of business.' Yemen's President Saleh was less delighted. Faced now with angry questions from his own countrymen, he gave orders that this sort of extrajudicial killing by the USA must never happen again on Yemeni soil.

Ever since Al-Qaeda was driven from its Afghan bases in late 2001, the Pentagon has been concerned about its operatives trying to regroup in East Africa, especially Somalia. The organization had a known presence in the region in the late 1990s, as demonstrated by the devastating twin bombings of the US embassies in Nairobi and Dar es Salaam that killed over two hundred people, mostly local Africans. Four years later Al-Qaeda struck again with the truck-bombing of an Israeli-owned hotel near Mombasa, and narrowly missed shooting down an Israeli airliner with a malfunctioning SAM missile smuggled across from Yemen. To try to prevent Al-Qaeda operations around the Horn of Africa the Pentagon set up CJTF-HOA, the Combined Joint Taskforce Horn of Africa, run out of the USS *Mount Witney*, a hi-tech US Navy command ship in the Indian Ocean, and drawing on around two thousand US Marines and Special Forces troops based at Camp Lemonier, an old French Foreign Legion base in Djibouti. There was also a naval taskforce involving British, French and Spanish warships circling the Arabian Sea and the Horn of Africa to try to disrupt the flow of arms in the region. In early 2003, as the world's attention began to focus on the impending conflict in Iraq, I flew down to Djibouti with a cameraman to make a film for *Newsnight* on just how the Pentagon was going about 'denying this area to terrorists', as they put it.

In the Joint Operations Room on board his command ship, the taskforce commander, Major General John Sattler, explained the rationale behind his mission. 'We've got six countries we're watching here: Yemen, Somalia, Kenya, Ethiopia, Eritrea and Djibouti. Now our concern is that the bad guys will try to move westwards to this part of the world from wherever they're hiding in South Asia and the Middle East and we aim to stop them.' Sattler, a big, plain-speaking US Marine Corps general, went on to tell me how they would do this. 'We've formed excellent relationships with all the host governments except for Somalia and we're training their guys in border security and counter-terrorism. We're working with their intelligence agencies so we can get real-time info on people on the ground. Heck, I've been in a few times to see President Saleh in Yemen and, I can tell you, he's right on-side.'

Yet again and again the vacuum of Somalia kept cropping up in our conversation. With no effective central government since 1991 the country has long been awash with warlords and weapons, a failed state to which America has been loath to return after getting such a bloody nose in the backstreets of Mogadishu in 1993. Early reports of Al-Qaeda setting up bases there after 2001 were probably exaggerated, but it was easy to see how its operatives could take advantage of the anarchic situation of fiefdom and thuggery. CJTF-HOA had no foothold on the ground there, although the CIA had reportedly been running a network of paid informers inside the capital, Mogadishu. In Djibouti's Camp Lemonier there were blackened Special Forces helicopters ready to fly combat teams on missions into Somalia, but the troops I met in Djibouti were bored and frustrated. We flew with them by helicopter up to a remote firing range near the Eritrean border, the Special Ops soldiers wearing ostentatious Superman 'S's on their uniforms, refusing to put on helmets and not flinching when the helicopter's flares went off with a bang by accident as we touched down on a bare mountain-top. The next day we watched them use laser sights to guide in a pair of US Marine Corps jumpjets that then obliterated their target, a rusting hulk of an old tank. It was impressive to watch, but I could not help thinking this was the wrong sort of war to be training for here in the Horn of Africa. Al-Qaeda and its shadowy operatives are unlikely ever to present themselves as open targets in broad daylight, choosing instead to mix with the local population and exploit anti-Western sentiment and an easy supply of weapons wherever they find them. The war against terrorism in East Africa is essentially a war of intelligence, and I suspect that the Supermen of Special Ops in Djibouti have had some very dull months in camp there.

*

I made one more trip to Yemen before my fateful visit to
Riyadh largely put an end to my go-anywhere-anytime field-
reporting days. In December 2003 I got a call from someone
close to the Yemeni president. 'Frank, you've got to get down
here quickly,' he said. 'There's an amazing story about Al-
Qaeda. Believe me, it'll be worth your time.' I put down the
phone and went straight to see Kevin Bakhurst, the editor of
the ten o'clock news. 'It's a fishing trip,' I told him as he
swivelled round to face me in his glass goldfish bowl of an
office. 'It's a gamble. It could be a great story, it could be a
complete waste of time, I can't tell. The Yemenis won't tell me
much over the phone.' Bakhurst did not hesitate. He gave me
one of the best cameramen in the business, Tony Fallshaw,
and we were soon on our way to Sana'a airport. A minor
customs official there tried to throw his weight around,
making us wait on a bench while he blew cigarette smoke at
us, but I took the opportunity to pass round a photo I had
had taken of myself with the president when I had interviewed him. It worked wonders and we were through
customs within seconds.

The story turned out to be an intriguing one, though not
quite as dramatic as we had been promised. The Yemeni
Justice Ministry, under pressure for detaining so many
suspects to keep the Americans happy, had come up with a
novel approach to winning hearts and minds. It had set up
a team of religious scholars to go round the prisons and convince Al-Qaeda supporters of the error of their ways, using
the tenets of Islam rather than the threat of punishment to
make them turn their backs on violence.

We were ushered into a book-lined meeting room to meet
a group of 'former' Islamist fanatics who had apparently
repented in prison and had now been released after signing a
pledge not to support terrorism. They looked a tough lot and
seemed none too pleased at having a TV camera trained on

them. The man sitting next to me looked exactly like Ramzi Bin Al-Shibh, the Yemeni member of the Hamburg cell, with his thin face, wispy beard and sneering lips. As if reading from a prepared script, he and the other former convicts declared their opposition to violence and their commitment to peace. I was not convinced. Twenty-five years of living in and visiting the Middle East had given me a good idea of when someone was telling the truth or not. These men may have signed a pledge of peace, but I could see the anti-Western hostility in their eyes. It mattered not a jot to them that I spoke Arabic and went to great lengths to explain to Western audiences the root causes of Muslim anger; all they could see was a *kafir*, an unbeliever, and worse still, one from a 'Crusader nation', Britain. I asked them what had made them change their minds, but my questions were making them uncomfortable so the cleric leading the discussion changed the subject.

Judge Hammoud Hittar seemed an impressive character, dressed in a neatly wrapped turban and expensive-looking *thaub*. A learned scholar of Islam, he told me how he used this knowledge to outmanoeuvre fanatical prisoners when it came to discussions on Islam and *jihad*.

'Sometimes it can take months,' he said, 'before we convince someone to renounce violence.'

'But surely,' I asked, 'isn't there a risk that some people will just say anything and sign anything in order to get out of prison and then go back to plotting attacks?'

Judge Hittar was realistic. 'Maybe,' he admitted. 'But then we watch them carefully after they come out, and besides, they have pledged on their family honour to behave.'

The British Foreign Office was impressed with Hittar, so much so that they invited him to London a few weeks later and asked him to address an audience of counter-terrorism specialists on the lessons Yemen had learned in adopting this unusual method of combating violent religious extremism.

But the US Embassy in Sana'a, I learned, took a fairly dim view of this programme, suspecting that it was a way for dangerous men to get back on the streets, where their number-one target was the US Embassy. Washington preferred a more direct approach to tackling terrorism and we were apparently the first journalists to be given a glimpse of it. In a barren, rocky gully in the desert outside the capital we were taken to see the US Army's Green Berets training Yemen's secretive Counter-Terrorist Unit. The Americans were huge men in shirtsleeves and dark woollen deerstalker hats and they all seemed to be called Hank and Al. We found them taking the Yemenis through a hostage-rescue scenario, showing them how to force entry into a hollow, plywood hut with no roof, then take out the targets inside. The Yemeni troops were on a high. Just that week they had brought about the capture of the country's most wanted terror suspect, Muhammed Al-Ahdal, without a shot being fired. A tip-off from an informer had led them to surround a house in Sana'a where Al-Ahdal was getting married. At dawn they sent in a messenger to tell him his situation was hopeless and that for the sake of his new wife and relatives he should surrender. Unusually, for someone supposed to be an Al-Qaeda fanatic, he did just that.

In Sana'a I stumbled on a story that had never been made public. A diplomat I knew vaguely at one of the Western embassies in the capital told me he had some information that was too sensitive to discuss over the phone. We should meet face-to-face, he said, so I suggested a night-time rendezvous on the roof of one of the centuries-old mud-walled houses in the Old City, which had been turned into a cheap hotel for backpackers. I knew that the rooftop was one of the most secluded places in Sana'a and it would be almost impossible for anyone to eavesdrop on our conversation.

Leaving Tony, my cameraman, at the hotel, I made my way

through the silent backstreets shortly before midnight. It was a route I knew well, having first explored this part of the capital as a backpacker myself in 1985, but I always found it enchanting. The narrow, twisting alleyways with their ancient, carved wooden doorways, the white stucco patterns beneath the crenellated rooftops, the glimpses of walled gardens where date palms ringed small allotments of verdant vegetables that fed several families and their livestock, all added to the impression of a timeless world that hid a thousand secrets.

Entering the seven-storey building, I ordered a pot of mint tea from the bleary-eyed boy on reception and asked for it to be brought up to the roof. He disappeared behind a curtain while I climbed the hundred or so stone steps, emerging at last on to a whitewashed rooftop bathed in the silver light of a full moon. Far away on the horizon I could just make out the dark silhouette of the volcanic mountains that ringed Sana'a, reminding me that we were over eight thousand feet above sea level up here.

My contact was bang on time, ducking his head to pass through the low doorway that led out on to the roof and taking a few minutes to get his breath back. We exchanged small talk until the mint tea arrived, leaning on the parapet and admiring the view; he then told me what was on his mind.

I ought to know, he said, that just three months earlier the British Embassy had been the target of a failed Al-Qaeda suicide-truck-bomb plot and that two other Western embassies had also been targeted. Since the British Embassy building was situated on a busy crossroads the bombers' plan was to drive at full speed through the main gate with a truck-ful of explosives then detonate it in the inner courtyard, obliterating the front half of the Embassy. The would-be bombers came from Arab countries outside Yemen and they had reached the stage of making reconnaissance circuits of the Embassy walls, filming as they drove. But their plan was foiled by Yemeni intelligence after one of them was caught having a very un-Islamic affair with a Yemeni woman.

I thanked the diplomat and walked back to the hotel through the darkened streets. The following day we confronted the British ambassador, Frances Guy, with the story and she acknowledged how serious it had been. While of course it made a great story for the BBC's ten o'clock news, I was appalled. It was now December 2003, one month after the devastating bomb attack on the British consulate in Istanbul that killed the consul-general and many others. The circumstances were almost identical, with the target's location, on a busy crossroads in town, allowing a truck to be rammed straight at the gates and into the courtyard. Yet the plot to blow up the British Embassy in Yemen was discovered in September – two months *before* the Istanbul attack. In Yemen the British security officer had immediately demanded concrete barriers be placed in front of the gates to thwart any future attacks. He had overcome budgetary protests and got his barriers, yet no one seemed to have got the message that similarly vulnerable British missions in the region were likely targets for truck bombs. When I put this to a Home Office security official back in London, he replied defensively, 'Well, Istanbul is a long way from Yemen.' The bottom line, I believe, is that if lessons had been learned quickly from the Yemen plot then the Istanbul consulate attack could have been prevented, or at the very least mitigated.

London: Spooks and Sources

LIVING IN CAIRO HAD BEEN GOOD professionally, but a disaster on the family front. Like many foreign correspondents' partners, Amanda had not appreciated being left alone for long and indeterminate periods of time while I shuttled around the Middle East, bouncing from one story to another. The BBC had rather planned on my doing a third year out there as Middle East Correspondent, but Amanda had other ideas: 'You can do another year here in Cairo if you like,' she told me, 'but we're going home.' So that settled it.

We returned to London at the worst possible time of year. It was mid-January 2002, bitterly cold, and at first we were living out of suitcases in a hotel room. My job situation was precarious: the Cairo contract having finished, the BBC had offered me just a four-month attachment with *Newsnight*. 'After that, it's up to you to find a programme to take you on.' I was rather miffed about this – it felt as if I was starting right back at the beginning again – but *Newsnight* was quick to make the most of my Arabic and soon started sending me back to the Middle East on short reporting trips. In fact at

one point, after several days of working particularly hard, I
decided not to answer the home phone, but the next thing we
knew the *Newsnight* driver was knocking at the door, saying,
'Sorry, Mr Gardner, they need you to go to Beirut.'

It was still less than six months since 9/11 and I found
myself being increasingly drawn towards investigative stories:
how much did Western intelligence know about Al-Qaeda?
What support was there for Bin Laden and his ideology in the
Middle East? Where could he be hiding? With less than a
week to go before my attachment ended and I was officially
out of a job, I was offered a correspondent post, 'following
up on 9/11 stories for the main news bulletins'. Again, it was
to be one of these infernal temporary contracts – the BBC
offered three months, I insisted on six. And then, suddenly,
things just snowballed. I found myself doing live interviews
outside the Foreign Office on the latest arrests of Al-Qaeda
suspects, and interviews by satellite from our Washington
bureau. I needed a title, and since 'War on Terror
Correspondent' would have sounded ridiculous I suggested
'Security Correspondent'. A new role was born.

Just as I was finding my feet in this new job I had a call
from the Foreign Office. It was someone in the news department whom I knew from my days in Yemen. 'Would you like
to be able to speak to someone in the intelligence services
from time to time, Frank?' he asked. My antennae began
twitching; was this an approach to recruit me, I asked. The
diplomat laughed. 'No. It's just that there is someone in each
service who is officially allowed to brief the media on intelligence issues and there are a number of journalists here who
have this access.' That figured, I thought. There was no way
that the broadsheet newspaper correspondents could have
known some of the things they wrote about so authoritatively
if they were not being briefed by someone inside the
intelligence community. Still, I was wary of anyone in
government trying to tap me for my sources, and had no

intention of becoming a mouthpiece for the intelligence services, so I went to our first meeting very much on my guard. After all, it was only eight years since it had been official government policy not even to confirm the existence of MI6.

The media officer from MI6 turned out to be a perfectly ordinary and likeable human being. I am not sure quite what I had been expecting: a man in a trenchcoat and trilby, perhaps, staring straight ahead while sitting down beside me and whispering, 'It is always cold in Minsk in March.' But of course our meeting was nothing like that. We ordered cappuccinos and got down to setting out the ground rules. There had to be trust, he said, which meant never revealing his name and never attributing anything directly to 'the Service' (MI6). If I did so I would no longer be given this access, it was as simple as that. I asked why the media was being given this access in the first place.

'We want to try to ensure the coverage is accurate without compromising operations,' I was told, 'because, let's face it, the media is prone to sensationalism.'

'All right,' I replied. 'Now I have a few guidelines of my own. Please never ask me to reveal any of my journalistic sources. I am happy to discuss the Middle East in general terms, but I won't tell you anything I am not already broadcasting on air.'

The officer nodded and drained his cup. It has always been of paramount importance to me that I maintain a strict journalistic neutrality, whatever private feelings I may have about the topic I am reporting on. And yet some of my BBC colleagues remained convinced that since I had access to intelligence-agency spokesmen, ergo I must surely be working for them. Quite how they imagined I would have time to moonlight for the spooks in between doing live interviews for *Breakfast News*, Radio 5 Live, News 24, BBC World and World Service radio, and editing TV reports for the one, six and ten o'clock news bulletins was not clear.

There followed an introduction to another media officer, this time from MI5, who were rather further along the curve than MI6 in their approach to public relations. Whereas 'C', as the head of MI6 is known, intentionally had no public persona, the Security Service's director-general, Eliza Manningham-Buller, had begun making a number of public speeches to selected audiences. With her background in Irish counter-terrorism she had grasped the seriousness of the terrorist threat from Al-Qaeda and saw it as her duty to reveal the nature of that threat. As part of my effort to broaden my base of sources in government, I also managed to arrange a one-off meeting with the public-relations team from the highly secretive government listening station, GCHQ. But if I had any hopes of getting titbits of gossip about intercepted Al-Qaeda chatter from GCHQ, I could forget it. I learned nothing, as they were authorized to talk only about the boring logistics of their move to new premises.

Frustratingly, though, the intelligence community in Washington seemed to be as leaky as a sieve. Journalists on the *Washington Post* or the *New York Times* were always being given scoops, claiming to have been shown exclusive extracts from classified CIA, Pentagon or Congressional reports. The UK media rarely seemed to be able to match such sensational stories and when they did it was usually quietly denied by the people who knew. Far from the spooks spoon-feeding the media stories, my experience of dealing with them has been more akin to getting blood out of a stone.

In the aftermath of 9/11, British intelligence began taking a closer interest in the various Islamist activists living in the UK, some of whom had fought in Afghanistan and other *jihadi* fields of combat. Since the mid-1990s London had been home to just about every Middle Eastern opposition movement in existence: Algerian, Iraqi, Saudi, Egyptian and others. The British government's policy towards them had been what it called one of 'watchful tolerance': as long as the dissidents did not break UK law they would reside here as political refugees. In fact Britain rather prided itself on being a safe haven for people who faced imprisonment, torture and execution in their home countries, even though some of these men were considered to be terrorists elsewhere.

Britain's Middle Eastern dissidents took full advantage of these liberal policies. They churned out propaganda against their countries' governments, held countless meetings, some open, some closed, and even set up satellite broadcasts to audiences back home. They also largely welcomed the attentions of us journalists, who gave them an outlet in the Western media for their stories of government corruption and human-rights abuses. We in turn got a plethora of sources and a different – if sometimes warped – perspective on what was going on in their home countries, which we could never have got from official sources or from the news wires.

Back in the mid-1990s many of us in the media had assumed that MI5 was watching the dissidents closely. After all, some of these men were not just opponents of their own governments, they were also bitterly opposed to the West and its policies in the Arab world. We were wrong. MI5 back then had very few Arabists on its books and it was not overly concerned by the activities of the Arab émigré community in Britain. Its inerests lay closer to home, in the form of the IRA's threat to target mainland Britain. For them, it was a question of priorities: the IRA posed an immediate threat to British lives; the Islamists didn't. But the bombings in France were about to change that.

During the summer of 1995 Algeria's principal rebel group, the GIA, took its battle on to the streets of France. It set off bombs in the Paris *métro*, killing eight people and causing horrific wounds to over a hundred others since the bombs were packed with nails inside gas canisters; it also tried unsuccessfully to target a high-speed train to Lyons. GIA's rationale for these attacks was that since the French government supported the military-backed government in the former French colony of Algeria, then France was, by extension, a legitimate target. The French security services reacted to the bombings with speed and vigour, rounding up numerous suspects and driving many others into hiding. To the frustration of the French, many of the suspected militants they hoped to question simply disappeared into the growing North African community in London. The British government effectively shrugged its shoulders, saying no UK laws had been broken.

But in the late 1990s, as the threat to Europe from a tiny minority of North African extremists gradually became apparent, MI5 began to look more closely at those extremists living in Britain. It acquired copies of some of the grisly videotapes that were circulating in the extremist underworld in London, Birmingham and elsewhere: tapes from Bosnia, and from North Africa showing ambushes on Algerian army convoys, where the rebels would line up captured conscripts and calmly slit their throats. Yet turning round British intelligence to face the threat of Al-Qaeda-inspired terrorism was rather like getting an ocean-going supertanker to change course.

For decades MI6 had been concentrating on fighting the Cold War, amassing a wealth of in-house expertise and a network of agents familiar with the inner workings of the Warsaw Pact countries of Eastern Europe. Likewise MI5, the Security Service which looks after domestic intelligence-gathering in the UK, had focused much of its efforts on counter-espionage, trying to prevent communist-bloc agents from stealing Britain's secrets. Both services had also spent a lot of time confronting the threat from the IRA. But now they were fighting a new, obscure and extremely dangerous enemy in the form of Al-Qaeda and its affiliated operatives.

When the news broke in May 2002 that a plot to ram explosives-laden dinghies into Western warships in the Strait of Gibraltar had been thwarted, my persistent questioning was eventually rewarded with a detailed explanation of the intelligence background. It was one of the very few intelligence operations that Whitehall officials were allowed to discuss with the media, perhaps because it had been so conclusive. Working together, British, French, Spanish and Moroccan intelligence had intercepted the plan to launch the dinghies from Morocco's Mediterranean coast. They had used, I was told, intelligence gleaned from a Moroccan prisoner in Guantanamo Bay which had led investigators there to uncover a network of Saudi and Syrian extremists living in Casablanca. There were several arrests and a trial, although this did not prevent the Casablanca bombings the following year that killed over forty people.

By the summer of 2002 the whole issue of the US military prison camp at Guantanamo Bay had become deeply controversial. The Pentagon had already suffered a PR disaster in January when the world's media witnessed the arrival of hundreds of Al-Qaeda and Taliban suspects off transport planes from Afghanistan. They were herded into cages, hooded, manacled, shackled and dressed in bright-orange jumpsuits, a detail later copied by followers of Al-Qaeda when they seized hostages in Pakistan and Iraq. President Bush had designated the prisoners as 'enemy combatants' and his defence secretary, Donald Rumsfeld, had branded them as 'some of the most dangerous terrorists on the face of the earth'. But the numbers were so large – over six hundred inmates – that it seemed doubtful that they could all be key operatives. Most of these men had been swept up by US or Afghan forces following the rout of the Taliban in late 2001, some were Arab aid workers arrested by suspicious police in Pakistan or even sold on to the Americans as 'terror suspects' by unscrupulous kidnappers, and some turned out to be innocent Afghan taxi-drivers. I became convinced that the USA was holding its so-called 'high-value suspects' elsewhere well out of the public eye, somewhere like Bagram airbase in Afghanistan, or on board a warship in international waters, or possibly in obscure countries where there would be few witnesses to interrogation. But I was still curious to see first-hand how Guantanamo Bay fitted into the US-led War on Terror, and that summer I got my chance. The Pentagon's Joint Southern Command granted access for a team of four of us from the BBC to fly in with our portable satellite dish and pay a rare visit to the prison camp.

It was a convoluted journey to reach Guantanamo Bay: London to Washington to pick up the crew, then down to Miami and Puerto Rico, where we boarded a US Navy plane at dawn for the short flight across the Caribbean to Cuba. I had been to Havana and the Cuban coast on holiday in the 1990s and had been expecting lush, tropical scenery. Instead, the plane banked over the barren, desiccated eastern tip of Cuba, where low, cacti-covered hills were bound by a razor-wire fence that marked the border between this leased US colony and Fidel Castro's socialist paradise. We were ordered to line up behind our bags on the edge of the runway while a team of sniffer dogs probed and slavered their way round our kit, before we were driven through the hills down to the coast and Camp Delta, the new purpose-built prison camp that had replaced the infamous transparent cages of Camp X-Ray.

Understandably perhaps, the US military was paranoid about security, letting us film almost nothing of Camp Delta. We were given a very narrow arc, about thirty degrees, within which we could point our camera and most of that was blocked by a corrugated-metal shipping container, part of the ongoing construction work to upgrade the camp into a more permanent structure. Al-Qaeda's chief strategist, Dr Ayman Al-Zawahiri, had recently issued a statement saying it was the duty of Muslims to try to free their brothers from jail in Guantanamo Bay and the Americans were taking no chances: they had round-the-clock surveillance of the harbour with heavily armed patrol boats manned by the US Coast Guard. We were allowed no contact with the inmates, in fact we could not even see them, but we were allowed to interview some of the US military prison staff. One NCO let slip that there had been up to thirty attempted suicides amongst the prisoners and that made instant news. Another told us that some of the more hardcore prisoners had thrown their own faeces and urine at him when he entered their cells. Most interesting to me was the chaplain, an amiable, overweight Friar Tuck character who was sweating profusely in the Caribbean heat.

'Some of these guys thought I was the devil incarnate when they first met me,' he told us, referring to the Afghan and Arab prisoners. 'I mean, I was the first Christian they had ever met and they reckoned I had a long spiky tail or something. But after a while they found I wasn't so bad and they began to open up a little. I do believe I have offered them some comfort in these difficult times.' Over all, I found the attitude of the US military guards to be one of defensive defiance, a sort of 'Hell, yeah, of course these guys are dangerous, why shouldn't we lock 'em up?' It did not seem to trouble anyone I met that incarcerating prisoners without trial or access to lawyers might be wrong or damaging to Muslim perceptions of the West. It had, of course, been only ten months since the 9/11 attacks on New York and Washington and America was still reeling from the loss of its invincibility, but I would say that the priorities at Guantanamo Bay in August 2002 were, in descending order:

1. interrogate the prisoners for information on impending Al-Qaeda attacks,
2. interrogate the prisoners for background information on

how they had been recruited, where they had trained, who they knew and so on,

3. ensure none of them escaped to pose a danger to the USA,
4. at some time in the future – but no rush here – try the detainees before military tribunals in lieu of civilian courts.

Other BBC correspondents have had better luck at Guantanamo Bay. One infuriated his escorts by managing to have a shouted conversation with some prisoners, while Gavin Hewitt timed his visit perfectly to coincide with the release of the British captives whose detention without trial had been a source of mild friction between Washington and London. Intelligence officers from both MI5 and MI6 had been going over to Guantanamo Bay to interview some of the detainees, just as they had done in Afghanistan in the months after 9/11. In most cases the British government did not believe that the British detainees posed a threat to UK security; there were other detainees around the world of far more intelligence value whose names were not coming up in association with Cuba, and these were the ones they were most interested in.

Personally, I think Guantanamo Bay has been disastrous for the USA and the West in general. It may have given some people in the Pentagon and the Bush administration a warm feeling inside to sweep up several hundred Islamist suspects from Afghanistan and Pakistan and cart them all off to a remote colony out of reach of civil courts or human-rights campaigners. Some valuable intelligence about Al-Qaeda may well have been gleaned in the early weeks after the camp was set up, but the damage done to Muslim and Arab perceptions of Western justice has been exponential. For every suspect locked away in Guantanamo Bay without trial – and without even a prospect of a trial for years – untold numbers in their home countries have turned against the USA, disgusted that the country which claimed to champion democracy around the world should have such scant regard for human rights. Until the US-led invasion of Iraq, Guantanamo Bay probably did more to reverse the tide of global sympathy for the USA after 9/11 than anything else; it effectively played right into Al-Qaeda's hands, allowing their recruiters to say, 'Look, we told you so. America just wants to humiliate and punish Muslims, it doesn't care about your rights. Believe us when we say the War on Terror is a war against Islam.'

Attacks by Al-Qaeda and its affiliates did not stop with 9/11, but they changed direction, sometimes targeting holiday resorts where Westerners gather, like Bali and Sharm El-Sheikh, sometimes targeting Jews, as in Mombasa, Tunisia and Casablanca. In Britain there was much media speculation about whether the country was a target, and I was criticized in 2002 by a retired newspaper editor in his opinion column for saying that it was. Accusing me of scaremongering, he wittily described me as 'the BBC's Insecurity Correspondent', but I had my reasons to be pessimistic and they had nothing to do with what the politicians or police chiefs in London were saying. A wide body of opinion in the Middle East still holds Britain responsible for the creation of the state of Israel, blaming this country in part for the misery of millions of Palestinians living either as refugees in Jordan, Lebanon and elsewhere, or living under Israeli military occupation in their own land. As Washington's closest ally, Britain is often seen as being complicit in US policy towards Israel and the Palestinians, whereas in reality the British government has worked hard to win a fair deal for both sides. A serving British ambassador in the Middle East told me he had personally seen Tony Blair lecture the Israeli prime minister, Ariel Sharon, about the need to give Palestinians more freedom. But Britain's influence in the region is a pale shadow of what it used to be, and its ineffectual efforts are often mistaken for a lack of interest or even acquiescence to a deeply unsatisfactory situation on the ground. Then there is the question of Britain's friendly relations with Middle Eastern regimes which Al-Qaeda sees as 'corrupt and apostate', notably Saudi Arabia, Jordan and Egypt; Al-Qaeda's ideologues have long called on the West to sever its ties with such governments, believing that once this happens they will collapse under a wave of popular resentment. More recently, Britain's role in the military campaign against the Taliban and Al-Qaeda in Afghanistan has put us firmly on their target list.

So when, in February 2003, the government deployed the Army to Heathrow in response to a terror alert, I did not see this – as some did at the time – as a political gimmick to get the public to back the coming invasion of Iraq. The Heathrow alert had nothing to do with Iraq; instead, it came from a captured Al-Qaeda supporter whose information had proved to be right before. He had let slip that there was a plot to bring down an airliner at Heathrow using a surface-to-air missile. The information passed up the chain of Britain's intelligence apparatus until it reached Sir David Omand, the National Intelligence and Security Coordinator; he now had the problem of what to do with it. Sir David told me later that year that he had gone straight round to Number Ten Downing Street, where Tony Blair was in his living room watching football on TV with their baby Leo. 'We have three choices,' Sir David told the prime minister. 'We can close Heathrow altogether, which would obviously be disastrous for business and tourism; we can do nothing, which in the circumstances would not be an option; or we can trigger a full-scale security alert.' The two men agreed to opt for the latter and the following day there was a meeting of the Cabinet Office Briefing Room, an emergency committee convened in times of national crisis. It was chaired by Tony Blair and attended by Sir David Veness, the head of Scotland Yard's Special Operations at the time (he later went off to work for the UN in New York), as well as a senior military officer and Alastair Darling, the transport secretary. David Blunkett, the home secretary, was said to be in a foul mood because nobody had consulted him until then. It was agreed that a large security presence was needed to deter the would-be attackers by making Heathrow a 'hard target'. Veness said he did not have the manpower to cover Heathrow sufficiently, including the land around its runways, at short notice. The Army said they could do it but they wanted their men armed and protected in their armoured vehicles. Hence the deployment to Heathrow of a cavalry unit in light reconnaissance vehicles (which the media wrongly called 'tanks'), while, out of public sight, plain-clothes soldiers from the Special Air Service patrolled the ground beneath the flightpaths around and beyond the runways. Was it an over-reaction? Not according to most of the passengers the BBC interviewed at Heathrow, who said they found the military presence 'reassuring'. However, the actual threat never materialized, and no surface-to-air missiles or their owners were discovered. That could mean the information was wrong or that the security alert did its job; we will never know.

Nine months later, on 3 November 2003, the first direct Al-Qaeda-inspired attack on British interests took place in Istanbul. I was on board a long-haul flight to Heathrow from Islamabad, having just spent a few weeks on the road reporting from Afghanistan and Pakistan, and as the plane taxied towards the terminal I was looking forward to a hot bath and an afternoon in the park with my family. It was not to be. The voice of the Emirates crew's First Officer crackled over the PA system: 'Could Mr Frank Gardner please make himself known to the ground staff immediately on arrival.' Stepping into the air corridor, I was told there had been a massive explosion at the British Consulate in Istanbul and another at HSBC; I was needed to appear live on the one o'clock news. I looked at my watch: it was ten past twelve. I had less than an hour in which to find a taxi, get into London to Television Centre, phone Amanda to break the news that I would probably not be home now till nearly midnight, and, most critically, make the necessary calls to find out exactly what had happened, and who were the most likely suspects.

My first call was to our news desk, where the BBC's invaluable John Witney had taken the initiative to get me tannoyed on the plane. I jotted down the details as my taxi lurched through Hounslow, occasionally dropping my mobile when we swerved round a bend. Two blasts – one at the British Consulate, another at HSBC, many casualties, no immediate claim of responsibility: all indications that this could be the work of individuals inspired by Al-Qaeda. Al-Qaeda attacks usually have a number of identifying features: no warnings, multiple synchronized explosions often carried out by suicide bombers, often using truck bombs, Western or Jewish targets, and maximum possible loss of human life. That morning's explosions in Istanbul ticked all the boxes. But I have never gone on air with just my opinions alone if I can avoid it, so my next two calls were to two Arab experts I know who independently follow Al-Qaeda's activities and have proved accurate in their assessments in the past. They were both convinced this was the work of a group inspired and possibly directed by Al-Qaeda.

I then phoned the intelligence agencies, knowing only too well that it was far too early for them to have formed a view but aware that any snippet they could give me – even if it proved in the end to be wrong – would throw some colour on this developing story. Had they, for example, been aware of any recent 'chatter' (internet and telephone gossip between Al-Qaeda supporters) that mentioned a target in Turkey? What had been the threat assessment for Istanbul prior to this attack? What groups did they know that might be responsible? What were their Turkish counterparts telling them? The media officers in MI5 and MI6 did not have all the answers – actually they didn't have any, or if they did they were not going to share them with me. I could appreciate that it would hardly help their work if they revealed too much to the media of what they knew about their terrorist opponents, but on the other hand I often have the impression that in their shadowy struggle against Al-Qaeda the intelligence agencies are somewhat embarrassed to admit how little they do know in some situations, evidence of the extreme difficulties they face in getting human informers inside the top layers of Islamist terrorist cells.

By one o'clock I was on the set of the lunchtime news, just. There was make-up over my stubble and I was still in the same white shirt I had worn to go birdwatching the previous evening in the Himalayan foothills outside Islamabad, but when Anna Ford asked me for my assessment I at least had some details to give her and the few million people watching. By the time I went live on the six and ten o'clock bulletins I had had a chance to phone more people, including the CIA's Public Affairs Office, which rarely gives out anything beyond the obvious ('We have reason to believe this was a terrorist attack') but is always good for a quote ('Don't say "CIA", say "US security officials"'). But it was in those first, frenetic fifty minutes that having good contacts paid off. When the proverbial hits the fan you do not have time to start cultivating new contacts and persuading people who do not know you to part with sensitive or even commercially valuable information. You have to call the people you know well, listen to their views, assess them and move on.

Four months later, on 11 March 2004, Al-Qaeda struck Madrid's suburban commuter trains with ten rucksack bombs, killing nearly two hundred passengers in the worst terrorist attack on mainland Europe to date. I took the call from the indefatigable one o'clock news just as I was dropping the children off at school. 'There've been some

left: Amanda in the Wahiba Sands, Oman, 1993.

left: My official BBC mugshot, shown on television each time I was interviewed from Dubai; viewers never knew I was usually on the phone wearing swimming shorts.

left: With Sasha and Melissa on the Mount of Olives, Jerusalem, 2001.
below: In Cairo's Islamic quarter with Raouf Ibrahim, the BBC's invaluable driver.

above: Cairo skyline, our block at centre left: the wiring was somewhat pharaonic.
left: Omani Bedu women of the Bani Wahiba inspect our camera.

Osama Bin Laden: he initially chose the BBC for his first television interview in 1996.

Saddam's torched yacht, Basra, 2003.

below: With the Riyadh bombing forensic investigators, 2003.

above: In a Pakistani village in the Tribal Territories near Peshawar, 2003; here we found the Taliban to be popular; the USA was not.

right: Phil Goodwin, me and Dominic Hurst at Shkin Firebase, south-east Afghanistan, 2003.

above: Yemen's newly formed Counter-Terrorist Unit, 2003.

below: Historic Sana'a: the Yemeni capital was like a living museum.

left: Simon Cumbers: murdered by Al-Qaeda on 6 June 2004.
below: My hour of agony: at first no one helped me as I lay bleeding from eleven bullet wounds.
bottom: The Saudi police scooping me off the street and into their patrol car.

OPPOSITE PAGE:
My Riyadh medical report and a photo of my torso taken on the night I was shot. Seeing this picture has made me realize how far I've come.
bottom, left: April 2005: my first day back at work and an emotional interview with Dermot and Natasha on BBC Breakfast News.
bottom, right: Back at my old desk at the BBC after five hospitals and twelve operations.

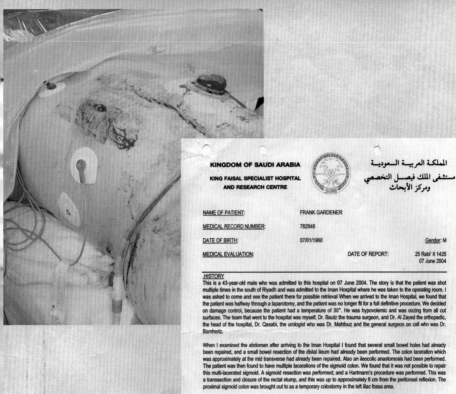

KINGDOM OF SAUDI ARABIA

**KING FAISAL SPECIALIST HOSPITAL
AND RESEARCH CENTRE**

المملكة العربية السعودية

مستشفى الملك فيصل التخصصي
ومركز الأبحاث

NAME OF PATIENT:	FRANK GARDENER
MEDICAL RECORD NUMBER:	782848
DATE OF BIRTH:	07/01/1960 Gender: M
MEDICAL EVALUATION:	DATE OF REPORT: 25 Rabi' II 1425
	07 June 2004

HISTORY

This is a 43-year-old male who was admitted to this hospital on 07 June 2004. The story is that the patient was shot multiple times in the south of Riyadh and was admitted to the Iman Hospital where he was taken to the operating room. I was asked to come and see the patient there for possible retrieval. When we arrived to the Iman Hospital, we found that the patient was halfway through a laparotomy, and the patient was no longer fit for a full definitive procedure. We decided on damage control, because the patient had a temperature of 30°. He was hypovolemic and was oozing from all cut surfaces. The team that went to the hospital was myself, Dr. Bautz the trauma surgeon, and Dr. Al Zayed the orthopedic, the head of the hospital, Dr. Qasabi, the urologist who was Dr. Mahfouz and the general surgeon on call who was Dr. Bamheriz.

When I examined the abdomen after arriving to the Iman Hospital I found that several small bowel holes had already been repaired, and a small bowel resection of the distal ileum had already been performed. The colon laceration which was approximately at the mid transverse had already been repaired. Also an ileocolic anastomosis had been performed. The patient was then found to have multiple lacerations of the sigmoid colon. We found that it was not possible to repair this multi-lacerated sigmoid. A sigmoid resection was performed; and a Hartmann's procedure was performed. This was a transsection and closure of the rectal stump, and this was up to approximately 8 cm from the peritoneal reflexion. The proximal sigmoid colon was brought out as a temporary colostomy in the left iliac fossa area.

EXAMINATION

On examination of this patient, there was a pelvic hematoma and multiple gunshot wounds. He had retroperitoneal ... ve solved this instability, the patient was then closed at that stage when he was hemodynamically ... ssure on leaving the Iman Hospital was 120 systolic, and the patient had been covered to prevent heat ... sferred the patient to King Faisal Specialist Hospital, and he arrived here shortly after midnight on 7 ... arrival, the patient had a temperature of approximately 30°, and he was found to have almost ... c blood pressure upon arrival to the emergency room where we stopped before going to the intensive ... ent was fluid resuscitated and after about half an hour, the patient had stabilized.

MEDICAL EVALUATION

برقيا: التخصصي   تلفون: ٧٢٧٢-٤٦٤ (٩٦٦-١)   فاكس: ٤٨٣٩-٤٤١ (٩٦٦-١)   تلكس: ٤٠١٠٥٠: تخصصي مع   ص.ب: ٣٥٤

...yadh 11211   Telex : 401050: RYSPEC SJ   Fax : (966–1) 441–4839   Telephone: (966–1) 464–7272   Cable : Specialist

...15)   I.C. 202040

above: Meeting the Queen to receive my OBE in October 2005: I was wearing callipers and palace officials were terrified I was going to topple on to Her Majesty.

left: Supported by my parents outside Buckingham Palace, 2005 – a proud moment for so many reasons.

explosions in Madrid, the Spanish think it might be ETA,'
said the producer. I did not have a great deal of expertise on
ETA, but as the death toll mounted my suspicions increased
that something more sinister than this Basque separatist
movement might be to blame. Once again, I had less than an
hour in which to get myself into the studios and make the
vital phone calls before starting a round of appearances on
News 24 and BBC World. JTAC, the government's Joint
Terrorist Analysis Centre that sits inside MI5 headquarters
and assesses the threat to UK citizens globally on a daily
basis, was keeping an open mind but tending to listen to the
Spanish government, who thought it was ETA. The Spanish
counter-terrorism people had an excellent reputation (unlike
those in some other Western European countries), honed by
decades of combating ETA, so JTAC's inclination was to
follow their lead. But in investigating the Madrid bombings
the Spanish were fatally influenced by politics. While the
politicians of Prime Minister José María Aznar's government
were busy telling Spanish journalists that ETA was obviously
to blame and that 'anyone who doubted this was being
irresponsible', the Madrid police were discovering an
abandoned van containing tapes of Koranic recitations and a
pile of detonators for explosives. They also traced the mobile
phone in the one rucksack bomb that had failed to detonate
back to a phone shop used by North African immigrants
suspected of belonging to the Moroccan Islamic Combat
Group, an extremist group linked to Al-Qaeda. It took
Britain's intelligence community forty-eight hours to concur
that their early inclinations towards ETA being the probable
culprits had been wrong and that Al-Qaeda had, after all,
been to blame. In Britain there was no harm done, but for
Spain's government the mistake – or, as many suspected, the
deceit – was unforgivable. In the nationwide elections two
days later a furious electorate punished Aznar's right-wing,
pro-Bush government by voting it out of office, ushering in a

new prime minister, Señor Zapatero, who had pledged to bring Spanish troops home from Iraq. Al-Qaeda was delighted. For the first time they believed they had managed to change the course of politics in the West, using terrorism to influence an election that resulted in the withdrawal of a major NATO ally from a *jihadi* battleground, Iraq. In fact Al-Qaeda was so encouraged by this development, as they saw it, that soon afterwards Osama Bin Laden issued an audio statement offering Europe a *hudna*, a truce, if it withdrew its forces from Islamic lands, i.e., Iraq and Afghanistan. Bin Laden made the point that it was nonsense to claim, as some had in Washington, that Al-Qaeda hated the West for its lifestyle. 'Do you see us bombing Sweden?' he argued. 'No, we do not attack Sweden because it has no troops in our lands.' At the time, in the early summer of 2004, there was a brief flurry of debate in the British and European media about the rights and wrongs of doing a deal with Al-Qaeda, but it was hypothetical anyway. No one in Whitehall seriously considered making any kind of a treaty with Al-Qaeda, and ministers have since pointed out that Al-Qaeda was attacking Western targets – notably New York and Washington – long before Coalition forces entered Iraq or Afghanistan.

Incredibly, even after the Madrid bombings, there were some who still thought the terrorist threat to Britain was the political invention of a cynical government. That delusion was to be shattered horribly on 7 July 2005, of which more in the final chapter. Yet who could blame them? The massive bungle over Iraq's alleged Weapons of Mass Destruction (WMD) had led the British public to distrust the authorities when they spoke of secret intelligence. It will be a very long time indeed before a government in power can expect to convince Parliament and the public with the words, 'Trust us, if you had seen the intelligence we have.'

8

Iraq and Afghanistan: the New *Jihad*

O SAMA BIN LADEN – AND WHAT WAS LEFT of Al-Qaeda in early 2003 – sat out the Iraq war on the sidelines. They have made up for it since. Sitting in his hideout, probably in Pakistan or Afghanistan, Bin Laden issued a desperate, last-minute appeal to Iraqi and other Muslims that was broadcast by Al-Jazeera as an audio statement on 11 February 2003. Bin Laden told Muslims it was their sacred duty to go and defend Iraq from invasion and occupation by the 'crusaders' (Al-Qaeda's term for any Western military presence in the Middle East).

'We are following up with great interest and extreme concern the crusaders' preparations for war to occupy a former capital of Islam [Baghdad],' said the Al-Qaeda leader, 'to loot Muslims' wealth, and install an agent government, which would be a satellite for its masters in Washington and Tel Aviv, just like all the other treasonous and agent Arab governments. This would be in preparation for establishing the Greater Israel.'

In his lengthy broadcast, Bin Laden advised Iraqis to use the ground to their advantage and dig plenty of trenches. He boasted that this was how three hundred of his *mujahideen* had survived massive aerial bombardment by the Americans in the mountains of Tora Bora in late 2001. US soldiers, he said, had no combat spirit, they were 'completely convinced of the injustice and lying of their government. They also lack a fair cause to defend. They only fight for capitalists, usury takers, and the merchants of arms and oil, including the gang of crime at the White House.'

At the time, Bin Laden was wasting his breath. Almost everyone in the Arab world had deep misgivings, to say the least, about a US-led invasion of Iraq, but few were prepared to act to stop it. Amr Moussa, the articulate head of the Arab League, spoke for many when he complained shortly before the invasion: 'You cannot deliver democracy to the Middle East at the end of a tank barrel.'

Bin Laden said, 'Regardless of the removal or the survival of the socialist Ba'ath party or Saddam, Muslims in general and the Iraqis in particular must brace themselves for *jihad* against this unjust campaign and acquire ammunition and weapons.' In other words, he did not care if Saddam's regime lived on or died. All that mattered was preventing another Muslim country from being invaded and occupied by the US-led Coalition.

Let us be very clear about Iraq and Al-Qaeda. In the run-up to war in early 2003 there was not one single major intelligence agency that believed there was any institutional link between the regime of President Saddam Hussein and Al-Qaeda. God knows, the White House and the CIA did their level best to find one. But months of research, analysis, quizzing of informants and trawling through intercepted telephone conversations could find only occasional, exploratory contacts between Iraqi officials and Bin Laden's followers, mostly from the time when he was living in Sudan in the early 1990s. By 2003 the consensus in the international intelligence community was that Saddam and Al-Qaeda were not on the same team.

The nearest anyone could come to a connection between them was the Islamist group Ansar Al-Islam and its protégé, Abu Musab Al-Zarqawi. But Ansar Al-Islam had set up base close to the Iranian border in a remote, mountainous corner of Iraqi Kurdistan that was outside the control of Saddam's forces. In August 2002 Western intelligence agencies believed they had tracked Al-Zarqawi to Baghdad; they believed the Iraqi authorities knew of his presence but they did not detect any signs of cooperation. Yet while there was little sign of Al-Qaeda activity in Saddam Hussein's Iraq, within a year of invasion that country was to become the primary cause célèbre for Al-Qaeda and the international *jihadi* movement. The US-led invasion and occupation was to transform what was once a brutal, repressive but essentially secular dictatorship into the biggest live laboratory for terrorism. Iraq effectively became a recruiting agent for violent *jihadi* Islamists from all over the Arab world and even Europe.

I first entered Iraq by mistake. In the aftermath of the Gulf War that drove Saddam's troops out of Kuwait in February 1991, the Iraq–Kuwait border was just a line on the map with little to demarcate it on the ground. I was running the Middle East office of the British merchant bank Flemings at the time and I had arrived in Kuwait to pick up the pieces of our Kuwaiti business after seven months of Iraqi occupation and six weeks of war. Over seven hundred Kuwaiti oil wells were blazing out of control, having been set on fire by retreating Iraqi troops as a last act of vandalism, and it had been a rocky final approach to the airport with the little Kuwait Airways Boeing jolting and shaking as we descended through the black smog.

Six months after liberation, Kuwait City was still a mess, with rubble piled up in the souk and Iraqi sandbags still facing out to sea where the US Marines had been wrongly expected to come from. Graffiti daubed on a roundabout in blood-red paint read 'Tank U Thatcher'. (Although John Major had become prime minister by the time Kuwait was liberated, it had been Margaret Thatcher who formed the initial coalition with President George Bush Snr to free Kuwait. I took a photograph of this Anglophilic graffiti, thinking it would be amusing to present it to Mrs Thatcher the following week at a British Embassy reception. She was curiously unappreciative and asked me to give it to a tall, rather coarse-looking man beside her. 'This is my son Mark. He'll look after it.')

My boss Rupert Wise had come with me to Kuwait to show me round and he introduced me to a powerfully built young Kuwaiti with a muscular chest that strained against the clean white lines of his traditional *dishdasha* robe.

'This is Sheikh Khaled Al-Sabah,' said Rupert. 'He stayed in Kuwait during the occupation and helped the resistance.'

Khaled winced with embarrassment at so formal an introduction, mumbling something modest as we took our seats at an outdoor restaurant serving plates of sizzling grilled kebabs beneath a dusty date palm.

The three of us drove up to Mutla Ridge, a low sand hill north of Kuwait bay where the retreating convoy of Iraqis had been caught by the US Air Force in a hail of cannon fire from the air, a so-called 'turkey shoot' that generated horrific images of blackened corpses frozen in agony as the looters had tried in vain to escape from their blazing vehicles. The hundreds of tanks, trucks and looted civilian vehicles had all been bulldozed off the road and now stood abandoned in the sand. Belts of live ammunition lay all around, there were unopened crates of rocket-propelled grenades and ammunition boxes marked 'GHQ Jordan'. Some passing Scottish soldier had left his mark on Kuwait by graffiti-ing a lorry with the choice words 'Fuck the Poll Tax'.

Sheikh Khaled Al-Sabah suddenly became very animated. On a windswept sand dune he had come across an Iraqi military intelligence file. 'I can't believe it!' he said, pointing at a weasel-faced man on the opened page that flapped in the breeze. 'I know this man, he used to come to my house every day! I always knew he was an Iraqi intelligence agent but I never thought his own people were keeping tabs on him.' Khaled told us how, as a member of Kuwait's ruling Al-Sabah family, he had had to adopt a different name while he stayed on incognito during the Iraqi occupation. 'I know you are a clever man and you know many people,' the Iraqi agent had said to Khaled, 'so we will pay you one thousand dinars for every Al-Sabah family member you can lead us to.' 'Don't worry,' bluffed Khaled Al-Sabah. 'If I catch any of those rotten Al-Sabah I will kill them myself with my bare hands!'

Soon after that Khaled and I set off to explore the war-ravaged northeast of his country, driving along the coast road that runs next to Kuwait's Bubiyan Island, one of the two islands which Saddam claimed were Iraqi when he invaded. It was as if the Iraqi army had left yesterday. There were hastily abandoned sandbag trenches and small piles of antiquated Russian gas masks lying on the sand. Knocked-out T55 tanks were everywhere and we passed a bridge that had been destroyed in the middle by an RAF laser-guided air-to-ground missile. As we drove northward the sky grew darker and ever more menacing from the burning oil wells and we passed more than one black, stinking lake of oil. Just short of the Iraqi border we reached the oil field of Sabratayn, where the air was thick with the smell of sulphur. Our ears were deafened by the roar of half a dozen blazing well-heads, where multinational crews of specialist firemen were battling in vain to put out the flames. Pessimists predicted the fires would burn for years, but in fact the last one was snuffed out in November, nine months after they were started. The desert here was notoriously dangerous as it was littered with land-mines, making it unsafe to stray off the road.

We drove on, past a wrecked Iraqi tank that had been

flipped upside-down like a toy. Some local wit had graffitied it with the Arabic words '*Hadithat al-muroor faqat*', 'Just a traffic accident'. We passed a torn barbed-wire fence, then a long low building with an Arabic slogan on it. There was an unfamiliar flag hanging limply from the flagpole: it was red, white and black, but was lacking the additional green of the Kuwaiti flag. 'Oh my God!' cried Khaled, slamming on the brakes and turning to face me. 'We're in Iraq! We've got to get out fast!' As a Kuwaiti prince, Khaled would have been a rich prize for an Iraqi patrol, although he had taken the precaution of placing a false ID on the dashboard just in case.

As we hurtled back across the Kuwaiti border we ran into a Kuwaiti army jeep that had come after us to warn us that we were straying into enemy territory. They took us to their base, a forward observation post a mile from the border, where they served us tea in a shallow shell-scrape, an office swivel chair perched incongruously behind a heavy machine gun that pointed towards Iraq. 'Sometimes they do some shooting at us,' said their officer, Captain Al-Otaibi. 'Then we shoot a few rounds back. But praise be to Allah no one has been hurt so far.'

We had been foolish and lucky. Iraqi raiding parties were active in the area, crossing the unmarked border at night and probing deep into Kuwait, often retrieving military hardware left behind in Desert Storm. A few weeks after our visit some Western caterers were captured by the Iraqis, who claimed they had strayed over the border. After a lot of huffing and puffing from Baghdad they were eventually released, but to avoid such incidents Kuwait built a broad sand berm and trench all along the border from the Gulf to the edge of Saudi Arabia.

It took a long time after Desert Storm for the BBC to be allowed back into Iraq, but the charms of the BBC's Rageh Omar eventually led to the opening of an office in Baghdad.

In November 1998, only a month before the Pentagon's Desert Fox bombing campaign against military targets around Baghdad, I had the opportunity to slip once again into Iraq through the back door and find out what life was really like in the country's second city, Basra, unencumbered by some government minder tugging at my elbow. With the blessing of the UAE government, a ferry company in Dubai had decided to reopen the old maritime passenger and cargo service to Iraq's port of Umm Qasr, right at the top of the Gulf between the Kuwaiti and Iranian borders, on the few short miles of coastline Iraq possessed.

There were over 100,000 expatriate Iraqis living in the Emirates, and with no commercial airlines flying into sanctions-bound Iraq this new route promised to be a lifeline for them, offering a comfortable forty-hour voyage instead of having to fly first to Amman in Jordan and then make the bone-jarring twelve-hour drive across the desert to Baghdad. At first the US Consulate in Dubai was very unhappy about this scheme, fearing it would allow Iraq to break UN sanctions, but they arranged for the ferry to be inspected and on a warm autumn evening we slipped out of Dubai's Port Rashid and steamed north for Iraq.

After a day and night at sea, we passed the Kuwaiti coastline on our left, then an Iraqi oil terminal on our right that jutted far out into the Gulf. As the ship slowed to negotiate the narrow channel that led to the port of Umm Qasr, we drew level with a flat, steamy marshland littered with triangular signs warning of mines; clusters of dead, decapitated date palms stretched to the horizon. This was the scene of the dreadful battles of attrition between Iran and Iraq in the 1980s, where hundreds of thousands perished in slow-moving trench warfare that gained little ground for either side. Everyone on deck fell silent, lost in thought as we passed this ghostly battlefield.

Long before we docked we could see the lines of buses

parked beside the harbour. This was a tremendous PR opportunity for Saddam's regime and it was not going to be passed up. Hardly anyone lived in the tiny port of Umm Qasr, so the government had bussed in hundreds of citizens from Basra to form a welcome crowd on the jetty. There were the posters of Saddam plastered on to wooden signs and waved before the cameras, there were the moustachioed, green-clad security people watching everyone from behind big, aviator sunglasses, and there, for the first time I had heard it, the crowds were chanting their patriotic ode to Saddam: 'With our blood, with our souls, we sacrifice ourselves for you, Saddam.' A hapless sheep was dragged to the water's edge where it had its throat slit; watched by nodding policemen, some very overexcited young Iraqis put their hands in the blood then smeared it over the ship's hull. Watching and filming all this, I sensed already that this was a very different country from freewheeling, apolitical Dubai, and I was eager to disembark and explore.

Incredibly, nobody had told the Iraqis there were Western journalists on board, so after a brief discussion with the ship's owners port passes were issued to myself and an Australian reporter writing for *Gulf News*. We walked down the gangplank, hired a taxi, headed for Basra and that was it: we were inside Iraq with no visas and no minders. There were several military checkpoints on the short journey up to Basra – the Iraqi military was on high alert, expecting a major US assault from the air, and there had indeed been a recent bombing raid on a radar installation nearby – but our port passes got us through; the soldiers took us for sailors.

Basra in 1998 was in a terrible state. As the principal city of the Shi'ite-dominated south, it had been starved of investment for nearly a decade, suffering both from sanctions and the displeasure of Saddam Hussein. Saddam loathed the southern Shi'ites, exacting terrible vengeance on them for their short-lived uprising following the Gulf War to liberate

Kuwait. Thousands were rounded up, interrogated, tortured, executed and buried in shallow graves. Now, a city that had once been rather wistfully dubbed the Venice of the Gulf had its canals clogged with garbage, old prams and a thick green scum. A foul stench rose up from these foetid waterways, yet a few desperate fishermen still cast their lines into the canals; I made a mental note not to eat fish here. Yet there was a palpable vitality and resilience on the streets. Basrans were getting by somehow, haggling and trading in the street markets, clutching fistfuls of dinars, all imprinted with the face of Saddam. The telephone system was so dilapidated that I could not find a line clear enough to file my radio report, so I spent much of my time perched on a footbridge filming the pedestrians down below as they thronged near a blue-tiled mosque, mingling with olive-uniformed soldiers and villagers on horse-drawn carts. My last memory of Basra in 1998 was of waiting for a taxi beside the Shatt Al-Arab waterway, close to a crossroads and a hospital. I never imagined I would return to that same spot five years later and see it swarming with khaki-clad British troops.

I have had mixed feelings about the invasion and war in Iraq. Writing this now, in early 2006, after watching the litany of mistakes by the Coalition and the ensuing carnage suffered by Iraqi civilians, it is all too easy to say the whole thing was an ill-conceived disaster. Certainly, the primary reasons given by the US and British governments for the need to overthrow Saddam Hussein have proved to be fallacious. Three years after the invasion none of the alleged weapons of mass destruction had been found, showing that Western intelligence analysis on Iraq – or the government's presentation of it – was catastrophically wrong. The US-led invasion and occupation of a sovereign Arab and predominantly Muslim country was always going to be deeply unpopular in the Arab world, but the situation could still have been salvaged had the

Coalition got it right in the ensuing months. Instead, far too little planning was undertaken for the 'post-combat phase'; too many people in Washington appear to have believed the story spun to them by certain Iraqi exiles that the Iraqi population would welcome the invaders with flowers and goodwill.

Amongst the many strategic mistakes made by the Coalition since April 2003, the following have been the most serious. Allowing widespread looting and ransacking of government offices, museums and other public buildings in areas under Coalition military control sent a message to the Iraqi population that the often brutally enforced system of order and control they had known all their lives had now been replaced by one of anarchy and uncertainty. The idea was to give Iraqis a 'taste of freedom' after decades of dictatorship, but in practice, emptying the ministries of their facilities, fittings and files greatly complicated the task of getting Iraq's infrastructure back on its feet. Then the decision to disband the Iraqi army created at a stroke 400,000 disgruntled, armed and unemployed young men who became instant potential recruits for the insurgency. Banning members of Saddam's ruling Baath Party from taking up senior posts may have been popular with much of the population, but these were the only people on the ground with practical experience of managing the country. Thirdly, the lack of any effective border controls in the first few months allowed nationalist and Islamist insurgents to bring in thousands of new recruits to their cause across the Syrian and Iranian borders. Cross-border smuggling had existed for years before the US-led invasion, so Al-Qaeda and other groups were able to capitalize on established routes and connections to stoke the insurgency, as if breathing new life into glowing embers.

Then there was Abu Ghraib. The scandalous abuse of Iraqi prisoners by sadistic US jailers in a prison already notorious for its brutality under Saddam has played right into the hands of the insurgents. Likewise, the isolated but still damaging reports of occasional human-rights abuses of Iraqi civilians by British forces in the south. Whatever else the Arab world thought of America and Britain, it at least respected their human-rights records. Arabs are acutely aware of their own governments' appalling track history in this department and they believed that, by comparison, Western democracies had an in-built respect for justice and fair treatment for those in captivity. Abu Ghraib shattered that belief. To the Arab world it was immaterial that the scandal involved only a tiny handful of wayward individuals amidst an army of 150,000; the damage was done. The well-publicized photographs and details of naked human pyramids of Iraqi prisoners, some tethered like dogs on leashes, were abhorrent to the whole world, but in the Middle East they crossed major cultural taboos. Public nudity is considered *haraam*, forbidden by Islam, especially in the presence of a female jailer, while dogs are largely considered low and unclean animals; one of the worst Arabic insults is '*ya kalb!*', 'you dog!' So with the revelations of Coalition prisoner abuse in Iraq, one of the last pillars of the Coalition rationale for invasion collapsed in Arab eyes: the notion that Western forces came in to protect Iraqi human rights sat uncomfortably beside pictures of a hooded prisoner who had been told that his fingertips were wired up to an electric generator and that if he lost his balance and fell off a box he would receive several thousand volts. There was no possible justification for these abuses. Even if you were to believe that torture is warranted if it can prevent mass casualties in a future terrorist attack, these prisoners were hardly the master planners of Al-Qaeda; they were, at most, low-level insurgents with no proven connections with international terrorism. Their mistreatment was purely for sport, of the sickest, most degrading kind. In early 2006 I heard a senior US Army officer conceded the damage done. 'We must operate in an environment of consent,' he told a London conference, 'and Abu Ghraib reduced that environment considerably.'

Yet back in March 2003, on the eve of the US-led invasion, it was not just Western intelligence that was wrong about Saddam's alleged WMD. Even countries like France and China that opposed the war had their suspicions about what Saddam was up to. What else, they reasoned, could possibly account for his continual obstruction and defiance of UN weapons inspections? Ever since the Gulf War of 1991 Saddam's government had lied and obfuscated over the true nature of its attempts to acquire banned weapons programmes, owning up to them only when it was presented with incontrovertible evidence that they had been discovered. So when Iraq said it had destroyed all its weapons after 1991, frankly, nobody believed it.

For the Bush and Blair governments, it was obviously extremely embarrassing that years after the invasion still no WMD had been found, but we should not forget the other perspective. If Saddam's regime had remained in place it would only have been a matter of time before UN sanctions were either lifted or ceased to be effective. Once that time came, either Saddam or his son Qusay would, in all probability, have accelerated Iraq's programme to acquire the components for WMD, and there is ample proof from the work of the Iraq Survey Group, which scoured Iraq from 2003–4, that Saddam's regime maintained an active interest in acquiring banned weapons. So when I say that I had mixed feelings about the Iraq war, on the one hand I felt that the invasion and occupation of a sovereign Arab country was both risky and wrong, and on the other I accepted that, thinking long term, the overthrow of Saddam's murderous dynasty had removed any possibility that the Hussein family may one day acquire WMD. After all, a regime that had invaded Iran, invaded Kuwait, slaughtered the Kurds and Shi'ites inside its own borders, and used both Scud missiles and chemical weapons against Iran in the 1980s could not be trusted not to use nuclear weapons if it could acquire them.

As a journalist, I had a bad Iraq war. A few days before US tanks rolled across the Kuwaiti border in March 2003, my boss Jonathan Baker gathered all the foreign correspondents together in a BBC room known as the Bridge Lounge. The cream of BBC journalists was being dispatched to the Middle East to cover this war and like a general on the eve of battle he ran through final preparations and plans, wishing everyone good luck and safe assignments as they departed for Kuwait, Jordan, Qatar and Iraqi Kurdistan. I was the only one in that room who spoke near-fluent Arabic and I felt I knew the terrain well, but because of the overriding fear that there would be some sort of revenge terrorist attack in Britain it was decided that as Security Correspondent I should be kept back at base in London. It was not necessarily a bad decision at the time, but for me it was intensely frustrating watching other correspondents trying to converse with the first Iraqis they met across the border; the Iraqi civilians usually spoke no English and my colleagues spoke no Arabic. 'No!' I would find myself shouting in the edit suite. 'That's not what he's trying to tell you!' Instead I had to content myself with reporting on how the Arab media was covering the war, a less dramatic story but one which was to have huge significance for Al-Qaeda's recruiting efforts. Whereas Western news bulletins tended to lead with the latest military advances towards Baghdad, the Arab networks often focused on some human tragedy, like an explosion in a marketplace that was being blamed on a US air-to-ground missile. Their TV pictures spared the viewer no grisly detail, beaming footage of dead, blood-spattered Arab babies and their mothers into living rooms right across the Middle East, while crowds of obedient Iraqis chanted their opposition to the war. The US and British forces had almost no Arab journalists embedded in their midst, partly because the military did not trust them, whereas Arab networks like Al-Jazeera had camera crews poised inside Iraqi cities and they were able to rush to whatever scene of human suffering the Iraqi Ministry of Information chose to let them film. The net result was that the Arab world saw a very different war from the one that Western viewers saw. In Britain we saw M1 Abrams tanks 'liberating' towns like Nasriyya, or lines of US Marines hunkered down on a sand berm and exchanging fire with Feddayeen troops loyal to Saddam. In Arab living rooms they saw a bloody invasion of a fellow Arab nation and the humiliating collapse of what was supposed to be one of the largest, most powerful armies in the world. Almost nobody liked Saddam, but he was the Arabs' problem and, naively or not, most Arabs would have preferred to deal with him in their own way. The final humiliation was the covering up of the face on Saddam's statue in Firdaws Square in Baghdad with an American stars-and-stripes flag. It did not remain there long – like President Bush's post-9/11 gaffe when he used the word 'crusade', it was quickly withdrawn – but the damage was done. The image was transmitted instantly around the world and the symbolism was disastrous for the Coalition: 'US global superpower conquers Arab country, humiliates its ruler and makes it a colony.' Osama Bin Laden must have been rubbing his gnarled hands together in glee at that image, knowing that recruits to Al-Qaeda would come pouring in after that. And they did. One bizarre moment in all of this was when I monitored Syrian TV to see how it was covering the defeat of a one-party Arab regime built around the cult of a dictator. On the day that Saddam's statue was torn down in Baghdad, Syrian TV aired an extensive documentary about early Islamic architecture. Next door's news was clearly not good news for the nervous regime of Syria's President Bashar Al-Assad.

In April 2003, after what felt like an eternity, I was at last assigned to Basra. I flew to Kuwait, picked up my press accreditation from some Coalition press office in a luxury hotel on the shores of the Gulf, and drove over the border with Bob, a designated BBC security escort, late of the 22nd Regiment SAS. The short war to depose Saddam was in its final days and there was a large BBC team up in Baghdad, but Basra was where the British troops were centred and I found our team based in the same palace complex as Britain's 12th Armoured Division. The palace was a collection of expensive, almost brand-new buildings built out of marble and white stone on the banks of the Shatt Al-Arab river and surrounded by a high wall. Cornering off some of the best land in the city, it had been intended for use by Saddam's delinquent sons, but had apparently rarely been used. Local Iraqis told me that any fishermen caught straying too close to its perimeter were automatically shot.

Saddam's regime may just have fallen but there were still plenty of stories to cover. The US Secretary of Defense, Donald Rumsfeld, flew into Basra for a one-day visit filled with theatre. When his plane landed on the runway black-clad US security men tumbled out of it 'to secure the area', watched by bemused British squaddies who had already secured the airport long ago. At the ensuing press conference Rumsfeld only took questions from his own travelling press pack from Washington, ignoring an awkward question I put to him. Journalists tend to remember these things.

I went up to the Iranian border at Shalamcheh to cover the tumultuous return to Iraq of the exiled Shi'ite cleric Muhammad Baqr Al-Hakim. It was a story made for television. At this bleak border crossing in the far south of Iraq, Iranian border guards in white gloves and helmets faced off with British soldiers in berets. There was a brief argument about exactly where the border lay, but no shots were fired and an international incident was averted. The Shi'ite crowds went wild with joy as Al-Hakim's convoy made its way slowly into Iraq, culminating in a massive rally at a stadium in Basra. But Baqr Al-Hakim had only three months to live; he was assassinated in August 2003 by a suicide bomber in the Shi'ite holy city of Najaf.

Basra was a lot safer then than it has since become, and several times I went out on patrol with the British troops to see how they were operating and interacting with local Iraqis. Sometimes this would be on foot and sometimes in convoys of Warrior armoured fighting vehicles – more for show than security, since almost no one was shooting at the Brits back then. When the patrol did hear the occasional burst of gun-fire it would almost invariably be what the soldiers called 'happy shooting', someone blazing off into the air with an AK-47 to celebrate something like a wedding, a common practice in some of the remoter villages of the Arabian Peninsula.

I really enjoyed the foot patrols, padding silently alongside the canals and riverbanks of southern Iraq, listening to the sounds of village life: the hoarse bark of a distant dog, the muffled revving of a pickup truck, a cacophony of frogs from close by, the soft call of an owl from the foliage of a date grove. The patrol commander would divide up the area into squares on the map, sending part of his force one way then joining up with them at an agreed point. Almost the only threat came from common banditry, which had long been rife here. When we came to a village, the British soldiers seemed to have established a rapport with the local Iraqis.

'Sullum alikkum,' a sergeant would call out in a Brummy accent.

'Wa aleikum assalaam!' would come a cry from a darkened doorway, in rather more authentic Arabic.

'Oh, 'ullo, Aly, how you doin', mate?' called the sergeant.

'Itfaddal! Please, come have tea with us.'

It was hearts-and-minds soldiering at its best and I believe it was genuine, rather than put on for my benefit as a journalist. Earlier in the day our crew had watched Royal

Engineers throwing up a metal bridge for villagers to use over a canal; they were working hard to sort out the shortage of fresh drinking water, and back at headquarters the officers were convening regular councils with tribal sheikhs and religious leaders to hear their complaints.

Basra and the surrounding area had sustained relatively little physical damage from the invasion and most Iraqis I spoke to then seemed well disposed towards the British, but always with the caveat that they expected them to leave as soon as some sort of order and infrastructure had been restored. Not everyone was thrilled to have been invaded: I attended a gathering of newly unemployed judges and lawyers who had prospered under Saddam. For them no curse was strong enough to condemn the British Army, but I learned later that they eventually got their jobs back.

But the vast majority of Iraqis I spoke to in Basra and the surrounding villages told me how relieved they were to be rid of Saddam Hussein at last. One man even berated me quite angrily for coming from a country that had held anti-war demonstrations. 'How dare you?' he rasped. 'You people did not have to live under that murderous bastard all your lives like we did. If you had, you would have welcomed this invasion, not opposed it.' It was only one man's opinion and there were plenty of others who took a very different view, but one afternoon I had an encounter that went a long way towards convincing me at the time that the overthrow of Saddam had been the right thing. A small group of pensive, quietly spoken Iraqis showed me round the torture cells at the Secret Police headquarters, now ransacked and empty. When you have been led by the hand round a cell by a man who shows you what was done to him by the state security apparatus it is hard to remain unmoved. These men were tortured for months on end, beaten with metal bars, electro-cuted on their genitals, hung up by their wrists with their arms behind their backs. The pain was excruciating, they said, the agony endless, and for what? They knew nothing worth telling their interrogators. Their jailers were just having fun.

For me, the most rewarding part of reporting from southern Iraq was meeting Iraqis, newly empowered to speak freely without Baath Party minders noting down their every word. In the evenings I would go with our Iraqi fixers to an open-air café, where we would sit in the stiflingly hot air playing noisy games of backgammon, drinking sweet tea and puffing away on a *narghila* water-pipe. This was the Middle East I have always loved: good company, quick, witty conversation and great atmosphere. It saddens me to think that if I had returned to Basra two years later I would have been risking kidnap or worse to go out at night in such a place.

But behind the scenes there were already dark forces afoot in May 2003; with Saddam and the henchmen of his ruling Baath Party no longer in power, old scores were starting to be settled. In the leafy date-palm-oasis village of Abu'l Khasab, south of Basra, I interviewed a ten-year-old boy who was plotting to murder his neighbour. As we squatted on rush mats in his family's spartan reception room, he told me he knew exactly which Baath Party official had ordered his father's execution some years ago. Now he said there was nothing to stop him from avenging the family honour – 'With this,' he said, cradling a rusty AK-47 that was almost as tall as he was.

A few miles away we found a man on a farm who was missing half his ears. As a deserter from Saddam's army in the mid-1990s he had been caught in a round-up, loaded on to a truck and taken under armed guard to Basra Hospital. 'When they strapped me down on to a trolley I did not know what to expect,' he told me, 'but I knew it was going to be bad. They found out my first name was Saddam so the doctor was allowed to be lenient. He said, "Because you have the same name as our President I will only slice off half your ears."

Then I felt this burning pain and I could feel something wet splashing down my neck. Now I am disfigured for ever.' Saddam the mutilated farmer seemed to have accepted what had happened to him; he was not plotting revenge.

When the US-led Coalition went to war in Iraq, I expected, as many did, that in the short term the threat of international terrorism would probably increase. But few could have predicted in March 2003 the depth, extent and sheer savagery of the insurgency that was to follow. When the first of Al-Qaeda's beheading tapes came into the BBC via the internet, I had the misfortune to have to 'package' it into a report for the lunchtime TV news. The victim was Nick Berg, an American telecoms engineer who had come to Iraq looking for work and who had ended up getting kidnapped and handed over to the most violent insurgency group in Iraq led by the Jordanian Islamist Ahmed Al-Khalayleh, who had adopted the *nom de guerre* Abu Mus'ab Al-Zarqawi.

'The tape is pretty horrific,' one of our videotape editors warned me. 'We've had a look at it and some of us just couldn't watch it.' I took a deep breath and slotted the tape into the machine then pressed 'play'. There was Nick Berg, seated cross-legged on the floor in a bare room and wearing an orange jumpsuit of the sort worn by the alleged terrorists incarcerated at Guantanamo Bay; he looked frail and frightened but unaware of what was about to happen to him. Standing behind him were four well-built men with their faces concealed by black ski masks, carrying machine guns and belts of ammunition. The man in the middle was Al-Zarqawi and he was reading out a statement in Arabic to the effect that Berg had been tried by an Islamic court and found guilty of being an enemy of Iraq and that his captors would now carry out 'God's will'. With that he withdrew an enormous knife, almost a sword, that he had been concealing inside his jacket. This was the signal for Al-Zarqawi's henchmen to put down their weapons and set about helping their leader to decapitate Nick Berg. Al-Qaeda's video technicians had not quite got the sound in sync with the pictures, as the tape had the hapless Berg screaming in terror while he was apparently still sitting immobile and saying nothing. But the video soon caught up with the audio as the men in ski masks pushed him over on to his side and held him down, crying, '*Allahu akbar!*' ('God is the greatest!') as Al-Zarqawi beheaded him and the camera zoomed in on this gratuitous, ghoulish bloodbath.

From their reactions on the internet I know that many Muslims found this utterly abhorrent and barbaric, especially the uttering of the sacred phrase '*Allahu akbar*' in conjunction with the cold-blooded murder of a non-combatant captive. 'This has brought shame on us,' wrote one Arab contributor. 'Slaughtering this man like a sheep is degrading.' Others, though, said he deserved it, claiming that as an American Jew (and therefore 'obviously a spy'), Nick Berg had no business to be in Iraq. Berg's executioners seemed to care little for what people said in the wider world, though. They had achieved their aim of horrifying the West and scaring many foreign contractors into leaving Iraq, thereby undermining the chances of the Coalition's nation-building succeeding. Their message was clear: anyone who cooperated with the 'puppet government' in Baghdad risked the same fate. Months later, lying in my hospital bed in Whitechapel, I watched the sad tragedy of the Liverpudlian Ken Bigley's capture and execution unfold. Al-Zarqawi's bloodthirsty and sadistic tactics were typical of Al-Qaeda's approach to asymmetric warfare. The Islamist extremists inspired by Osama Bin Laden and others were never going to be able to confront and defeat a Western army on a conventional battlefield, but they did know how to hit the West where it hurt. The fear engendered by these beheadings was exponential: for every foreign contractor kidnapped and beheaded on camera, perhaps dozens of others would be put off coming to Iraq, or, if already working there, intimidated into leaving early.

By late 2005 Iraq had become well established as the new *jihadi* battleground, the chosen destination for angry young Muslims to go and confront the USA and its allies. Saudis, Yemenis, Algerians and others, including Europe-based North Africans, formed a steady trickle of recruits that was funnelled into Iraq across the Syrian and other borders by an efficient network of sympathizers. Iraqis still made up the bulk of the insurgency, but a relatively high proportion of these non-Iraqi Arabs volunteered for suicide-bombing missions. Their preferred targets were US and Coalition troops, sometimes detonating a car full of explosives into a convoy of Humvee jeeps, sometimes remotely detonating a roadside IED (Improvised Explosive Device). But far more accessible and just as damaging to US-led efforts at nation-building have been the 'soft' targets: the suicide bombings of unprotected marketplaces or milling crowds of police recruits.

Iraq in the 2000s differs from Afghanistan in the 1990s as the magnet for *jihadi*s in one vital respect. Iraq is a real battlefield, whereas the thousands of young men who made their way to Al-Qaeda's Afghan training camps in the latter half of the 1990s were at little personal risk and so survived. After learning to fire a Kalashnikov and rocket-propelled grenade, listening to rousing and vitriolic anti-Western sermons and making some international personal contacts, they were free to move on, choosing either to put their skills into practice in their own countries' insurgencies or simply to lie low and blend back into the societies to which they had returned. In Iraq, many of the volunteer *jihadi*s have made a one-way journey, convinced they are guaranteed a place in Heaven for blowing themselves up and taking a handful of Iraqi 'collaborators' with them. But those who do return from the insurgency intact are often changed men, deeply imbued

with violence, having witnessed bloodshed of the most gruesome kind at first hand. The return of these combat veterans
to neighbouring countries like Saudi Arabia deeply worries
the authorities there. The longer the Iraq insurgency drags
on, the bigger the pool of battle-hardened *jihadi*s who will
one day turn their attention to new arenas in which to confront the hated West and its allies. Ironically, one of the few
things President Bush and Al-Qaeda could agree on is that
Iraq has become the front line in the so-called War on Terror
(which it never was before the invasion of March 2003).
Washington has considered it vital to defeat terrorism there or
risk a new failed state like Afghanistan in the 1990s. Al-
Qaeda has considered it a sacred duty to confront the
'crusading infidels' and drive Coalition forces out of Iraq. For
both sides the stakes are impossibly high; this is a war that
neither side can afford to lose.

Inevitably, the conflict in Iraq has distracted attention from
Afghanistan, nicknamed 'Op Forgotten' by the British troops
who served there in the early 2000s. Two years after the
Taliban had been dislodged from power I went with a BBC
team to see at first hand how the US military was fighting
the ongoing insurgency up in the wild mountains of the
southeast.

It was cold in Gardez in mid-November 2003. Crisp and
clear by day, this desert market town lay nearly eight
thousand feet up in the mountains and by nightfall it had us
stamping our feet and blowing into our hands. We were staying in a mud-brick fort, one of thousands scattered across
Afghanistan's bleak landscape. At each corner stood a raised
watchtower, with a rickety wooden ladder leading up to a
narrow parapet. This particular fort had been taken over by
a company of soldiers from the US Army's 10th Mountain
Division, men from upstate New York more used to freezing
winters than we were. They were mostly reservists, civilians

pulled out of their day jobs to be mobilized for months at a time in the name of fighting the Global War on Terror.

From the outside, their fortress base would have looked right at home in a nineteenth-century lithograph of the Khyber Pass. True, it bristled with sophisticated antennae and every so often a column of Humvees would come barrelling out of the gates, machine guns poking through the windows. But the basic idea was the same: high walls thick enough to withstand bombardment, no windows, and a massive gate strong enough to resist attack.

Six months before our visit this had been bandit country. Remnants of the Taliban and other anti-government forces were controlling the countryside, raiding at will, while corrupt police officers had been extorting money from the locals. Now the venal police chief had been sacked for embezzlement and the US Army had set up a Provincial Reconstruction Team or PRT, a robust military presence to protect the civilians doing the actual reconstruction, disarmament and electoral registration. By the winter of 2003 there were four of these PRTs in Afghanistan, manned by small detachments of troops from the US, Britain, Germany and New Zealand, and there were plans to open up others all over the country. As in Iraq, one of the principal problems in Afghanistan has been security. Without it, nothing gets done.

The Americans had made themselves at home in Gardez fort. They had had twenty-four-hour generators and big Texan steaks flown in from Ramstein Airbase in Germany. In their tiny mud-walled rooms, some of the officers even had their laptops hooked up to the internet. Down in the makeshift canteen there were fridges full of Dr Pepper soda drinks, and DVDs of Hollywood blockbusters showing in the evenings. You had to hand it to the US military, they certainly knew how to make themselves comfortable in a war zone.

We were in Gardez to report on how Coalition troops were trying to help rebuild Afghanistan after numerous wars and a period of paralysis under Taliban rule. In a way, we hoped our film would be a microcosm of the wider challenge this country faced. If peace and prosperity could be extended to the whole of Afghanistan then the Taliban and their Al-Qaeda partners would have little chance of returning. But if conditions for ordinary people were no better than they had been under Taliban rule then there was an increased risk of this country slipping into anarchy, a situation Al-Qaeda would be bound to exploit in the hope of re-establishing its Afghan foothold, which might make it logistically easier to plan major attacks on the West.

We had spent the afternoon at a half-built schoolhouse, watching the American soldiers on a 'presence patrol', stand-ing around in their wraparound sunglasses supervising construction while bearded labourers shovelled gravel and slapped on wet concrete. They seemed to be in a hurry to finish by dusk. The trouble with foreign troops getting involved in civil reconstruction in a country that is still suffering from low-level conflict is that the distinction between the troops and those they are trying to protect can easily become blurred, in this case making both fair game by those who wanted the US-backed government of President Hamid Karzai to fail. As far as the Taliban, Al-Qaeda and their sympathizers were concerned, Afghanistan in the early twenty-first century was a nation under foreign military occupation, and they believed they had a duty to resist every aspect of that occupation. While we were in Gardez we learned that a Taliban spokesman had given an interview in the town of Spin Boldak on the Pakistani border, in which he denounced all Western journalists and aid workers in the country as 'CIA spies' who were therefore ripe for punish-ment by having their throats slit. (The Taliban's outlook on life also included banning all music and television, ending women's education, forcing men to wear beards and blowing up the centuries-old Bamyan Buddha statues.) A few days

later gunmen on a motorbike rode up alongside a car carrying a French aid worker in Ghazni and shot her dead through
the window. Ironically, these kind of threats meant that in
Afghanistan the safest place for a Western journalist to be
was probably under the protection of the Coalition military;
it did not mean you agreed with their military aims, it just
made you a harder target to access.

In its effort to make Afghanistan a safer place, the UN had
set up the Disarmament, Demobilization and Reintegration
(DDR) programme, a scheme to try to disarm the notoriously
powerful and violent warlords and find useful, civil jobs for
their newly unemployed militias. While we were in Gardez we
had a chance to see it at first hand. On a flat, sun-beaten plain
just outside town we found a few dozen bearded Afghans in
scruffy military uniforms milling around a collection of
weapons that they had just handed over to the UN. There
were heavy mortars, field guns, anti-aircraft cannons and
heavy machine guns, all of Soviet era and some frankly
belonging in a museum. A young ex-British Army officer
working for the UN, Stephen Romilly, was dashing around
with a clipboard, stooping and squinting down barrels while
the Afghans wrestled with their weapons to prove they
worked, thereby earning them a few dollars from the UN.
Sometimes he would tell them to put more oil on and try
again, sometimes he would reward them with the coveted
splash of yellow paint which meant they had passed. Cheers
would then go up and the warlords would manhandle the
weapons over to a UN lorry that was waiting to tow them
away.

At this point the US Army showed up, driving on to the
plain in their armoured jeeps in a swirl of dust which settled
on the small armoury of surrendered weapons. The vehicle
that pulled up next to me had rock music playing inside.
Some of the infantrymen got out to greet the plain-clothes
US Special Forces soldiers already there. 'What's goin' on,

man?' said one of the new arrivals. 'Do they take credit cards for this stuff?!'

Back at Gardez fort we discovered that the Special Forces had their own secretive base attached to the one we were staying in. They were working closely with the Afghan Militia Forces or AMF, going out on night-time missions to investigate reports of Taliban activities or suspected arms caches. As journalists, we were not allowed to go near them or speak to them, but within our own mud-walled fort there were a number of curious characters lurking around. You could tell by their clothes that they occupied that murky netherworld halfway between soldiers and civilians. Bearded and dressed in beige cargo trousers, desert boots, dark jackets and woollen caps pulled right down to their eyebrows, they spoke in an American drawl and wore no rank. One of them told us he was 'with the State Department', another was 'attached to the UN'. Sure. We just assumed they were all CIA paramilitaries masquerading as reconstruction advisers. Up on the watchtower parapet, admiring the galaxy of stars, I got talking to one of these types. I am always deeply suspicious of any information coming from someone who won't tell me their full name or who they really work for, but this man certainly knew how to get my attention. US intelligence, he said, reckoned they had Osama Bin Laden boxed into a corner to the north of here and they were about to go after him with everything they had got. 'Where?' I asked. 'Oh, somewhere up north. It's a big one, they're even diverting some air assets over from Iraq and the Horn of Africa.'

That would be just our luck, I thought. Here we were, miles from Kabul, and they were about to capture Bin Laden. Great. The story of the year and I was not going to be there for it. I hurried down the ladder and went in search of my producer, Dominic Hurst. When I told him what this spook had let slip, his face displayed a mixture of excitement and fear. Missing the capture of Bin Laden would not have been great for his career prospects, either. We decided to get back to the capital the next day then head on up to the big Coalition base at Bagram to sniff out what was going on.

In Kabul we just had time to squeeze in an interview with the Interior Minister, Ali Jalali, in his newly painted office. In the Gulf Arab States I had grown used to such ministers giving out a Panglossian vision of their countries, insisting that everything was for the best, but Ali Jalali was refreshingly candid. Corruption was rife, he said, and there were serious problems with terrorism, crime, drugs and factional fighting. In the south and east the threat was from Taliban/Al-Qaeda-related terrorism, in the north it was from factional fighting between warlords, and everywhere there was crime and banditry. Like many Afghan officials, the Interior Minister blamed Pakistan for harbouring Taliban fighters; he denied they were gaining ground but insisted they were conducting hit-and-run raids from their logistical bases just across the border.

It was time to get over to Bagram, a huge, sprawling airbase and tented city on the Shomali plain. Once a major Soviet base and prize target for the *mujahideen* fighters in the 1980s, it now served as the Coalition headquarters in Afghanistan. On the way we passed an entire camel train of Afghan nomads winding their way south to warmer pastures for the winter. With camels and donkeys adorned with bells they plodded past us, the women in bright-blue and silver dresses, their eyes rimmed with antimony. It was a fleeting glimpse of an ancient world, one that pre-dated Al-Qaeda, joint task-forces or the so-called War on Terror. A distant burst of gunfire brought us back to the twenty-first century; a pair of Apache helicopter gunships was strafing a barren mountain-side, getting in some target practice before lunch.

Once through security and inside Bagram airbase we passed the US military's interrogation block, a large windowless building with no identifying signs. This was where the US Army brought in what they called their PUCs (Persons Under Control), which could be a hapless Afghan farmer who simply happened to be too close to a Taliban arms cache, or someone of major interest to the CIA such as a suspected Arab member of Al-Qaeda. The US administration has been extremely secretive about where they have been holding their 'high-value' prisoners, such as the self-confessed Al-Qaeda operatives Khaled Sheikh Mohammed and Ramzi Bin Al-Shibh. But secrecy does not always equate to security and some time after our visit a major Al-Qaeda captive from Indonesia managed to escape from Bagram base. Adding insult to injury, Al-Qaeda released a video of him boasting how he and others had got away, to the huge embarrassment of the Pentagon and the annoyance of the Indonesians, who now feared he would be back to bomb them.

We arrived at Bagram just in time for a press conference, held outdoors in a gravel compound with a large-scale map pinned to a board.

'We have launched Operation Mountain Resolve,' announced Colonel Rodney Davis, a big, bald, black officer from Virginia. 'Our troops are operating in some of the toughest terrain that the Coalition has ever been in here.'

'OK, but what about Bin Laden?' I asked.

The colonel exchanged glances with a junior officer. 'We can make no comment on his whereabouts at this time . . . but we think he's in Afghanistan.' Gosh, well that narrowed it down then.

After the press conference we followed Colonel Davis up to his office, where he sat back in a swivel chair and eyed us coolly. Dominic Hurst, my producer, had been joined by our cameraman, Phil Goodwin, an old Afghan hand who had covered the Taliban's taking of Kabul in 1996. We told Colonel Davis that we were hoping for a 'facility', a chance to film how US forces were tackling Taliban and Al-Qaeda forces close to the Pakistani border. Colonel Davis wanted us to go away.

'You BBC guys are not my favourite people,' he drawled. 'I consider you pretty much left of centre. You were against the war in Eye-rak, if I recall. So I would put Fox News out here on one side with the good guys and you over there on the other. So why should I give you a facility?'

It took several days to thaw Colonel Davis out, and then he arranged what was obviously a test to see if we could behave ourselves. He allowed us to film, under close escort, in the Joint Operations Centre, a huge air-conditioned tent from where the Coalition's operations all over Afghanistan were being run. First we had to wait outside while he went in and ordered all the analysts to sanitize the displays on their computers of any classified information. Then we were ushered into a secret world where row upon row of operators sat behind terminals in various clusters: air operations, fire support, logistics, intelligence officers, meteorological and terrain experts, and numerous Coalition liaison officers. There were over thirty nations and fifteen thousand troops involved in Afghanistan but it was clear that the Americans were doing the bulk of the combat operations in the unstable south and east. I caught a glimpse of a large, classified map detailing the routes and flightpaths for Operation Mountain Resolve, which of course meant nothing to me. An officer in charge of helicopter operations explained how these were usually conducted. Often, he said, Special Operations troops would go in first to survey the terrain on the ground, and their reports would be combined with satellite imagery to give commanders a good idea of what they were going into. Increasingly, UAVs or pilotless drones were being used to fly over an area and take pictures prior to an operation.

Colonel Davis decided we had passed the honesty test – we had not filmed anything we were not supposed to – and

Dominic, Phil and I were summoned up to his office. It felt like being called to the headmaster's study.

'I can offer you three choices,' he said, enjoying our obvious eager anticipation. 'I can send all three of you down to Kandahar for a "presence patrol", which I can't promise will be very exciting. I can send one of you – just one of you – to Kandahar for an indefinite attachment to US Special Forces.' The colonel was looking pointedly at me now, so I asked him what this would entail. 'Well, you would be going into villages, checking them out, inoculating tribesmen and camels and trying to befriend the locals. You know, hearts-and-minds stuff, but who knows what you might see. But there's only room for one of you, you'll have to keep up with the Special Ops guys and I can't promise when the mission will be over.' I glanced at Dominic, who was firmly shaking his head. 'Which leaves the third option,' said the colonel. 'I can get you by chopper down to the firebase at Shkin on the Pakistani border, but I can't promise you when we can lift you out.'

After a cold night in the tent we awoke soon after dawn to the sound of helicopters taking off en masse from Bagram airbase as part of the ongoing Operation Mountain Resolve. We had slept badly, since it had been rather like trying to take a kip at the end of a Heathrow runway. A-10 Warthog attack aircraft were taking off one after the other, while some of the transport planes coming in were so heavy we could feel the vibrations right through our camp beds. The Coalition was clearly throwing everything at this operation up in the mountains of Kunar and Nuristan. Then there was Colonel Davis, beaming his Hollywood smile as he saw us off. 'You're going to the worst place in the world!' he shouted above the roar of the rotors with an air of smug satisfaction. 'That place Shkin is evil, man, there are some b-a-a-a-d people down there on the border.' But we were happy; after days of negotiating, we were finally getting out of Bagram's depressing tented camp and heading for the wild frontier with Pakistan.

*

On a grey, misty autumn afternoon, the sort of day that would have held a whiff of bonfire smoke back in England, we lifted off the tarmac at Bagram in a Blackhawk helicopter and headed due south. Shadowed by an Apache helicopter gunship for protection, we flew fast and low over barren, desolate mountain ridges. Strapped in next to the window, I watched eastern Afghanistan slide by so close I felt I could almost touch it: brown, parched ravines; grey, dried-up riverbeds; the occasional shepherd staring up at us; abandoned, mud-brick villages; the rusting, burned-out carcass of a tank. This was still what much of twenty-first-century Afghanistan looked like outside the cities.

To the east the mountains soared to nearly fifteen thousand feet, their jagged crests laced with the first snows of winter. There seemed to be no sign of life here at all. But then, south of Khost, as we neared the Pakistani border, the landscape changed. Short, alpine fir trees sprang up on the slopes and as we swooped low over a ridge a broad, sunlit valley unfolded beneath us, ringed by mountains. Every single building was a fortress, surrounded by a high mud-brick wall a metre thick and surmounted by look-out towers. An hour into the flight we began to drop down towards Shkin firebase and the door-gunners readied their weapons, swinging their machine guns out through the windows on pivots, aiming them at the desert floor, fingers on the triggers. For the Americans this was hostile territory where the writ of the Kabul government ran thin and local loyalties were hard to divine.

In a swirl of dust and wind-blown bushes, we put down on the landing zone just outside the base. Like the fort we had stayed in at Gardez, it was a big, four-square mud-brick fortress, rather like the toy Red Indian fort I used to play with as a child. The base had a detachment of artillery, Special Ops soldiers (whom once again we were forbidden to speak to) and a huge radio mast for communicating with Coalition HQ in Bagram or for the soldiers stuck out here to make calls back to the USA. We drove through a huge gateway and were greeted by the base commander, a softly spoken Irish American who seemed to relish being out here on the frontline.

At dusk we went up to the look-out post, where the duty guards were scanning the horizon through binoculars, watching a lone pickup truck jolt unevenly over the rocks before it slipped out of view. The Pakistani border lay just six miles away along a low mountain ridge, and that, they said, was where most of the attacks came from at night. The Americans could not usually tell who was shooting at them until they returned fire and identified the bodies the next day. Mostly, they said, it was Afghan and Pakistani insurgents, but they had also come across Arabs and Chechens, remnants of a whole network of Al-Qaeda-run training camps that had flourished here in the 1990s. The previous year, before all the base's defences were in place, a force of nearly thirty Taliban/Al-Qaeda fighters tried to overrun it, rushing headlong at the fort in a suicidal charge. A US sergeant grimaced as he recalled how easy it was to beat them back, catching their attackers out in the open with machine-gun fire in a scene reminiscent of the First World War.

Darkness fell quickly, and at nearly eight thousand feet above sea level the temperature dropped like a stone. Beneath a clear, starlit sky, the American troops began to light fires inside the courtyard of their fort, the flickering light of the flames playing across their tired, drawn faces. Someone got out a guitar and began singing 'I don't belong here', but in fact morale seemed to be good. Most of the soldiers were just out of school and I was taken aback at their philosophical approach to life. A nineteen-year-old told me how two of his good friends had been killed out on patrol here, but he shrugged his shoulders. 'I'm just proud to be doing what I'm doing, but if it's my time it's my time.'

By nine p.m. our little BBC team was tucked up in our

sleeping bags, secure in a reinforced bunker room built into the walls of the fort. But this was not to be a quiet night. Fast asleep, I dreamed that someone was shouting 'Incoming!' as if I was in the middle of some Vietnam war film. It seemed remarkably realistic, though, and the shouts grew louder and more insistent. Suddenly I was wide awake; the base was under attack. In fact it was pretty ineffectual: just a salvo of four Chinese-made rockets that fell two hundred metres short of the base, exploding harmlessly in a dirt ravine. But the base was now a hive of activity. The Americans used their technology to pinpoint the exact location the rockets had been fired from and already they were returning fire, pumping out artillery shells into the mountains along the Pakistani border. They were sanguine about the results. 'Most times the Taliban set the rockets on a timer fuse,' said one of the sentries, 'so by the time they go off the people who set them are long gone, back over the border into Pakistan where we can't pursue them.'

At first light the next morning we joined the tail end of a patrol of jeeps heading up to the border to investigate the previous night's activities. We drove through a narrow gully, which seemed to me a frighteningly obvious ambush point, came up to a ridge and dismounted. The US infantrymen were, frankly, not as fit as they should have been and they found it tough going scrambling up these low hills. They fanned out, picking their way over the rocks amidst small juniper trees ripe with berries, some of the soldiers sweating and gasping to keep up. Birds I could not recognize swooped ahead of us, calling out as if to alert people to our presence. As our BBC team hung back, happy to film from a safe distance, the lead elements of the patrol blew the door open on the suspect compound up ahead. They found nothing inside, but now the nearby Pakistani border guards were in a flap. As I watched their observation post through binoculars I counted ten Pakistani soldiers with Kalashnikovs spilling out of their hilltop fort and scrambling down the mountainside to confront the Americans. They seemed very upset; obviously they viewed this as an incursion.

'Do not open fire!' radioed the patrol captain to his men up front. 'Those men are Pakistani border guards. I say again, do not engage them!' Mercifully no shots were fired, but the Americans had some complaints of their own. Why, they wanted to know, had those rockets been fired from right beneath the Pakistani border fort without the guards doing anything to stop the insurgents? Rather unconvincingly, the border guards said they knew of no such rockets, but we all suspected they had probably hunkered down in their bunker and hoped the problem would just go away. At this point a shout went up from one of the US scouts. Two rockets had been found intact, complete with timers and fuses that had failed to go off. They were Chinese-made, and attached to an alarm clock that was taken away for analysis. The US infantrymen took detailed photos of the scene to present to the Pakistanis the next day at their joint border conference to back up their demands that the Pakistanis do more to stop cross-border infiltration. It was a small incident, but indicative of the bigger problem along this wild, tribal border region. The Americans and their Afghan militia allies were not allowed to pursue anyone into Pakistan's Waziristan and northwest frontier provinces. But there, where local sympathies lay with the Taliban and to a lesser extent Al-Qaeda, it was easy for insurgents to lay up, replenish and re-arm, ready for the next raid back over the border into Afghanistan.

The Americans had little contact with the local population. Walled up in their fortress compounds, eating grilled steak and strumming guitars at night, theirs was a parallel world. Yet in the short time we were there, I never saw any morale problems; their black humour was summed up by a piece of graffiti scrawled on the wall of a urinal at Kandahar airbase:

> Osama Bin Laden: your time is short
> We'd rather you die than come to court.
> I have a question about your theory and laws.
> How come *you* never die for the cause?
> As is usual, you failed in your mission.
> If you expected pure chaos,
> You can keep on wishing!

Afghanistan has always been of enormous importance to Osama Bin Laden, his mentor Ayman Al-Zawahiri and the rest of Al-Qaeda's core, original leadership. This was where Afghan *mujahideen* and Muslim volunteers from the Arab world joined forces in the 1980s to humiliate and eventually drive out the mighty Soviet Red Army, killing over 100,000 of its troops. Of course things might have taken a very different course had it not been for the enormous financial, logistic and military assistance given to the *mujahideen* by the USA, Saudi Arabia and Pakistan, but Al-Qaeda's theorists still view the Soviet defeat as a purely Muslim victory over a godless superpower.

Bin Laden has always felt at home in Afghanistan's stark desert and mountain landscapes, which must have reminded him of his ancestral homeland in the Hadhramaut area of southern Yemen. The more remote his Afghan bases were from Western civilization, the more freedom he felt. For over five years, from 1996 to 2001, Bin Laden and his lieutenants had pretty much a free rein in Afghanistan, so close was their alliance with Mullah Omar and the ruling Taliban. The training camps that Al-Qaeda set up and ran during this time processed an estimated fifteen thousand Muslim volunteers from all over the world, including several hundred from Britain. A few of the international trainees were singled out as being exceptionally talented and went on to become Al-Qaeda operatives who were assigned missions such as the bombing of US embassies in East Africa or the attack on the

USS *Cole*. But for most who attended the camps it was primarily an opportunity to network, to share common beliefs and hatreds with others from as far afield as Indonesia, Algeria, Saudi Arabia and the British Midlands.

When the USA was attacked on 11 September 2001 Osama Bin Laden knew full well to expect an onslaught of US reprisals. The East African embassy bombings in 1998 had been followed by a cruise-missile strike on one of his bases, but this time there was likely to be an invasion of Western forces. So Bin Laden had already secured his escape route back over the mountains to Pakistan, bribing a passage to safety for him and his entourage well in advance of 9/11. The training camps were destroyed by carpet bombing from US B-52s but their occupants had long since dispersed, with Bin Laden reportedly telling them to filter back to their own countries, lie low and wait for the order to strike.

Since then, Al-Qaeda and the Taliban have proved surprisingly resilient. Thousands of heavily armed US troops, backed by satellite intelligence and close support aircraft, have failed to eliminate their remnants in southeast Afghanistan. Parts of that country have been made too dangerous for international NGOs to operate in and there are parts of Afghanistan where local people are far more afraid of the Taliban than they are of the US-led military Coalition.

The use of Pakistan as a logistical rear base has been crucial for the Taliban. Although the central government in Islamabad has been cooperating closely with the FBI and the CIA to stamp out Al-Qaeda, and several of its key operatives have been captured in Pakistani cities, the prevailing sentiment along the wild, tribal borderlands has remained in favour of the Taliban and against the USA and the Northern Alliance in power in Kabul. Both Al-Qaeda and the Taliban are convinced that time is on their side, that sooner or later US forces and their Coalition partners will leave Afghanistan, that the democratically elected government will be too weak to hold the country together and that gradually they will be able to re-establish themselves in much of the country. In several speeches intended for a Western audience Bin Laden and Al-Zawahiri have repeatedly demanded that Western forces withdraw from Islamic lands, notably Iraq and Afghanistan. But for the West there is a fundamental dilemma here. Keeping troops in such a remote, difficult and dangerous country is expensive and exhausting; it also fuels Al-Qaeda's claims of Western occupation and colonization. But to withdraw and allow Afghanistan to revert to an anarchic shambles in which Al-Qaeda could re-establish itself would be almost unthinkable. The challenge will be to build up a strong Afghan government with broad popular support that can eventually run the country without a Western military presence, while resisting the advances of those who would turn back the clock. It will not be easy.

9

From Riyadh to Rehab

THE INSURGENCIES IN BOTH AFGHANISTAN AND IRAQ WERE already well under way when Simon Cumbers and I made our fateful visit to Riyadh in 2004. Having stayed alive for the first vital minutes after I was gunned down, my destiny now passed into the hands of others.

While the Riyadh police were rushing me at breakneck speed, bleeding and screaming, to the Al-Iman Hospital on the evening of Sunday 6 June 2004, a few miles away on the other side of the city, in a heavily secured area known as the Diplomatic Quarter, a meeting was under way at the British Embassy. The ambassador, Sherard Cowper-Coles, was chairing a routine Heads of Mission meeting, pulling in staff from the Riyadh Embassy and its consular outposts in Jeddah and Dhahran. The meeting was interrupted by another diplomat rushing in with the news that two British journalists had been shot in Al-Suwaidi district. Sherard thought for a moment: there were only two journos he knew of who were working for the British media in the country at that time: me and Simon Cumbers. The ambassador immediately broke up the meeting, got straight into his chauffeured, reinforced car and headed south for Al-Suwaidi, accompanied by his body-guards, the Close Protection Team and Detective Inspector Wanless, who was on secondment to Riyadh from Scotland Yard's Anti-Terrorist Branch. The Close Protection Team were uncomfortable with Sherard going down to Al-Suwaidi, but he insisted on finding out what had happened and what could be done to help.

His first stop was the mortuary, where he was presented with the heart-wrenching sight of Simon Cumbers's body. Only two days earlier Simon had filmed an interview I did with the ambassador in Al-Khobar and we had all shared my Walkers shortbread fingers in his hotel room afterwards. Simon had been killed by our attackers. One of the nicest, most kind-hearted men I have ever met, Simon had never even had a chance to use his famous Irish charm to talk his way out of this situation.

By now it was almost dusk and the British ambassador was working the phone, speaking directly to the governor of Riyadh, Prince Salman Bin Abdulaziz, one of the inner circle of Saudi princes who rule the country. I had interviewed him once, three years earlier, at the official twentieth-anniversary celebrations of King Fahd's rule, but I doubt he remembered this. Prince Salman was appalled by what had happened and immediately ordered a team of top surgeons from one of the best-equipped hospitals in the world, the King Faisal Specialist Hospital in Riyadh, to come to my rescue. Later that night he told Paul Wood, one of my fellow BBC correspondents who flew in from Cairo immediately to see if he could help: 'We will get the people who did this, I can promise you that.' Prince Salman's intervention was fortunate, but I was about to have an amazing stroke of luck.

It transpired that a South African gunshot-wound specialist surgeon was working in Riyadh. It is a sad fact of life in South Africa that, working in Cape Town, Peter Bautz had seen more than his fair share of gunshot-wound victims from the area known as Cape Flats. It was my good fortune that this young, energetic trauma surgeon now led the emergency rescue team that raced over from the King Faisal Hospital. When they pulled up at the Al-Iman Hospital in the Al-Suwaidi district of Riyadh, the surgeons there had already been working on me for about an hour. It was not going well. In fact, to use a cliché, they were losing me. Dr Bautz told me later that had his team not arrived when they did, with their hi-tech equipment and expertise, I would have died that night. His team's hospital notes paint a picture of a man about to move on somewhere else:

> Upon arrival of Dr Bautz the patient was seen in the operating room with open abdomen, bleeding extensively. His body temperature was 30 degrees C (86°F) and he had disseminated intravascular coagulation. He was in hypovolemic shock and was oozing from all cut surfaces.

In other words I had lost so much blood that I was dangerously cold and my heart was only pumping blood to the vital organs. Months later, when I showed my Riyadh medical file to an Army doctor friend he went pale. 'Strewth! You had DIC! That's where you are so severely injured that the blood starts clotting all over the body. Your whole body effectively becomes one big wound. It's the endgame, one of the last things before death.'

I subsequently asked Bautz how they had brought me back from the brink. 'The DIC had everything thrown at it,' he told me in a text message, 'including two doses of Activated Factor 7, a miracle drug. It's verrry expensive!'

After working on me for several hours at the Al-Iman, Bautz and his team then loaded me into their mobile Intensive Care Unit for the transfer to the King Faisal Specialist Hospital. DI Wanless, the Scotland Yard anti-terrorist detective in Riyadh, was watching as they put me in the ambulance. 'I've seen a few dead bodies in my time,' he told me months later, 'and I thought you were a goner. Your face was ashen grey and you had tubes coming out of you everywhere. It's incredible to see you alive now.' He also said that Dr Bautz had shaken his head at this point and remarked, 'That boy's not well.'

When the ambulance pulled up at the King Faisal shortly after midnight I was still in a very bad way. The hospital report records:

Upon arrival the patient had a temperature of approximately 30 degrees and he was found to have almost impalpable systolic blood pressure. On examination, the patient had eleven bullet holes and three bullets in situ. On careful examination, the patient had been shot about six times with three through-and-through and three bullets in situ. The patient had entrance wounds mainly posteriorly indicating that he had been shot from the back. These are all classic entrance wounds with a perforating and surrounding area of contusion and abrasion. On examination of the bullets through the X-rays they measured approximately 8.5mm which is probably 9mm bullet size [it was]. These bullets look classically like that of a handgun probably semi-automatic or machine pistol type but certainly not that of revolvers. Because of the potential bleeding risk and the condition of the patient only one bullet was removed and this was from the abdominal wall. This was a copper-jacketed lead-filled bullet, it was carefully handled, wrapped, placed into sealed container which was witnessed by several people and given to the police after the surgery.

Bullets used for forensic evidence, I learned later, are always touched by hand, as holding them with metal instruments destroys the marks impressed on them by the gun barrel which can lead to the identity of the gunman, as indeed it did in my case. But on reading this on my hospital bed in London weeks later, I texted Bautz for clarification as to where exactly I had been shot. Back came the answer. One bullet in the left thigh/buttock area had gone in almost parallel to the skin and had then come out again within a three-centimetre tract. 'You had a severe case of acute lead poisoning.' Lead poisoning? Hang on, I thought, I've still got two bullets inside me. Another text to Bautz, another reply: 'Don't worry, each bullet now has a scar capsule around it.' Good. It's so reassuring to know these sorts of things. In fact 'lead poisoning' turned out to be hospital humour for being shot. Lead levels in the blood are apparently undetectable following the failed removal of retained bullets.

While Bautz and his team were battling to save me in Riyadh, three thousand miles away in England my parents were casually watching the ten o'clock news on BBC1. At the mention of two British journalists shot in Riyadh my father turned grimly to my mother. 'It's Frank,' he said. He spent the next few hours desperately trying to get information out of the BBC and the Foreign Office. All they knew initially was that one of us was dead and one severely wounded.

As soon as the BBC had got confirmation of our identities, two of its managers, Mark Damazer and Sarah Ward-Lilley, raced round to our house to break the news to Amanda before she heard it second-hand. She was just putting the children to bed. 'We have some bad news,' they said. 'Frank has been shot in Riyadh and he's in a critical condition. He's been taken to hospital there but there's a chance he won't make it. We'll fly you out as soon as you're ready.'

It was too much for Amanda to take in. 'Could you hang on,' she said politely, 'while I just read the children a good-night story?' A few minutes later she came back downstairs to where Mark and Sarah were waiting. 'Now,' she said, 'tell me what has happened.'

Amanda hardly slept at all that night. While the surgeons were fighting to save my life, she was trying to make sense of what she had been told. Our two closest friends, Aidan and Naomi Hobbs, were camped in our living room, also trying to take in the idea that I might already be dead. Amanda told them that if the phone went she did not think she could answer it, so Aidan volunteered to stay on phone watch, giving himself the terrible task of having to break the news to Amanda if the call came through that said, 'We are sorry, Frank passed away a few minutes ago.' On the other side of the world, Amanda's parents were boarding a plane from New Zealand, coming to offer whatever support they could, while her brother Mike dropped everything at the hotel he ran in Bangkok to escort his sister to Riyadh.

Meanwhile Amanda had the pressing problem of what to tell Melissa and Sasha the next morning, the start of the school week. The news was already on the radio, so she knew that the children's classmates and their parents would hear it as they drove in on the school run. She decided there was no point beating around the bush. 'Something bad has happened,' she told them, as she adjusted their uniforms at the breakfast table. 'Daddy has been shot in the hand and he's in hospital. I may have to go and be with him.' Sasha, who was five at the time, seemed to take this in her stride, but Melissa, who was a year older, was visibly shaken.

Amanda had hoped that spending most of the day at school might take the children's minds off what had happened, but Melissa kept going up to friends in the playground, saying, 'My Daddy's been shot.' The school thoughtfully appointed her a companion to accompany her for the next few days, but still she was asking questions that no six-year-old should ever have to ask: 'Mummy, if I was shot in the hand would I die?' and plaintively, resentfully demanding to know, 'Why couldn't the terrorists have shot Daddy with a water pistol instead of guns?'

Amanda now had the dilemma of whether to stay in London with the children or get herself out to Riyadh to be at my bedside. Saudi Arabia was obviously not safe for Westerners, she reasoned, and to run the risk of the children losing two parents did not bear thinking about, so she was hesitant to leave. Her parents made the decision for her when they got to London, taking over the care of Melissa and Sasha, who probably saw the unexpected arrival of their Pops and Gran as a huge treat. On Wednesday Amanda was taken shopping along with my researcher Katie Pearson for an *abaya*, the black cloak required to be worn by women in Saudi, and late that night they landed at Riyadh's futuristic King Khaled Airport, together with a delegation from the BBC and Simon's parents. 'It was very disorienting,' Amanda told me later. 'We were given a VIP reception because the British and Irish ambassadors were there to meet us. There were security men with guns everywhere.' Simon's widow Louise had just spent a harrowing day being taken under heavy security to the spot where the Saudi police said her husband had died, a version they later changed.

It was past midnight three days after the attack and Amanda was given the choice of going to the Embassy to get some sleep or going straight to the hospital to see me. Uncertain as to how critical my condition was, she chose the hospital in case I did not survive the night. It must have been quite a shock for her to see two armed guards posted outside my room. Having failed to protect us while we were filming, the Saudi authorities now seemed determined to prevent any-one from coming to finish me off. This extra security was probably just as well since hospital staff told her that gunmen had recently crept into another hospital, disguised as women, to try to kill a patient they had wounded earlier. In the light of this news Amanda now planned her own emergency con-tingency plan in case anyone had similar ideas for me. She prepared a sheet that could be pulled over me to cover my face and located a cupboard in which to hide herself. This may sound paranoid, but Riyadh at that time must have been a very frightening place for her and on each subsequent trip to the hospital she never knew quite what to expect.

All this time I was under heavy sedation, pumped full of a whole pharmacy of drugs and hooked up to machines that helped my body perform its most basic functions, like breathing. But my mind was far from still; in fact it was extremely active. The morphine-derived drugs I had been given after being shot were so powerful that I was having some bizarre hallucinations. I imagined that someone was asking me to hold up two pails of blood while the contents were mixed together for my blood transfusion. But something was wrong. The young German medical student in charge of mixing the blood was arguing with a nurse and now he had stormed off in a huff. 'Excuse me,' I said weakly, but no one could hear me and now I was being left to balance the pails of blood on my own. Of course none of this was happening except in my head – the hospital notes at the time did mention I was 'showing signs of delirium'.

For five days Amanda came to sit quietly at my bedside, reading to my motionless form, mopping my brow and holding my hand. As I underwent operation after operation, she lost count of the number of consent forms she had to sign, knowing each time there was always the risk it could go fatally wrong.

The Saudis continued to take a concerned interest in my case. On more than one occasion Prince Salman, the governor of Riyadh, visited me in my small room while I was still out for the count, accompanied by a retinue of up to thirty followers and bodyguards. The British, Irish and US ambassadors also came to visit my almost lifeless form. How ironic, I thought later, that only a few days previously I had called in on the US Embassy to hear their latest assessment of the Al-Qaeda threat, only to become one of their statistics myself. Still, the US ambassador James Oberwetter must have rated my chances of recovery as he left me a present of *Ghost Wars*, a six-hundred-page book on Al-Qaeda, Bin Laden and the CIA's covert war in Afghanistan.

Amanda's brother Mike, a former bodybuilder who had once run the gym at the Mandarin Oriental Hotel in Hong Kong, performed gentle physiotherapy on my arms, but they were slack and lifeless. The only reaction anyone got out of me was when Mark Perrow, my BBC line manager who had flown out to see me, joked that he had put me down for weekend duty in the newsroom; apparently my blood pressure went up noticeably.

Eight days after I had first gone under sedation on the night I was shot, I finally floated up to the surface and opened my eyes. Amanda's face smiled down at me. 'Honey, you made it!' she cried. 'You're my hero!'

I was groggy but full of questions. 'Where is Simon?' I asked.

Amanda's smile faded. 'He didn't make it, I'm afraid. I'm sorry.'

This was too much to take in and I closed my eyes again. Perhaps she was wrong. How could he not be alive any more? Surely if I had survived he must have done too. I simply could not comprehend the possibility that Simon's fate had been any different from mine.

The BBC was doing its best to get me repatriated to a UK hospital as soon as possible. Initial arrangements had been made for the RAF to fly me out to Qatar and from there to a UK airbase. But Dr Bautz was unwilling to risk the life he had just saved and each time they asked him when I could be released he would reply, 'Just give it one more week.'

I remember little of the hospital in Riyadh, hooked up as I was to tubes and needles; just the sweet-sour smell of urine and a perpetual, overwhelming thirst. My guts were so badly damaged that I was not supposed to drink anything, but

Amanda was allowed to give me tiny drops of mango juice which I sucked from a sponge on the end of a stick. She says I complained that it was never enough and also that I desperately wanted a monkey bar above my bed so that I could pull myself up. But I was not allowed to move, as the bullet wound to my right shoulder was still fresh and the bone there still damaged.

Eventually, after eighteen days at the King Faisal Hospital in Riyadh, Bautz relented and agreed to let me go home, but only after he had secured a telephone link with the pilot of the air ambulance. Sherard had had a quiet word with the Saudi Foreign Minister, whose government generously paid both the hospital bill and the cost of the flight home.

In convoy we drove under police escort through the streets of Riyadh to the military airport in the centre of this low-rise city, bypassing customs completely. I vaguely remembered passing through here in happier times with a junior prince, off to visit some tribesmen in the mountains of the Hijaz, but that was in another life. We then boarded a sleek executive jet with oval windows and swivelling armchairs that cruised at 45,000 feet. Strapped down on my stretcher, I was unable to appreciate its finer comforts, but I did feel I was in space. The sky looked so deep blue it was almost black and I was convinced I could see the curvature of the earth. Mike, my brother-in-law, was in hog heaven: he had found some fellow smokers up front. He spent the entire flight in the cockpit, helping the pilot and co-pilot kick up a dense blue fug.

We landed that afternoon at Luton airport, where the English summer welcomed us back with a blast of wind and drizzle. There was a small, very cold-looking reception committee waiting for us: a handful of BBC News managers, someone from the Saudi Embassy and the ambassador's security adviser, Nawaf Obaid, whom I had been on the phone to on the afternoon we were attacked. A whole hour was then spent transferring me into a little red helicopter for

309

the short flight to east London. Mike sidled up to me and said conspiratorially, 'So, Frank, who do you want to accompany you on the helicopter?' 'Amanda,' I croaked. His face fell. After his six-hour joyride in the Learjet cockpit, Mike had clearly thought he was on to a winning streak.

Unable to see very much from my stretcher, I felt the helicopter lift off, turn south then bank round and almost immediately, it seemed, steady itself for landing. We touched down into the wind on the roof of the Royal London Hospital in Whitechapel, my new home for the next four months. As the whine and backwash of the helicopter's rotors slowly subsided I was loaded into a lift and lowered into the bowels of the building. A second, slow-motion ordeal was about to begin.

I did not realize it then, but when I was delivered to the Royal London that afternoon I was still very weak and ill. When the lift doors opened I was wheeled on a stretcher past the hospital's consultants and registrars, earnest-looking men in pinstriped suits all lined up to receive me. It was my first sight of Frank Cross, a trauma surgeon whom Bautz had met and recommended to take charge of my recovery. A conversation developed over my head, literally, and I began to feel increasingly nauseous and begged to be put to bed. I was then brought up to the High Dependency Unit, a sort of halfway house between Intensive Care and a normal ward. On the way we passed a private room guarded by a cluster of armed police in bulletproof vests. I was alarmed to see guns again so soon so I asked a nurse what they were doing there. 'Oh that,' she said nonchalantly. 'The patient's a drug-dealer or something. Got shot in the neck in a drive-by last week. Police are just making sure the people who did it don't come and finish the job.'

It was not until over a year later that Frank Cross confided, 'When we first saw you we were very worried that you were not going to make it. You just didn't seem to have enough small bowel left to survive nutritionally.'

Partly for my own security and partly to ward off any press enquiries, I was given a pseudonym. To everyone's bemusement this was 'Dan Kilo, Unknown', an invention of the hospital's Emergency Department. Many trauma patients are brought in unconscious with no identity so they are named in alphabetical order. I rather liked Dan Kilo, it made me think of some comic-book hero. It also came in useful in preserving my anonymity, as before long an enterprising journalist from a Sunday paper crept into the hospital, pretending to be an old friend of mine, seeking an in-depth interview. He did not get past the nurses.

Inside the HDU ward there were monitors bleeping everywhere. The first thing I remember was a Bengali woman having some kind of fit in the bed opposite mine. She was moaning and wailing, shaking her head, her hands trembling, and I wondered what had happened that had so upset her. Once my bed was installed in its bay someone handed me a mirror and I saw myself for the first time since being shot. I was a shocking sight. My eyes were yellow with jaundice from my liver being thrown out of kilter by the cocktail of drugs I had been fed over the past three weeks. But what horrified me most was the sight of my legs, especially the left one. Lying slack and useless after being disconnected from my spinal nerves, the thigh was withered where the muscles had atrophied to little more than skin and bone, and I did not recognize it as my own. My arms were still slightly tanned from the Saudi sun but they were dreadfully shrivelled, the flesh hanging off the bone like that of someone more than twice my age. I had a cannula inserted into the back of my hand, which was purple, bruised and swollen. A large tube called a 'central line' for administering drugs ran into the side of my neck and to this was attached a whole cluster of drips like a bunch of grapes, so that it hurt to turn my head. I had often wondered what those tubes were that people had taped to the top of their nose on hospital programmes. Now I knew: a nasal-gastric tube fed through my nostril and all the way down the back of my throat into my stomach to provide basic nutrients. Another pair of much smaller plastic tubes provided oxygen; they smelt of stale cigarettes. I had a vacuum dressing on my abdomen where nine abdominal operations known as 'laparotomies' had been performed and the flesh was raw. When Bautz and his team had rescued me on the operating table of the Al-Iman Hospital my intestines had been in pieces, so now a colostomy bag was attached to my right side which a nurse came to check at intervals. My bladder was another war zone. I had never seen a catheter before, in fact I was not entirely sure what they were, but now the nurse pointed out two of them, like a salesman showing off the features of a new car. I had what is called a suprapubic catheter coming straight out of my abdomen where it was inserted through the abdominal wall into the bladder. I could see the second one, known as an 'in-dwelling' catheter, emerging to my alarm from the tip of my penis and connected to a urine bag. I was briefly thankful not to have been awake when that one was inserted. When no one was looking I took a quick peek down there; there was some colourful bruising but mercifully no bullet holes. Frank Cross told me later that when they first examined me my genitals were so badly bruised it looked as if I had been 'helping the police with their inquiries'.

My right leg was in traction for a hip fracture known as an 'acetabular' break. My left foot was drooping to one side in a very unnatural-looking position, while both my calves were encased in Flotrons, mechanically inflating stockings designed to stop potentially fatal deep-vein thrombosis. All in all I was still in quite a state and this was three weeks since the shooting. All the surgical attachments had been put in in Riyadh while I was out for the count, under general anaesthetic. And I still did not know about the paraplegia.

In those first few days I got so used to being injected, tested and monitored that one nurse's visit blended into another's. At one point a figure in a white coat loomed towards me with a Russian name on his white hospital coat. 'Lobotomy,' he said, in a deadpan voice but with a thick Slavic accent.

'Sorry, what?'

'I come for lobotomy,' he repeated.

This had to be either a joke or another blasted morphine dream. 'I think you've got the wrong patient,' I croaked.

He glanced down at his clipboard. 'You are Mr Gardner, no? Date of birth 1961?'

This was no longer funny. 'Yes, but . . . what did you say you're here for?'

'Phlebotomy. Blood test.'

Within days of my arriving in London I had some welcome visitors: first my daughters, and then my parents and in-laws. By this time I had had yet another tube inserted into me: a 'Hickman line' had been fed into my chest under local anaesthetic so that nutritional supplements could be fed straight into my body. Melissa and Sasha stared at me in horror, whispering to Amanda, 'What's happened to Daddy?' But if my parents were alarmed at my appearance they did not show it. For three weeks they had waited at home, consumed by worry and desperate for information. They had even gone to their GP and had vaccinations for Saudi Arabia (not something I had ever bothered with), preparing to fly out to Riyadh in their eighties until Amanda assured them I would soon be back in London. Now they were here in Whitechapel, smiling bravely at what must have been a startling sight. I was jaundiced and emaciated, I had not shaved since the day of the attack, and I must have looked like a ragged porcupine with all these tubes sprouting out of me. I was too weak to answer their questions with anything more than 'I don't know, I don't know.' My mother could see I was exhausted and she seemed content to just sit there beside the bed, while my father showed a boyish fascination with all the gadgets and bleeping monitors around me. I remember whispering to them, 'I'm so sorry about all this,' and my mother just squeezed my hand and smiled at me.

On the ward, life settled into a grim routine. I was given daily injections of Heparin to thin the blood and prevent clotting. The nurse always asked where I wanted the needle and I always pointed to my thighs as I had almost no feeling there. Annoyingly, though, whenever I grew hot I kept getting a sensation like being jabbed in the thigh with a sharp needle. I thought, 'This does not bode well for summer holidays.' There were daily blood tests from the veins in my arm and a blood-sugar-level test using a pinprick on my fingertips. This was not an issue the first few times, but very tedious once I had gone through every finger twice. I was still being fed intravenously, but now at last I was allowed small swigs of juice and even soft food. But my spine was a worry to the hospital's resident Libyan neurosurgeon; he was keen to open me up and remove any remaining grit and bone splinters that may have still been lurking in my lower back from the Riyadh shooting. I remember having dreadful headaches at that time, but as soon as I came round after the four-hour operation the headaches had gone and I felt wonderful. The surgeon had drained five millilitres of fluid from an abscess on the spine. Depressingly, though, he told me afterwards that he had seen some severed spinal nerves down there. Yet still I did not realize that I could be paraplegic – largely paralysed below the waist; I convinced myself that the numbness I felt in my buttocks and pelvis was just from lying too long in a bed.

After I had served my seven days in the High Dependency Unit, my kindly consultant Frank Cross arranged for me to be moved upstairs to a single room on Treves Ward, due to the horrific nature of my injuries. The walls may have been blotched and peeling but I did not care; getting a room to yourself on the NHS was a privilege not to be sneered at.

My cell-like room allowed me to have visitors whenever I wanted, which kept my spirits up considerably. Even without visitors, the room was rarely quiet for long. All day long the hospital's little red helicopter took off and landed on the roof above my head. I liked this, as the sound of the rotor blades and the smell of the Avgas fuel never failed to quicken my pulse and remind me that there was a big wide world beyond my window, and it reminded me of some of my more adventurous assignments in places like Afghanistan. The immediate view out of the window was not inspiring. All I could see was a couple of cranes and what looked like a half-built multi-storey car park. Life on the TV was rather more colourful: by day I watched Maria Sharapova slam and grunt her way to victory at Wimbledon. In the evenings I could hear some of the local lads gathering outside in the deserted east London building site, shouting, screaming, kicking cans and smashing bottles. Once there was a frightful cry of pain, which went on long after dark and brought back bad memories of lying alone and nearly bleeding to death in a street in Riyadh.

The nurses were nearly all angels. They seemed to have infinite patience with everyone, including me. Most were from either the Caribbean or Africa, part of the resource drain that is bleeding that continent of its most qualified medical staff. One girl was from Rwanda, and she told me how being half Tutsi and half Hutu had been no protection against the carnage and bloodlust that had rampaged through her country a decade ago, eventually killing 800,000 people. She and her family were lucky – they got out just in time, fleeing eastwards to Tanzania where they started a new life.

One of the first people to come and see me was the Saudi ambassador to London, Prince Turki Al-Faisal. I had already read the comments he had made to the press when we were attacked and it was obvious that he was personally aggrieved by what had happened to Simon and me. It was, after all, he who had given us visas at short notice and encouraged me to go, although of course he was in no way to blame for the attack. Unlike most other Saudi officials, Prince Turki had taken the view that his country had nothing to hide from journalists and they should be encouraged to see Saudi Arabia for themselves. It must have been very embarrassing for him that when we did just that, we got shot.

As Prince Turki walked down the hospital corridor to my room, escorted by Jonathan Baker, two of the nurses told me later that they noticed he was clutching a gift box of Ferrero Rocher chocolates. 'Ambassador, you are spoiling us,' they whispered, mimicking the television commercial, not knowing who he was. They could hardly believe it when Jonathan waved him into my room, saying, 'Ambassador, please, after you.'

For a busy ambassador, Prince Turki still managed to give the impression that he had all the time in the world for me. He seemed as at ease in my shabby hospital room with its peeling walls and faint whiff of urine as in the gilded confines of his Mayfair Embassy. We talked at length about the trip before I asked him if he thought it had been an opportunistic attack or a pre-planned one – in other words, a set-up. 'It seems that it was opportunistic but the investigation is still going on,' the prince replied before adding cryptically, 'and sometimes there are things which people would rather not say.'

That night a truly enormous bunch of flowers arrived with a courtesy note from the ambassador's office. It was so big it filled the window, but no sooner had a nurse put it up on the window-sill than two men from hospital security rushed in to check it over. I have no idea what they were looking for – bugs? Poison ivy? Combustible orchids? They would not say – but the flowers were allowed to stay and they lasted for nearly two weeks.

While I had still been under the surgeons' knives in Saudi, the BBC had chosen the Royal London Hospital to repatriate me to because it had such an excellent range of care. Sure enough, I had almost daily visits from what seemed like every team in the building. There were neurologists, urologists, orthopaedic surgeons (known unkindly in the trade as 'orthopods', as if they were some primitive form of swamp life), nutritionists and physiotherapists all knocking on my door. There was even someone called a Tissue Viability Nurse, who would come and change the dressing on my raw stomach wound.

My nutrition was clearly a worry since I only had one metre of functioning bowel remaining whereas most adults have seven. Several metres had been so badly shot up they had had to be removed in Riyadh; the rest had been clamped off until I was much, much better. This meant that everything I ate bypassed my intestines altogether, so I was assigned a team of dieticians to keep an eye on me. The team was under the direction of Professor Jeremy Powell-Tuck, the man who helped nurse the American illusionist David Blaine back to health after his forty-four-day starvation stunt in a box beside Tower Bridge in 2003. Powell-Tuck (or Bowel Tuck, as I kept thinking of him) arranged for me to be hooked up to something called Total Parental Nutrition or TPN. This was essentially a three-litre bag full of gunk that dripped slowly into my circulation overnight via the tube in my chest, feeding my body all the essential proteins, fats and nutrients that it was not getting from my meals. I soon discovered there was an entire industry built up around TPN. Small armies of technicians laboured in obscure warehouses to make these bags up, measuring just the right proportions of liquid ingredients. When it came to setting up the bag at night, it always took two specially trained nurses and their conversation was like the pre-flight checks on a 747.

'Patient number 3904556.'

'Check.'

'3.2 per cent sodium nitrate.'

'Check.'

'2.9 per cent amino something or other.'

'Check.'

Because of the risk of infection the TPN had to be set up and given under sterile conditions. Each bag came with a 'giving set' containing sterile gloves, swabs and so on. Standard procedure was for the nurse to flush through the tube that went into my chest with a syringeful of saline solution. This was intended to wash out any bugs that might have settled there and be starting to make themselves comfortable. But somehow, one of them slipped through the net and in July I contracted an infection on the inside of my chest wall. It was staphylococcus epidermis, a distant cousin of the dreaded hospital superbug MRSA, and I deteriorated with frightening speed.

As the cards and emails came in wishing me a full and speedy recovery, I began to do just the opposite. I developed a terrible fever that killed my appetite, made me listlessly wave away visitors, and stopped me doing any physiotherapy. By early evening I would be vomiting and shaking un-controllably. At this stage nobody knew what was wrong with me – they even tested in vain for malaria, not a major problem in Riyadh, a city slap in the middle of one of the driest deserts on earth. For two weeks they injected me and plugged me full of antibiotics, three different types, with needles and drips puncturing my arms, and I was wheeled down time and again to be X-rayed, CT scanned and generally prodded and poked.

My salvation came in the form of the son of a World War Two Polish fighter ace, Paul Sroden, who was a hospital registrar and took a personal interest in my case from the beginning. 'The trouble with you,' he said, smiling at me pityingly from the foot of my bed, 'is that you are a very com-plicated patient. Normally when someone is admitted here they have just one thing wrong with them but you've got everything going on!' Mr Sroden now suggested trying nuclear medicine to locate the source of my infection. This did not involve a trip to North Korea, just to a special lab below ground. They drew out 50ml of my blood, dropped in some radioactive isotopes with a half-life of eight hours and re-injected the blood. A few hours later they put me under a device called a 'gamma camera' to look for the result. Sure enough, there were the isotopes all clinging to the white blood cells, which in turn had flocked to fight the infection in my chest where the feeding line had been inserted. Twenty-four hours later they beat the infection with the appropriate antibiotic, Vancomycin. Brilliant.

In the one-sided gunfight in Riyadh in June, both my bladder and rectum had been punctured by bullet wounds. Now, in August, the urologists decided it was time to see if my bladder had healed. I was wheeled down to a lab and my bladder was filled up via the in-dwelling catheter with a liquid that showed up on X-rays. It was a good result, there were no leaks, but that was the easy part.

'They can take out his urethral catheter now,' I heard the urologist say.

'So, we'll just whip that out, shall we?' said the nurse when I got back up to the ward, glancing pointedly at my groin. Gloves on, sheet back, deep breath. But one gentle tug was enough to send me into paroxysms of pain in the genitals.

'I don't think I can do this,' I gasped.

'Well, honey, we can take a break for now but I'm going to have to come back and do it soon. You're just going to have to be strong.'

I took a gulp of water, ate some Cheddars, flicked between channels on the TV, anything to take my mind off what was to come. When the door opened and the rubber gloves came on again it occurred to me how useless I would be under torture. 'Just make it quick,' I said. 'Ahh . . . Aaarrrggh!' I could hardly believe what came out. The far end of the catheter looked like a folded-up cocktail umbrella!

I still had the other catheter attached to me, the one that had been inserted during surgery into the bladder through the abdominal wall, and since my genitals were in shock after the cocktail-umbrella treatment I decided to keep peeing through the catheter. After a few days I woke up one morning with a full bladder, as one does, and reached for the cardboard urine bottle. To my huge delight, a few drops came out from where nature intended. I was so excited I even rang my parents, who really ought to have been spared such details, to tell them the news. But the following morning the ward sister burst my bubble, so to speak. 'I'm afraid if it was only a few drops that was just stress from a full bladder. It's very common, we call it "firing off".' She was right. All my subsequent attempts to wet the inside of the cardboard bottle came to nothing. My worst fears were confirmed: the bullets had knocked out the sacral nerves that control the bladder. I was not incontinent, I was overcontinent, condemned to a lifetime of peeing through catheters.

As part of their comprehensive care, the consultants at the Royal London decided that it would be a good idea to have the inside of my head looked at while they were about it. A clinical psychologist was duly dispatched to my room, clutching notes.

'Now tell me,' she began, without looking at me, 'why are you here exactly?'

I wondered if this was perhaps some sort of philosophical question about God, the universe and the meaning of life, but decided to play it straight.

'Um . . . it's all in the notes,' I told her.

'Well, I haven't read those. Was it a car accident?'

Oh lordy, I was too tired for this. I began telling her the basic details then stopped halfway, suddenly feeling it was all a waste of time. If this woman couldn't be bothered to find anything out in advance about her next patient then I certainly didn't feel like baring my soul to her.

The BBC sent me a superb Royal Navy psychologist who had counselled other journalists after traumatic incidents. Neil put me at ease immediately, and not just because he had read my medical notes. As a military doctor he understood about gunshot wounds, firefights and the effect they can have on people. We talked for what seemed like hours. All right, I admit it, I talked for hours while he mainly listened. Maybe I was just having withdrawal symptoms from being on air and Neil was my captive audience. But it felt wonderful to tell the whole grisly story to someone who was a dispassionate listener, someone whose emotions had not been hurt by it all.

We fairly quickly established that in terms of mental health I had been lucky. Despite the vivid horror of my experience I had so far been spared the nightmares, flashbacks, anxiety attacks and other symptoms of Post Traumatic Stress Disorder. I could deal with what was in the recent past. All my exertions, I told him, were going into getting better, all my anxieties were about what sort of physical state I would end up in. Was I going to be paralysed for life? Would I ever run, walk or even stand again? If I was to be crippled for life then what kind of a husband and father would that make me? These were the questions that kept me awake at night.

At about this time I had a visit from General Sir Peter de la Billiere, who commanded British forces in the Gulf War of 1991, and his wife Lady Bridget. Sir Peter and I had worked together in the Gulf soon afterwards for Flemings bank and they had come to our wedding. Now Sir Peter had written *Supreme Courage*, a large and impressive book on the history of the Victoria Cross and some of those from all over the Commonwealth who had won it in battle. To my considerable pride he wrote in the inside cover: 'To Frank, a man of great courage. See you fighting fit before long.'

Over the summer a number of my BBC colleagues came to

see me, many of whom had been to far more dangerous places than I had. Brian Hanrahan, who had covered the Falklands War; Orla Guerin, the Middle East correspondent, who put on a flak jacket for her job like other people put on socks; Ben Brown, the ten o'clock news special correspondent, who had been to just about everywhere on the planet where people were shooting at each other, yet always managed to return with a perfect tan and no injuries; John Simpson, who had had a narrow escape the previous year when the US Air Force shot up the convoy he was travelling with; Stuart Hughes, a producer who had lost half his leg to a landmine in the Iraq war; Caroline Hawley, the Baghdad correspondent, who shared the Cairo bureau with me for a couple of years and who now worked in an atmosphere of constant fear of car bombs, kidnappers and snipers; and Tony Fallshaw and Duncan Stone, two of the bravest and best cameramen in foreign news. All of these people and others, I believe, showed amazing courage in pursuing their stories in dangerous conditions and yet now I found myself being drawn involuntarily into their Club of the Brave.

There was also a deluge of cards, letters and emails, mostly from friends, but a few hundred from members of the public who had got used to seeing and hearing me on BBC News and felt they almost knew me personally. I read every one of these and treasured them but I could not begin to respond to them. Several were from Muslims, both in the UK and in the Middle East, hugely and unnecessarily apologetic for what their co-religionists had done to me in the name of their version of Islam. One even commiserated with me on 'the martyrdom of your cameraman'. Many of the British Muslims who wrote to me were furious that Islamic extremists had attacked us, saying the gunmen were not proper Muslims and that they had brought shame on their religion. One Asian girl in Luton with beautiful handwriting wrote that although she thought the West deserved to be punished for its policies in the Middle

East she cried when she learned that I had been shot; I was not sure how I felt about that. From Jeddah a Saudi couple I have known for years wrote to tell me they went straight to Mecca to pray for my survival on the night I was shot. (Having now seen my medical records, I think I needed every prayer on offer.) Aly, a Pakistani friend in Dubai, told me how he had been on a flight when I was attacked and had sat there, tears rolling down his face, staring at the on-board news which read: 'Frank Gardner shot in Riyadh, condition critical.' It must indeed be very strange to see the name of someone you know so well alongside such dire public news. A Christian hermit on an Atlantic island sent me a collection of her poems, some of which struck quite a chord with me. A Welsh couple sent me a gorgeous sheepskin rug from their farm in the hills. The Home Secretary David Blunkett, the UN Secretary-General Kofi Annan and the EU's foreign policy chief Javier Solana all sent me personal letters of commiseration; Paul McCartney sent me an autographed note after he had heard my story from one of our producers at an anti-landmine conference. There was even a letter from a fan on the inside: a convict in Wormwood Scrubs who wanted to meet up when he got out. James Maughan, who had been my best man at our wedding, sent me a collage of photos from some of the many Latin American and Asian countries we have travelled round together, as well as a box of cocoa-dusted truffles from Zurich; these cheered me up enormously. Jo Cayford, a BBC producer friend just back from Moscow, brought me one of those wooden matryoshka dolls, except that instead of being the usual stout, red-cheeked babushka it was of Osama Bin Laden; I unscrewed it and there inside was a smaller wooden doll of the Taliban's Mullah Omar; inside him was Saddam Hussein; then Ayatollah Khomeini; and finally the smallest doll of all was Yasser Arafat. There was also an email from Disco Ron in Hong Kong, the friend who had taken us skiing in Lebanon in 1992 and for whom life was obviously still one long fiesta. 'Yo dude,' it read, 'I'm in town. Let's go party!' I looked at the date this email was sent. It was three weeks after I had been shot and must have been about the time I was spiralling downwards with that dangerous chest infection. Of all my friends, only Disco Ron had not heard what had happened to me and, strangely, this made me smile.

As if to test my tolerance for pain once more, the white coats decided I needed a skin graft from my inside thigh to patch up the raw but granulating wound over my stomach. Back I went under the knife while the plastic surgeons did their work. When I emerged from surgery there was a thick bandage over the 'donor site' on my thigh which itched like mad. I was told it would stay in place for two weeks and I was not to scratch it. When the bandage came off it revealed a neat, rectangular patch of vivid, suppurating sores. 'Excellent,' said the plastic surgeons. On my abdomen the graft had taken, which was a relief since if it had not they would have had to rip another patch of skin off my leg and start all over again. Back on went the vacuum dressing, draining the site of excess fluid. When the surgeons came into the room a few days later to inspect their work they were delighted. To me, my abdomen looked like a horror show. Only a very thin, bright-pink membrane covered my intestines, which coiled and uncoiled themselves beneath it like a snake slowly digesting its lunch. Was this what I was going to be stuck with for life? It was all too reminiscent of that scene in *Alien* where the monster bursts out of John Hurt's abdomen. 'Just don't put it in the sun,' warned the plastic surgeons. As if.

By now I had been in hospital for over two months and it was starting to dawn on me just how serious my injuries were. I had absolutely no movement below my hips, although my legs and feet were in pain all day every day, and I still had this huge raw wound in my belly. I asked the lead neurosurgeon what my chances of walking again were. 'If I were a betting man,' he said, 'I'd say you probably won't walk again. But with nerve damage you can never be sure.'

That was a black day. Naively, I had thought that hard work through physio would be enough to get me back on my feet. I envisaged kick-starting recalcitrant nerves with some sweaty sessions on a static bicycle. Perhaps a bit of gentle hydrotherapy in a warm pool. The idea that I could be paralysed for life had simply not registered until then. I sulked for a day, pouring my fears out to Amanda. Then one evening, while jiggling my hips to keep the blood circulating in my legs, I discovered a muscle twitch in my inner thigh. There was life down there after all, this was a breakthrough. I pressed the call button for the nurse, who was almost as thrilled as I was. The on-call house doctor duly confirmed my hopes: there was nerve activity below the waist. But the next morning Frank Cross brought me down to earth. 'Don't get too excited,' he said, 'it's just the first slippered footstep on a long road to recovery.'

Once I had got over the debilitating effects of that chest bug I picked up in July, I started to get visits from clean-looking girls in crisp white uniforms. They were the physiotherapists, or 'physio terrorists' as they were known, although given what had happened to me everyone was too polite to use that phrase in front of me. I was asked to lift miniature sandbags above my head in bed and out to the sides. I quite enjoyed this – it felt good to use the half of my body that was not paralysed – but this was just the warm-up. After a couple of weeks they got me sitting up on the edge of the bed with my legs dangling down to the floor. This I hated. For a start, I felt dizzy and disoriented sitting up after being supine for so long, and secondly my feet swelled up with the rush of blood, turned purple and hurt like mad. But what really depressed me was the sensation I felt for the first time of having two dead logs for legs. I had to use both hands to lift each leg across the bed and down. There was no touch sensation or motor movement in them at all. Weird.

Of all the physios at Whitechapel, one stood out. Julie Hicks was a slender blonde from New Zealand, in fact she came from the same part of North Island as Amanda's family, but that was not her prime qualification. Julie was a neuro-physio, which meant she understood which muscle movements corresponded to which nerves. She was also tough as nails. Once, when I was perched on the edge of the bed facing her as she knelt, I lost my balance and pitched forward, inadvertently headbutting her on the forehead. Anyone else would have sworn or at least said 'Ow,' but Julie just smiled and said 'Oh, hello' in a sort of easy Antipodean backpacker way. I was impressed, and when I eventually moved from the Royal London I hired her – at the BBC insurers' expense – to come and keep up the physio work three times a week.

There were some brighter moments in Whitechapel to distract from all the pain and probing. Once I had recovered from the infection and fever, my family and friends started a Murmansk run of gourmet food. Naomi and Aidan, who had rushed over on the night of the shooting to be with Amanda, made regular weekend visits with a Thermos bag full of home-cooked chicken wrapped in pancetta and herbs. My parents came up from the country to Waterloo and then took the Tube through London to visit me at least twice a week with slices of country ham and succulent French peaches. I took great delight in recounting these meals the next day, in mouthwatering detail, to the posse of dieticians who came in to check up on me. I may not have been regaining weight but I was certainly rediscovering a love of food.

Best of all were the intimate dinners that Amanda arranged. With a nod from the nurse we would be left undisturbed while my wife lit candles in the room, against every hospital regulation, and laid out a white tablecloth. She then unpacked our Wedgwood wedding china and two crystal wine glasses, filling them with iced mango juice or tropical fruit cocktail. We would then feast on chopped avocado and pasta that melted in the mouth followed by little cartons of chocolate mousse. Afterwards we would snuggle up on the bed and watch black-and-white classics like *Casablanca* on the little TV/DVD that the BBC had bought me. The only hard part was when Amanda had to leave, often close to midnight, and I would go to sleep alone once again.

In my last week in Whitechapel I was taken down in the lift to somewhere which, for me, held almost as much terror as an Iraqi interrogation chamber: the Colo-rectal Department. The white coats wanted to know if I still had muscle tone down there and proposed a series of progressively uncomfortable tests. I cannot imagine what had possessed the tall and beautiful girl who greeted me to make a career out of inserting things up people's bottoms, but she did her best to put me at ease. 'You make yourself comfortable and face the wall while I get everything ready.' Make myself comfortable? My injuries, combined with the nerve damage and four months of lying in bed on my bum, had left me so sensitive down below that I found myself involuntarily recoiling at the slightest touch.

She showed me a very thin catheter. 'Now, Frank, I'm just going to insert this, then inflate it, like so . . . OK, you should now feel as if you need to pass wind.' I did. 'And now . . . this should feel like you need to empty your bowels.' It did. 'And this . . . should feel like you're absolutely desperate to go.'

'Arrgh! Yes, it does! Make it stop!' I half expected her to say, 'Tell us the truth, Frank, and I can make the pain go away.'

The colo-rectal nurse had a whole raft of other devices lined up for me, including something that – and I am not joking here – was bubbling away in a miniature steel cauldron. But since I howled at the first touch of her little finger the rest of the exercise had to be aborted and I was wheeled back up to the ward in disgrace. Later my consultant, Frank Cross, came into my room and sat down for a chat. When I told him what had happened he confessed sheepishly that he too had baulked at a similar test.

By now Melissa and Sasha had got used to seeing me in hospital and they became a familiar sight on the ward. One of their favourite games was to put the unused cardboard bedpans upside-down on their heads so they looked like cowboy hats. 'Howdy doodie!' they squawked, their shrill voices carrying way down the corridor. Another time Amanda found them playing doctors, having got hold of a stethoscope that they clamped to each other's chest, their little faces solemn with concentration. But the journey from our home to the East End of London had been proving increasingly tedious for my family. Often it could take up to two hours each way thanks to cancelled Tube trains or solid traffic. Amanda began urging me to ask for a transfer to a hospital closer to home. But I replied that I was reluctant to leave since I was getting such good care. Amanda then accused me of suffering from Stockholm Syndrome, whereby prisoners fall in love with their captors. She was right. Despite all the unpleasant medical procedures I had grown quite comfortable in my little room up on the fifth floor. It was time to move to the Chelsea and Westminster Hospital.

They took me in an ambulance, which was a novel experience for me (my rescue in Riyadh having been courtesy of a police patrol car) and I loved it. Lying prone and strapped on to a stretcher, I had Amanda beside me and a constantly changing kaleidoscope outside the window. I saw the Tower of London slide past at an unexpected angle, then a long avenue of plane trees all green and glistening with rain-washed leaves. There was Big Ben, leaning crazily towards me through the treated glass of the ambulance, then more plane trees and suddenly we were in Chelsea.

It was a shock to be back on a public ward after the cosseted privilege of a room to myself for the past four months. At first I disliked it intensely since my fellow patients all seemed to be grumpy old men with nothing much wrong with them. They would grumble and moan to the nurses and then get up and go off to the loo. I thought, 'I can't do that.'

But after a day or two I began to take an interest in them. A couple of beds down lay Ted, a jovial wino who was using the place like a hotel, letting himself out each morning then boozing the day away with his mates in Fulham Broadway. He would roll back in at eight p.m., happily drunk, and regale me with stories of his National Service days in Berlin, guarding Rudolph Hess in the 1950s. Sadly for him he was spotted in the pub by one of the doctors and was promptly given his marching orders. Ted's best friend on the ward was a tiny bearded East Ender of no fixed address. Whenever he was asked to fill in a form he would shake his head sadly. 'Can't read,' he would grunt. Right opposite me was the patient from hell. He would rumble and grumble throughout the night, then empty his guts into his incontinency pads just before each mealtime, effectively putting everyone off their food. There was Sven, a noisy Scandinavian drug addict who told me he had been injecting for nearly forty years and was now having a stab at methadone. Whenever his fix was late he would threaten to go out on to the street and buy heroin from a dealer instead. Sven had a large, suppurating wound on his leg and after a while word got out that he had contracted MRSA. He was swiftly moved to an isolation room while an inquiry was conducted as to how we had found out (we had overheard the nurses discussing him).

At about this time I had a visit from the Chronic Pain Team. Even their name had a ring of despair about it but I was open to all suggestions. Like most spinal-cord-injury patients I had been suffering a lot from pain in the legs where the nerves had been all jangled up by my injuries. The worst kind of pain felt like I was being kicked on the shins, quite hard, by someone with steel toecaps. It would hit me without warning, causing me to hunch up in agony until it passed. At all times I was aware of a low, aching pain in my legs which sometimes felt like pins and needles. It was not as painful, but was enough to stop me getting to sleep at night. The pain team prescribed a daily course of neuropathic painkillers; they also had a clinical psychologist who tried, unsuccessfully, to get me to 'breathe through the pain'. I would challenge anybody to 'breathe through' being kicked on the shins.

Being in hospital in Chelsea did wonders for my morale as people flocked to my bedside. My dear friend Khaled Al-Sabah, who had crossed the border into Iraq with me in 1991, generously gave me a brand-new Sony Ericsson P900 mobile phone (my blood-stained BBC mobile was still in the tender care of Scotland Yard's Anti-Terrorist Branch). He also brought me a bottle of exceptionally good claret, which we drank out of plastic cups with our lukewarm takeaway pizza. Jo Cayford, from the BBC, brought me back a tub of caviar from Moscow – I enjoyed the look on the nurses' faces when I asked if they would be so good as to bring me my caviar from the communal fridge. John Simpson and his wife Dee ambled over from their Chelsea pad, he fresh from a difficult and dangerous assignment, I fresh from having my colostomy bag changed. Others insisted I get into a wheelchair so we could go off to a restaurant for the evening.

The first time this happened I did something of a double-take. As I wheeled into an Indian restaurant the waiter bent down towards me and said, 'I must tell you, sir, that we don't have disabled access to toilets on this floor.' I thought, 'Why is he telling me this? I'm not disabled.' And then it hit me. Of course. Disabled. That's me now. All those little wheelchair signs are going to be part of my world, so I had better get used to asking where the disabled loos are. Up until then I had not paid much attention to what sort of wheelchair I had, telling myself it was just a temporary phase for a few months until I got my legs back. While I still thought that, I did notice that the hospital wheelchair I had been issued with was of a very poor design. Julie, my physio, was horrified when it started to tip backwards as I mounted the tiniest of kerbs. The footplates scraped along the ground half the time, which meant I had to be wheeled backwards into some places, which I hated as it made me feel like even more of an invalid than I already was.

Despite my paraplegia I was still the healthiest patient on the ward, so before long it was decided that I should be sent to a physio rehab unit for a few months until my intestines had recovered enough to be operated on. The Royal National Orthopaedic Hospital at Stanmore in Middlesex is a bizarre place. Situated on the outer reaches of northwest London, it has a leafy, rural feel to it. It is within earshot of the M1 yet there are deer foraging here in woods and fields. The buildings were in a decrepit state; the corrugated roofs were overgrown with grass and moss, and rainwater often trickled into the corridors. There has since been a multi-million-pound fundraising drive to update it. Yet despite having the air of a 1950s National Service boot camp, it has a reputation for being one of the best places in the country for rehabilitating spinal-injury patients. Unfortunately, nobody explained to me before I went what I could expect to achieve there. I arrived thinking they were going to be concentrating my efforts on walking again; I even told friends at the BBC that they would be trying to get my legs working again. But I was quickly disillusioned.

On day one, the consultant, Dr Gall, came in to give me an 'Asia' test (standing for American Spinal Injuries Association). This involved pushing and tweaking my legs to see how much sensitivity and movement I had left. It was one of the most depressing hours of my life.

'Can you move your toes?'

'No.'

'Can you lift your foot up?'

'No.'

'Can you lift your knee up?'

'No.'

On almost every test I was scoring 0 or 1 out of 5, indicating nothing more than a flicker of life at most. The consultant shook her head sadly.

Next came a sensitivity test in a sensitive part of the body. A Jordanian doctor asked me to roll on to my side and pull down my tracksuit bottoms. He then took out something that looked like a map pin and slowly, deliberately, jabbed me in the anus. I felt it all right, I virtually hit the wall with pain. 'Good,' he said. 'If you have sensitivity there that means your injury is incomplete. You are what we call "sensory incomplete", which means you might have a 20 per cent chance of walking again. But every patient is different.'

I was keen for them to leave the room, but the ordeal was not over. 'Now we need you to roll over on to your back,' said the doctors. Another jab in another sensitive part of the body, more pain and more nods of approval. I half expected them to move on to my eyeballs.

I was now left alone with my thoughts in a small dark room. There was a window, but it looked out on to a corridor. From somewhere down the passageway I could hear children laughing and playing, and suddenly I felt very, very low. My own children were far away on the other side of London and I would not be tucking them into bed tonight or any time soon. How long had it been now since I had last read them their bedtime story? Four months? Five months? It seemed like a lifetime since I had slept under the same roof as my family and I missed them desperately. On top of this I was having to cope with near continual, undulating pain in my legs, wandering like a torchbeam from my foot to my calf to my shin, then back again.

The next morning I was introduced to my new physio-therapist, Almari from South Africa, and the special physio gym in which she worked. It was unlike anywhere I had ever seen. Housed in a sort of well-lit warehouse, it consisted of padded plinth beds, wooden standing frames with sheepskin straps, parallel bars, powered rowing machines and a versatrainer on which paraplegics could exercise their limbs. Some patients were on their backs having their flaccid legs manipulated, others were strapped into the standing frames, one was on the assisted cycle machine (it does the pedalling for you) and one was being wheeled in, still in his bed, then winched up in a sort of garden-compost sack then transferred on to a tilting table where he was slowly raised to near vertical. A group of three patients with lesions quite high up their spines was gathered for a balance and coordination lesson, passing a rubber ball endlessly backwards and for-wards to each other. Everyone's wheelchair paraphernalia seemed to have jaunty, toytown names like 'Quickie' and 'Action 3'. I noticed how incredibly skinny everyone's legs were, especially the calves. A typical example was Ray, a big, broad-shouldered Jamaican with huge biceps and tiny match-stick legs encased in girlie white stockings to prevent deep-vein thrombosis.

Almari was all business and she needed to be; she was an expert in rehabilitating spinally injured patients while I was new to this, and at first we did not see eye to eye. I was only interested in working towards getting back up on my feet, but she made it clear from the outset that I was extremely unlikely ever to be able to walk again without artificial help. Instead, she gently insisted on spending session after session on 'transfers', using my arms to shift myself from wheelchair to plinth and back again. I found this frustrating and boring and it was probably not a barrel of laughs for her either, but I later realized it was an essential building block for any kind of mobility.

Physiotherapy was doubly difficult for me because of the other medical problems caused by my multiple gunshot wounds. Since Dr Bautz's emergency surgery in Riyadh had effectively sealed off my intestines, whatever I ate came out minutes later through a hole in my side into the plastic ileostomy bag attached to my abdomen. For seven months, until they reconnected my guts in 2005, the effluent was so undigested that it had no bad odour; I even recognized things I had recently eaten. But since it came almost directly from my stomach it was highly acidic, the stomach containing a powerful concentration of hydrochloric acid. This acidic brown matter would often leak under the bag's adhesive seal, burning my skin red raw. Sometimes I would detect a leak during my daily hour of one-on-one physiotherapy, forcing me to cancel the rest of the session and wheel myself back to the ward for emergency repairs. On most nights I would have to wake up several times to empty the bag, keeping a careful record of volume on the instructions of the gastro consultant in Chelsea. Apparently more than 1.5 litres a day meant I was losing too much liquid and would become dehydrated. 'Your nutrition is highly precarious,' he told me. Altogether it became a major distraction from physio.

There were also sessions with Emma Linley from Occupational Therapy, a down-to-earth girl who later featured on the front pages of the newspapers holding hands with another patient, Abigail Witchalls, who was brought to Stanmore after being stabbed in the neck while wheeling her son in a pushchair near a quiet village in Surrey. Emma taught me how to get dressed in the mornings, coaxing my inflexible, paralysed legs to bend just a little bit more so I could get my socks on and tie my shoelaces, and showing me how to hitch up the waistband of my trousers by rolling from side to side on the bed. I was enrolled in wheelchair-skill lessons, learning how to do a 'back-wheel balance' whereby you tip the chair back to lift the front wheels up over a kerb. To be honest, I was not very interested in my wheelchair because I had convinced myself that I would be up and out of it somehow before long. But Emma's report for my Disability Living Allowance laid it out in black and white: 'It is estimated that Frank will be a long-term wheelchair user.'

Stanmore had its own resident urology nurses who doubled as sexual-function counsellors, spinal-cord injury having a habit of damaging this as well as bladder and bowel control. One day when I was lying on my bed exhausted after a physio session, one of these nurses came barrelling out of her Viagra-stocked storeroom to tell me about ISC.

'ISC?' I asked. I had never heard of it.

'Intermittent Self-Catheterization. It's what we encourage all the patients to do if they can.' OK, so this was a bladder thing, not a sex thing, but I still did not like the sound of it. The nurse had a kind, motherly face and I would much rather have talked to her about almost anything else other than this, but she pressed on.

'Now, Frank, like most of the patients here you're finding you can't urinate naturally any more and I know you have a permanent catheter sitting in your bladder, but in the long term this is not very healthy. The bladder doesn't like foreign objects and it can give rise to urinary tract infections or even bladder stones and, believe me, you don't want to get those. So –' She paused for effect, having softened me up with these dire warnings. 'That brings us to ISC.' The nurse now produced a catheter that was – and I am not exaggerating – as long as my arm.

'I'm going to show you how to use one of these on this rubber model and then you can have a go.'

Oh great, I can't wait, I thought. I watched in horror as she withdrew the oiled tube from its cellophane wrapping and then proceeded to insert it into the tip of her model penis then feed it all the way up inside it.

'Now you may find,' she went on gaily, 'that you meet a bit

of resistance at this point. Don't worry, that's the valve at the entrance to the bladder. You just have to keep pushing it upwards and then the urine will start to flow out.'

When it came to trying this on myself I baulked the first time, then on the second attempt I got as far as that resistance at the valve and just could not go on. This was one instance where I was actually at a disadvantage over the other paraplegics on the ward, since unlike them I still had sensation down there, and a year later I still had not steeled myself to start shoving a very long tube up my private parts four times a day.

A few weeks after arriving at Stanmore I was moved on to a public ward, the Spinal Injuries Ward, and started to get to know some of the other patients. Their stories were tragic and moving, made all the more so by the sound of gentle sobbing I could sometimes hear at night; it was the sound of very disabled men mourning the loss of their legs, saying goodbye to the independent life they had taken for granted and which now they would never have again. There was Robbie, a Scotsman who had been hit by a bus and spun round then almost immediately run over by a car. He lay in bed, smiling apparently cheerfully, yet being paralysed from the neck downwards he was unable to feed or wash himself or carry out any other bodily function. There was Neil, another tetraplegic (paralysed from the neck down), who told me he had been pushed off a three-storey building by someone he knew. He said he had spent eight hours lying in a coma and was only discovered in the morning. 'I'd give anything to have my arms like you've got,' he told me, 'so I can get the bastard that did this to me.' Another patient bent on revenge was John, a tall Vinnie Jones-like character with a James Bond ring tone on his mobile. He told me he had been deliberately run over by his sister-in-law on the gypsy commune they lived on. 'She hates my guts,' he said, 'and one day she just drove her Land Rover straight at me, knocked me down and went over me chest. I had tyre tracks all across me body afterwards.' There were also two Jamaican friends from north London, one of whom had a bullet lodged in his spine. 'They're yardies,' said one of the nurses to me in a conspiratorial whisper. Every time I wheeled past them they shouted 'Respect!' and knocked knuckles with me; I liked to think this was because we had all survived potentially lethal gunshot wounds.

I discovered by chance that there were at least two failed suicides on the ward. One was a girl who had thrown herself under a Tube train in London. The other was Simon H. Tall and powerfully built, he had been a champion martial artist, competing in Taekwondo and Ultimate Fighting competitions at international level. He had fallen in love with a Swedish girl and moved to Stockholm with her, but when the relationship turned sour he returned to England and grew increasingly depressed. Eventually he climbed up on to the roof of the four-storey government building where he worked, tied one end of a rope around his neck and the other to a hard point on the roof, and jumped off. The rope snapped. By chance, just as he was falling towards the concrete, someone happened to open a window below which deflected him towards a patch of grass. He came to, to find himself still alive and now completely paralysed from the waist downwards. Simon H. was a very private person but I discovered he was a talented artist; for hours he would stand upright in the standing frame, held in place with padded straps, drawing brilliant but frightening cartoons of patients cowering in bed while demonic nurses came out of the furniture and advanced on them with lethal-looking hypodermic syringes. Already popular with the nurses, he was elevated to hero status after an incident on the ward. A new patient, Terry, had arrived with a nasty attitude. He openly admitted to having spent the last ten years in a Belgian jail – we never learned his crime – but it was his racism that grated.

When one of the nurses told him his racist comments were unacceptable, he threatened to 'cut her up', and wheeled himself back to his bedside locker where he produced a knife. Simon, who even in his wheelchair could probably have felled him with a single blow, calmly talked him out of using the knife. The police were called and Terry was taken away.

I had my own demons to fight at Stanmore. Mostly it was the prospect of being confined to a wheelchair for the rest of my life that terrified me. But one day a visiting friend brought me a DVD of the latest Tom Cruise film, *Collateral*. When it came to the bit where Cruise's hitman character guns down a gang of thugs in a backstreet, I sat bolt upright in bed. This was suddenly, chillingly familiar: the roar of the pistol going off, followed immediately by the clink of the ejected cartridge case hitting the metalled surface of the road. I had forgotten that, but now Hollywood had brought it back in sharp relief; I could remember it as clearly as if it were yesterday, that deafening roar as the Al-Qaeda gunman's pistol went off, pointing directly at the centre of my body, the earth-moving thump of each bullet as it slammed into me and then that high-pitched, almost musical tinkle of the cartridge case landing on the tarmac beside me. It was all too real. But I did not want to have a problem every time a gun went off on television, so I 'inoculated myself' by pressing pause, rewind, then play, pause, rewind and play, until I was thoroughly bored of that sequence. I don't have a problem with on-screen gunshots now.

In November I had two major emotional hurdles to get over: my first visit home and the memorial service for Simon Cumbers. Emma, my occupational therapist, warned me that going home for a visit can be quite upsetting. As we drove in her car from Stanmore past the rising skeleton of the new Wembley Stadium, she explained why.

'When spinally injured patients go home for the first time after their injuries they're suddenly confronted with a glimpse of their past life,' she said. 'Often the house they lived in before is not going to be suitable for them now they're in a wheelchair.'

I thought about where we lived, a typical late-Victorian terraced house, tall and narrow with thirty-six stairs and lots of half-floors and landings. I had a bad feeling about this. Although I had practised car transfers at Stanmore, it was still a major operation to get me out of Emma's car, on to a sliding board and across that into my wheelchair, all the while holding up the traffic in our narrow street. I felt intensely self-conscious as I was wheeled up over the kerb, through the piles of dry autumn leaves and up to our front door. One of our neighbours waved cheerfully but I did not feel like talking to anyone. I could not wait to be off the street and inside.

Then it was through the same front door that I had trotted briskly out of, rucksack over my shoulder, just five months before, and into our narrow hallway. Amanda was waiting for us with fresh-brewed coffee and warm croissants. We soon found we could only just turn me round to get into the living room and it took both Emma and Amanda to lower me down the two steps into the kitchen. I felt very much an invalid. We had no bathroom on the ground floor and Emma's expression was pretty grim. By the end of the visit – which included me having to shoo the others out of the living room so I could go to the loo in a bag – it was painfully obvious: no amount of adaptations were going to be enough here, we would have to sell our family home and move out. We did not break this straight away to the children when they were collected from school that afternoon. Instead, Amanda told them there was a surprise in the living room, where I lay hidden under a rug. Then Sasha spotted a foot and squealed, 'It's Daddy! He's come home!'

The day of Simon's memorial service was crisp and blue, and London seemed to sparkle in the pale sunlight of early November. The service was to be held in the seventeenth-century St Bride's Church, the journalists' church just off Fleet Street, and Louise Bevan, Simon's widow, had been working on it for months. She did him proud. The service, complete with a choir singing from the Messiah, was by invitation only, yet there were a good three hundred people there, with friends and colleagues having flown in from news bureaux on three continents. There were Simon's friends from his days at Channel 4, ITN, London News Network and APTV (now APTN), and of course his family from Ireland, whom I had not met before. Louise had organized a tot of Bushmills finest ten-year-old Irish whiskey for everyone in the church, 350 glasses in all, during the singing of 'Jerusalem', a touch which everyone appreciated. Afterwards Simon's mother Brona threw her arms around me and just held me.

Just as everyone was heading from the church to the reception, Simon played his final joke. A rumour came out of Jerusalem that Yasser Arafat had died in Paris, which prompted all the BBC and other news people to dash around with mobiles clamped to their ears. The rumour was false: Arafat still had a week to live.

For all of us there, Simon's memorial service was very, very hard and I found I was unable to talk about it for a long time afterwards. Orla Guerin, the BBC's Middle East correspondent who had recently been awarded an honorary MBE for her journalism (like Simon, she was from the Irish Republic), tried to inject a lighter note in her speech. 'As Simon is probably watching me right now I will try to do this in one take,' she said from the pulpit as she began listing the many ways in which he had been such a pleasure to work with. But when she remembered how on every assignment Simon had never failed to mention his beloved Louise, Orla broke down and we cried with her. After all my months in hospital it finally hit home hard: Simon was dead, because of the trip we had gone on together. I had survived and he had not. I would have given anything to wake up and realize it had just been a terrible dream, that Simon was still doing what he loved, making superb films or just making everyone around him smile and laugh.

Back at Stanmore Orthopaedic Hospital, the nurses and dinner ladies could see how upset I was in the days that followed and they were especially kind. One of my favourite nurses, Anne-Marie, who confided that she was the daughter of the High Commissioner of Sierre Leone in London, went to a lot of effort to massage my legs to try to reduce the agonizing nerve pain I was suffering. Since on these occasions sleep was out of the question, we would stay up chatting for hours, with her perched on the end of my bed. Another favourite was Eileen, who had grown up tough in rural Ireland in the 1950s. She told me she was one of seventeen children – seventeen! – although five had died very young. She remembered her ten-month-old brother dying of pneumonia because the doctor could not reach their house in time. In rural Kilkenny, she said, they had been desperately poor. Unable to afford a football, they used to play with a pig's bladder until it burst, a story which somehow made me wince with empathy. Much of the family's money, she said, used to go to the priests, who would announce in church exactly how much each person had given, thereby shaming them into giving more. Once, a distant relative arrived from America with oranges and the family could not believe their luck.

In mid-November Amanda took off for a well-earned hen weekend in Paris and I arranged with friends to break out of Stanmore for a day and take Melissa and Sasha to the London Wetland Centre in Barnes, a wonderful expanse of lakes and marsh in southwest London where ducks and geese fly in from Siberia to spend the winter. We had brought the girls here before I was injured and they had loved using my binoculars and peering out of the wooden hides, but this outing was to be unexpectedly hard for me. My friends Aidan and Steve were attentive and playful with the girls, who loved them as surrogate uncles, but as I sat in my wheelchair, unable to join in their chasing games, I began to realize what I had lost through disability. Whereas before I would have whirled them round or plopped them up on my shoulders, now I could only watch from the side, feeling like a passive grand-parent out for a spin in the park. I thought, 'I'm forty-three, I'm not ready for this.' When I told Amanda later, she sensibly told me to stop being so morbid. 'Ah, cheap thrills,' she said. 'Anyone can whirl them round but they'll soon grow out of that. You're their daddy and now they've got you back.' That same week Margaret Hassan, the CARE charity worker abducted by gunmen in Iraq, was murdered by her captors, which rather put my problems in perspective.

Back in the physio gym at Stanmore, I had one more battle to fight. I was determined to start walking in callipers as soon as possible, but the hospital had a policy of not letting patients do this until at least a year after their injury and it had only been six months in my case. I persisted, making such a nuisance of myself that the orthopaedic surgeon agreed to have me X-rayed. When he looked at the results he pro-nounced there was no reason why my spine could not tolerate my walking in callipers, so off I went to the Orthotics work-shop to have warm plaster of Paris smeared over my legs from which they then fashioned the callipers. They were bigger, heavier and clunkier than I had hoped for, with great metal hinges and plastic ridges that came right up to the groin and buttocks, and they were quite a struggle to put on. But when I took my first steps in them between the parallel bars I found it surprisingly easy. The callipers encased my legs like a couple of rigid tubes – without them my legs would have collapsed beneath me – so that, using my hips and thighs, I could move forward one step at a time. It felt fantastic to be up and on the move again, even if it was only a pale imitation of walking.

I must have been so encouraged by this development that when I gave my first interview since the attack, on the *Today* programme on Christmas Eve, I mistakenly gave listeners the impression that all was going to be well. John Humphrys, after quizzing me about what I remembered of the attack, then asked me how I was, healthwise. Although I replied that I was in a wheelchair, I think most people had the impression that this would be temporary, like someone with a leg in plaster after a skiing accident. Cards and letters started to come in congratulating me on my 'full recovery'. 'No!' I felt like screaming. 'You don't understand! I'm paraplegic, disabled, crippled for life. I need to make that clear.'

At Christmas I was allowed home for a few days, reunited at last with my family in our newly rented two-bedroom flat, where Melissa and Sasha were squeezed into bunk beds but where at least I could roll into the room and read them their bedtime stories. My father bought us tickets to Tchaikovsky's ballet *The Nutcracker* and so we headed off to the South Bank, where the disability people made a welcome fuss of me and took us backstage in the interval to meet the ballerinas. The dancers from Moscow greeted our daughters in Russian and let them touch their elaborate lace dresses – at least one experience, I told myself, they would never have had if this whole horrible thing had not happened to us. On Christmas Day my parents came up to join us and we raised a toast to survival, but when we went for the traditional walk after lunch I realized that in my wheelchair I was finding it hard to keep up with my parents, who were nearly twice my age. It brought back distant memories of trying to keep pace with them on walks in the Alps when I was eight, and I thought sadly that my dreams of hiking over mountains until I was well into my seventies were probably not now going to be realized.

In January 2005 I turned myself in to the Chelsea and Westminster Hospital for a scheduled operation I had been dreading: anastomizing my intestines. It was a five-hour surgical procedure to open up my abdomen yet again, scrape off the scar tissue and reconnect my intestines after seven months. In recovery, I felt that I was right back where I had been six months before, with a nasal-gastric tube down my throat, green bile rising up, and a very painful abdomen where the surgeons had pulled the two sides together over my bowels and stitched them together. A long livid scar stretched from my chest down to my groin, but there was a welcome bonus: my tummy button was back in the middle instead of round by my ribcage. The thin pink membrane that had been all that separated my guts from the outside world was now covered with normal flesh, which meant I would no longer have to hide from the sun on holidays. But I had terrible nausea, and when after a few days I tried some soup I soon threw it all back up. I even managed to vomit in front of my boss, Jonathan Baker, nearly causing him to follow suit.

While I was still in recovery, a Kuwaiti patient was wheeled in. He had been stabbed and robbed, he was frightened, and he tried to get up and walk out, ripping the epidural out of his back. There was clearly a language barrier between him and the nurses but I was too exhausted to interpret. Eventually I could stand it no longer and I waded in. Fu'ad, the Kuwaiti, was so grateful, but what must he think of our country? I thought.

Six weeks after my op, the surgeons pronounced me fit enough to resume aggressive physiotherapy, including standing upright in the standing frame. A weighing chair was fetched to check my weight. I had gone from eleven stone down to eight: I had not weighed so little since I was in flannel shorts. My bum was so scrawny that my sacral bones sat directly on the chair with very little natural padding. My tolerance for sitting was limited to a few hours at a time, and I had to use an inflatable plastic cushion to go beneath me in the bath. My new colostomy bag filled with air every thirty minutes, with a noise like a whoopy cushion. If this continued once I returned to work and happened while I was broadcasting live, it would give a whole new meaning to being 'on air'.

In April 2005, ten months after being shot, I went back to work at the BBC. Everyone made a huge and slightly embarrassing fuss of me as I wheeled myself back through the glass doors of Television Centre, a journey that some, I suspect, probably thought I would never make. For the first and probably last time in my TV career I was directed down a corridor to one of the celebrity dressing rooms, where make-up and managers fawned over me in equal measure. It made a pleasant change from nurses with hypodermic needles. Then it was up a ramp and on to the set of Breakfast News, where Dermot and Natasha gave me one of the kindest, most compassionate interviews I have ever known. After so many years of covering the news as a reporter it felt very strange to be making it, but also a little disconcerting to be greeting old friends at belly-button height. Jonathan Baker, who had worked so hard to get me safely back from Riyadh, arranged a wine-and-sandwich reunion lunch for me with all the World Affairs correspondents. I gave a short speech, mumbling something about how good it was to be back, and then took a renewed interest in two of my colleagues who were also disabled, Stuart Hughes, who had lost part of his leg to a landmine in Iraq but now went jogging with his prosthetic limb, and Driss Makaoui, a Moroccan producer with lifelong polio, callipers, crutches and biceps the size of a tree trunk.

It was an emotional but happy time for me, seeing so many friendly faces, so many people who had steeled themselves to hear I had not lived through that first night after the attack, and had then willed me to recover. The TV presenter Fiona Bruce and her team in Manchester made a whole programme about my ordeal for BBC1's *Real Story*. They even tracked down Peter Bautz, the surgeon who saved me, in his new workplace in Australia. 'Frank fell into the category of the very, very seriously injured,' he said. The film showed me struggling to walk with callipers at Stanmore, and in a rather pathetic attempt at a walking piece-to-camera I recounted how all of us there in the Spinal Injuries Unit dreamed every night that we were able-bodied again and how when we woke up we wished the dream was reality and our waking hours had been just a nightmare. People came up to me in the street for weeks afterwards to tell me how the film had inspired them, which made me glad I had taken part in it.

The following month I felt strong enough to make a day-return trip to Geneva to interview a half-brother of Osama Bin Laden for the six o'clock news. This was perfectly safe – Yeslam Bin Laden is a peaceful, legitimate businessman – but the trip was still a mistake. The interview went fine, although our guest admitted he had barely known the maverick member of the Bin Laden family, but I was exhausted by two flights and a fourteen-hour working day. I was simply not capable of working the kind of hours I had done before my injuries.

I had hoped that after twelve surgical operations my ordeal in hospitals would have come to an end, but not quite. In the summer of 2005 a CT scan revealed two sizeable bladder stones, each measuring over 2cm across. Just as the doctors had feared, they were a by-product of having had a catheter inserted through my abdominal wall for so long.

'We'd better book him TCI,' said the urology nurse.

'TCI?' I asked. 'What's that?'

'Oh,' she replied, 'it's just short for "To Come In".'

In September I was admitted to hospital to have the bladder stones removed. A doctor came over to my bed, drew the curtains and explained what they were going to do to me.

'You laser them, right?' I asked.

'I'm afraid not. We use a process known as cysto-litholopaxy. We insert a device up through the penis which then uses crocodile-like jaws to crush the stones into smaller fragments which can be drained out.'

He saw my look of abject horror and added, 'Don't worry, you will be under general anaesthetic while we do this.'

I noticed the doctor's name was Khaled Shendi, a place in northern Sudan. Sure enough, he was from the town of Shendi, which I had once passed through on the roof of a train. When I told him I had spent the night sleeping on a slab at Khartoum General Hospital back in 1983, he could hardly believe it. He said he had been a junior doctor in training there at that time.

But despite this pleasant interlude, I could not take my mind off the grisly operation I was about to undergo. This time even the anaesthetic was abnormally painful. After a cannula had been inserted into a vein in the back of my hand, I remember staring up at the ceiling art and complaining of an intense burning pain spreading up my hand into my arm. I felt like Keanu Reeves in *The Matrix* after he took the hallucinogenic pill. Later the surgeons presented me with a test tube containing some of the debris they had removed: it resembled something from the Geological Museum. For days afterwards I was bleeding from the most sensitive part of my anatomy, and an infection led to a fever that it took nearly a week to bring down with antibiotics.

Meanwhile, I was struggling to keep up my physiotherapy sessions with the tireless Julie, in between working long hours after the London bombings, writing this book, catching up lost time with my family, and then getting set back several days when I was in too much pain to walk with callipers. A major landmark for me came in the summer of 2005, when for the first time since my injuries I attended a company's annual party standing up in callipers, supporting myself on a frame and watched over by my loyal and conscientious researcher, Katie Pearson. I was extremely wary of being knocked over so I backed myself up against a wall and 'held court', as it were. A retired general came up to me to say how proud it had made him to see me 'walking' in with the frame. He told me that when he had heard my interview about the attack on Radio 4 on Christmas Eve, he was so choked with emotion he had had to stop the car before he drove into a hedge.

In September 2005 I returned to Stanmore's Spinal Injuries Unit for a week's physiotherapy. I had a single goal in mind: to conquer the stairs. At first, the ever-sensible Almari, my physiotherapist, was reluctant to let me try, seeing how unsteady I was when walking with callipers and crutches. But I persisted and with her help I made it up a flight of twenty steps, going up backwards, which for some reason is easier, using one hand on the railing and the other on a crutch to power myself upwards. It was slow and exhausting and I found myself letting out a Serena Williams-like grunt each time I launched myself up a step, but it gave me a huge sense of achievement: these were the first stairs I had climbed in sixteen months.

Less encouraging was a visit to the bone-density clinic. A few minutes under the laser scan revealed that I had developed osteoporosis in my hips and legs: through lack of use, the bone density had declined to a worrying level. This came as a shock, as it had never occurred to me that I would need to worry about something like this for at least another thirty years.

'Just make sure you don't fall over,' smiled the technicians.

'Why?' I asked. 'What will happen?'

They exchanged knowing glances; probably every conversation went like this. 'Well, you're quite likely to fracture your bones, that's all.'

That's all? Argh. I just could not face the prospect of being laid up again in a hospital bed – or any bed, for that matter – for months on end. My consultant, Dr Gall, was brisk and breezy, though. In her soft Scottish brogue, she reassured me that this was a common condition – even astronauts get it when they spend too long in space, she told me – and it was reversible. I would just have to carve out some time each day to walk in my callipers, however much it got in the way of whatever else I was doing.

Being told I had osteoporosis at forty-four was a bit of a blow, but it was hard to feel sorry for myself when I looked around the ward at my fellow patients. This time I was the only one with an injury low down on the spinal column; the others all had neck injuries, which meant they could hardly move anything below the shoulders. As I wheeled myself back from a session in the gym I would see them being hoisted, helpless as a baby, from their chairs on to their beds. Nurses would feed them and bathe them, and often the sickly smell of evacuated bowels would hang over the ward. In the world of spinal-cord injury and paralysis, no two cases are identical and everyone compares their own condition to those of others. I could see that the tetraplegics eyed me with envy, but I in turn found myself envying a patient who had been confined to a wheelchair after her epidural went wrong, but who was now up and walking around with only a stick for support. She, of course, envied all the completely able-bodied nurses and physios around her.

Stanmore in the warm, soft light of late summer was a good place to practise my calliper walking and I soon found the confidence to break out of the gym by myself and totter slowly along a path through an orchard. As I paused to lean against some railings, I caught my reflection in the window of the gym. I saw a man in a T-shirt standing almost upright, leaning forward as if to chat to a friend; he looked fit and slightly tanned. Suddenly I recognized in that reflection my old self, the person I had been for so many years before I was gunned down and crippled. It was like looking at an old photo album, but this was not the past, this was here and now. I realized in that moment that, despite everything that has happened to me and all the painful and unwelcome changes I have had to go through, I can make this thing work. I can, I think, rediscover the love of life that made every day worth living and will do so again. I will get through this.

ماذنه جامع القلوون ، خان الخليلى

۱۱۸۲ / ۱۰ / ۱٤ . مصر

10

Making Sense
of It All

No evidence has come to light which
suggests that Mr Cumbers and Mr
Gardner had been targeted before
they entered the Al-Suweidi area.

Joint UK/Saudi Investigators' Report

W HO SHOT US IN RIYADH AND WHY WERE THEY SO
determined to kill us? These were the questions that
played over and over in my mind throughout those long
months in hospital. Had we been followed from our hotel?
Set up by our Saudi minders? Was there anything I could have
said or done that could have saved us from those bullets?

I was to get my answers. Sir Sherard Cowper-Coles, the
British ambassador in Riyadh who had helped save my life on
the night of our attack, lobbied hard for a full investigation
by the Saudi authorities. Sharing their findings with
foreigners, let alone a journalist, was not something that
came naturally to them, but in the early summer of 2005 I got
a call from SO13, Scotland Yard's Anti-Terrorist Branch.

After months of delay, the Saudi secret police, the *Mabahith*, were finally here in London to give Louise, Simon's widow, and me a face-to-face account of their investigation.

June 29th was a fabulous summer's day, the sort of day when the last thing you feel like doing is sitting in an office and hearing how someone tried to murder you. But we had work to do, so it was off to the Yard, through security, and up in the lift to the Anti-Terrorist Branch Commander's office. The London bombings were still a week away and SO13 had plenty of time to give us. The view across London was spectacular, right across Parliament, the Thames, the London Eye and out to the low hills of Kent on the horizon. Reluctantly, I swivelled my wheelchair round, turned my back on the view and prepared to meet the Saudi detectives.

One by one they filed in, five of them in all, clearly edgy but bearing formal messages of goodwill from their Ministry of Interior headquarters in Riyadh. I later learned that it was quite unprecedented for the *Mabahith* to come over to Britain to talk to victims of Saudi terrorism like this. 'They would have been nervous,' a diplomat told me. 'They probably gave you false names to protect their identities. Remember, these are people very much in Al-Qaeda's sights back home.' For seven hours we sat there, breaking only for lunch in the police canteen. Fortunately, our Saudi visitors did not seem to notice that the roast of the day was a great glistening joint of gammon, pork being *haraam*, forbidden, to Muslims.

I listened, spellbound, as the Saudis gave us a blow-by-blow account of how they believe the attack on us was carried out. 'We are sorry we have taken so long to come here,' said their team leader, a genial captain, 'but we have been working on new information which we want to tell you about now. In fact there were not five people who attacked you, but six. The sixth person's name is Adel; we have him in custody, but he is

very severely wounded from a recent gun battle. We are
keeping him alive so he can tell us everything and we can
bring him to justice.'

The Saudi detectives then painted a quite terrifying picture
of what happened that Sunday in June 2004. While we
were filming in Al-Suwaidi district, they said, a team of
four Al-Qaeda members happened to be travelling from the
north of Riyadh to the south where we were, for a meeting
with the leader of Al-Qaeda in the Arabian Peninsula,
Abdulaziz Al-Muqrin, and his entourage. Soon after the two
groups met up they drove past us and spotted us filming,
and immediately pulled into a nearby sidestreet to discuss
what to do about us. Al-Muqrin decided we should be
killed, since we were Westerners and therefore 'infidels', non-
Muslims, and this was Arabia, the land of the two holy
mosques. (If we had had a police escort I am convinced
they would have left us alone.) A senior member of the
group, Faisal Al-Dakheel, took charge. One member was
assigned to kill the infidel cameraman, another the infidel
reporter. So while I was delivering my piece-to-camera and
Simon was filming, our fates were already being decided
in the neighbouring street. They were to use the personal
weapons they always carried, in this case automatic 9mm
pistols. The Al-Qaeda leader, Al-Muqrin, was to sit back at
some distance in his Nissan Pathfinder jeep to watch the hit
go down.

It began with a man called Abdullah Al-Subaei walking up
to me and greeting me in Arabic, '*Asalaamu aleikum*,' 'Peace
be upon you.' He was the young, almost pleasant-looking
man I remembered approaching me. When I responded in
Arabic, giving the stock response to his greeting, that
apparently threw him. Perhaps I was a Muslim. But why did
I look like a Westerner? Then he remembered his orders. He
was here to kill me. So he pulled out his pistol and at that
point I ran for my life. The police believe I was then brought

down with a pistol shot from Faisal Al-Dakheel, who had dismounted from the second vehicle, the van I remember with the sliding doors.

'He fired seven bullets at you. Three of them missed, four of them hit you,' said the detectives. How on earth he could have missed at point-blank range I don't know, but since I was on the ground and he was standing that would explain why the bullets I took in the lumbar/pelvic area were all from behind. Faisal Al-Dakheel had stood there and shot me repeatedly while I lay helpless in the dirt. Since the hospital records show me as having been hit by six bullets with a total of eleven wounds, someone else may well have joined in. Then, when I was lying motionless on the ground hearing those footsteps approaching, one of the cell members got out and tried to buckle the numberplate of the minivan so it couldn't be recognized. 'We had a lot of trouble over that van,' said the detectives. 'They hid it inside a garage for weeks, that's why we could not locate it at first.'

My attackers then drove off, which I also remember. As for what happened to Simon, their story differed considerably from what we had always been told. When the British and Irish ambassadors had gone to the scene of the crime three days after it happened, together with Louise, a BBC delegation and a close protection escort, they were shown a place about a kilometre away where Simon had reportedly been killed. They were told he had run for his life all that way, carrying his heavy camera, but unable to find cover had been shot dead. Now they were saying he had died instantly, almost as soon as the attack began. Louise, understandably, has been pressing the Saudis ever since for evidence of how her husband died.

Simon Cumbers, said the Saudi detectives, had made a dash for the door of our own van as soon as he realized we were under attack. But they said he was shot inside the van and died instantly, while the driver accelerated away to safety. It was to be a further eight months before this story was finally backed up by hard evidence.

In Scotland Yard, the Saudi detectives now asked me if I felt strong enough to see photos of what had become of the terrorists who attacked us. I did. Five out of the six were dead, they said, all killed in shoot-outs with the security forces last year. Only Simon's alleged murderer, Adel, was still alive and he was the one critically injured. One by one they silently passed me a set of gruesome A4-sized photos. There was Al-Muqrin, the local Al-Qaeda leader in Saudi Arabia, eyes closed, beard blood-stained, killed in a gun battle only a few days after our attack. There too was Faisal Al-Dakheel, the man I'm told shot me in the back and left me for dead. He was apparently killed in the same shoot-out in June 2004, but his once cruel-looking features were now unrecognizable. The photo they showed me was of someone with a face puffed up in death, with one side distorted by wounds. There were others they showed me, all hideously disfigured. As if reading my doubts, the detectives assured us they had done DNA checks on all the corpses. 'We are still investigating,' they said. 'We will tell you if anything changes.'

So there it was, closure of sorts for me. An apparently opportunistic attack, a case of bad luck, the wrong place at the wrong time. But when I think of what these people did it disgusts me. To say 'Peace be upon you' and then immediately pull out a gun to kill you makes a mockery of the universal Muslim greeting of peace and goodwill. To shoot another human being, an unarmed civilian, when he is already wounded and helpless on the ground and begging for mercy, is surely despicable in any religion. 'I pray every day,' said a normally gentle Saudi friend of mine on the phone a few days after my meeting with the detectives. 'I pray that the people who did this are burning in hell right now. They have brought shame on our religion and on our country. They are beyond forgiveness.'

*

The first anniversary of the Riyadh attack in June 2005 was tough on all of us. For Amanda, it brought back vivid memories of those terrible days when she thought she had lost me, of flying out to Riyadh not knowing if she was already a widow, of sitting day after day at my hospital bedside, signing countless consent forms for emergency operations while I lay inert and motionless, hooked up to drips and monitors. For me it was not so much the past that troubled me, it was and still is my new-found paraplegia. I never thought that one year after the attack I would still be in a wheelchair, unable to do the things I had taken for granted all my life. But I can only imagine what this anniversary must have been like for Simon's widow, Louise, and for his family back in Ireland.

The tragedy of Simon's death has introduced me to this kind and big-hearted family which I would never otherwise have met. In April I went over to Dublin with my own family to see them and to appear on RTE's *Late Late Show*, which is considered Ireland's premier TV show, going out live every Friday night and watched by over six million people. In the chic bar of our hotel, Andrea Corr the singer and Colin Farrell the actor were mingling with guests, but on the other side of town I was bracing myself to appear before a live studio audience, not something I had done before. I found it immensely calming to see Bob Cumbers, Simon's father, and the rest of his family, sharing a few drinks before the show in the Green Room. Then, just after I had been wheeled up a ramp on to the set during a commercial break and seconds before the lights came up and the host Pat Kenny began the interview, disaster struck. A well-meaning but clumsy make-up lady insisted I needed a dab of powder beneath the eyes and promptly jabbed her thumb into my eyeball. Tears immediately flowed down the right side of my face and I could see some of the audience shaking their heads sadly, probably whispering, 'Poor lad, he's obviously terribly upset.'

I knew I would find it difficult to talk about Simon, but I could have done without appearing to be in tears before the interview had even started. But Pat Kenny was a pro and he deftly steered the interview between humour and sadness, at one point stepping into the audience to interview Bob, who reeled off the details of his son's impressive and multi-talented journalistic career.

The next day Bob Cumbers and I made the journey I had thought so often about while I was in hospital: to lay flowers at Simon's grave in Greystones, County Wicklow. It was one of those soft, muted Irish days when it was hard to tell which season you were in. A fine drizzle fell about the gentle hills and a mist enveloped the shores of the Irish Sea as we approached the cemetery. 'Simon and his cousins used to spend all their summers in Greystones,' said his father, and his widow Louise had chosen it as the final resting place for the man who was everything in her life. Simon loved mountains so he was buried in the shadow of County Wicklow's Sugar Loaf Mountain.

Bob and I had the cemetery to ourselves and I cannot remember how long we stayed there, Bob standing, me sitting in my wheelchair, while the rain fell without a sound, both of us deep in our private thoughts. It was one of the saddest moments of my life, staring immobile at that simple grave-stone. 'Simon Peter Cumbers 1968–2004 Rest in Peace'. He was just thirty-six years old when a Saudi terrorist shot him, and all for some twisted, pointless cause. There were others at the BBC who knew Simon much better than I did, but he was one of those rare people with such natural charisma you only had to be with him for five minutes and you felt you had known him a lifetime. Unhealthy as it was to think such thoughts, I could not help thinking, 'Oh Simon, if only you had got away, what times we would have had on each anniversary of the shooting, meeting up in the corner of some pub, toasting our lifelong bond of survival against adversity.'

Yet, although I am not especially religious, I know that Simon is up there somewhere, willing me to pick up my journalistic career from the point where it was so very nearly terminated.

In the best of Irish traditions Bob and I went straight from the cemetery to the pub. He took me to Johnny Fox's, reputedly the highest pub in Ireland and a clandestine gathering place during the rebellion against British rule in the last century. Outside, the rain fell in sheets, but a log fire crackled in the bar and more than one Guinness drinker came up to tell us how much Simon's story had touched them when they watched it on the *Late Late Show* the previous night. I found it awkward, to say the least, looking up at people from my wheelchair; it was not a situation I had ever expected to be in. But knowing where Simon's final resting place is and being able to picture it whenever I want has given me a certain peace of mind.

Somehow, I have found a way to deal with the horror of being shot. It happened and I can't undo it. Coming to terms with being disabled is a different matter. Almost everything has changed. At the risk of sounding morbid, so many of the things I enjoyed have been taken away – jogging along the Thames towpath with friends at the weekend, roller-blading with my daughters, chasing them through the park and showing them how to climb trees, and trekking through jungles, deserts and mountains, which I enjoyed more than anything. Almost every single aspect of daily life requires an effort that was not needed before, from lifting up my legs with my hands to swing them off the bed, to lowering myself into the bath using just my arms, from straining forward and nearly falling off my wheelchair to unload the dishwasher, to having to project my voice upwards so it can reach everyone else at their head height. Every single journey I undertake, whether it be a taxi ride to west London or a flight to a European city, necessitates help from other people somewhere along the way. Before, I revelled in spontaneity, being able to just sling a bag over my shoulder and walk out of the door in five minutes flat; now I have to go through a mental checklist. Do I have enough medication for where I am going? Are there going to be steps involved, in which case who is going to get me up and down them? Is the vehicle I will be travelling in going to have room for my wheelchair, and will I be able to lift myself up on to the passenger seat? Does the place I am going to have disabled-access toilets? Will the lift be so small that there is no room for the wheelchair, meaning I cannot actually get upstairs to join everyone else for lunch? And how long can I last before I have to lie down on my side to ease my emaciated backside, numb with pressure from sitting on the chair for too long?

I have surprised myself that I am not more angry about what happened in Riyadh. I mean, just how pointless and senseless was this stupid attack? It was utterly cowardly too, picking on two defenceless, unarmed non-combatants who had taken the time and trouble to come and see the situation in Saudi Arabia for themselves and try to explain it to a global audience – not some government-sanitized, state-censored version, but the views of ordinary people, including their many grievances against the West and their own governments. That my reward for this should be several bullets in the guts and a lifetime of paraplegia is of course immensely unfair. But what's done is done. Tempting as it is to think, 'If only we had not gone,' 'If only we had left a day earlier,' 'If only I could have talked the gunmen out of those last four bullets that did me the real damage,' I know such speculation is pointless.

But in July 2005 the whole of London was to witness the horror of Al-Qaeda-inspired terrorism. Both MI5 and SO13, Scotland Yard's Anti-Terrorist Branch, were aware that

Britain was a prime target for fanatical Islamists, but having already intercepted a number of plots they knew of no specific terror cell with both the capability and the intent to mount an imminent attack on mainland Britain. With both those criteria unfulfilled, the Joint Terrorism Analysis Centre had lowered the secret national-threat assessment from Severe General to Substantial in June. There was still a threat, but nobody knew which direction it was coming from.

By 7 July 2005 I had been back at work for nearly three months and was feeling stronger. I was also starting to put the horrors of the previous year behind me. In the relatively quiet months of early summer I had revived many of my old contacts and forged some new ones. Now I was off to Germany, where I was giving a lecture, and taking my family with me for a short holiday. We loaded the suitcases into the taxi, collected Sasha from her ballet exam and headed west for Heathrow. But something was wrong.

The traffic was worse than usual and there was talk on the radio about a power surge on the London Underground; curiously, my mobile could not get a signal from inside the taxi. While Melissa and Sasha chattered excitedly about the open-air swimming pool we would be going to in Germany, I asked the cab-driver to turn up the radio. It seemed there had been two incidents on the London Undergound and there was talk of explosions. Amanda and I exchanged glances: this did not sound good. One explosion could have been an accident, two sounded like a terrorist attack. I tried again to phone the BBC newsdesk but could not get a signal, since of course most of the capital was on the phone. The reports on the radio were now confirming there had been bomb explosions with several people killed; there was nothing for it but to divert to the BBC studios. Our holiday was over before it had begun. Sasha's little face began to crumple with tears. 'Does that mean we're not going to Germany at all?' she sobbed.

'I'm afraid so,' said Amanda. 'Daddy has to go to work now.'

I sent the family back home in the taxi and we agreed they would stay indoors for the rest of the day, while I raced as fast as my wheelchair could carry me up to the live on-air studios.

Although the casualties were a fraction of those in New York and Washington on 11 September 2001, I still had that same nervous feeling throughout the day, uncertain whether the attack was over or whether this was just stage one of an elaborate plan. I remembered Al-Qaeda's fondness for simultaneous strikes causing maximum human casualties. But when the day passed with no further attacks I suspected the worst was over, for the time being.

Despite what had happened to me in Riyadh the previous year, I felt strangely detached from the carnage in central London. It brought back no memories, for my attack had been an intensely personal one where my assailants had effectively singled us out for 'execution', targeting only us and not our Saudi minders. But of course the intent was the same: to murder Western civilians in cold blood.

Even before Al-Qaeda released the posthumous video testimony of Mohammed Siddique Khan, the presumed leader of the July London bombers, there were indications that this attack was inspired by, if not actually sanctioned by, Al-Qaeda and its anti-Western worldview. Firstly, the targets: choosing to hit a 'soft' Western transit hub at rush hour with the maximum chance of high casualties was almost an exact repeat of the Madrid bombings of the previous year. Al-Qaeda has always had a fascination with targeting Western transport systems, and its planners have long ago figured out that setting off bombs in dark tunnels hundreds of feet below ground would add a particular dimension of horror to any attack. (The UK government also expected such an attack, which is why the emergency services practised reacting to a mock chemical-bomb attack on Bank Tube station in

September 2003.) Secondly, the modus operandi: Al-Qaeda saw the effectiveness of Lebanese Shi'ite suicide bombers in the early 1980s and copied it for themselves. This was pure asymmetric warfare, pitting a single man driving a truckful of explosives against an enemy he could not hope to defeat on the battlefield, yet who now suffered over 240 deaths in the case of the attack on the US Marines' barracks at Beirut airport in 1983. In London, Anti-Terrorist Branch detectives quickly worked out from the forensic evidence that the July bombers had blown themselves up. Then there was the simultaneous, coordinated nature of the attacks, again a habit of Al-Qaeda and its affiliates, as evidenced in New York, Madrid, Bali and several other locations. There was also no warning and no immediate claim of responsibility, just to keep the investigators guessing.

In the days and weeks that followed the London bombings, I went into overdrive at work. Two things made a particularly strong impression on me: the reaction of the Arab world, and the testimony of the survivors I interviewed as they tried to cope with what had happened to them.

Inevitably some pro-*jihadi* websites hailed the attacks as just retribution for Britain's policies in Iraq and elsewhere, just as they claimed that Hurricane Katrina was divine punishment from God on America. Some media commentary condemned the attacks but declared them inevitable since Britain had invaded and occupied a sovereign Arab country on a fabricated pretext. But the overwhelming reaction was one of shock and sympathy for the British people, more so than for almost any other country attacked that I can think of. Arab journalists pointed out to their readers that millions in Britain had opposed the war in Iraq and still did; a Saudi correspondent told his paper that the streets of London were not what you would imagine – they were totally cosmopolitan, he said, full of every colour and creed, so an attack on London was like an attack on the world. Whatever Arabs think of British government policy, and it is rarely compli-mentary, most of them retain a great affection for London, a place which many view as their second home. They love its freedom of expression, its lively press, its open, grassy parks so popular with Gulf families in the summer. And young, holidaying Arabs love the shops, cafés and amusement arcades of Bayswater and the West End. America used to be a favoured destination, especially for Saudis who used to fly direct from Jeddah to Orlando, but 9/11 has changed that and many Gulf Arabs no longer feel welcome there. So the principal Arab reaction to the July bombings was one of out-rage, potentially a hugely significant factor if the West is ever to come close to defeating Al-Qaeda-inspired terrorism. Sadly, that sympathy began to wane almost immediately as the death toll in Iraq continued to mount, and the widely held perception that the War on Terror is a war against Muslims still carried currency in so much of the Middle East.

So will Britain be attacked again or was this a 'one-shot punishment' for perceived misdemeanours? Almost certainly there will be plans afoot to stage further attacks on British interests – there were three thwarted plots in the months immediately after July 2005. Even if British troops withdrew immediately and totally from Iraq and Afghanistan and there was to be some miraculous solution to the Palestinian–Israeli dispute, there will probably always be a hard core of fanatics determined to strike at a country they see as hostile to their beliefs. The secret to defeating them in the long term rests partly, I believe, in winning over the mid-dle ground of mainstream Muslim opinion, both in Britain and around the world. That will not be achieved by clever words of persuasion, instead it will take actual deeds on the ground: genuine progress towards a viable Palestinian state ('Britain helped create the problem so Britain must help solve it' is a widely held view), the eventual withdrawal of all British and Western forces from Muslim countries (Iraq is the sorest point here, but the situation is more complex in Afghanistan where Al-Qaeda and the Taliban can hardly wait for them to leave so they can re-establish themselves), and concrete steps towards making British Muslims feel their voices and concerns are not simply being ignored.

The second, lasting impression came from a radio documentary I made for Radio 4's *Broadcasting House* programme on the wounded and traumatized survivors of the July bombings. The editor had rightly guessed that the victims would feel some empathy with me, as a fellow victim of terrorism; in fact the feeling was mutual. Often I would find myself talking quietly to survivors long after I had put down the microphone. Their descriptions of what it was like down in those darkened, smoke-filled Tube carriages in the minutes after the explosions were haunting and terrifying. An Australian girl, Gill Hicks, told me how her legs had become bloody, truncated stumps yet she clung to consciousness and hung on for help. I recognized that same survival instinct I remembered kicking in for me in Riyadh, but after that we differed. A brave and magnanimous person, she told me she felt only pity for the bombers who had robbed her of her legs; for my part, I could never forgive the people who had robbed me of mine and murdered my cameraman. They had a free choice and they chose to do what they did.

Working hard helped to take my mind off my own physical state, but some months after I left Stanmore hospital I had a call from a fellow patient. Simon H. had gone home at around the same time as I had and now he wanted to meet up. We got together in a café in west London, two paraplegics sitting there gossiping over coffees in our wheelchairs. He seemed robust and was as powerfully built as ever, in fact he was thinking of applying to go on the next *Beyond Boundaries*, a BBC2 reality endurance programme that took parties of disabled people across difficult terrain in places like

Nicaragua. He was also showing his hospital sketches to someone who thought they could be published. We made it a regular thing, meeting up every other Friday, but then one day Simon H. phoned me in distress. Did I know, he asked, if doctors could legally have him 'sectioned' (restrained under observation for his own safety and that of others)? I asked him why. It turned out that he had deliberately swallowed a large amount of painkillers and had woken up in hospital. It was his second suicide attempt.

Simon H. managed to avoid being sectioned, but I begged him not to try anything like that again. He was clearly finding his new life as a paraplegic extremely tough; he sounded surprised that I was not taking any antidepressants. The next time we met he was in obvious physical pain, wincing and gripping his legs as spasms of nerve pain racked his body, a sensation I know only too well. He mimicked putting a gun to his head and grimaced.

Two weeks later I had a call from his mother: Simon H. had finally taken his own life. He had joined a gun club in the US over the internet, flown to Las Vegas by himself, taken a day of instruction, then turned the pistol on himself. I was saddened, but somehow not surprised – this was his third and final attempt to commit suicide.

A rather different character was Stu. Like me, he was a gunshot-wound victim, having been shot and robbed by bandits in Guatemala on New Year's Day 2001. They had left him on the jungle floor, bleeding and paralysed from the chest downwards. But two days after he arrived in a Texas hospital he was out of bed and in a wheelchair. Stu had a can-do attitude to everything. When I met up with him for the first time he had just come back from a month in Cameroon, exploring remote bird habitats in a dug-out canoe, with his wheelchair wedged in the back. Now he was planning to swim with killer whales in Norway's Arctic Ocean. Stu had a healthy disdain for his paraplegia; it was almost as if he didn't notice it.

I decided that if anyone was to be my role model for pursuing an active life after such appalling injuries, it should be Stu.

For me, the avalanche of mail sent in by the public has been recognition enough for surviving six bullets and then coming back to work. But there was more to come. Not long after returning to my old job – and even my old desk – at the BBC I got an official letter from the prime minister's office at Number Ten Downing Street:

Dear Sir,

The Prime Minister has asked me to inform you, in strict confidence, that he has it in mind, on the occasion of the forthcoming list of Birthday Honours, to submit your name to The Queen with a recommendation that Her Majesty may be graciously pleased to approve that you be appointed an Officer of the Order of the British Empire . . .

I am, Sir, Your obedient Servant . . .

I was in mild shock. So this is how people get their gongs, I thought. I had always wondered how it worked. I duly kept it secret for nearly three weeks, telling only my parents and Amanda, until at last my name appeared in the Queen's Birthday Honours List. By happy coincidence, I had agreed to be the compère that same day at our children's school carnival. My parents drove up from the country and glowed with pride as the headmistress announced my honour to the assembled parents and pupils. I wheeled myself up the ramp to the stage, but no sooner had I begun to do the commentary on the parade of children in their costumes than I was interrupted by an RAF flypast for the Queen's birthday. 'Ah, they really shouldn't have,' I said into the microphone. 'I mean, it's just an OBE!'

Four months passed and then came the day of the investiture at Buckingham Palace. I was allowed to bring three guests to watch the medal being pinned on to my chest in the ballroom, so here was a dilemma. Amanda would obviously come, but should we bring our children or my parents? Melissa and Sasha, who have finely tuned antennae for picking up words like 'palace' and 'queen', overheard our discussion and got very excited and begged to come too. But we decided that after all my parents had been through this was the least we could do to reward them; we also felt it would mean more to them, since having lived through the reigns of three sovereigns, George V, George VI and Queen Elizabeth, they had an in-built respect and fascination for the Queen and the pageantry of the Palace.

After a warm autumn, the morning of 13 October 2005 dawned cold and rainy and there were few people outside the gates of Buckingham Palace. But the weather made no difference to us. The all-important Royal Standard was flying from the flagpole: the Queen was in residence, which meant she would be doing the honours. (Earlier, I had not been able to resist winding up my poor mother by telling her the Palace had informed me that 'since the Queen was away in Balmoral it would be Viscount Linley awarding the medal'. Baah.)

Police in black anoraks searched the bonnet and boot of our car and then we were through the gates, past the sentries in their chocolate-box uniforms and into the Quadrangle, where a line of pages in red waistcoats was waiting to escort guests upstairs. Over twenty investitures are held each year, mostly at Buckingham Palace, and there were at least a hundred recipients here today, together with their guests, yet the Palace staff still made everyone feel as if they were the most important person in the building. Except for the Queen, of course.

The week before the investiture, I had said on Radio 4's *Desert Island Discs* that I was determined to attend social events standing up in my callipers, instead of being two feet below everyone else in my wheelchair. Well, today, of all days, was an occasion to be upstanding and looking the Queen in the eye, I thought. I had strapped on my clunky callipers as soon as I woke up, but as the time came to shuffle the final few yards to Her Majesty I grew suddenly nervous. The red carpet stretched ahead of me like an aircraft-carrier runway and I could sense the palace flunkies watching me nervously as I gripped the bars of my rolling zimmerframe. What if I lost my balance and toppled over in front of a thousand guests, live television cameras and in the presence of the sovereign?

'Mr Frank Gardner,' announced the chamberlain, 'for services to journalism.' I could hear the equerry whispering in the Queen's ear, 'Riyadh ... 2004 ... survived' as I concentrated on covering the ground up to the dais. I attempted a bow then looked up at her, recognizing the face so familiar from close-ups on television and feeling as if I knew her already, which was ridiculous.

'How very gallant of you to come like this,' said the Queen, pointing to my callipers.

'Thank you, Your Majesty,' I gasped; I was quite out of breath after hobbling just thirty yards across the ballroom.

'So are you still recovering?' she asked.

'No, I think this is probably it,' I replied, and then told her how I had hung on to life in Riyadh for the sake of my family. She asked me if I had returned to work, and this was my cue to shamelessly promo a programme I had been working on. 'I gather you are an avid Radio 4 listener, Ma'am?' I said.

'Yes, I do enjoy listening to it.'

'Well, you may like to tune in this Sunday morning to Broadcasting House. I've done a special report on the survivors of the London bombings and how they're coping with their injuries, which you may find quite moving.'

'Oh,' said the Queen, 'yes, I will do.' And that was it: out came the royal handshake, which was the signal that the audience was over and my time was up.

That evening I was back on parade for a BBC party in my honour; it was one of the happiest moments in my career.

There in a large room were gathered over one hundred of my closest colleagues, many of whom had known me ten years ago when I was making the difficult transition from banking to journalism. As I tottered in on my callipers – for most people this was the first time they had seen me standing up since the shooting – the James Bond theme played over the sound system. Wine flowed, canapés were passed round and Helen Boaden, the Head of News, gave a speech that made me blush for its tributes. When I looked around the room at such stellar broadcasting figures as Kate Adie, Brian Hanrahan and Jeremy Bowen, I thought, 'This is mad. What an earth am I doing getting an OBE for services to journalism at the age of forty-four?' But if you take six bullets and survive, there's a good chance people will credit you with rather more than you deserve.

Going home that night in a taxi, through the rain-washed streets of London, I felt better than I had in a long while. I knew that nothing was going to bring back Simon or the highly active, spontaneous life I had led before Riyadh, but I was alive and fit and happy. As Amanda had said when I first came out of heavy sedation in hospital: 'You made it! Now we get to spend the rest of our lives together.'

Afterword

 طَرَب ضِنا في وكالة الغوريه في مصر ب ٢٧ / ٢ /١١٨٢

BEING SHOT – DELIBERATELY, METHODICALLY AND AT CLOSE range – by people who know exactly what they are doing is one of those very personal close encounters you never think will happen to you. It has, of course, changed my life and those of my family.

While I don't spend every day wondering why it happened, there is no getting away from the fact that I am now based in a wheelchair. This was not something I ever planned for, in fact I always imagined I would in time be a fit seventy-year-old, still striding up hillsides, keeping pace with my children. Being made paraplegic while you are still relatively young and fit is an absolutely catastrophic blow. But I know I am luckier than many others who have sustained Spinal Cord Injury: I still have my upper body, I have a loving family, a caring employer and I live in a city, London, that is increasingly conscious of the need to make adaptations for people with disabilities.

In the months after I emerged from hospital many people wrote to me. Some of the best advice I received was from Stu,

370

shot in the chest by Guatemalan robbers. When you first come to terms with your new life, he told me, it can be fairly depressing, but you have to focus on what you can still do, not on what you used to do. How right he is. Had I been a professional tennis coach my career would now be in serious trouble, but as it is, I am finding that I am busier than ever, trying to navigate our audiences through the complexities of terrorism, security and the Arab and Islamic world.

I never imagined, when I signed up to study Arabic in my teens, that I would come to apply it to something so murky or violent as Al-Qaeda-related terrorism, but since 2001 I have found it to be invaluable. I continue to believe that we need to understand as much as we can about each other's cultures, religions and societies. In a very small way, I hope that this book will give readers a glimpse of a different Middle East, one beyond the headlines, where my own tragic experience only came after twenty-four years of good ones. My abiding memory of the Muslim world is not facing the pistol barrels of a handful of fanatics, but of sharing the lives of good, ordinary people in Egypt, Jordan and elsewhere.

I suspect it is still some way off, but one day I hope that we will live in a world where the phrase 'Middle East' does not have so many violent connotations, where the Islamic world can be appreciated for its culture and its contributions to civilization instead of being viewed with suspicion in the West, a world where there is no place for the blinkered bigots such as those who shot Simon Cumbers and me, nor for those who say that Arabs and Westerners cannot be friends.

Acknowledgements

To Dr Peter Bautz, my brilliant South African surgeon, for saving my life in Saudi Arabia and to all his team at the King Faisal Specialist Hospital in Riyadh. To Sir Sherard Cowper-Coles, HM Ambassador in Riyadh, for going the extra mile to get me to hospital on the evening we were shot. To HRH Prince Salman Bin Abdulaziz Al-Sa'ud, Governor of Riyadh, for putting his city's best medical team at my disposal. To HRH Prince Sa'ud Al Faisal, Saudi Foreign Minister, for arranging a flying ambulance back to Britain. To Frank Cross and his team at the Royal London Hospital in Whitechapel for all their expert trauma care, and to the surgeons of Chelsea and Westminster Hospital. To Dr Gall, Almari Smit and Emma Linley at the Spinal Injuries Unit in Stanmore, and to my neurophysiotherapists, Julie Hicks and Leigh Forsyth, for patiently introducing me to the grim realities of my new life as a paraplegic. To every nurse who looked after me – well, almost every one.

To the BBC, especially Jonathan Baker, Mark Damazer and Sarah Ward-Lilley, for offering every possible support right from day one; I forgive the BBC's news managers now for all the wrecked weekends and cancelled evenings that come with being in the news business. To my excellent agent Julian Alexander at LAW for helping to turn a concept into a book, and to the BBC's Vin Ray for recommending him. To Simon Taylor and my publishers, Transworld, for backing this book with so much enthusiasm and professionalism. To Louise Cumbers and Bob Cumbers for proofreading the difficult passages about Simon. To Frank Cross, again, for his medical advice on the rehab chapter, and to David Pearce for his insights into Yemen. My thanks to David Budge for his sobering eye-witness account of the Riyadh bombing of 2003. To Adam Kelliher, for thinking up the snappy title for the penultimate chapter. To the many hundred of kind people out there, Muslims, Christians, Jews and others, who sent me letters, emails, poems and prayers to raise my spirits while I was in hospital and since.

To my parents who, after twenty-five years of worrying about their son being in the Middle East, finally saw their worst fears realized. To my wife, Amanda, for going through hell and never once complaining, and to my daughters, Melissa and Sasha: you were all worth surviving for.

Picture Credits

All photos have been kindly supplied by the author except for the following: Osama bin Laden: © Reuters/CORBIS; Simon Cumbers: © Louise Cumbers; FG on Breakfast News and FG at his desk: BBC; FG receives his OBE: courtesy BCA Films.

Index

Hassan, Margaret 342
Hawkins, Neil 30
Hawley, Caroline 322
Heath, Ted 148
Heathrow airport alert (2003) 257–8
Henderson, Vic 168–9
Hicks, Gill 364
Hicks, Julie 326, 347
Hittar, Judge Hammond 242
Hizbollah 195
Hobbs, Aidan and Naomi 305
Holland 21
Horn of Africa
 US attempt to prevent Al-Qaeda operations in 239
Howaitat tribe 97
HSBC (Istanbul)
 bomb attack on (2003) 258–9
Hughes, Stuart 322, 345
Hull, Ed 234
Humphreys, John 343
Hurghada (Egypt) 50–1
Hurst, Dominic 288–9, 290, 291
Hussein, King 91

Intelligence services, British 247–8, 259–60
 and Al-Qaeda 251, 252
 and plot to launch explosive-laden dinghies into Western warships in Strait of Gibraltar 252
 taking interest in Islamist activists living in UK 249–50
 see also M15; M16
Intifada 194–8
IRA 251
Iran
 and Lockerbie bombing 211
Iran–Iraq War 27–9, 115, 269
Iranian embassy siege 24
Iraq 364
 abuse of Iraqi prisoners in Abu Ghraib 272–4

and Al-Qaeda 263, 264–5, 272, 276, 281–4
Al-Qaeda beheading tapes 281–3
Coalition and mistakes made by 271–3
invasion of Kuwait (1990) 115–16, 117
post-war Islamist insurgency 281–4
state of Basra in 1998 270–1
suicide bombing missions 283
torturing of prisoners by Secret Police 279–80
and UN weapons inspectors 157, 274
US flying missions over 160
war with Iran 27–9, 115, 269
and weapons of mass destruction (WMD) 262, 271, 274, 281
Iraq Survey Group 274
Iraq war 271–2, 274, 275–9, 281
 and Al-Qaeda 276
 British soldiers based in Basra 277, 278–9
 view of by Arab world and media coverage 264, 275–6
Islam
 spread of 32–3
Israel 40, 58–9, 132–3, 256
Israeli Defence Force (IDF) 195, 196
Israeli–Palestinian conflict 193–8
Istanbul
 bomb attack on British consulate and HSBC (2003) 245, 258–9

Jalali, Ali 289
Jasra Ball 135
Jeddah (Saudi Arabia) 122
Jerusalem 62–4
John Paul II, Pope visit to Egypt 185–6
Johnson, Paul 13
Joint Terrorist Analysis Centre (JTAC) 360
Jordan 91–107, 194, 257